Dakini's Warm Breath

Dakini's Warm Breath

THE FEMININE PRINCIPLE IN TIBETAN BUDDHISM

Judith Simmer-Brown

Shambhala
BOSTON & LONDON
2002

Shambhala Publications, Inc.
Horticultural Hall
300 Massachusetts Avenue
Boston, Massachusetts 02115
www.shambhala.com

9 8 7 6 5 4 3

Printed in the United States of America

♾ This edition is printed on acid-free paper that meets the American National Standards Institute z39.48 Standard.
Distributed in the United States by Random House, Inc., and in Canada by Random House of Canada Ltd

The Library of Congress catalogs the hardcover edition of this book as follows:
Simmer-Brown, Judith.
Dakini's warm breath: the feminine principle in Tibetan Buddhism/Judith Simmer-Brown.
p. cm.
Includes bibliographical references and index.
ISBN 1-57062-720-7 (alk. paper)
ISBN 1-57062-920-X (pbk.)
1. Ḍākinī (Buddhist deity) 2. Buddhism—China—Tibet.
3. Femininity—Religious aspects—Buddhism. I. Title.
BQ4750.D33 S56 2001
294.3′42114—dc21 00-046359

Contents

Illustrations

PHOTOGRAPHS

FIGURES

Preface

WHEN I WAS NINETEEN, I was first enveloped by the feminine principle, albeit in a hidden form. As I arrived on the Delhi tarmac straight from Nebraska and inhaled the scent of smoke, urine and feces, rotting fruit, and incense, I knew I was home. From that moment on, the sway of brilliant saris, the curve of water jugs, the feel of chilis under my fingernails, and the pulse of street music called me back to something long forgotten. As I gazed into the faces of leprous beggars, wheedling hawkers, and the well-oiled rich, I was shocked into a certain equanimity I could not name. The only way I could express it was to say that I suddenly knew what it meant to be a woman. On subsequent trips, I have had similar responses, the slowing of my mind and a deep relaxation in the pores of my body, calling me from ambitions of daily life to an existence more basic and fundamental, calling me home.

As a graduate student in South Asian religion in the late sixties, I discovered feminism. For many years, my feminist journey paralleled my academic and spiritual ones, and I found few ways to truly link them. Looking back at my papers and essays, I can see that I was trying to find a place for myself as a woman in academe. At the same time I began Buddhist sitting meditation practice, *zazen*, in the Japanese Sōtō tradition. In my first teaching job, I was the only woman my academic department had ever hired. When I was inexplicably terminated, departmental memos gave as the reason that my husband was a university administrator and I "didn't need the money." I joined a class action suit against the university and eventually won. During the turmoil, Buddhist meditation gave me a quiet center from which to ride out the maelstrom.

Later, eschewing another full-time academic appointment for full-time intervention with rape victims, my feminism emerged full blown. I saw myself burning in all women's rage, rage against the violence, the brutalization and objectification of us all. Even as I became outraged, I continued to sit. Alternating confrontation therapy with convicted rapists and long periods of intensive meditation, I learned that rage is bottomless, endless, the fuel for all-pervading suffering in the world. I began to feel directly the sadness at the heart of rage, sadness for all the suffering that people—female and male, rape victim and rapist—have experienced. I knew then that feminism saw a part of the truth, but only a part. Having experienced my own suffering, I began to sense its origin and to glimpse its end.

That is when I came to teach Buddhist Studies at Nāropa University, at the end of 1977. Several years earlier, I had met my teacher, Ven. Chögyam Trungpa Rinpoche, and recognized at once that I had everything to learn from him. He completely knew the rage and he knew the sadness, and yet he had not lost heart. He thoroughly enjoyed himself, others, and the world. And he introduced me to a journey in which I could explore rage, sadness, passion, and ambition and never have them contradict my identity as a woman and a practitioner. My feminist theories wilted in the presence of his humor and empathy, and my consuming interests turned to Buddhist practice, study, and teaching.

Ven. Chögyam Trungpa Rinpoche was one of the first Tibetan lamas to teach in North America. Born in the eastern Tibetan province of Kham in 1940, he was recognized as an incarnate teacher (*tülku*) of a major Kagyü school when he was only thirteen months old.[1] He was enthroned at Surmang Monastery and rigorously trained in Kagyü and Nyingma Buddhist philosophy and meditation until the Chinese invasion of his country. Like many lamas in Kham, he fled Chinese persecution during the Tibetan uprising of 1959, leading a large number of monks and lay devotees to safety in India. There he served as spiritual adviser to the Young Lamas Home School in Dalhousie, India, until 1963, when he was encouraged by His Holiness the Dalai Lama to study at Oxford University.

In 1969, after a solitary meditation retreat at the Padmasambhava cave in Taktsang in the kingdom of Bhutan, Trungpa Rinpoche radically changed his approach to teaching and meditation. Realizing that the Buddhist teachings would never take root in the West unless their cultural trappings were cut away, he gave up his monastic vows and married a young British woman. He also decided to teach in North America and established meditation centers in Vermont and Colorado in the early 1970s.

The America that Trungpa Rinpoche entered then was ripe with social and cultural ferment. Feminists were active and vibrant, but some did not find in political activism the experience of wholeness they sought. Many feminists like myself turned toward spirituality to complete their journeys, but most sought spirituality that did not involve the patriarchal oppressions of institutional religion.[2] From that perspective, I had made a peculiar choice. Tibetan Buddhism in its Asian and North American manifestations at that time had male teachers, strong hierarchical patterns, and neither sympathy for nor openness to feminism. I was fresh from the gender wars of lawsuits and rape trials, but still Tibetan tantra drew me. Meeting Rinpoche, I knew I could bring everything with me and that nothing would be confirmed or denied. And I knew that healing would happen only if I was willing to risk everything.

For his part, Rinpoche spoke inscrutably and enthusiastically of what he called "the feminine principle" in Tibetan Buddhism. He presented this material in a completely unique way for a Tibetan lama, couching traditional and fundamental insights of tantra in language accessible to citizens of the late twentieth century influenced by feminism. In his public and private teachings, he wove in what he called the Mother, who "safeguards against the development of ego's impulses."[3] He said that because she was unborn she was also unceasing,[4] and his explanations did nothing to clarify this conceptually. I understood I could access these teachings only through deeper meditation practice. He encouraged me, teased me, and devastated me in a variety of ways; I can never forget the accuracy and warmth of his compassion. He introduced me to the ḍākinī, and I know that she is inseparable from his mind.

Whereas Trungpa Rinpoche was best known to the public as unconventional in his lifestyle and teachings, with his students he was meticulous, generous, and exacting in his presentation of Tibetan tantra. He required rigorous practice as prerequisites, and he introduced the stages of practice in turn. He closely supervised the translation of ritual texts, standardizing the English in consultation with the most respected teachers of his lineages. And he monitored the progress of his many students both personally and through a network of his students who were trained as meditation instructors. He also insisted that the teachings be reflected in our everyday lifes, our homes, families, and relationships, and tested our understanding at every turn.

I gratefully threw myself into this regimen, appreciating its demands for direct, experiential understanding and commitment and for its accessibility to Americans. My practice evolved and so did my study as Rinpoche gradually taught more traditionally and invited the greatest Kagyü and Nyingma lamas of the exiled Tibetan communities of India and Nepal to teach his students. He also encouraged the development of my academic studies in Buddhism. From the beginning, I was pushed to teach at Nāropa University and within the Buddhist community, which forced me to integrate study and practice in a most public and personal way.

I presented my first academic paper on the ḍākinī in the spring of 1987, a memorable time because it occurred within months of both the birth of my first child and the terminal illness and death of my beloved teacher. In the years since Rinpoche's death, I have had the opportunity to study with the best of the realized lamas of the Kagyü and Nyingma lineages, who generously took on the guidance of the "orphaned" students of their friend Trungpa Rinpoche. Slowly during these years, as I continued my study and practice, I became more committed to an extended work on the ḍākinī, but because of teaching and domestic demands, this seemed impossible. Finally in the spring of 1993, with two young children at home, I was granted a one-semester sabbatical from Nāropa University and began my work in earnest.

Impressed with the enormity of the challenges and depressed by my inability to meet them, I scheduled an interview with the young and dynamic female incarnation Ven. Khandro Rinpoche, to ask prepared questions on the ḍākinī. A tiny, spirited woman with a penetrating gaze and gentle demeanor, Rinpoche spoke fluent English in rapid staccato sentences. As the interview progressed, she questioned me closely about my project and its aim and intention, and generously urged me to persevere. I explained my doubts, but Rinpoche declared how necessary such a book would be, pointing out my particular qualities and responsibilities to write it. As a rare Tibetan woman *rinpoche,* she had experienced her own challenges in receiving a full monastic education and the respect accorded an incarnation. On her first American tour, she had been assailed with questions about women and the feminine wherever she taught. As a result, she had come to deeply understand the concerns that Westerners, practitioners and nonpractitioners alike, share regarding gender in Tibetan Buddhist practice.

At first I had approached Rinpoche out of curiosity. After all, her very name, Khandro Rinpoche, means "ḍākinī incarnation." As I came to see, if one looked only at her gender, most of what she had to offer would be lost. Her unusual background, combining traditional Tibetan monastic education with Western convent-school training, made her a brilliant bridge between traditional and contemporary perspectives. And her own gifts in directly imparting her insightful, immediate understanding of the Buddhist teachings are remarkable. In wise and humorous counsel, she advised, "If being a woman is an inspiration, use it. If it is an obstacle, try not to be bothered." When she departed, I sat down at the computer and in seven weeks had a rough skeleton of the book. Khandro Rinpoche continued in subsequent years to encourage the project, generously granting me repeated personal interviews, communicating by letter, and reviewing an early draft of the entire manuscript. To say that her inspiration has been essential is an understatement.

In the succeeding years, many doors have opened to me in support of this book. I interviewed a number of lamas with whom I had studied and found them generous and helpful in countless ways, answering questions, guiding the structure of the work, correcting my mistakes and confusions, and encouraging me. I would never have undertaken such a project without the insistence and encouragement of these lamas, and I owe them a debt of gratitude for any measure of understanding of the ḍākinī that I may have. The structure, design, and conception of the book have been shaped by their direct suggestions and guidance.

For me, the encounter with the ḍākinī has inspired an intense personal journey. My early interest in her was born of my feminist sensibilities and concerns that women practitioners of Tibetan Buddhism need "positive role models" on our spiritual journeys. Yet the journey took me much farther than those limited goals. I have sought her traces in my practice and study for over twenty-five years. Gradually my motivations for meeting the ḍākinī have changed. I have seen that she required me to be willing to shed all these reference points of ego and identity in order to enter her domain. At the same time, she demanded that I bring everything along, all neurosis and confusion, all arrogance and rage, all concepts of feminine and masculine, to offer into her blazing gaze. Even while she has shown her face to me in glimpses, she has become more elusive, taking me with her on a boundless journey. I pray that she remain my unanswerable question, my seed syllable, my Tibetan *koan,* for this life.

The inspiration of this book is my encounter with the symbol of the ḍākinī, who personifies in Tibetan Buddhism the spiritual process of surrendering expectation and concept, revealing limitless space and pristine awareness. But while her feminine face drew me inward, what I have found is far beyond gender concerns. She is a powerful religious phenomenon, a fertile symbol of the heart of wisdom to be realized personally by every practitioner and to be respected and revered throughout the Tibetan tantric tradition. Her manifestations and meaning are profound, experiential, and hidden from rational strategy. Yet she appears everywhere in tantric literature and practice, mystifying and intriguing all tantric practitioners.

Methodology in Interpreting Tantric Sources

A study of the ḍākinī requires a methodology that employs both scholarly preparation and training in Vajrayāna Buddhist practice traditions. These two orientations must be combined because Vajrayāna Buddhist scholarship demands that traditional tantric texts be interpreted through the oral instructions of a qualified guru. As has often been said, tantric texts are written in "twilight language" (*sandhā-bhāṣa, gongpe-ke*), which, as the *Hevajra-tantra* states, is a "secret language, that great convention of the *yoginīs,* which the *śrāvakas* and others cannot unriddle."[5] This means that the texts of Buddhist tantra cannot be understood without the specific oral commentary by authorized Vajrayāna teachers.[6] For this reason, while I have consulted many translated texts and scholarly sources on Vajrayāna Buddhism, I have also taken every available opportunity to consult tantric lamas from the Kagyü and Nyingma traditions for guidance, interpretation, and commentary on the written sources.

The Kagyü and Nyingma schools are two of the four major schools of Tibet, and although they have distinct histories and styles, their lines of transmission have for centuries intertwined and complemented each other. The Nyingma school (literally, the "old" translation tradition) represents the form of Buddhism introduced to Tibet in the eighth century by Padmasambhava, with a strong emphasis on yogic practice, visionary experience, and decentralized institutional structure. The Kagyü is one of the major Sarma schools (literally, "new" translation) that appeared in the eleventh to twelfth centuries and is noted for joining a strong yogic and visionary tradition with monastic discipline and centralized hierarchy. Both schools place meditation practice and realization above scholastic training, and although many treasured lamas of these traditions have been thoroughly trained in monastic colleges, they are regarded above all as meditation masters.

The core material for this study surveys representations of the ḍākinī in selected texts in translation from these two Tibetan schools, in addition to Indian tantric texts that have been valued in Tibet. The primary texts consulted have been selected tantras (*gyü*), hagiographies (*namthar*), and realization songs (*nyam-gur*) of the Vajrayāna. These texts are from the so-called higher tantras,[7] those tantric traditions that accelerate the path to enlightenment by employing extraordinary means to arrive at the essential point. Of special importance have been the "mother tantra" texts (*ma-gyü*), which especially emphasize the ways of bringing passion to the spiritual path. In the Sarma tradition, the tantras consulted have been especially the *Cakrasaṃvara-tantra* and related tantras of the Saṃvara group (*Abhidānottara-tantra, Saṃvarodaya-tantra*); the *Hevajra-tantra;* and to a lesser extent the *Guhyasamāja-tantra.*[8] In the Nyingma tradition, the Mahāyoga and Anuyoga tantras are associated with skillful means and wisdom respectively, closely paralleling the approach of the Sarma traditions. These Nyingma tantra texts are not available in translation, but the Nyingma also considers the Guhyasamāja and Cakrasaṃvara tantras to be important canonically.[9] The original languages of these texts include Buddhist Sanskrit, Apabraṃśa, Central Asian languages, and Tibetan, and I have relied on the published and unpublished work of many translators.

I have also consulted the hagiographies of many *siddhās*, or tantric adepts, both male and female. From the Kagyü lineage I have drawn from the namthars especially of Tilopa, Nāropa, Marpa, Milarepa, Gampopa, Machik Lapdrön, Niguma, Sukhasiddhi and the Karmapas.[10] From the Nyingma lineage, the hagiographies of Guru Rinpoche, Yeshe Tsogyal, and Maṇḍāravā[11] were most helpful, as well as individual accounts of the great treasure-discoverers (*tertöns*) such as Jigme Lingpa and Pema Lingpa.[12] I also consulted the classic collections and histories by Butön, Tāranātha, Gö-lotsawa Zon-nupel, and more contemporary collections by Dudjom Rinpoche and Tulku Thondup Rinpoche.[13] I also collected available accounts of encounters between ḍākinīs and great women teachers of these two lineages for study of gender specificities.

Whenever possible, I have relied on the commentarial traditions of Tibet, especially the oral commentaries of Kagyü and Nyingma lineage masters. Wishing to present the tradition in its own terms as much as possible, I have often placed the commentary and interpretation of lamas of these lineages above the commentaries from other scholarly sources. On the other hand, developments in Tibetology have greatly influenced this book, especially the intelligent work of recent scholars who utilize disciplines such as the history of religions, literature, gender studies, anthropology, and art history in interpreting Tibetan sources.

Some of the commentaries came in private interviews, conducted especially for this book, with thirteen Kagyü and Nyingma lamas in exile. In each case, I approached the lama in question with the basic outline of the book project and a summary of the material I had already received from my root teacher. Often I first encountered reticence, even suspicion. The ḍākinī lore is one of the most revered and guarded of Tibetan esoteric symbolic teachings. Many diaspora Tibetan lamas have become concerned about interpretations they have encountered among Western observers, especially on topics as vulnerable to feminist scrutiny as the ḍākinī and related understandings of sexuality. These lamas have seen their most sacred understandings interpreted through the lens of feminist critique in destructive ways that they feel denigrate the lama, the profound practices, and the effectiveness of teaching environments in the West. They closely quizzed me as to my intentions and understanding, and also wanted to know what I had learned from other lamas on this subject.

Almost all of these lamas agreed to speak with me on tape, knowing that I would include their comments in this book. In many cases they gave me specific teachings to include, suggesting a structure and focus for the book. Most encouraged me to complete this study, and several urged me onward. I can only speculate on the reasons for their generosity. First, I was a student of one of the most respected and successful Tibetan teachers in the West, one who had paved the way for their own teaching opportunities. Second, I have taught Buddhist studies for over twenty years at the only accredited Buddhist college and graduate school in the Western higher education system, a school for which they had respect, however little they may have known about its approach. Third, most of them already knew me at least slightly and knew something of my practice and commitment to propagating an authentic understanding of the Tibetan teachings. Several lamas offered more information and support than I requested, suggesting that I come back the following day for more teachings and conversation. While no lama said so explicitly, it was clear that there were specific topics that were not to be included out of respect for the secrecy of the teachings, although, to my surprise, very few topics were deemed too secret to include.

I have also relied on the tireless and selfless work of translators, many of them first-generation American Buddhists themselves, who have lived for many years with lamas and have endeavored to make the essential teachings of Tibetan Buddhism available in English or other Western languages. Some of these translators have academic credentials and appointments; many do not, and serve in often marginal livelihoods that support their translation activities in dharma centers throughout the world. Their contribution to a genuine understanding of Tibetan Buddhism cannot be overestimated. My Sanskrit and Tibetan are sufficient to appreciate the monumental tasks they have undertaken and to standardize terms in these languages here.

It has also been important to this study to place the symbol of the ḍākinī in its characteristically Vajrayāna formulation within the context of earlier Indian Buddhism. Scholarship that examines the Vajrayāna in isolation from Indian sources has tended to miss elements of meaning that have been central to Tibetan understandings of Vajrayāna ritual and practice. For an interpretation of the meaning of a Vajrayāna symbol to be effective, these foundations must be discussed and integrated. For this reason, the themes and symbols of Tibetan tantra are placed in the context of earlier Indian Buddhism.

As background, I have endeavored to locate the meaning of the ḍākinī specifically within the tradition of Tibetan tantra, as distinguished from the ḍākinī and other feminine forms of "great goddess" or tantric traditions in India. This is important because of the dangers of mixing Hindu and Buddhist tantric traditions when interpreting symbols, manifestations, and meanings. Because Hindu and Buddhist tantras of medieval India used many of the same "twilight" conventions, scholars often assume that the two traditions of interpretation are the same. This is a common pitfall because the commentaries on Hindu tantra are more accessible to the noninitiate, and so generalizations from Hindu tantric literature sometimes creep into interpretations of Tibetan sources. For this reason, chapter 2 identifies similarities and differences between the ḍākinī in Hindu and Buddhist tantric traditions.

The methodology of this book has also been deeply influenced by academic studies of gendered symbols in various religious traditions. Their reflections and methods have helped shape my understanding of patterns and meanings in the tapestry of ḍākinī lore. These works have recognized that gendered symbols have unpredictable but often separate meanings for women or men in the societies in which the religions are practiced. The discoveries of the differing patterns of practice and understanding of gendered symbols have expanded my appreciation of the ḍākinī in new directions, freeing me from the too-narrow assumptions of feminist perspectives and scholarship, which often bring contemporary values to bear on the interpretation of historical material. This book may be sympathetic to certain feminist concerns, but it does not follow feminist methodology.

Gender symbols have a specific context of interpretation in the traditional Tibetan mileu, one removed from issues of the personal identity of individual men and women. Rather, gender symbols are used to animate and express the dynamic world of duality, which is viewed as a painful alienation from the truth of things as they are. In the Vajrayāna Buddhism of Tibet, duality need not be painful alienation. Properly understood, it can be seen as a wisdom display in which all the enlightened qualities are present, symbolized by the feminine and masculine joined in ecstatic union. When the conventional world of duality is seen in this way, it is already liberated. In this context, any study of the feminine in Tibetan Buddhism must also include the masculine, the *heruka* who is a symbol of skillful means and compassion. The heruka is contrasted with the ḍākinī, but most of all the symbol of their union (*yab-yum*) is explored and interpreted in traditional context. Chapter 4 critically reevaluates the understanding of sexual imagery and its role in tantric iconography and practice.

This study interprets the subtle meanings of gender symbolism in Tibetan religion. There may be fascinating interplay between gender as symbol in Tibetan Buddhism and the impact this symbol might have on the lives of Western-convert Buddhist practitioners for whom gender and identity are inextricably joined. Certainly my questions of the lamas often reflected this interest, and their answers probably reflected some degree of their assimilation of Western views of gender. For example, I asked various lamas how they understood living human men and women to manifest in accord with religious symbols. They consistently answered, unhesitatingly, with a coherent description of what they considered masculine and feminine temperaments to be while insisting that these traits were not inherent and could not be conventionally seen. Discerning them was considered part of "sacred outlook," the practice of seeing purity in every circumstance, which is foundational in Vajrayāna Buddhism.

Throughout this book I carefully outline the structure of the feminine principle in traditional expression, drawing on text, ritual, meditation, and iconography with available oral instruction. And yet the structure of the topics, my interpretation of their meaning, and the overall understanding have come from my perspective as a contemporary Western woman practitioner. This is particularly true on the topic of subjectivity, which is woven through the entire work. My reflections on the interplay between traditional and contemporary contexts come in the conclusion.

The methodology of this work is perhaps wildly messy. Traditional sources, sometimes over one thousand years old, are interpreted in a historically and culturally different context. In this case, we have the perplexing complication of texts from as early as eighth-century India[14] that became influential in Tibet by the twelfth century. These texts are commented upon by twentieth-century Tibetan lamas, who because of the Tibetan diaspora have been trained in Indian *shedras*[15] by refugee masters, conveyed sometimes through translators in English to an American scholar-practitioner. The consistent element, appropriate to Tibetan Buddhism, is that these teachings have been conveyed personally from teacher to disciple through an oral tradition of communication that has probably changed in context and content over the centuries. But for Tibetans, the very symbol of this transmission is the "warm breath of the [mother] ḍākinīs" (*khandro khalung*). It is personal, fresh, and alive, born of immediate insight, the direct communication between teacher and disciple.

Chapter 1 explores interpretations of the ḍākinī from recent generations of Western scholars and translators and assesses the adequacy of these interpretations. Especially at issue are the prevailing modes of feminist and Jungian paradigms. After an assessment of these methods, more appropriate methodologies are proposed that draw from the academic disciplines of the history of religions and gender studies. This chapter also explores the influence of religious symbols on the development of personal subjectivity as a prelude to an understanding of the ḍākinī as the symbol of spiritual subjectivity for the Vajrayāna practitioner.

Chapter 2 gives the context, Indian historical background, and overview of the ḍākinī in the Tibetan tradition. The ḍākinī is defined and differentiated from her Hindu tantric cousins, and her types in tantric Tibet are detailed. Finally, a fourfold model is proposed for understanding the ḍākinī in a wide variety of her meanings in Tibetan tantra.

Chapter 3 explores the most subtle level, the "secret ḍākinī," the Great Mother Prajñāpāramitā, the essence of the wisdom-mind of the practitioner. Chapter 4 describes the "inner ḍākinī" as the dynamic visionary form invoked in deity meditation who vividly illustrates the contours of this wisdom-mind. Chapter 5 traces the "outer ḍākinī," the energetic expression of the wisdom-mind as it takes subtle-body form in the practitioner of tantric yoga. Chapter 6 examines the "outer-outer ḍākinī," the human woman, living, interacting, and teaching. Insight into the ḍākinī's nature, developed through Vajrayāna meditation, propels the practitioner to cut through obscurations to the pure enlightened nature; thus, the ḍākinī is essential for the ultimate attainment of buddhahood. These chapters draw from tantric biographies, songs, and practices, giving shape to the feminine.

Chapter 7 interprets the ḍākinī's hagiographic lore, in which she engages directly with yogins and yoginīs as messenger, guru, and supporter in tantric practice. This section identifies the ḍākinī's characteristic style, the times and places of her appearance, her particular qualities of teachings through blessings of her body, and the qualities of the encounters. A special section contrasts the features of ḍākinī encounters with female yoginīs as opposed to yogins and interprets their meaning for male and female practitioners.

Chapter 8 describes the ḍākinī as protector of the tantric teachings through the power of indecipherable language—the auspicious coincidence of appropriate time and place for teachings—and as midwife of the transmission of teachings. She also is responsible for engendering new lineages of instruction.

The conclusion reflects upon interpretations of ḍākinī stories and their relevance for an overall understanding of the ḍākinī. The book concludes with an exploration of its central image, the warm breath of the mother ḍākinīs.

Acknowledgments

It is humbling to reflect how many generous people have contributed to and participated in the writing of this book. First and foremost, I must thank my teachers, especially my root teacher Chögyam Trungpa Rinpoche, whose passing was thirteen years ago today. He embodied the feminine principle and introduced me to that aspect of myself. His son and successor, Sakyong Mipham Rinpoche, has been most kind in his permission to publish these materials and in his support, encouragement, and brilliant teaching. I wish to thank those generous lamas who gave special help with specific parts of the project: Khenchen Thrangu Rinpoche, Khenpo Tsultrim Gyamtso Rinpoche, my special teacher Dzogchen Pönlop Rinpoche, and Ringu Tulku Rinpoche from the Kagyü lineage; and Dzigar Kongtrül Rinpoche, Khandro Rinpoche, Chagdud Tulku Rinpoche, Tsoknyi Rinpoche, Sogyal Rinpoche, Namkhai Nyingpo Rinpoche, and Ngakpa Dawa Chödak of the Nyingma lineage. It is important to acknowledge, however, that the structure and content of this work are my own, and I take full responsibility for any and all mistakes in interpretation.

I am grateful also for the help of many friends and colleagues who have supported and encouraged this project. Reggie Ray suggested I undertake it and gave invaluable early suggestions. Martha Bonzi's personal encouragement and generous financial support for one semester's work was strategic in realizing the first phase. Nālandā Individual Assistance Trust provided financial support for technical aspects. I wish to thank Nāropa University, especially President John W. Cobb, for the year's sabbatical leave and faculty development grants that so directly nurtured this book. Judy Lief contributed early impetus and inspiration for the book and commented insightfully on an early version. John Rockwell has given inestimable guidance and moral support, twice reviewing the entire manuscript and discussing fine points. Clarke Warren and Jenny Bondurant provided clarifying suggestions on the entire draft. James Meadows and Bea Ferrigno furnished early editorial help. Sarah Harding corrected the Tibetan and provided overall suggestions, and Ann Helm and Scott Wellenbach of the Nālandā Translation Committee double-checked Tibetan phonetic spellings and Sanskrit listings. L. S. Summer ably transcribed hours of taped interviews, and Misha Neininger and Angelika Pottkamper saucily aided in reading extensive German sources. Ark LeMal provided both technical support and therapy when computer problems arose. I wish to thank my Nāropa faculty colleagues: Cynthia Moku, for permitting use of her exquisite drawings of ḍākinīs throughout the book; and Joshua Mulder, for giving permission to photograph his art in progress—stunning larger-than-life sculptures that are being created for the Great Stūpa of Dharmakāya at Rocky Mountain Shambhala Center in Red Feather Lakes, Colorado. Special thanks to Marvin Ross, who beautifully photographed these sculptures.

Rita Gross has been my conversation partner on these issues for over twenty years. Amy Lavine offered perceptive advice on methodology, feminism, and gender studies; her enthusiasm buoyed me at low moments. Jules Levinson, Larry Mermelstein, David Kinsley, and Nathan Katz supplied important advice at key junctures. Joan Halifax, Keith Dowman, Tsultrim Allione, and Ngakpa Chögyam offered welcome perspective, advice, and encouragement. Sangye Khandro's suggestions refined the title of the book. David Germano and José Cabezón offered translations and leads for ḍākinī stories. I wish to express my appreciation to my Nāropa University students, upon whom many of the early ideas of this book were tested. Nāropa University Library's Ed Rutkowski and Philip Merran kindly procured my obscure interlibrary loan requests during the research phase.

Many Shambhala saṅgha friends have been most helpful and supportive through lively interest, suggestions, and moral support—I could never have continued without them. Students and faculty of the Ngedön School have dialogued with me about much of this material. I want to thank Conner Loomis and the Women Who Run With Scissors for moral support and feedback. Other important supporters, directly or indirectly, have been Cindy Shelton, Daniel Berlin, Denise Wuensch, Janet Solyentjes, and Giovannina Jobson. I have nothing but admiration and appreciation for my Shambhala editor, Kendra Crossen Burroughs, who truly served as midwife, confidante, and mirror in her expert editorial guidance. Thanks also to Eden Steinberg, Emily Bower, and Tracy Davis for their meticulous editorial support.

The greatest supporter of all has been my partner, best friend, and husband, Richard Brown, who has consistently and warmly believed in this project and has effected its completion in countless daily ways. He and our children, Alicia and Owen, have provided me with the real incentive to persevere, and I look forward to spending more time with them now that the book has reached completion.

Dakini's Warm Breath

Introduction

ENCOUNTERING THE DAKINI

When the great yogin Padmasambhava, called by Tibetans Guru Rinpoche, "the precious teacher," embarks on his spiritual journey, he travels from place to place requesting teachings from yogins and yoginīs. Guided by visions and dreams, his journey takes him to desolate forests populated with ferocious wild animals, to poison lakes with fortified islands, and to cremation grounds. Wherever he goes he performs miracles, receives empowerments, and ripens his own abilities to benefit others.

When he hears of the supreme queen of all ḍākinīs, the greatly accomplished yoginī called Secret Wisdom,[1] he travels to the Sandal Grove cremation ground to the gates of her abode, the Palace of Skulls. He attempts to send a request to the queen with her maidservant Kumarī. But the girl ignores him and continues to carry huge brass jugs of water suspended from a heavy yoke across her shoulders. When he presses his request, Kumarī continues her labors, remaining silent. The great yogin becomes impatient and, through his yogic powers, magically nails the heavy jugs to the floor. No matter how hard Kumarī struggles, she cannot lift them.

Removing the yoke and ropes from her shoulders, she steps before Padmasambhava, exclaiming, "You have developed great yogic powers. What of my powers, great one?" And so saying, she draws a sparkling crystal knife from the girdle at her waist and slices open her heart center, revealing the vivid and vast interior space of her body. Inside she displays to Guru Rinpoche the maṇḍala of deities from the inner tantras: forty-two peaceful deities manifested in her upper torso and head and fifty-eight wrathful deities resting in her lower torso.[2] Abashed that he did not realize with whom he was dealing, Guru Rinpoche bows before her and humbly renews his request for teachings. In response, she offers him her respect as well, adding, "I am only a maidservant," and ushers him in to meet the queen Secret Wisdom.

This simple maidservant is a messenger of her genre, the ḍākinī in Tibetan Buddhism. As can be seen from her name, Kumarī, "beautiful young girl, the crown princess," she may be humble in demeanor, but she is regal and commanding in her understanding of the nature of reality. Like many ḍākinīs, she teaches directly not through words but through actions. Specifically, she teaches with her body, cutting open her very heart to reveal her wisdom. She holds nothing back, sharing her nature with Guru Rinpoche himself. Kumarī demonstrates that her body is not as it appears. While she may be young, graceful, and comely, the object of desire, she shows her body to be empty and as vast as limitless space; in her heart is revealed the ultimate nature of reality. And within its vastness are all phenomena, all sense perceptions, emotions, thoughts, and cognitions as a maṇḍala of deities arrayed in the vivid splendor of their raiment, ornaments, and jewelry, with demeanor both peaceful and wrathful. Looking into her heart center, the practitioner is looking into a mirror, seeing the mind and the entire world in dramatically different perspective. One cannot see such a sight without being transformed.

Kumarī represents the most significant class of enlightened female figures in Tibetan Buddhism, the wisdom ḍākinī. In yogic literature and lore, she and her sisters appear to practitioners, men and women alike, during rituals and during retreat to give teaching, direction, and challenge in meditation practice. According to the Tibetan tradition, as a female she has a unique power to transform the practitioner and to confer power. Her power comes from her lineage of realization, representing the enlightened nature of mind of both yogins and yoginīs. Her mind is the expression of the essence of pristine wisdom, the fundamental wakefulness inherent but undiscovered in all beings. Her female body is vibrant with vitality, uniquely bearing and birthing that pristine wisdom.

Yet at first the great Guru Rinpoche, considered the second Buddha and known for unfailing omniscience and sophisticated skillful means, does not recognize her. What does this mean? The biography of the great

Retinue ḍākinī, maidservant of the queen of ḍākinīs.

master is known in Tibetan as a liberation story (*namthar*) that portrays the inner spiritual journey to enlightenment. The events in this biography are not historical fact in the Western sense. They trace in mythic, symbolic, and visionary fashion the transformation of conventional mind into awakened awareness. This biography and others like it in the Tibetan Vajrayāna tradition are beloved blueprints for the spiritual journey of every practitioner.

Why does Guru Rinpoche not recognize Kumarī as a realized ḍākinī-woman? This event in Vajrayāna lore is paradigmatic. In many sacred biographies, even the most realized teachers do not immediately recognize the ḍākinī, whose ambiguous, semiotic quality accounts for the richness and variety of her lore. She may appear in humble or ordinary form as a shopkeeper, a wife or sister, or a decrepit or diseased hag. She may appear in transitional moments in visions, her message undecipherable. If she reveals herself, if she is recognized, she has tremendous ability to point out obstacles, reveal new dimensions, or awaken spiritual potential. It is essential that the Vajrayāna practitioner not miss the precious opportunity of receiving her blessing. But when the time is not yet ripe, or when inauspicious circumstances are present, the ḍākinī cannot be seen, contacted, or recognized. When this occurs, the potency of the moment is lost and realization is missed.

Missed Opportunities, Skewed Interpretations

The ḍākinī lore has sparked enormous interest in recent decades, as Western scholars and interpreters have endeavored to comprehend her meaning. Speculation about the ḍākinī has been an implicit part of scholarship on Varayāna Buddhism from its inception as a Western academic discipline. Nevertheless, the lack of agreement concerning her meaning and the attempts to interpret her according to various biases are reminiscent of Guru Rinpoche's mistake. In an important essay surveying Western interpretations of the ḍākinī, Janice Willis concluded that there is little consensus concerning her meaning, and "little precision in the various attempts to further delineate and characterize [her] nature and function"; finally, she "remains elusive to academic or intellectual analysis."[3] She has, for the most part, not been recognized.

Certainly there have been fine preliminary studies of the ḍākinī, beginning with the scholarship of David Snellgrove, who traced the development of the ḍākinī from her "gruesome and obscene" origins to her "more gentle aspects" in Tibetan depictions as symbols of transcendent wisdom.[4] Herbert Guenther shed light on her meaning in symbolic context, associating her directly with teachings on emptiness and the spiritual goals of tantric Buddhism.[5] Recent scholars such as Martin Kalff, Adelheid Herrmann-Pfandt, Anne Klein, and Janet Gyatso[6] have continued to contribute to a comprehensive understanding of the ḍākinī. Yet certain biases have inhibited further development of an interpretation of ḍākinī lore.

Two pervasive paradigms have prevailed, sometimes facilitating understanding, but finally inhibiting an appropriate explanation of the ḍākinī in the Tibetan Varayāna tradition. The first, prevailing model is that of the anima in Jungian psychology, an archetype of the feminine closely associated with the unconscious, embedded in the psyche of the male. The second, more recent model derives from feminist sources, which treat the ḍākinī as a female goddess figure who may be, on the one hand, a creation of patriarchal fantasy or, on the other, a remnant of some prepatriarchal past who champions women in androcentric settings. Each of these paradigms has obscured an accurate understanding of the ḍākinī in her Tibetan sense. The adequacy of these models is examined and assessed in more detail in chapter 1.

Ambiguity regarding the ḍākinī's identity is not found only in Western scholarly sources. Tibetans also consider the ḍākinī ambiguous and often hesitate to conceptualize, systematize, or formulate her meaning. Yet, at the same time, Tibetan lamas and rinpoches who travel and teach in the West are increasingly troubled by the ḍākinī's appropriation by various Western communities. They are particularly bothered by feminist criticism. At a recent dinner with several Tibetan lamas, I discussed the progress of my book. One remarked to me, "Everywhere we go, everyone always asks us about ḍākinīs." Yes, I replied, Western students are very interested in ḍākinīs and in enlightened women teachers. "No," he corrected me. "They don't ask because they are interested. They ask to embarrass us. They want to criticize our tradition." He and the other lamas went on to describe how they felt that such questions were attacks on Tibetan Buddhism and how they perceive feminist critique as a rejection of the very heart of their tradition.

Certainly this atmosphere affected my research. Several of my interview subjects questioned me closely about my intention and method and eventually expressed displeasure with interviews they had conducted with others who were writing books, saying that "the teachings had been perverted." One lama asked me to come back for more material the following day, commenting, "If you are writing such a book, you must get it right." This lama asked me on several occasions to turn off my tape recorder so that he might speak frankly about his concerns for the future of the Tibetan tantric tradition.

How can this concern be heard? Just as Tibet has captured the utopian imagination of American culture, the romance of Tibet has sparked deep ambivalence in American Buddhists and others that is surfacing in a variety of ways.[7] Especially at issue are questions regarding spiritual authority and potential, imagined, or real "abuses of power." Feminists within, but especially outside of, American Vajrayāna communities have been among the most vocal critics of the spiritual authority of the Tibetan guru. At the same time, the ḍākinī has been appropriated by some as a symbol of either female power or patriarchal exploitation.[8]

This appropriation has been met by Tibetan lamas with a mixture of disappointment and outrage. Just when the esoteric Vajrayāna teachings have been made most available to Western students, these teachings have been used as weapons against the very teachers who have presented them. The ḍākinī, traditionally viewed as the most precious symbol and secret of the inner spiritual journey, has been reshaped into gynocentric crusader or misogynized victim. The irony of this dilemma holds little humor for Tibetan lamas in diaspora making a concerted effort to safeguard and propagate their own precious traditions and lineages. The gender wars in American Buddhism are viewed as a fundamental distortion of the teachings.[9]

From a feminist point of view, one might consider their responses to be patriarchal entrenchment that deserves no sympathy from Western practitioners. But the tremendous complexity of these matters reflects in part the sorry state of gender relationships in Western culture. Women's and men's liberation movements have remained primarily in a political or oppositional mode that has insidiously promoted the disempowerment of both men and women. While various forms of feminism have attempted to address this, their methods have often promoted a merely political vision incapable of healing the whole wound.

When political or oppositional methods have been carried into religion, religious communities have become the battleground. This has definitely been the case in these recent developments in American Buddhism, which threaten the integrity of the transmission of Buddhist teachings.

Certainly, there are wholesome and important aspects to this warfare: the social and political dimensions of patriarchal institutional religion need scrutiny and adjustment in order to respond to concerns about gender equality and responsible uses of power. But there is the enormous danger that the gender wars will obscure the central point of a spiritual path. For anyone, feminist or otherwise, who wishes to step into the vortex of spiritual power of a vital contemplative tradition like Tibetan Buddhism, a certain nakedness is required. One's politics, convictions, gender identity, and emotions are exposed to a perspective that transcends all of those aspects of one's identity. Yet all are potent fuel for the spiritual journey. If one is ready to include every political instinct, every conviction, every emotional reaction in one's spiritual practice, unflinchingly staying with all the painful aspects, there is tremendous possibility for transformation, both personal and situational. Only this can heal the gender wars in American Buddhism.

This book is not intended to contribute in any way to the gender wars, for it seems they have completely missed the point of the fundamental teachings of Tibetan Buddhism in general and the ḍākinī tradition in particular. Watching these controversies rage has provided the ground for quite a different approach to the ḍākinī lore, one based not on politics, sociology, or feminism but on looking at the phenomenon of the ḍākinī as a central religious symbol in Tibetan Buddhism.

At the same time, it is probably mutually beneficial for the ḍākinī lore to be made more explicit in Western Tibetan Buddhism. Ḍākinīs represent the domains conventionally attributed to women, such as embodiment, sexuality, nurture and sustenance, and relationship.[10] But for ḍākinīs, these domains are transmuted into realms that are not merely conventional but are much more profound than the concerns of daily existence. When ḍākinīs take human form as teachers and yoginīs, they deal with many issues that may prove obstacles to ordinary women, such as discrimination, rape, social limitation, and abuse. But these ḍākinī women serve as models for how obstacles may be turned into enlightenment. In short, the ḍākinī lore provides genuine support for women practitioners, whether Tibetan or Western, to develop confidence, perseverance, and inspiration in their meditation practice. But this lore also provides support to the spiritual journeys of men, showing the locus of wisdom in realms that male practitioners often ignore.

Another point must be addressed. In a traditional Tibetan context, until recently, it would probably be inappropriate to write a book on the ḍākinī. Much of the material here could not be found in any written Tibetan text. The ḍākinī lore has been carried through oral transmissions for centuries, passed on from teacher to student in an intimate setting that would not be appropriate to share publicly. This is not because there is anything scandalous, shocking, or dangerous in its content. Rather, its secrecy is based upon the personal spiritual power implicit in its understanding. When the practitioner has insight into the nature of the ḍākinī, Vajrayāna practice has the potential to become intimate, pervasive, and transformative.

As this tradition has been brought to the West, and indeed depends for its future survival upon Western support, it is important that fundamental misunderstandings of the ḍākinī lore be addressed. If the ḍākinī can be removed from the naïve and destructive realms of gossip and politics, the tremendous power of Vajrayāna practice and its relevance for Western Buddhist practices may be tapped. These teachings may have the potential for liberating the very views of gender that have blocked much spiritual progress in Western culture.

The Ḍākinī as Symbol in Tibetan Buddhism

It is clear that Western interpretations have failed to resolve the many conflicting manifestations of the ḍākinī. The problems of interpretation are obvious when we survey the uses of the term *ḍākinī* in Tibetan Buddhism. In sacred biographies, she is depicted in a personified manner as an unpredictable, semiwrathful, dancing spirit-woman who appears in visions, dreams, or the everyday lives of yogins or yoginīs. Her demeanor changes in various contexts: she may be playful, nurturing, or sharp and wrathful, especially when protecting the integrity of tantric transmission. She also guards the most private details of the practice, so that only those with the purest motivation are able to penetrate their essence. Without the blessing of the ḍākinī, the fruition of Vajrayāna practice is said to be inaccessible.

It is important to note that the word *ḍākinī* is also used in nonpersonified senses, especially in the meditation and ritual literature. In classical formulation in the unsurpassable Practice Vehicle (*Anuttara-yoga-yāna*),[11] she is depicted on four levels of meaning. On a secret level, she is seen as the manifestation of fundamental aspects of phenomena and the mind, and so her power is intimately associated with the most profound insights of Vajrayāna meditation. In this her most essential aspect, she is called the formless wisdom nature of the mind itself. On an inner, ritual level, she is a meditational deity, visualized as the personification of qualities of buddhahood. On an outer, subtle-body level, she is the energetic network of the embodied mind in the subtle channels and vital breath of tantric yoga. She is also spoken of as a living woman: she may be a guru on a brocaded throne or a yoginī meditating in a remote cave, a powerful teacher of meditation or a guru's consort teaching directly through her life example. Finally, all women are seen as some kind of ḍākinī manifestation.

The most appropriate methods for interpreting the ḍākinī place her squarely within this broad Tibetan Vajrayāna context of meditation and meaning. There she functions as a complex but unified religious symbol of meditative realization, whether or not personified. The methods required to interpret her meaning are associated with the interpretation of symbols. As Janice Willis wrote:

> In a tantric universe replete with symbols, *ḍākinī*, one may say, is *the* symbol par excellence; and being preeminently, constitutively, and inherently *symbolic*, the *ḍākinī* always remains a symbol within the "Tibetan symbolic world." As such "she" serves always only to represent and suggest—even for the tantric adept—other and deeper, non-discursive experiential meanings.[12]

As a classical symbol, the ḍākinī has two dimensions. In the first, the ḍākinī with all her complexity represents the inner wisdom-mind of the tantric practitioner appearing in concretized form to accentuate obstacles and to indicate the practitioner's inherent wakefulness. In a second dimension, the ḍākinī symbolizes the ancient wisdom of the guru and the enlightened lineages of teachers under whose protection the tantric practitioner meditates, navigating the perilous waters of the tantric journey. These two aspects merge when the ḍākinī reveals to the practitioner an ancient wisdom legacy that is simultaneously recognized as the inner wisdom-mind of the tāntrika.

Yet it is of central importance in Tibet that the ḍākinī is represented as female or, in the nonsubstantial sense, feminine.[13] As a gendered symbol the ḍākinī provides special challenges if the interpreter is to avoid the extremes expressed above. The discoveries of scholars such as Caroline

Walker Bynum, who interprets gender symbols in medieval Christianity, have been most helpful.[14] For example, meaning given to gender symbols in a Tibetan setting contributes in unexpected ways to the social roles of women, to gender attitudes, and to the success of women on the spiritual path. On an ultimate level, the limitless and vast qualities of mind are referred to as the Great Mother (*Yum Chenmo*), while conventional understandings of motherhood are nowhere present. Or, appearance in a semi-wrathful dancing feminine form is experienced differently by the yogin and the yoginī in ways one could not predict, as discussed earlier. From this perspective, a study of the ḍākinī in all her symbolic dimensions has tremendous potential to shed light on her identity and to bring new perspectives to the meaning of gender.

CHAPTER ONE

Gender, Subjectivity, and the Feminine Principle

IN INTERPRETING THE ḌĀKINĪ lore in Tibetan Buddhism, certain challenges arise. How is the ḍākinī to be understood—as a human woman, a goddess, an archetype? What is the significance of her gender for the Tibetan tradition and for contemporary Western interpretation? How relevant are previous interpretations of the ḍākinī for an authentic understanding of her significance? Given the meaning of the ḍākinī in Tibetan Buddhism, what tools of interpretation are most appropriate?

This chapter surveys selected Western interpretations of the ḍākinī, derived primarily from Jungian and feminist models, and assesses their adequacy. These models are contrasted with traditional understandings of the ḍākinī in Tibetan sources, in which she represents the most profound discoveries of tantric meditation. Then an appropriate Western model of interpretation is proposed, depicting the ḍākinī as a symbol but not an archetype; as feminine in gender but not a conventional female. In this context, the ḍākinī has significance in the practice of both women and men tāntrikas and is supplicated as a major support, second only to the guru. Lastly, the ḍākinī is depicted as the symbol of the spiritual subjectivity of the practitioner, evoking complete awakening.

Jungian Interpretations of the Ḍākinī: "Fantasy of Opposites"

The earliest model applied in Western interpretations of the ḍākinī was the Jungian anima archetype, reflecting C. G. Jung's general influence on the early generation of Western studies of Tibet. When W. Y. Evans-Wentz edited the early translations of Tibetan tantric texts, he asked the Swiss psychiatrist to write psychological commentaries for two of the four works.[1] Jung had been deeply influenced by exposure to these tantric texts, and it is clear from his writings that he "mined Asian texts (in translation) for raw materials"[2] for his own theories. One wonders how much his views of the anima were shaped by his study of the few translated Tibetan texts to which he had access. Throughout the *Collected Works,* he spoke of deities of Tibetan maṇḍalas as symbolic expressions of the importance of the anima. But when describing the deities, he followed the example of Arthur Avalon's translations, making little distinction between Hindu and Buddhist tantra, referring to the central deities as "Shiva and Shakti in embrace."[3] In his commentary on the *Pardo Thödröl,* in which he encountered ḍākinīs of the pardo in wrathful forms, he called them "sinister," "demonic," "blood-drinking goddesses," in "mystic colors."[4] Here he made no mention of the anima principle. Ironically, Jung would have denied for Tibetans a relationship between the ḍākinī and the anima, for he felt that the "Eastern view" was too introverted to require it; and he suggested that the extraverted quality of the Western soul-complex required "an invisible, personal entity that apparently lives in a world very different from ours."[5] Instead, he would have spoken of the ḍākinī as "psychic data, . . . 'nothing but' the collective unconscious."[6]

Jung's writings nevertheless set the stage for the tendency to psychologize and universalize the interpretations of various tantric principles. Giuseppe Tucci applied Jung's ideas in elucidating the maṇḍala, and Mircea Eliade drew on both of them for his work on the subject.[7] The influence of the Jungian milieu was apparent in commentaries by Lama Govinda and John Blofeld.[8] But the overt associations between the ḍākinī of Tibet and the Jungian anima were not explicit until 1963, when Herbert Guenther identified the contrasexual dynamics of each. As Guenther commented on the appearance of the ugly hag to the scholar Nāropa:

> all that he had neglected and failed to develop was symbolically revealed to him as the vision of an old and ugly woman. She is old because all that the female symbol stands for, the emotionally and passionately moving, is older than the cold rationality of the intellect which itself could not be if it were not supported by feelings and moods which it usually misconceives and misjudges. And she

> is ugly, because that which she stands for has not been allowed to become alive or only in an undeveloped and distorted manner. Lastly she is a deity because all that is not incorporated in the conscious mental make-up of the individual and appears other-than and more-than himself, is, traditionally, spoken of as the divine.[9]

In referencing this personal commentary on the ḍākinī appearance, Guenther remarked that "this aspect has a great similarity to what the Swiss psychologist C. G. Jung calls the *anima.*" The notion that the ḍākinī, like the anima, represents all that man is lacking and for which he yearns has pervaded Western scholarship since the early 1960s.[10]

Jung's anima is the image of the female in the individual male unconscious, shaped by individual men's unconscious experiences of women early in life. These images are further nurtured by the much deeper archetypal collective unconscious. The anima represents the intuitive, nurturing, erotic, emotional aspects of psychic life often neglected in male development. For men, this contrasexual image is the gateway to the unconscious, in which real women, or dream or symbolic images of women, lead him to the depths. Jung referred to the anima as "the image or archetype or deposit of all the experiences of man with woman,"[11] placing the subjectivity of the experience firmly within the purview of the man. She is the key to wholeness, through whom he is able to access the hidden parts of himself.

Jung identified the anima with personal subjectivity, the inner life, which is the reverse of the public persona, in which one's private dreams, impulses, and imagination hold sway. For the male, the (inner) anima represents all that the (outer) persona cannot manifest: the emotional, intuitive, and invisible. The anima is the personal link with the collective unconscious and provides the balance with the persona, which is always concerned about image, order, and societal values—hence she is called the subject.[12] The anima is the link with the deeper and more spiritual forces, which manifest to the conscious mind as symbols and shape every decision, act, and perspective.

Jung accounts well for the power of symbol in human experience, for it is through symbols that the conscious mind accesses the rich pattern of meaning available from the unconscious. The unconscious holds personal memories that influence the individual, but it also holds a deeper layer of primordial images common to all humans. These living psychic images are called archetypes, inherited by all humans at birth. Symbols manifest the primordial material to the individual through dreams and imagination, as well as in religious and cultural myth, ritual, and iconography.

There are definite benefits in regarding the ḍākinī through the lens of the anima construct.[13] Like the anima, the ḍākinī manifests in a manner that is immanently personal while representing a perspective on reality that is vaster and more profound. She appears in dreams, meditation, or visions, taking a variety of forms, both wrathful and peaceful. She is frightening, for she represents a realm beyond personal control, and she wields enormous power. And through the sacred outlook that is part of the Vajrayāna commitments, she is every human woman encountered. If she is recognized, she can transform the individual in ways that lead to greater awakening; thus she is said to hold the keys to transformation.

There are other ways in which the comparison between the anima and the ḍākinī can be misleading. The first, most problematic area relates to Jung's ideas concerning the contrasexuality of the individual and the anima. Jung's ideas about the anima (and the corresponding animus, the inner subject of women) have come under scrutiny because they essentialized gender notions, caricatured masculine and feminine traits, and fell into what James Hillman called the "fantasy of opposites." It is important for Western interpreters of the ḍākinī to understand these criticisms, for the same charges could be made against their work.

In the fantasy of opposites, everything in human experience is polarized into oppositions, which are further qualified by other opposites. The female ḍākinī is the messenger only for the male yogin, and in this relationship all gender traits are stylized into opposite tendencies, forcing all human experience into stereotypic views of gender. When this contrasexuality has no corresponding ḍāka for the female practitioner, many problems arise for Western interpreters.[14] This fantasy of opposites has placed undue pressure on the anima to serve whatever is neglected in human psychology, and because of this the precise meaning of the anima paradigm has become seriously diluted in Jungian studies. Under the rubric of this fantasy, there is a rich trade of "smuggled hypotheses, pretty pieties about eros, and eschatological indulgences about saving one's soul through relationship, becoming more feminine, and the sacrifice of the intellect."[15] When this fantasy of opposites is applied to the symbol of the ḍākinī, much is projected onto her that is not indigenous to her tradition.

The contrasexual dilemma also relates to another area in the overapplication of the anima paradigm to the understanding of the ḍākinī. In placing subjectivity firmly in the male prerogative, Jung neglected the spiritual subjectivities of women with relation to the anima.[16] Preoccupied with his theories, Jung confused the anima with real women and expected them to fit the image he had discovered in his own psyche. Then he developed a corresponding contrasexual theory of the animus, which he described as the inner unconscious of women, a theory to which his women patients could not fully subscribe.[17]

Similar perplexities can be found in the interpretation of the ḍākinī when scholars have tried to understand the application of the anima paradigm to the experiences of women and men. As greater numbers of hagiographies of yoginīs emerge, it is clear that ḍākinīs play a key role in the spiritual journeys of Tibetan women practitioners, guiding, teaching, and empowering them. The content of these appearances, however, is different for women than for men, as we will see in chapter 7.[18] In addition, in relationship with the male yogin, the ḍākinī is not all that "other," for she embodies many qualities that she shares with him. Yogins also experience visionary relationships with male gurus and *yidams* that are significant in ways similar to those with visionary ḍākinīs.[19] Several women scholars have challenged the contrasexuality of the ḍākinī. As Janice Willis commented, "The ḍākinī is the *necessary complement* to render us (whether male or female) whole beings." And Janet Gyatso concluded that it is inadequate to consider the ḍākinī as an "other," for "Buddhist women need ḍākinīs to help them loosen their attachments too."[20]

A second general area of concern about Jungian interpretations of the ḍākinī comes from Jung's reification of the psyche and of archetypes and its incompatibility with Buddhist principles, especially the teaching concerning *śūnyatā*, or the emptiness of inherent existence both of the self, in whatever guise, and of projections.[21] Jung understood the archetypes such as the anima to be a priori categories with status and inescapable power, analogous to God. He used words such as "sovereign, ominiscient, and unchanging" to refer to the archetypes. "The archetypes are the great decisive forces, they bring about the real events, and not our personal reasoning and practical intellect. . . . The archetypal images decide the fate of man."[22]

The first problem with this interpretation has to do with Jung's ideas concerning projection. For the human who has not yet individuated, the archetypes are manifest through projections, which are taken to be real. For Jung, the projections are less real than the anima and less real than the psyche that perceives them; the projections are mere phantoms of the vital power of the archetypes. For this reason, Jung became trapped in a subject-object dualism in which the subject was more real than the object. This dooms Jung to solipsism, a closed world in which the perceived is nothing other than an expression of the self that perceives it.[23]

Jung's stance on this matter creates special difficulties in gender discussions. By implication, the polarity between male and female is insurmountable, causing unendurable alienation and suffering. If the perceiving subject is more real than its projections, the "other" can never be reconciled, and the psychic and spiritual search is doomed. When both sides of the polarity are grounded in emptiness, this potential alienation is nothing but a temporary obscuration.

These flaws also raise concern when they are applied to Tibetan Buddhism, in which the unconscious has no ultimacy. The ḍākinī is a symbol that expresses in feminine form the fundamental ground of reality, which is the utter lack of inherent existence of every phenomenon, whether relative or absolute. Applied to Jungian notions, Buddhism discovers that the self has no inherent reality, nor does the psyche, the projections, the unconscious, or the archetypes. All phenomena arise as dreams within the vast and luminous space of emptiness. The ḍākinī is, above all, a nonessential message of this realization. Her nature is beyond limitation of any kind, including gender. For this reason, the ḍākinī is a symbol in the sense described above, capable of inspiring a transformation beyond gender issues, social roles, and conventional thinking of any kind.

As for the irreconcilability of masculine and feminine that remains in Jung's interpretation, the Tibetan spiritual path transcends these dualities in enlightenment, in which duality has no snare. The highest realization is one in which gender dualities are seen as "not one, not two" and all apparent phenomena are understood for what they are. There is finally no projector, no projection, and no process of projecting. This is called *Mahāmudrā*, the great symbol, in which all phenomena are merely symbols of themselves.[24]

In the context of our previous discussion of the complexity of symbols in influencing the subjectivities of women and men, it is clear that there are certain limitations imposed by a Jungian interpretation. The contrasexual framework of the anima and animus overly manipulates the dynamic of gender symbols in a way that conforms no more to the power of gender symbols in Tibetan religion than it does to the actual experiences of men and women. In my interviews with Tibetan lamas, they described the ḍākinī's influence on yoginīs and yogins in a fluid fashion without consistent contrasexual symmetry.

However, there are some real benefits in employing Jungian ideas in interpreting the ḍākinī. Once the contrasexual dilemma (expressed in the fantasy of opposites) and the reification of the psyche and archetypes have been corrected, the anima sheds light on an understanding of the ḍākinī, as we have discussed. But those who employ an understanding of the anima in interpreting the ḍākinī must have a broader range of interpretation at hand in order to comprehend the unique elements of the ḍākinī symbol.

The pervasiveness of the Jungian paradigm in examination of the ḍākinī emphasizes contrasexuality, the ultimacy of gender imagery, and psychological interpretation. These emphases have precipitated a blizzard of feminist objections, and no wonder. However, that critique may be directed more toward Jungian tenets than toward Tibetan Buddhism, which has not been properly represented in Western interpretation.

Feminist Interpretations of the Ḍākinī: Problems and Promise

In Western Judeo-Christian religion, prevailing patriarchal patterns have inspired a variety of feminist responses as women and men seek a religious life that promotes awakening free from gender bias. Some of these responses have discarded Christianity and Judaism completely, finding them irredeemably patriarchal, particularly in the male identity attributed to the godhead. These proponents have often turned to new religious forms, some of them consciously reconstructed, based on so-called prepatriarchal goddess religions.[25]

Given the patriarchal legacy of Western religion, it is understandable for feminisms to seek their religious birthright outside of Western sources. India and Tibet have been natural places for feminist spiritualities to turn, because of their rich heritages of goddess traditions in religious contexts in which the ultimate reality is not gendered. For this reason, the work of feminist scholars of Buddhism has been influential in unearthing legacies that might nurture a feminist religious life.

Recent work focused on the ḍākinī has been strongly influenced by these feminist considerations. This work has fallen into two general critiques. One identifies the ḍākinī as a construct of patriarchy drawn by a primarily monastic Buddhism in Tibet into the service of the religious goals of male practitioners only. The second perspective identifies the ḍākinī as a goddess figure in a gynocentric cult in which females are the primary cult leaders and males are their devoted students. These considerations have done much to simultaneously polarize and confuse those who wish to understand the ḍākinī in her Tibetan context.[26] The central concern of these interpretations is the ḍākinī's gender.

The German scholar Adelheid Herrmann-Pfandt published a comprehensive scholarly study of the ḍākinī drawn from Tibetan tantras and biographies.[27] The feminist critiques in this work were built upon a Jungian interpretation of the ḍākinī, and her monograph has influenced recent American studies such as Shaw and Gyatso. Herrmann-Pfandt noted that while Tibetan tantra was more inclusive of the feminine than Indian Mahāyāna Buddhism, women were exploited on a subtle level since the ḍākinī was understood only in terms of the male journey to enlightenment. The central point of her focus on the ḍākinī was her contrasexuality in relationship with the tantric yogin. Whether as visionary guides to the yogin or as human counterparts, women in tantric texts were not depicted as autonomous beings who could use the ḍākinī imagery in service of their own liberation. Herrmann-Pfandt's conclusions were that the ḍākinī is an example of the exploitation of women, while her human counterpart is subservient to the yogin in a patriarchal religious context.[28]

June Campbell's *Traveller in Space* critiqued Tibetan Buddhist patriarchal monastic and religious systems, demonstrating that women have been systematically excluded from Tibetan religion, serving only in marginal observer roles. She criticized the patriarchal matrix of power in which young boy tülkus are taken from their mothers' arms at a young age to be enthroned, raised, and trained by an exclusively male monastic establishment. Human women are removed from any actual influence in these young lamas' lives; instead, they are replaced by an abstract "feminine principle," manifesting as mythical ḍākinīs or Great Mothers and remaining ethereal and idealized, sought after by lamas "in reparation for their own damaged selves."[29] Campbell critiqued Tibetan notions of the ḍākinī, remarking that she is "the secret, hidden and mystical quality of absolute insight required by men, and . . . her name became an epithet for a sexual partner." The lama, however, retains the power of the teachings and transmits their meaning while using the abstract feminine as a complement. The female body and subjectivity are then coopted completely by the patriarchal system. This, she maintained, is damaging for women, for they can never be autonomous teachers or even practitioners in their own right, and they are kept under the dominion of male Tibetan hierarchies. For this reason, the ḍākinī can only be understood as a symbol of patriarchal Buddhism that guards male privilege. Campbell concluded that ḍākinīs, "travellers in space," are emblems of patriarchy, inaccessible to and even dangerous for the female practitioner, whether Tibetan or Western.[30]

While certain feminists have labeled the ḍākinī a purely patriarchal construct, others have idealized her as a goddess with special saving power for women alone. Miranda Shaw's *Passionate Enlightenment* reassessed women's historical role in the formative years of Indian Vajrayāna. Although her focus is primarily Indian Buddhist, her work has often conflated Indian and Tibetan, and Hindu and Buddhist, sources. The result is a depiction of a medieval Indian gynocentric cult in which women have a monopoly on certain spiritual potentials and are ritually primary while men are derivative. This is the reason, she wrote, that "worship of women (*strīpūjā*)" is shared by tantric Hindus and Buddhists. The theoretical basis of this is that "women are embodiments of goddesses and that worship of women is a form of devotion explicitly required by female deities."[31] For Shaw, the Tibetan version of the ḍākinī is a cultural remnant of the prepatriarchal period of tantric Buddhism in India. She suggested that women played pivotal roles in the founding of tantric Buddhism in India, serving as gurus and ritual specialists with circles of male disciples. As Buddhism spread to Tibet, women no longer played ritual or teaching roles. Instead, as Shaw argued, Tibet shaped the ḍākinī symbol into an abstract patriarchal ideal who serves the spiritual paths of male yogins only, in betrayal of her historical roots.

These interpretations of the ḍākinī have certain common features that merit general discussion. All have inherited from Western scholarship's Jungian bias certain contrasexual assumptions regarding the ḍākinī's role on the tantric path. These assumptions follow the contours of the fantasy of opposites, in which gender becomes stereotypic, essentialized, and androcentric, unlike many of the source materials themselves. This creates a theoretical model in which the feminine is idealized and made to serve "all that man is lacking and for which he yearns." With this interpretation as background, it is no wonder that feminist critics would challenge this ḍākinī as a construct of male fantasy and an abstract patriarchal principle. When one calls into question the Jungian bias of Western scholars, the basis of this feminist critique is also disputed.

An additional problem arises when mythic and symbolic material is taken to have historical significance. In her desire to "reclaim the historical agency of women,"[32] Shaw employed methods of feminist historiography to reconstruct a history of women in early tantric Buddhism in India. Drawing from early tantras attributed to ḍākinīs, she interpreted these to be authored by historical women and from their coded language constructed a gynocentric cult in which women were the ritual specialists and men were the apprentices. Employing "creative hermeneutical strategies,"[33] Shaw concluded that these sources reveal a great deal about women and gender relations in the tantric movement. In her account, the ḍākinī appears as support and patron of women qua women, serving as their exclusive protector in a gynocentric cult. Certainly there is ample precedent for Shaw's method, but it is difficult to discern anything authentically traditional about the ḍākinī from her interpretations, as she drew historical conclusions from symbolic tantric literature. In this case, as in the critiques of Campbell and Herrmann-Pfandt, the conflating of historical and symbolic has probably created greater perplexity over the identity of the ḍākinī than the Tibetan tradition could have ever produced.

These feminist interpretations of the ḍākinī have followed certain methods that draw conclusions about the historic or contemporary lives of women from a study of feminine symbols, in this case in Tibetan culture. This methodology has been critiqued in many works; in the case of Tibet, Anne Klein and Barbara Aziz have demonstrated that there is a distinction to be drawn between the seemingly egalitarian symbol of the ḍākinī and the lives of women in Tibet.[34] Certainly they and other scholars have indicated the strong connection between these two realms of experience, but the actual nature of the connection is not easily discerned. In order to enter this realm, one must delve more deeply into the realm of religious phenomena, especially symbols.

In order to responsibly analyze issues of gender in religious phenomena, three kinds of phenomena must be distinguished, each requiring differing methods: tenets or doctrines, social institutions, and systems of symbol and ritual. Studies of gender in the Buddhist tradition suggest a general pattern of institutional patriarchy accompanied by a contrasting doctrinal promise of the inherent spiritual capabilities of women.[35] This means that in the institutional structures of authorization of teachers, monastic education, writing and recording of texts, and ritual specialization, women in Asian traditions have been excluded from more than occasional positions of power and responsibility.[36] Insofar as women have been seen as threats to the renunciant path of male practitioners, attitudes toward them have been misogynistic, regarding them as evil seductresses who were snares of the tempter, Māra. Yet the core teachings of Buddhism reflect confidence in women's wisdom and potential for enlightenment. Still, when examining only the doctrinal and institutional aspects of Buddhism for gender bias, it is easy to become disheartened. Little has been done in the area of symbol and ritual, especially within Tibetan Buddhism, which is particularly rich in these aspects.

Symbols have tremendous potential to shape the spiritual journeys of male and female practitioners of Tibetan Buddhism. Gender symbols are pivotal in Tibetan symbol systems, providing expression for the dynamic qualities of phenomenal existence. Enlightened feminine and masculine symbols populate the painted scrolls and ritual texts of Tibet, suggesting a sacredness of gender so longed for in Western religion and feminism. How are these symbols to be understood? Do they have relevance for understanding the identities and values of humans? Such questions suggest the complexities of examining gender symbolisms and their implications for human life. In examining these symbols more deeply, it is important to identify their structure and presentation as well as the contexts in which they are practiced.

At the same time, there is a stream of the feminist critique regarding the ḍākinī that must be seriously considered in order to fully portray the actual power of gender symbols within culture. This is important because, while symbols have a distinct realm of structure and meaning, they deeply influence institutional life and doctrinal development in any tradition, though not in predictable ways. Whether or not one is sympathetic to feminist concerns, this feminist critique must be understood and considered. It says this: when female representations such as the ḍākinī pervade the Tibetan Buddhist symbolic world, they appear as abstract representation for the benefit of male practitioners only. Whether these female symbols are depicted as chaste or dangerous, visions of beauty or horror, cultural patrons or destroyers, they are described through the eyes of male practitioners, whether hierarchs or laymen. When women are defined in a patriarchal society like Tibet, their gender "can be exploited as a movable entity to be used to reflect men's sense of 'other' or to be abstracted to the transcendental, when the acknowledgment of her subjectivity, by-and-for-herself, becomes problematic for them."[37] June Campbell and Adelheid Herrmann-Pfandt have suggested that this is the case with the ḍākinī symbol, an abstract, objectified feminine as seen through the true religious subject of Buddhist culture, the male.[38] According to this view, women practitioners are deprived of their personal subjectivity.

In order to follow this critique, it is important understand the meaning of *subjectivity* in the context of feminism: a sense of agency and power at the heart of personal identity.[39] The critique continues: if religious practice is to be personal and dynamic, practitioners must experience spiritual subjectivity in which their full engagement is apparent. This is difficult in androcentric settings in which power rests in male hands and women are objectified in a variety of ways. In patriarchy, the male is considered the paradigm of humanity, and the female is a variation of the norm. Because of this, media of communication, ways of knowing, and social forms shaped by men are considered normative.

Because women's styles and forms often rest outside these norms, they are viewed as objects from the point of view of male privilege. Women achieve a temporary, precarious seat within normative realms only by receiving approval from men when they exhibit compliant qualities of objectified beauty, service, and submission. From this perspective, women do not fit within the androcentric definition of humanity and are objectified as the "other," treated as things to be controlled, classified, idealized, or demonized.

In religious life, according to this critique, males are the religious subjects who name reality, institutional structure, religious experience, and symbolic expression, and women are presented only in relation to the experience of men, as seen by men.[40] In the case of gender symbolism, female representations are depicted in an abstract form in service of male spirituality and through male projection and idealization. From this perspective, the Virgin Mary is the idealized purity of unconditioned love, Athena represents civility overcoming raw emotion, and Sītā is the ideal and submissive wife. But from the view of certain feminist critiques, these feminine symbols all serve the male subject.

It is true that subjectivity is of vital importance to women's experience, for it relates to the formative and meaningful aspects of female identity, which stand in contrast to culturally constructed male styles. For example, a specific female subjectivity values those experiences unique to biology and processed through Western patriarchal culture—experiences of birthing, mothering, and nurturing. These experiences have fostered in many women's lives a subjectivity that values nonconceptual, nonverbal wisdom as opposed to conceptual or logical knowledge, and that understands a somatic, visceral awareness associated with embodiment. The tendency to use this orientation as a stereotype of a universalized biological difference has, of course, been rejected by many feminists as an essentialist approach to sex roles.[41] Yet women's subjective experience has often been denigrated or ignored in androcentric settings.

In androcentric settings, the critique continues, women often have difficulty placing themselves within religious life as active subjects of their own spiritual experience, especially in relation to gender symbols. Within their traditions, few choices are available. Either women can ignore their female gender and identify themselves as a kind of generic "male," dismissing any obstacles they may face in the practice of their spirituality. In this case, women may avoid gender symbols of any kind as reminders of the peril of gender identity in religious practice. Or they can make a relationship with their female gender by seeing their bodies and emotions through men's eyes. Feminine symbols provide a paradigm for the objectified female, and women may subjectively experience their own gendered bodies in this abstracted way.

Liz Wilson explored the issue of gendered subjectivity in Buddhism in her work on representations of women's bodies in first-millennium Buddhist India and Southeast Asia.[42] While women were widely excluded from monastic life, their bodies appeared prominently in hagiographic literature as powerful objects of male desire and renunciation. When they were young and beautiful, women's bodies enticed men into fantasy and lust; when they died, their bodies rotting in the charnel ground evoked deep abhorrence. When women were depicted in rare instances as subjects in this hagiographic literature, how did they experience their own bodies? Wilson showed that nuns from the *Therīgāthā* became enlightened contemplating the impermanence of their own bodies. The former courtesan Ambapāli examined her body in her declining years, as if standing in front of a mirror, surveying sagging flesh and deepening wrinkles in a classic contemplation:

My hair was black, the color of bees, curled at the ends;
with age it's become like bark or hemp—
not other than this are the Truth-speaker's words.

My hair was fragrant, full of flowers like a perfume box;
with age it smells like dog's fur—
not other than this are the Truth-speaker's words. . . .

Once my two breasts were full and round, quite beautiful;
they now hang pendulous as water-skins with water—
not other than this are the Truth-speaker's words.

My body was once beautiful as a well-polished tablet of gold;
now it is covered all over with very fine wrinkles—
not other than this are the Truth-speaker's words.[43]

Ambapāli compared her aging body with the desirable, objectified form seen by her patrons when she was in her prime. Finding it to be other than its previous projections, she saw nothing of value remaining in cyclic existence. In this contemplation, Ambapāli followed the androcentric convention of contemplating the decaying body, attaining enlightenment by interacting with herself as an object.[44]

For feminism, neither ignoring one's female gender nor subjectively experiencing oneself through patriarchal eyes is a satisfactory option.[45] The natural responses are those pursued by our feminist critics. Either one must disown the ḍākinī as a construct of patriarchal fantasy having little of genuine benefit for women practitioners, or one can attempt to reconstruct a utopian, gynocentric past in which women were the agents of ritual or symbol.[46] Although each of these options pursues the ḍākinī, she actually becomes lost in what is an essentially ideological though well-intentioned endeavor. What is needed is a fresh reexamination of the ḍākinī in her Tibetan context, utilizing methods from the history of religions and from gender studies to identify her meaning as a gendered symbol of Tibetan Buddhism. Yet, in these investigations, it is appropriate to take up the topic of subjectivity in this broader context to identify the dynamics of the ḍākinī symbol in meditative practice and ritual celebration, which we will do in the next section.

The Complexity of Religious Symbols: Spiritual Subjectivity

Subjectivity is an important topic in the study of religion, especially the power of symbols to evoke a sense of inner meaning in the lives of women and men. Symbols are a structure of signification that has at least two levels of import. One level is primary and literal, drawn from ordinary experience, expressible in words and ordinary images, and susceptible to conventional interpretation. This first draws us to another level that is profound and directly inexpressible and that lends itself only reluctantly to interpretation. The second level comes before language or discursive reason and defies any other means of knowledge. It is not merely a reflection of objective reality but reveals something about the nature of the world that is not evident on the level of immediate experience. Psychoanalysis and the arts speak of this area as the unconscious or the creative; in the history of religions it is called the sacred.

In Tibetan tantra, symbols are of central importance, and ḍākinīs are the prime purveyors of symbol with their physical appearance, their gifts, and their styles of communication. Their meanings are difficult to discover, and they are often not recognized even by the initiated. But for those who are spiritually prepared and open, the depth of the ḍākinī teachings is realized and the ḍākinī's gifts can be received.

Exploring symbols is always personal. They lead into a more intimate experience of meaning on an inner reflective level at the same time that one is exploring the dynamics of the evident world. Symbols bridge these two worlds and as such awaken individual experience into realization and action. From this point of view, one's place in the cosmos is not an alien one; instead, in a symbolic sense, one is completely at home. In this way, the meanings arising from exploring symbols reverberate through experience, sensitizing one to a new realm of understanding.

Symbols find expression in concrete elements of our world. They are expressed in images, through iconography and art; they are expressed in words, in ritual and narrative; and they are expressed in actions. Yet, when we attempt to express the deeper experience of symbol, we must do so metaphorically, poetically, or artistically, for these expressions themselves are merely tools, which are not identical with the symbol itself. Ḍākinīs speak often in highly symbolic language employing ordinary, earthy imagery in order to convey subtle, personal meanings. For example, the visionary ḍākinī offers treasure boxes, skulls, or shells, but these gifts cannot express the profundity of the recipient's experience. "Language can only capture the foam on the surface of life," wrote Paul Ricoeur.[47] Symbols are opaque, for they are rooted in inexpressible experience, and "this opaqueness is the symbol's very profundity, an inexhaustible depth."[48]

For this reason it can be said that symbols are truly multivalent, simultaneously expressing several meanings that do not appear related from a conventional point of view. The wrathful appearance of a ḍākinī who gnashes her teeth and threatens the practitioner may be experienced blissfully and joyfully; the beautiful ḍākinī vision or dream may be experienced with great fear and trepidation. Symbols have the ability to convey "paradoxical situations or certain patterns of ultimate reality that can be expressed in no other way,"[49] communicating on several levels at once and evoking meaning far beyond the literal words.

The greatest power of symbolism is in the formation of personal subjectivity. Subjectivity in this sense refers to the dynamic empowerment of personal inquiry, emptying the narrow, self-centered concerns into the vaster perspective evoked by the symbol.[50] Ḍākinī visions have the power to arouse the tantric practitioner in all areas of spiritual practice, for she represents his or her own wisdom-mind, the nature of which is inexpressible. Symbolic representations and appearances have tremendous power to shape the spiritual subjectivity of all religious practitioners, engaging them at the heart of their own spiritual journeys. We can develop no self-knowledge without some kind of detour through symbols, and through telling ourselves our sacred stories we come to know who we really are. This process of self-disclosure is the cultivation of subjectivity.

In the context of Tibetan symbol systems, popular hagiographies of saints serve as narrative symbols of the practitioner's journey. When the poet-yogin Milarepa was undergoing tantric training under his master Marpa's guidance, he was asked to erect a series of stone towers in the rough landscape of eastern Tibet.[51] As he finished each, his master changed his mind and demanded that Milarepa tear it down, returning the rocks and soil to their original places. With great physical hardship, personal frustration, and despair, Milarepa did as his master asked. When the practitioner contemplates these tales, the inner landscape of the spiritual journey is illuminated; its contours become more familiar and meaningful, transforming frustration and obstacles into inspiration.

Symbols are not mirrors of the self or of a socially constructed reality; rather they are windows to realms beyond thought or meaning. Ricoeur speaks of the symbol giving rise to thought,[52] and when we encounter symbols in a dynamic and personal way, a sense of meaning develops as a subjective reality. In Tibetan Buddhism, these symbols are especially encountered in ritual practice. Meanings that arise in ritual practice are not the same from individual to individual; they rely on the whole context offered by the rituals themselves and on the connotations that we bring to them. The result of this engagement cannot be precisely predicted. Yet, because of the larger context in which symbols are formed, there are consistencies in subjective experience.

The formation of subjectivity is not, of course, immune to gender issues. Symbolic narratives are full of gender dramas identifying the masculine with heroic value and the feminine with objectified, weak, or dangerous qualities. These heroic myths, which have played so prominent a role in the interpretation of symbols in the West, do not compel women in the same way as they do men, for they ignore the subjective, nonverbal wisdom and embodied sexuality that is central to women's experience. How can the gender biases of symbol systems be contravened so that symbols can have unmediated power in shaping the subjectivities of both women and men?

Ricoeur outlined levels of a symbol that give a clue to appropriate methods for interpreting it in a gender-neutral manner. The primary level of the symbol is that experienced preverbally, through dreams and visions, and this level has the most direct influence on the shaping of personal subjectivity. This can be seen in the tāntrikā's visionary and meditative experience, either in encounters with the ḍākinī described in the hagiographies or with the levels of meaning in personal tantric practice. Secondary symbols appear in narrative or stylized ritual, expressed in metaphorical or poetic language, one step removed from personal experience but with direct power to evoke personal subjectivity. The accounts of ḍākinī encounters may fall into this category when they interpret rather than give the actual details of the encounters. Tertiary symbols take the form of doctrine, philosophic expression, or societal forms, and they are most subject to the gender biases and interpretations imposed by culture. Examples of tertiary symbols can be found especially in the derived understanding of the kinds of human ḍākinīs in tantric literature. While this material is important, it plays a secondary role in our study of the ḍākinī symbol.

Ricoeur suggested that encountering a symbol requires a dynamic engagement made up of two aspects. First, the subject must consent to the symbol, engaging with its power and letting it reverberate in her or his experience. In Vajrayāna, this consent is associated with devotion to the tantric guru and maintaining the commitments and vows, without which the practice cannot bear spiritual fruit. At the same time, the subject must allow the emergence of a critical quality that Ricoeur terms "suspicion."[53] This attitude of suspicion requires us to question aspects of our experience of the symbol, identifying its essential qualities as opposed to phantasms created by cultural overlay. Vajrayāna practitioners are encouraged to bring their critical intellect and curiosity to bear in ritual practice, even while retaining the fundamental consent necessary for successful accomplishment of the practice. A healthy balance of these two views is necessary in order to personalize and deepen one's understanding of the power of the practice beyond mere forms.

In this context, it is important to scrutinize a symbol, deconstructing its levels to the most personal. In the case of the ḍākinī, this entails deconstructing the overly theoretical or mythologized dimensions of her manifestation in favor of her visionary and essential aspects as they are experienced by the Tibetan Buddhist practitioner. For example, when the ḍākinī is directly experienced in the practice of her ritual and in formless practice, her reality is unmediated. When she is encountered through hagiographic accounts, the subjective experience of her meaning is possible especially if the ritual or visionary experience accompanies the reading. The most removed aspect of the ḍākinī is the doctrinal formulation in which overlays of interpretation obscure her meaning. When the symbols are allowed to directly influence the practitioner's spiritual subjectivity, the authentic experience of the ḍākinī symbol is available. The direct experience of the ḍākinī happens especially in the context of consent, in which the practitioner is devoted to the guru and maintains the Vajrayāna commitments. Having fully consented, the subject may reconstruct the symbol into meaningful myths, stories, and paradigms concerning the ḍākinī. This dialectic of consent and suspicion becomes the essential way in which the full range of the ḍākinī symbol may empower the subjectivity of the practitioner.[54]

In the study of the ḍākinī, it is essential to emphasize how she is described in terms of dreams and visionary experience on the one hand and meditative and ritual expression on the other. Hagiographic material is also an important facet of her interpretation, especially when informed through the perspective of meditative realization. This preference suggests a methodology that ranks doctrinal formulations and metaphysical speculation at a lower level. However, in order to find coherence between the symbol of the ḍākinī and the rich commentarial traditions of Tibetan Buddhism, it is important to contextualize the symbol of the ḍākinī within an overall understanding of Vajrayāna.

There is no evidence that gender symbols play favorites in the structuring of gendered religious experience. For example, feminine symbols cannot be said to serve in the formation of the subjectivity of only women, nor masculine symbols to have power only for men.[55] In Tibetan Buddhism, the rituals of female deities are essential for both men and women practitioners, as are the rituals of male deities. Symbols of both genders function in an interconnected way in vital symbol systems, such that feminine symbols have potency for both men and women, though in somewhat different frameworks of interpretation.

Ironically, the importance that feminism (or patriarchy, for that matter) places on gender identity may prove an obstacle to experiencing the full power of symbols in the formation of spiritual subjectivity. For example, if practitioners with feminist inclinations insist on the practice of only female deities, a whole dimension of tantric ritual is missed. When we identify too fully with our gender, it may be impossible to discover the transformative effect of symbols. As a woman, can I fully identify with the confusion of the isolated yogin who supplicates the ḍākinī for help, or with the travails of a beleaguered male disciple confronting the demands of the male tantric guru? If I cannot, I have shut myself off from much of the symbolic power of tantric Buddhism.

One of the reasons this is true is that the cultivation of spiritual subjectivity entails stepping beyond the confines of rigid control. Ricoeur was perhaps the most articulate in demonstrating that symbols shape the formations of the self through an intimate process of opening and letting go of ego-centered concerns. As he so vividly noted, when reading a text that conveys symbolic content, "I unrealize myself."[56] When humans experience themselves as spiritual subjects, they find that they are agents who, in the process of spiritual transformation, open to power beyond the narrow confines of the self. This means giving up their hold on concepts of gender identity, along with other ego-centered concerns.

The way in which subjectivity unravels concepts concerning personal identity is traced in Buddhism in the process of meditation. Anne Klein described how meditation practice places attention first on the *contents* of mind, but viewing thoughts, emotions, and sense perceptions from the perspective of how the mind *is.*[57] One generally regards personal subjectivity according to the plotlines of identity—I am a woman, I am a Buddhist, I am reading this book, I am thirsty, my neck aches. But when one exposes the experience of subjectivity to meditation practice, one finds a more subtle sense. First the attention is placed on these details, steadying and settling the mind. Then one notices the patterns of mental contents and, eventually, recognizes the dynamic of the mind itself.

One discovers that pervading all the contents of experience is an awareness of the present moment, an awake and clear cognition that illumines the details of mental processes. This cognition is not composed of thoughts, emotions, or sense perceptions, though it pervades them; its experience is nonconceptual and nonverbal. This awareness is inherent in the nature of the mind and depends on nothing outside of itself. It is through this awareness, according to Buddhism, that humans can be said to have subjectivity at all. This fundamental "subjectivity without contents" is the empty center of all our experience, which Klein called "a different experience of subjectivity, of mind itself."[58]

The most intimate level of the experience of the symbol of the ḍākinī is this nonconceptual "without contents" level, as we shall see in chapter 4. But the contentless subjectivity discovered in Buddhist meditation is not averse to contents; in fact, it ceaselessly gives rise to symbols that wordlessly express the profundity of its meaning. The ḍākinī in her most profound level of meaning is beyond form, gender, and expression, but "she" gives rise to bountiful forms and expressions, which sometimes take the female gender as a way to express "her" essence. In this communication, the ḍākinī holds the key to understanding the relationships between emptiness and form, between wisdom and skillful means, and between female and male. This communication has a liberating message to offer the Western practitioner burdened by the politics of gender and confused by the dualities of cyclic existence.

In recent scholarship on gender symbolism, feminist assumptions concerning the limitations of androcentric symbols have been given new perspective. Women and men experience religious symbolism in different but personally transformative ways.[59] In her research on the religious lives of medieval Christian women, Caroline Walker Bynum discovered that feminine symbols functioned in a different way for medieval women than for medieval men. While both men and women saw God as male and the soul as female, she argued that this interpretation socially empowered women while reversing cultural views of power and status held by religious men. For example, when men became "brides of Christ" their symbolic understanding reversed their culturally based gender experience. There was no question that the medieval women she studied perceived themselves as spiritual subjects. While they actively engaged in prayer, *ascesis,* and good works, contemporary questions of *personal* gender identity had no role in their spiritual lives.[60]

Bynum's work led her to the conclusion that a study of symbol, myth, and ritual does not lend itself as easily to feminist methods of scholarship as do studies of institutional structure and theology. Her conclusions on the complexities of gender are two. First, in accord with the discoveries of feminism, it is clear that all experience is gendered experience. There is no generic human, and the experiences of men and women in every known society are different precisely because of gender. Second, religious symbols transform gendered experience beyond societal expectations and endow it with abundant religious meaning. There is no way to accurately predict the effect of a gender symbol on the perceiving subject, for the symbol may support, reject, or invert cultural meanings of gender. When one asks what a gender symbol means, one must also ask for whom.[61]

These conclusions, of course, question the narrow range of interpretation of the ḍākinī symbol that has characterized Western scholarship for at least the past twenty years. These approaches suggest that the gender of the ḍākinī may have something to do with understanding the female gender, but a great deal to do with meanings having nothing to do with gender. Openness to the full range of the ḍākinī's meaning yields the full richness of her symbolism.

From this perspective, we may understand why the encounter with the ḍākinī is important for every tantric Buddhist practitioner, whether male or female. She represents the most intimate aspects of the spiritual path. She is the fundamental nature of the mind; she guards the gates of wisdom for the practitioner and the lineages of tantric teachers; she holds the key to the secret treasury of practices that lead to realization; and she manifests variously in her support of authentic meditation. To limit her meanings only to those of gender concerns would be to miss much of what she has to offer.

However, as we shall see in chapter 7, she is experienced slightly differently by male and female practitioners. The ḍākinī appears in visionary form to both yogins and yoginīs at key points in their spiritual journeys, at times of crisis or intractability. But in her appearances to the yoginī, the ḍākinī is more predictably an ally and support, often welcoming her as a sister and sometimes pointing out her own ḍākinī nature. For yogins, the ḍākinī is more likely to to be perceived in threatening form, especially as a decrepit hag or an ugly woman of low birth. These appearances have the effect especially of shocking the yogin out of intellectual or class arrogance and turning his mind to the dharma.

Among the ḍākinī's many gifts, she gives a blessing of her radiant and empty body to her subjects. The ways in which she bestows her body gifts differ slightly, depending upon the gender of the recipient. The ḍākinī acts as a mirror for the yoginī, empowering her view of her body and life as being of the same nature as the ḍākinī's. For example, contact with the ḍākinī restores health and extends life for all practitioners; for the yoginī, this contact rejuvenates her sick and aging body quite literally. In terms of sexual yoga, the ḍākinī gives her body gifts in the form of sexual union to yogins, whereas for yoginīs she selects suitable consorts.

Finally, the yoginī is likely to manifest as a ḍākinī at some point in her spiritual development. For some yoginīs, the physical marks of a ḍākinī are present at birth; for others the signs and powers manifest at a later time. But the yoginīs in the namthars are likely to be perceived as ḍākinīs by their students at the point of their full maturation.

The patterns with regard to ḍākinīs accord in some ways with preliminary observations made by Bynum and her colleagues concerning certain patterns in men's and women's experience of gendered symbols drawn from a variety of religious traditions. Men and women in a given tradition, working with the same symbols and myths, writing in the same genre, living in the same religious circumstances, display consistent patterns in interpreting symbols:

> Women's symbols and myths tend to build from social and biological experiences; men's symbols and myths tend to invert them. Women's mode of using symbols seems given to the muting of opposition, whether through paradox or through synthesis; men's mode seems characterized by emphasis on opposition, contradiction, inversion, and conversion. Women's myths and rituals tend to explore a state of being; men's tend to build elaborate and discrete stages between self and other.[62]

In chapter 7 we will examine these hypotheses to see whether women's experience of the ḍākinī differs in any way from men's and what the meaning of possible differences might suggest.

Gender in Traditional Tibet

Tibetan Buddhism developed its own unique understanding of gender, though in a context somewhat different than the contemporary concerns of Western culture. Questions of personal identity and gender are generally considered a contemporary Western phenomenon. In traditional Tibetan culture before the Chinese occupation in the 1950s, every detail of cultural life was infused with religious concerns such as the appeasement of obstructing spirits, the accumulation of merit, and the attainment of enlightenment. There is every indication that in areas of Tibet outside of Lhasa, these conditions remain to a greater or lesser extent.[63]

For Tibetans, concepts of "feminine" and "masculine" have been important only to the extent that they reflect this ultimate dynamic in ritual and meditation. Gender has been understood to be beyond personal identity, a play of absolute qualities in the experience of the practitioner. For Tibetans, the "feminine" refers to the limitless, ungraspable, and aware qualities of the ultimate nature of mind; it also refers to the intensely dynamic way in which that awareness undermines concepts, hesitation, and obstacles in the spiritual journeys of female and male Vajrayāna practitioners. The "masculine" relates to the qualities of fearless compassion and actions that naturally arise from the realization of limitless awareness, and the confidence and effectiveness associated with enlightened action.

From this sacred view, the embodied lives of ordinary men and women can be seen as a dynamic and sacred play of the ultimate expressing itself as gendered physical bodies, their psychologies, and their states of mind. For traditional Tibetan Buddhism, this dynamic is merely one among a universe of polarities that are ordinarily taken as irreconcilable. For the mind ensnared in dualistic thinking, these polarities represent the endless dilemmas of life; for the mind awakened to the patterns of cyclic existence, these extremes do not differ from each other ultimately. Seeing through the seeming duality of these pairs, using the methods of Vajrayāna practice, transforms the practitioner's view.

As we discussed earlier, this general sacred view of gender was not necessarily reflected in Tibetan social life.[64] In general, women have enjoyed more prestige and freedom in Tibet than in either China or India, wielding power in trade, in nomadic herding, and in the management of large families. Still, generally speaking, women were subject to their fathers and husbands. Their spiritual potential was generally valued, but, as in the Indian context, women were generally denied full monastic ordination, education, ritual training, teaching roles, and financial support for their dharma practice. And while there exist hagiographies of remarkable female teachers and yoginīs of Tibet, it is clear that these women were rare exceptions in a tradition dominated by an androcentric and patriarchal monastic structure and system of selection of reincarnated lamas (tülkus). In these aspects, the patterns from the Indian heritage of Buddhism were carried on to Tibet.

Buddhist teachers in Tibet often engaged their potential disciples by encouraging them to contemplate the fruitlessness of worldly concerns, whether they be gain or loss, pleasure or pain, fame or infamy, or praise or blame.[65] Painful situations in everyday life were considered excellent incentives for dharma practice. When such realities as the fragility of life and the certainty of death are contemplated, the mind naturally turns to dharma practice. When women contemplate the intractable obstacles they face because of their gender, these are not feminist reflections; they are dharmic contemplations that initiate them to the tantric path. Princess Trompa Gyen summarized her dilemma to her guru in this way:

Our minds seek virtue in the Dharma
but girls are not free to follow it.
Rather than risk a lawsuit,
we stay with even bad spouses.
Avoiding bad reputations,
we are stuck in the swamp of cyclic existence. . . .
Though we stay in strict, isolated retreat,
we encounter vile enemies.
Though we do our Dharma practices,
bad conditions and obstacles interfere. . . .
Next time let me obtain a male body,
and become independent,
so that I can exert myself in the Dharma
and obtain the fruition of buddhahood.[66]

Her guru responded with an even more dismal depiction of her situation, observing that she wandered hopelessly through cyclic existence. He pointed out, "having forsaken your own priorities, you serve another,"[67] moving from parents and siblings to husband and in-laws, slaving in the home of strangers, suffering but getting no gratitude. He concluded with the admonition, "A girl should value her own worth. Stand up for yourself, Trompa Gyen!"[68] And he urged her to renounce these patterns and to practice the dharma.

This is the perspective that both Gross and Aziz took when observing that the Tibetan word for *woman* (*kyemen*), which literally means "born low," is not a point of doctrine but an insight from Tibetan folk wisdom that accurately observes the constrictions and difficulties of a woman's life under patriarchy.[69] But the traditional Tibetan understanding reflects that the difficulty of a woman's life, which is readily acknowledged to be greater than that of a man's, provides her motivation to practice the dharma. Reversing the oppressions of patriarchy would merely yield different kinds of suffering. The depictions of the hardships of Tibetan yoginīs in sacred biographies are not thinly veiled feminist tracts; they are acknowledgment of the specific difficulties that women experience, which lead to a life of committed practice and successful realization.

A common theme in Tibetan tantric lore is the superior spiritual potentialities of women. Women are, by virtue of their female bodies, sacred incarnations of wisdom to be respected by all tantric practitioners.[70] Padmasambhava spoke of men's and women's equal suitability for enlightenment, noting that if women have strong aspiration, they have higher spiritual potential.[71] Namkhai Norbu Rinpoche was heard to say that women are more likely than men to attain the rainbow body through the practice of Dzogchen, citing the great patriarch Garap Dorje on the matter.[72] There are a number of reasons for this. Having overcome more daunting hardships than men, women have superior spiritual stamina and momentum. Embodying wisdom, they have greater potential for openness and intuitive qualities. But the pitfalls for women are also uniquely difficult, and developing such religious potential entails overcoming emotionality, ego-clinging, and habitual patterns just as it does for men.

In traditional Tibet women pursued religious vocations as best they could. Spiritual practice has always been an essential part of laywomen's lives, as can be attested even today by observing Tibetan communities. Or those women who wish to devote themselves to religious pursuits as men do could become either celibate nuns or tāntrikās, noncelibate practitioners of Vajrayāna yogas. Nuns may live together in small nunneries close to their natal home, usually lacking in resources for support of education, spiritual instruction, or even appropriate food, shelter, and clothing for members.[73] Tāntrikā women may live in monastic compounds or with family members, remaining in semiretreat in the upper reaches of the home. Or they may dwell in solitary retreat punctuated by pilgrimages to visit sacred sites or spiritual teachers residing either in monasteries or in solitude.[74]

The limitations on women's institutional influence in Tibet are seen in a variety of ways. In a study of the commentarial texts of the Tibetan canon, there is little evidence of women's contributions to or even their presence in monastic life and lineages. But when study turns to the ritual and yogic dimensions of Vajrayāna Buddhism, there is greater evidence of women's participation. Especially in Tibet's oral traditions, the influence of women has been evident, in storytelling, poetry, and both secular and religious songs. Examples can be found especially in the songs of Milarepa, the siddhas, and the music of the Chö and Shije traditions.[75]

In addition, certain shamanic transmissions of the yogic tradition have always been carried by women, such as the *delok* possession, in which a woman literally dies in a visionary descent to hell realms, returning again to her human body with memories and insight gained from the experience.[76] Sometimes women have served as oracles, mediating specific deities who guide the sacred and secular affairs of monastery, government, and village.[77] Women have also consistently played important roles in the discovery of termas, or hidden treasure texts, but were usually cautioned not to propagate their discoveries for a requisite number of births.

Until recently, Western Tibetology has paid the greatest attention to the institutional manifestation of the tradition, almost completely neglecting the contributions, insights, and transmissions of women, which have often been seen as superstitious or merely folk traditions. Barbara Aziz noted that this is probably because the patriarchal nature of Western scholarship, which honors monastic traditions and classical texts, reinforces the patriarchal habits of Buddhist institutions in Tibet.[78] Recent works have begun to correct this imbalance, showing greater interest in the shamanic or yogic aspects of Buddhism and the oral traditions and the less institutionalized aspects of the Tibetan tradition. As scholarship in this area grows, more will be known about the transmissions and contributions of Tibetan women.

Of relevance to a study of women's religious lives in Tibet is the work of Geoffrey Samuel, who argued that in the study of Tibetan Buddhism many complexities are resolved in distinguishing between two general, complementary components of religious life: the monastic (clerical) and the yogic (shamanic).[79] The monastic aspects of Tibetan society concern the institutional life in which discipline, conduct, education, and power are governed by the monastic disciplinary code and by goals other than, but not necessarily contrary to, enlightenment. In contrast, the yogic dimension places its emphasis upon spiritual and societal transformation through yogic practice, relying on views of reality other than prevailing conventional norms. The yogic dimension also includes many folk elements with pragmatic ends other than enlightenment.

Samuel described how these two complementary aspects may interweave in the activities of a particular lama, yogin, or lay practitioner, and they certainly have intertwined in the development of religious institutions. But these two aspects are "rooted in fundamentally different orientations towards the world and towards human experience and behavior."[80] Yogic Buddhism focuses on transformation and means of transformation. In its folk dimensions, yogic Buddhism may wish to transform conventional circumstances, as by extending life, attracting wealth, or averting disaster; or it may seek only the ultimate transformation, enlightenment. It employs a variety of ritual and visionary methods, but its power rests upon direct perception of the nature of mind and reality, which is said in Tibet to be the essence of the Buddha's experience of enlightenment.

Monastic Buddhism shares with yogic Buddhism the ultimate goal of enlightenment, but it has other goals, related to monastic disciplinary codes and the continuity of monastic lineages and education. Monastic Buddhism places greater emphasis on the gradual path based upon purifying one's karma through accumulation of merit, renouncing unvirtuous actions, scholastic mastery of texts, debate, and preserving the monastic tradition. In this last area, monastic Buddhism is concerned with power and succession and institutional life.

This study focuses on the yogic tradition, especially as it was practiced and understood in eastern and central Tibet in the Kagyü and Nyingma lineages. These traditions have emphasized personal transformation based upon direct experience of a mode of reality more basic and meaningful than conventional reality, cultivating extraordinary powers of communication and understanding in their adepts, and opening the way to enlightenment, which is ultimate freedom. In most literate and complex societies, yogic-style shamanism has been subordinated to cultural structures such as the state or institutionalized religion such as the monastery. Samuel argued that Tibet is unusual in its successful retention of a vital and energized shamanic dimension with influence upon every aspect of culture, especially outside of Lhasa and central Tibet.[81] Of relevance for this study is the fact that shamanic or yogic cultures of Tibet have relied on the visionary and symbolic dimensions of religion, nurturing their development in ritual practice and spiritual transformation. These are the areas in which the participation and leadership of women have been more evident. It is also the area in which the ḍākinī has been a central symbol of spiritual transformation.

If we are to employ Ricoeur's strategies to retrieve the authentic symbol of the ḍākinī, we must turn to the shamanic or yogic traditions of Tibet, in which visionary experience and ritual practice have been so central. These strategies suggest that scholastic or doctrinal presentations are of less importance to a proper understanding of the ḍākinī symbol. The shamanic traditions have been preserved primarily in the oral teachings of the Kagyü and Nyingma lineages, and it is here that we find women's participation and the prevalence of the ḍākinī symbol.

Although Tibetan women have played a minor public role in institutional Buddhism, they have emerged in yogic lineages as teachers and holders of special transmissions and practices. They have served as founders of new lineages of teachings, as in the case of Machik Lapdrön; they have played important roles in the hidden-treasure (terma) traditions of Tibet, beginning with Yeshe Tsogyal; they have developed unique practices, as did Gelongma Palmo, who conjoined Avalokiteśvara practice with fasting in *nyungne* meditation;[82] they have appeared as partners and "secret mothers" of great yogins, teaching privately or through their life example, as in the case of Dagmema;[83] they have been renowned yoginīs practicing in retreat, as in the contemporary examples of Ayu Khando[84] and Jetsün Lochen Rinpoche.[85] These women played yogic rather than academic or monastic roles, probably because monastic education and leadership were traditionally denied them by the Tibetan social structure. A rare exception can be found in Jetsün Mingyur Paldrön, the daughter of the Mindröling tertön Terdag Lingpa, who was known for her penetrating intellect and great learning. She was responsible for the rebuilding of Mindröling monastery after its destruction by the Dzungars in the early eighteenth century.[86] Studies of Tibetan women have appeared elsewhere, as we have discussed, and are not the specific focus of this book. However, insofar as these Tibetan yoginīs have been considered human ḍākinīs, they fall within the purview of our study and will be treated in the discussion of embodied ḍākinīs in chapter 6.

The ḍākinī symbol continues to be the living essence of Vajrayāna transmission, the authentic marrow of the yogic tradition. While monastic establishments and philosophic systems may exhibit elements of patriarchal bias, this living essence carries no such bias. It is essential to study the ḍākinī in her own context to understand the power and importance of this symbol for the authentic preservation of the yogic traditions of Tibet. Vajrayāna Buddhism places emphasis upon oral instruction in the guru-disciple relationship, preservation of texts and teachings, and solitary practice as a way to safeguard these meditation and symbolic traditions. These aspects form the matrix of the study of the ḍākinī.

Symbolism and Subjectivity: The Feminine Principle

What is the significance of the gender of the ḍākinī? This is a central enigma of her manifestation, and considerations of this question will arise throughout the chapters that follow. In previous interpretations of the ḍākinī, such as those influenced by Jungian psychology and by feminism, her gender has been the predominant factor. In the Jungian versions, her female gender has been abstracted, essentialized, and androcentrized. Feminist materials reacted to previous substantializing of gender issues even while they perpetuated them, causing reactive interpretations that also focus unduly on the ḍākinī's gender. It is clear that neither of these two general paradigms effectively addresses the ḍākinī in her Tibetan context.

When we deal with the ḍākinī as a religious symbol, her gender becomes more complex and multivalent. On an ultimate level, the ḍākinī is beyond gender altogether. As Janice Willis wrote, " 'she' is not 'female.' Though the ḍākinī assuredly appears most often in female form (whether as a female deity, or a female human being), this is but one of the *myriad* of ways Absolute Insight chooses to make manifest its facticity."[87] "She" is in essence the vast and limitless expanse of emptiness, the lack of inherent existence of all phenomena expressed symbolically as space, that which cannot be symbolized. But in the true Tibetan Vajrayāna sense, "she" manifests in a female-gendered form on various levels. She also manifests in meditation phenomena that have no gendered form, such as in deity yoga, in the subtle-body experience of vital breath in the energetic channels, and in the experience of transmission from a tantric guru.

The ḍākinī is, from this perspective, more than a singular symbol and more than a feminine deity. She represents a kind of "feminine principle,"[88] a domain of spiritual experience beyond conventional, social, or psychological meanings of gender. This domain of the feminine principle permeates many levels of Tibetan Buddhist practice and understanding, each integrated in some way with the others. While the feminine principle takes a feminine form, ultimately there is nothing feminine about it. Additionally, because the term refers to emptiness, the absence of inherent existence of any kind, either ordinary or divine, the word *principle* does not really apply either.

Yet understanding the ḍākinī in this way is challenged most by the claim, central to Tibetan interpretation, that all human women are finally an expression of the ḍākinī. This creates a delicate situation that has often been misinterpreted. When Tibetans speak of all women as expressions of the ḍākinī, it is to indicate a sacred outlook concerning gender. This statement is not an invitation to make the ḍākinī and her realm a feminist bastion. As a young Nyingma lama, Ven. Tsoknyi Rinpoche, explained to me in a kind of epiphany, "Women are part of the ḍākinī—ḍākinīs are not part of women!"[89] And, he continued, men are also emanations from the ultimate masculine principle. From the point of view of sacred outlook, human women are the display that emptiness takes when it expresses itself in form. Taking the form at face value in a substantial way causes the observer to miss the essential nature of the form. That is why the ḍākinī is a symbol. When we see the symbolic nature of the ḍākinī, there is fresh insight about the nature of all phenomena.

For these reasons, I have chosen throughout my book to speak of the "feminine," not of the "female." The Tibetan point of view, as I understand it, is that the English word *female* is embedded in substantiality, in inherent existence, in ego, in affirmative personal identity. When ḍākinīs are spoken of as "female," mistakes can be made in interpretation. In the introduction to Maṇḍāravā's sacred biography, Janet Gyatso emphasized the femaleness of the great ḍākinī, proclaiming that "her female gender has a great significance of its own," and that she was a "female heroine in her own right."[90] Her interpretation of Maṇḍāravā emphasized the "feminist themes" of the work, the subversion of patriarchy, kinship structures, marriage, and power relationships. This prompted a preface with a disclaimer by the gifted American translator, herself a devout practitioner, who wrote, "I feel I must mention that the views and comparisons presented in the introduction that follows do not completely reflect my views and reasons for translating this precious revelation treasure. The basis for the difference of opinion centers around the interpretation of the feminine principle and how it pertains to the path of Vajrayāna Buddhism."[91] In our conversations, the translator expressed her opinion that Gyatso misunderstood the fundamental qualities of Maṇḍāravā's ḍākinī manifestation.

The ḍākinī's depiction in feminine form has symbolic power in the meanings that she reveals, for the ḍākinī is the symbol of tantric wisdom in the nonconceptual sense. Specifically, she is the inner spiritual subjectivity of the tantric practitioner herself or himself, the knowing dimension of experience. This subjectivity is not the personal, identity-oriented subjectivity that is discussed in feminism, psychology, phenomenology, or even postmodernism, for that matter. It is "subjectless subjectivity," an experience of the nature of mind itself, when mind is understood as no object of any kind. But this subjectless subjectivity is not adverse to contents. According to Anuttara-yoga-yāna, all phenomena of gendered human life arise from the vast space of this subjectivity—and every aspect is seen to be a vividly clear, luminously empty symbol of mind's nature. Spiritual subjectivity accessed in tantric practice sees ordinary phenomena in a transformed way, as the dance of emptiness.

The subjective voice is often a feminine voice,[92] and for the tantric practitioner the ḍākinī is the inner catalyst, protagonist, and witness of the spiritual journey. Representing the inner experience of the practitioner, she joins the guru to the disciple, the disciple to the practice, and the practice to its fulfillment. At the same time, the ḍākinī is the "other." As an outside awakened reality that interrupts the workings of conventional mind, she is often perceived as dangerous because she threatens the ego structure and its conventions and serves as a constant reminder from the lineages of realized teachers. She acts outside the conventional, conceptual mind and has therefore the haunting quality of a marginal, liminal figure.[93]

Simultaneously the ḍākinī is more intimate than the tongue or the eyeballs and yet is feared as the "other," the unknown. Like the nature of mind in the Mahāmudrā tradition, she is too close to be recognized, too profound to fathom, too easy to believe, and too excellent to accommodate.[94] This is one reason that she is not immediately recognized by the most realized practitioners even when she is consistently present. The ḍākinī is the most potent realized essence of every being, the inner awakening, and the gift of the Buddha. The encounter with the ḍākinī is the encounter with the spiritual treasury of Buddhism, the experience of the ultimate nature of the mind in its dynamic expression as a constantly moving sky-dancing woman. She represents the realization of this nature, as well as the means through which the nature is realized.

TWO

The Dakini in Tibetan Buddhism

QUESTION: What are ḍākinīs?
VEN. CHÖGYAM TRUNGPA RINPOCHE: One never knows.[1]

To him who sees the mind's nature
And dispels the mists of ignorance,
The ḍākinīs show their faces;
Yet, in the realm of reality,
There is nothing to be seen.
Without deliberate "non-observation" in one's mind,
All dharmas rise and are illuminated by themselves.
This is preached by all ḍākinīs.[2]

IT IS PERHAPS FOLLY to attempt to systematically describe the ḍākinī, for she manifests in forms consistent with her nature. Scholars of Tibetan Vajrayāna have despaired at her definition, calling the term *ḍākinī* "semantically ambiguous, multivalent,"[3] "curious,"[4] and "impossible to pin . . . down or limit . . . to a single definition."[5] In interviewing lamas on the topic of the ḍākinī, I usually asked the same questions and received a wide variety of answers. A catalog of ḍākinī definitions could fill a large ledger. It is said that the ḍākinī follows no philosophy or system, that her activities obey no external laws or patterns. Nevertheless, with oral commentary a certain consistency emerges regarding the ḍākinī symbol. Through tracing

The ḍākinī as the meditational deity Vajrayoginī.

her attributes, activities, and manifestations, we can perhaps develop an appreciation for her faultless and uncompromising representation of the spiritual path of the Vajrayāna Buddhist practitioner.

Ḍākinī Development in India

Ḍākinī is a term derived from Indian regional Prakrit or possibly Sanskrit,[6] vulgar in connotation, attributed to a minor player in the pantheon of deities associated with indigenous non-Brahmanical traditions of India. Ḍākinīs were demonic inhabitors of cemeteries and charnel grounds, delighting in the taste of human flesh and blood and dancing with ornaments fashioned from the bones of decaying corpses. They were identified as witch-spirits of women who died in pregnancy or childbirth. Unfaithful wives were also suspected of becoming ḍākinīs. When angered, these witches were capable of causing pestilence among humans, especially fever, obsessions, lung diseases, and infertility.[7] They were wrath personified, joining the slaughter on the battlefield, intoxicated from thirstily sucking the blood of their victims.

Ḍākinīs were considered one class of the minor deities who served under the command of such dominant non-Brahmanical deities as the wrathful goddesses Durgā or Kālī, or the god Śiva in his form as Gaṇapati, "lord of the categories."[8] It is significant that ḍākinīs sucked blood, the precious *rasa* or vital bodily juices in Āryan tradition, which according to caste law must be kept pure and integral in order to preserve the sacredness of the body.[9] Those who violate that purity were viewed in Āryan society as unimaginably vile and dangerous. Like their famous champions Kālī and Durgā, ḍākinīs represented forces marginal to mainstream Āryan society—female, outcaste, impure—and therefore were powerful outlaws.

The ḍākinī's feminine gender is associated in some scholarship with contemporary rituals in Indian culture related with sexuality, menstruation, and childbirth.[10] In India, women are viewed as more libidinous than men, making demands upon them that cannot be satisfied. When refused, popular Indian culture suggests, some women might become witches (in Hindi, *dakan or dahani*)[11] who would exact their revenge by feasting on the blood of their decapitated male adversary. Husbands and sons are considered particularly vulnerable. Particularly during menstruation, when women are secluded, their danger and power are associated with polluting menstrual blood. "The association of seclusion and blood brings to mind accounts of the *dakan,* or witch. She also is said periodically to shut herself in a darkened room and abandon herself to her hostile desires, drinking the blood of some, eating the livers of others of those who have slighted her."[12]

Her non-Brahmanical roots tie her to what have been described as prepatriarchal Dravidian cultures, known for their Mother Goddess traditions, yogic practices, artistic sophistication, and reverence for trees and animals. What little is known concerning these cultures comes from preliminary archaeological work; however, it is theorized that various religious movements in the subcontinent had their impetus in the resurgence of interest in Dravidian preoccupations colored by the spiritual influence of the Vedas. Several of these movements have relevance for this study: the *śramana* movement (seventh to fifth centuries B.C.E.), which gave rise to the career of Siddhārtha-Gautama, the historical Buddha; and the development of esoteric cults of tantra, which eventually developed Buddhist and Hindu strains.

Until the rise of tantra within Indian traditions, the ḍākinī remained a minor figure. In India and Nepal between the seventh and ninth centuries C.E., ritual texts called tantras began to appear in manuscript form,[13] characterized by a preoccupation with the divine power of the absolute coupled with an emphasis on feminine symbolism. One of the most important such texts, which has been associated with the ḍākinī, is the *Cakrasaṃvara-tantra,* with close associations with the Śiva-Bhairava cults of Hinduism. Certainly the practices associated with the tantras predated this period, but their exact chronology and history remain obscure. According to these tantric texts, the absolute was singular in ultimate essence, manifesting with female and male aspects. Alone, the male aspect was impotent and could act only through his female consort (his *śakti,* in Hinduism), who was hypostatized as a goddess. She became an all-powerful creator and sustainer of the cosmos, and in Śākta tantric traditions of Hinduism she became ultimately primary.

With the development of the various tantric traditions of India, various non-Brahamanical goddesses were elevated to supreme status in a Mother Goddess cult related to this śakti. Accompanying these tantric movements were the emergent Purāṇa texts, which highlighted mythological elements and the importance of devotion. Examples of the elevation of the goddess can be found in the examples of Durgā and Kālī, and with them their retinues were also elevated. The ḍākinī stepped into the foreground as one of the minor deities of the non-Brahmanical pantheon.[14]

It is important to note that the early tantric traditions of India were diverse. Most of them carried a preoccupation with the powerful goddess, but the understanding, interpretation, and application of this interest developed in quite different ways as tantra interacted with the other classical strains of Indian thought and practice. For example, in Śaivite traditions, the male deity was supreme, with a powerful but ultimately subordinate consort. In the Vaiśnava tantric traditions, the śakti is often seen as the creative aspect of the male godhead, which gives rise to the cosmos, perhaps in the form of speech or seed syllables.[15]

Many scholars hold that Buddhist tantra developed at an earlier time than the various schools of classical Hindu tantra and that deities of the Buddhist tantras were later assimilated into Hindu deities.[16] From their point of view, the ḍākinī probably was interpreted according to Buddhist understandings before she appeared in Hindu tantric texts.[17] In her later Hindu incarnations, the ḍākinī served variously as a goddess of the *cakra* centers of the body in tantric yoga or as an attendant to the main śakti goddess in tantric temples and cults.

The elevation of the goddess to cult status in mainstream Hinduism emerged in the sixth century C.E. with the Purāṇic text called *Devī-Māhātmya,* in which the Great Goddess is extolled as the source of all creation.[18] With this text and the commentaries that followed, the Great Goddess is interpreted and understood through classical themes from the Vedas, the Upaniṣads, the six philosophic schools, and the epics. In short, the feminine principle of śakti from the Indian tantric tradition was assimilated into Brahmanical themes in classical Hinduism, and the Goddess became an essential "theological" dimension of the Hindu tradition. Within this cult, she became more than just an individual goddess and emerged as *the* Goddess, the essential feminine aspect of the divine, associated specifically with creation.[19]

To understand the feminine principle in Tibetan Buddhism, it is important to briefly review the process that occurred in the Hindu tradition. To be accurate, the textual portrayals of the feminine in the Indian tantras must be interpreted in the context of the traditions in which they became meaningful. The diverse Hindu tantric traditions are characterized by an emphasis upon the feminine śakti,[20] interpreted differently in various Hindu traditions. The śakti might be the active and creative power of a specific male deity, embodied as his female consort, as in the case of Śiva's wife Pārvatī. The śakti may also be understood as a generative power possessed by a single, supreme god or goddess associated with the creation of the cosmos, as in the case of Kālī. Or, most abstractly, śakti may be viewed as the power of creativity inherent in the universe. In any case, śakti is viewed as a feminine power associated with cosmogonic forces.[21]

Buddhist tantra, especially in Tibet, interpreted the feminine principle differently. As tantric Buddhism developed in India and Tibet, the qualities associated with the feminine were distinctively Buddhist, with little importance placed on the physical creation of the world. Instead, Buddhist presentation of the feminine echoed its central teachings of impermanence, emptiness (*śūnyatā*), penetrating insight (*prajñā*), and compassion. The term *śakti* appears in the early Buddhist tantras only infrequently.[22] When tantric Buddhism is called Śākta Buddhism because of the supposed "confluence of Buddhism and Śāktism,"[23] there is clearly a misunderstanding of the complex factors at work in the development of these tantric interpretations. The tendency of some scholars to move freely among the tantric traditions, blurring the distinctions in the interpretation of the ḍākinī and the feminine in Tibetan Buddhist, Indian Buddhist, Nepali Bajrācārya, and various Hindu tantric schools, raises serious methodological questions.

The ḍākinī's Indian origins in the Buddhist tantras and biographies of the great yogins and yoginīs are, of course, extremely important. However, in her development in Tibet, the ḍākinī evolved from a minor goddess figure to a central symbol of meditative experience in iconography, ritual, and meditation. Also, in Tibetan religion the integrity of the oral tradition of instruction, transmissions, and the ḍākinī's secrecy remains. When we examine the ḍākinī in her Tibetan context, we find her in a vital, living tradition of tantra.

The second reason it is important to review the place of the ḍākinī in the Hindu tradition is to clarify the Buddhist style of assimilation that is documented in many studies of the development of Buddhist literature, language, mythology, iconography, and cosmology. Specifically, Buddhist assimilation refers to the practice of embracing indigenous or prevalent teachings, norms, or mythologies and gradually (or not so gradually, in the mythology of Tibet) negating them or subordinating them to the more universal teachings of Buddhism.[24]

The process of assimilating the early tantric ḍākinī began in the Mahāyāna traditions of India. There, she was considered a barbarian, associated with the most vile of beings, because of her cannibalistic tendencies.[25] In the *Laṅkāvatāra-sūtra,* in a particularly vehement chapter on the evils of meat-eating for the practicing yogin, the Buddha warns of the disastrous results that come from the uncompassionate act of consuming meat:

> [The meat-eater] is ill-smelling, contemptuous, and born deprived of intelligence; he will be born again and again among the families of the Caṇḍāla, the Pukkasa, and the Ḍomba. From the womb of Ḍākinī he will be born in the meat eater's family, and then into the womb of a Rākshasī and a cat; he belongs to the lowest class of men. . . . [Meat-eating] is forbidden by me everywhere and all the time for those who are abiding in compassion; [he who eats meat] will be born in the same place as the lion, tiger, wolf, etc. Therefore, do not eat meat which will cause terror among people, because it hinders the truth of emancipation; [not to eat meat] is the mark of the wise.[26]

It has been theorized that this uncharacteristic section of the sūtra was written somewhat later than the rest, shortly before 443 C.E., as an expression of defensiveness in the face of the early encroachment of such tantric ritual practices as eating meat and drinking wine.[27] Certainly it was around this time[28] that the ḍākinī, who had played a minor role in non-Brahmanical India, was elevated in stature with her mistress Kālī in selected early tantras,[29] and independently in other tantras, some of which are considered sacred to Buddhism.

In later Indian Buddhism, the tantric ḍākinī became important in biographical literature and in the recorded tantras themselves, retaining her fierce and unpredictable ways. David Snellgrove has described how non-Buddhist deities were assimilated into certain Buddhist tantras from the retinues of Śaivite communities.[30] These deities appeared with outcaste consorts, surrounded by retinues composed of horrific ḍākinīs bearing emblems of their unconventional, esoteric status: skull-cups of blood, human flesh, excrement, and urine.[31] These figures contrast with peaceful female goddess figures, female bodhisattvas such as Tārā and Paṇḍaravāsinī, who are more Buddhist in origin. As monastic and institutional Buddhism assimilated tantric elements, the interpretation of the ḍākinī developed in important ways as well.[32]

It is in Tibetan texts that the ḍākinī took center stage in Vajrayāna teachings. In the early Indian Buddhist tantras, she perhaps paralleled the early śakti as consort née wild sprite who imbued the yogin with spiritual power. But as the ḍākinī became assimilated into classical Buddhism, her meanings came to reflect the most treasured and profound of teachings, especially those related to emptiness and wisdom. As we shall see later in the chapter, the Tibetan assimilation of the ḍākinī portrays the various stages of her transformation, with examples in each of the categories of malicious flesh-eating witch, powerful protector of the teachings, and, in the most profound cases, enlightened female being who serves as buddha or guru with special methods and styles of transmission.

This is not to say that the ḍākinī subsumed all female protectors, great beings (*mahāsattvas*), or female deities in Tibetan Vajrayāna.[33] There are many female manifestations in Vajrayāna, falling under the seven general categories of buddhas, bodhisattvas, gurus, yidams, ḍākinīs, dharma protectors, and regional protectors.[34] Strictly speaking, Tārā the savioress, for example, is generally considered a great bodhisattva rather than a ḍākinī, and Palden Lhamo (Vetalī) the fierce one is usually called a dharma protector. But ambiguity concerning the appearance and form of the ḍākinī still pervades these various categories. The ḍākinī is the only one of these seven general categories that belongs exclusively to the female gender, and female representatives of all seven are at times considered ḍākinīs.[35] For example, the guru Machik Lapdrön is commonly called a ḍākinī, as is Vajravārāhī the female yidam. But when this is indicated, there is usually lore that supports this classification.

It is also interesting to note that ḍākinīs populated the ranks of the indigenous Bön pantheon of deities. Per Kvaerne describes them as "semidivine," manifesting often in human form in the characteristic dancing posture. Many times they were depicted as historical figures such as female sages or shamans with many superhuman capacities. The most famous ḍākinī of the Bön tradition is Chosa Bönmo, who lived in the eighth century during the religious struggles of King Trisong Detsen. She was appointed by the king to mediate the conflict with the Bön priests. Other ḍākinīs were consorts of famous Bön shamans, such as Nyibarma, depicted in iconography in union with her consort, naked and with ornaments similar to those of her Buddhist counterpart.[36]

In Tibetan Buddhism, the profile of the ḍākinī is unique in that she has been elevated to a status beyond a specific named ḍākinī to a feminine principle that is at the heart of Vajrayāna teachings.[37] The essence of this feminine principle is wisdom, defined as insight into emptiness. That essence arises in a variety of expressions in the symbol of the ḍākinī in the Tibetan Vajrayāna tradition: limitless space; intense heat; incisive accuracy in pointing out the essence; an emanation body that is itself a powerful teaching tool; the power to transmute bewildering confusion, symbolized by the charnel ground, into clarity and enlightenment; and an unblinking stare from her three eyes, which galvanizes the experience of nonthought.

The Meaning of the Ḍākinī in Tibetan Buddhism

Given the tremendous evolution and assimilation of the ḍākinī in the development of Buddhist tantra in India, it is difficult to render the Sanskrit as a single English term.[38] I use the well-known Sanskrit terminology for that reason, and because the Tibetan tradition privileges those elements that have been inherited from the Indian sources. The etymology of *ḍākinī* has been the subject of some debate by Vajrayāna scholars; the term is generally interpreted as "she who flies through the sky."[39] Related forms of the word appear as *ḍāginī* (a Prakrit form) and *śākinī* ("she who is powerful").[40] In any case, it is difficult to derive the Vajrayāna Buddhist understanding of the term unless one turns to Tibetan.

Because it is the feminine form that most often appears, the feminine translation of the word is customary, *khandroma,* which is most literally translated as "she who goes through the sky." This is a shortened form of the full Tibetan term *khekham su khyappar droma,* which is literally translated as "she who flies everywhere in [the limitless limits of] the realm of space."[41] Perhaps this can best be rendered as "sky-dancer," as the ḍākinī is often iconographically depicted as dancing,[42] which suggests constant movement in space. From her earliest appearances in Indian pantheons, her powers of flight were important, although she is not always seen flying in her Tibetan depictions. For this reason we must examine the meaning of "sky" and "dancer" beyond the merely literal level.

According to Tibetan commentaries, the first part of her name, *kha,* refers to space or sky, the boundless expanse of emptiness (*śūnyatā, tong-pa-nyi*) which is the ground of all experience in the Vajrayāna Buddhist context.[43] According to the teachings of the sūtra tradition, emptiness is described as beyond concept, but the skillful means of this philosophic tradition limits its expression to words and concepts. In the Vajrayāna, understanding of emptiness is evoked through iconography, symbol, and liturgy. In this context, the ḍākinī awakens the experience of groundlessness and lack of reference point through her soaring in space or the sky (*kha*). She abides nowhere but arises continually in the practitioner's experience as an emblem of space.[44]

The second part of her name, *dro,* indicates movement and life itself.[45] Emptiness is not mere blankness but a mode of being, in which manifestation arises freely, never compromising the power of emptiness. In fact, manifestation in the case of the ḍākinī aids the practitioner, for she points out the dynamic of emptiness in phenomena through her very being (*dro*). This quality of movement is one of her most consistent traits, and it refers not only to the movement of her physical form but also to her ability to change form and to appear and disappear at will. The emblematic expression of movement is found in iconographic depictions of her dancing, stepping forward, or flying. These movements relate on an exoteric level to the ḍākinī's role as a helper or leader on the path; esoterically, they point not to herself but to the medium, the limitless space, in which she moves. She represents the inner experience of space, which is the inspirational impulse at the heart of enlightenment.[46] *Ma,* the feminine ending, suggests that it is *she* who dances in the limitlessness of the sky, for as a feminine form she has a unique ability to point out emptiness directly.

Other terms are also translated as equivalent to the Sanskrit *ḍākinī.* Most common is the Sanskrit *khecarī* or *vyomacarī,* in Tibetan *khachöma,*[47] which means "she who enjoys or rules the sky."[48] She thrives in vast luminous space and dances as an expression of that enjoyment. The meaning appears to be almost equivalent to the more prevalent *khandroma.* One also sees the terms *ḍākki, ḍākkima,* and *ḍākima* in Buddhist tantric literature; these have an intimate, affectionate connotation.[49]

In Tibetan, the word *khandro* is actually of indeterminate gender. Although usually interpreted to be feminine, it could also be translated as "male sky dancer." Part of this is due to the nature of the Tibetan language, in which gender is not explicitly indicated by syntax, except in cases where the gender-specific Sanskrit has been translated; however, in Tibet it is culturally and contextually implicit that the khandro is female unless otherwise designated.[50]

The masculine counterparts to the ḍākinī, known in Sanskrit as ḍākas, appeared in the Hindu pantheon as male ghouls and flesh-eating warlocks, also attendants to Durgā, Kālī, or Śiva, and they also were transformed with the development of the ḍākinī in tantric India to represent a more profound aspect. They are depicted as male sky dancers who serve as consorts of ḍākinīs and spiritual mentors in their own right for yogins, yoginīs, and human ḍākinīs. In the transmission of Buddhism to Tibet, it appears that the ḍāka was transformed into the *pawo* (*vīra*), which means hero or fearless warrior. When paired with ḍākinīs, their female counterparts are often called *pamos* (*virinī*) and sometimes called yoginīs, or *naljormas*.[51] When the male heroes come to be interpreted as having the power of full realization, they are called herukas, which we will discuss below. However, the ḍākinī emerged in Tibet as a symbol in her own right, sometimes accompanied by a consort but often alone. The ḍāka or vīra became a rare companion in biographies and visionary accounts.

Similarly, ḍākinīs were more prevalent in texts of Tibetan Vajrayāna early in its history and in its Indian sources. The more contemporary hagiographies of Tibet reflect a lower profile for ḍākinīs, especially in accounts of the spiritual journeys of monks. Yet there is every indication that ḍākinī visions have continued to play a strong role in the spiritual journeys of noncelibate yogins, yoginīs, and tertöns, if we are to take contemporary anecdotal, oral accounts seriously. As discussed in the previous section, the yogic strands of Tibet have emphasized visionary experience and personal transformation, while the monastic institutions focus on scholastic learning, ritual performance, and monastic community issues in which women and transformation play but a supporting role. The ḍākinī, with her orientation toward the visionary and transformative paths of meditation, would naturally be more directly invoked in the yogic movements of Tibet, and insofar as these strands are separated from the textual centers, ḍākinīs would be found more explicitly in the oral lore.

General Classifications of Ḍākinīs

The ḍākinī populates the texts, lore, and practices of the Tibetan Vajrayāna tradition, playing a variety of roles with many classifications. The two most important are the worldly ḍākinī (*jikten kyi khandro, loka-ḍākinī*), originally related to the demoness of pretantric tradition, and the wisdom ḍākinī (*yeshe khandro, jñāna-ḍākinī*), the fully enlighted ḍākinī. In their Indian forms, the distinctions between these two ḍākinīs were clear and consistent; in Tibet, these ḍākinīs often overlap in appearance and function, with dynamic play. Sometimes the worldly ḍākinī is converted into a wisdom ḍākinī, and often a wisdom ḍākinī takes on worldly, ghoulish qualities.[52]

WORLDLY ḌĀKINĪS

The ambiguity of the ḍākinī is part of her Tibetan lore. In her manifestations as a flesh-eating demoness, she may be acting on behalf of negative forces opposed to spirituality. She may be an attendant force, acting as a protective aide to her liege, who may be a realized being or merely a powerful shaman. Or she may be fully realized herself, acting as a teacher, messenger, or protector of the dharma. For example, when the flesh-eating worldy ḍākinī acts on behalf of the dharma, she eats not the body but the ego-clinging of her victim, thus liberating the practitioner into deeper realization.[53]

The lore of Tibetan Buddhism demands that lamas and tantric practitioners learn how to identify types of ḍākinīs in order to interact with them properly. There are many accounts of highly realized yogins or yoginīs who do not recognize the ḍākinī in their midst at all, or who mistake a worldly ḍākinī for a realized one, or vice versa. Making such a mistake can have disastrous results. Trusting a worldly ḍākinī with intimacy and secrets can lead to death and the destruction of one's own teaching lineage. Missing an opportunity to receive teachings from a realized ḍākinī can lead to years of fruitless practice, frustrating obstacles, and general lack of synchronicity with the teacher and his or her transmissions. For this reason there are many guidelines, recorded and oral, on how to recognize ḍākinīs. When these sources are consulted and followed and one still makes mistakes, it is said that this is because the general circumstances are not ripe.[54]

The great teacher Pema Lendreltsel (1291–1315) received as hidden treasure teachings (terma) the original transmission of the *Khandro Nyingthik* (*Heart Essence of the Ḍākinī*), an important cycle of meditation texts that originated with Guru Rinpoche and the ḍākinīs. After transmitting them to the third Karmapa, Rangjung Dorje, at age twenty-five he met a beautiful woman in the Nyel district, and, thinking her to be a realized ḍākinī, for a month "he took care to have body contact with her in conditions of secrecy."[55] Subsequently, he had a dream in which it was revealed that his consort was a mere demoness. Mortified, Pema Lendreltsel became entangled in a terrible scandal that led to the death of one of his disciples and eventually his own death, endangering the transmission of the Heart Essence teachings.[56]

The Tibetan manifestation of the worldly ḍākinī is closely related to her Indian precursor, for she arises as a demoness or ghoul with her arsenal of powers and armies, who cause calamity or mischief depending on the seriousness of their intention. Her fondness for the taste of human flesh and blood continues from her earlier forms. These ḍākinīs roam about, unaffiliated and untamed, creating chaos in many situations, fickle and terrifying. They embody worldly magic and power, haunting their victims in cemeteries and charnel grounds, where dead bodies decay. They also inhabit mountains and springs and serve as regional protectors. In a description of modern conditions in a place said to be especially sacred to the ḍākinī, Dudjom Rinpoche wrote that the women of the region belong to an ancient race of ḍākinīs and still "have power over the arts of magic gaze, transformation of objects by means of certain gnostic spells, and some minor sorcery."[57]

In their fiercest mode, they are called *shasa khandro*, or flesh-eating ḍākinīs.[58] They are classified into twelve different specialists in consuming the human body, such as breath-takers, flesh-eaters, blood-drinkers, and bone-chewers.[59] The hagiography of Guru Rinpoche, in which he was exiled to the charnel ground, describes worldly flesh-eating ḍākinīs in this way:

> *There are to be seen countless ḍākinīs:*
> *some of them have eyes that dart out sun rays;*
> *others give rise to thunderclaps and ride water buffaloes;*
> *others hold sabres and have eyes which inflict harm;*
> *others wear death's heads one above the other and ride tigers;*
> *others wear corpses and ride lions;*
> *others eat entrails and ride garuḍas;*
> *others have flaming lances and ride jackals;*
> *others in their numberless hands carry many generations of living beings;*
> *others carry in their hands their own heads which they have severed;*
> *others carry in their hands their own hearts which they have torn out;*
> *there are others who have made gaping wounds in their own bodies and who empty out and devour their own intestines and entrails;*
> *there are others who hide and yet reveal their male or female sexual organs, riding horses, bulls, elephants.*

In the central lake Cloud of Purification is the charnel ground,
the haunted place where others cannot venture.
There they stand, sucking the substance out of life.[60]

These flesh-eating ḍākinīs wielded power primarily because of their dominion over the realm of human death and destruction, and they haunted their victims with their utter disregard for the human horror at such devastation. Their haunting took the form of sucking out the precious blood of their victims.

It is important to note that there were many demoness figures in Tibetan Buddhism from the earliest time, both Indian assimilations and those indigenously Tibetan. The malevolent *sinmo* (rākṣasī) was the most famous of the indigenous ones; along with her masculine counterpart, the *sinpo,* she represented resistance to the introduction of Buddhism to Tibet. Under Songtsen Gampo, the land of Tibet was depicted as a supine sinmo who had to be bound down and rendered helpless before Buddhism could successfully enter.[61] Other such demoness figures include the *yakṣas* (*nöjin*), earth goddesses, *senmos*, female *vetālas* (*tramen*), female *māras* (*dü*), and female *nāgas* (*lu*). All of these demonesses were encountered by Guru Rinpoche and the great siddhas of India and Tibet, who tamed them and had them vow loyalty to the dharma. The ḍākinīs or khandromas in their worldly forms were similarly tamed in many cases, but they stand in a special relationship with the spiritual teachings of Buddhist tantra. They were the demoness forms who ascended to the central realizations associated with the nature of mind, yogic practice, and protection of the innermost aspects of transmission. Yet they retained the accoutrements of their demonic forms, which remain powerful even in their untamed state.

Ḍākinīs, like other beings such as gods and goddesses, live long but temporary lives, subject to sickness and death.[62] Because these ḍākinīs have no inherent spiritual inclination, they have untamed emotional tendencies and are capable of turning their power toward vindictive chaos. Humans can offend or incite them by violating their realms of authority, causing a stain (*drip-pa*) on the relationship.[63] This can lead to a variety of responses, including attacks, from the volatile ḍākinīs.

When shepherds from the village of Dinma Drin built a huge fire in the forests in the Lachi Snow Range, the home of the worldly ḍākinī Tseringma,[64] she was deeply affected by the fiery smoke and became mortally ill. In revenge, she and her retinue of ḍākinīs exuded vapors that brought a great plague upon the village, infecting the inhabitants with severe contagious diseases causing the vomiting of blood, dizziness, and fever. Many humans and livestock died. When asked what had occurred, Tseringma explained that "it is the common oath of all worldly ḍākinīs that if one of us has been made unwell or unhappy, we are all offended and the devas and spirits support us, throwing the world into confusion."[65]

A specific kind of powerful worldly ḍākinī is the *mamo*,[66] who is depicted as an extremely fierce and ugly demoness, black with emaciated breasts and matted hair. Mamos were among the local spirits subjugated by Guru Rinpoche upon his grand entry to Tibet. They were assimilated by Buddhism from the *māra*s of India, who attacked the Buddha under the tree of enlightenment, sending down rains of weaponry and pestilence. They also were assimilated from the *mātṛkā*s, non-Brahmanical mother demonesses who endanger fetuses and abduct small children.[67] Mamos are particularly ferocious inhabitors of charnel grounds and are among the most feared malicious spirits of Tibet. They appear with a variety of leaders, armed with sacks full of diseases, magic notched sticks, black snares, and magic balls of thread.[68] They are considered one of the eight classes (*lhasin degye*) of gods and demons often mentioned in Vajrayāna texts, and when incited they can arouse all eight kinds to follow them in attack. The mamo is known for causing havoc with a roll of her magical dice, creating pestilence and warfare.

As we said, worldly ḍākinīs are closely related to the māras of India, who haunted the Buddha under the tree of awakening. In this role, they took whatever form might correspond to the vulnerabilities of their target, including beguiling and seductive forms of exquisite beauty. When that ruse failed, they again became vicious ghouls and demonesses. When the yogin Kambala meditated in an isolated cave at Panaba Cliff, the local mamo ḍākinīs plotted to obstruct his meditation. Noticing that he was particularly reliant upon a tattered black woolen blanket that also served as his only robe, they asked to borrow it. Sensing the power of the blanket, they tore it into shreds and devoured it, burning a final scrap in his cooking fire. In anger Kambala magically transformed the mamo ḍākinīs into sheep and sheared them, so that when they returned to their original forms their heads were shaven. Fearing the power of his realization, the mamos vomited up the shreds of blanket, and Kambala collected the pieces and rewove them. From that day, he was called Lvapa, or "master of the blanket."[69]

In corresponding masculine form, the worldly māras attacked Yeshe Tsogyal in her penultimate meditation in the cave at Nering Senge Dzong in their most seductive forms as virile young rakes:

> On another occasion, the spirits took the form of a band of handsome youths, their faces beautiful and complexions wholesome, good to smell, well built and sturdy—a joy to look upon. To begin with they spoke to her respectfully, addressing her as "Mistress" and "Lady," but later they called her "girl" and "Tsogyal," and began to speak to her with words of desire. They started by teasing her playfully, but little by little they uncovered their manhood, saying things like, "Hey, girl, is this what you want? Do you want its milk?" And they put their arms around her waist, fondling her breasts, playing with her sexual parts, kissing her, making love in all sorts of ways. Some of the young men disappeared, subdued by the strength of the Lady's concentration. Others, through the concentration that perceives all things as illusion, faded away, mere phantoms. Still others, through the counteractive meditation of a Bodhisattva, were changed into blackened corpses, hideous old men, lepers, blind men, cripples, and idiots, all of them loathsome. And being thus transformed, they disappeared.[70]

Having vanished, these ḍākas again became malicious demons who rained down pestilence, weaponry, and disaster. While these demons manifest most often in female form, in cases like these the masculine manifestation more appropriately addresses the yoginī's potential vulnerability.

These worldly ḍākinīs often swear allegiance to a more powerful mistress or master and serve in support of their liege's agenda. In Tibetan mythology, the liege could be a demon, a shaman of a folk tradition, a Bön priest, or a Buddhist teacher. It was customary in Tibetan circles that a lesser demoness would be bound by oath (*tamla tak*) to the superior power, in a vassal-liege relationship.[71] Mamos serve a variety of masters and mistresses, such as Palden Lhamo, the protector of the city of Lhasa, or the meditational deity Vajravārāhī, the supreme wisdom ḍākinī.

When Virūpa was studying at Nālandā, he visited Devīkoṭa, a nearby shrine. There a worldly ḍākinī approached him and gave him a lotus flower and a cowrie shell, marking him as under her power. When he tried to get rid of these gifts, they stuck to his hands, arousing the pity of everyone around him. A ḍākinī protector advised him to flee immediately in order to free himself from their spell, and he escaped. At nightfall, the flesh-eating ḍākinīs sought to kill him for sport, but he ran to an inn and hid under an overturned cauldron, meditating on emptiness. During the next years he studied and practiced fervently in order to develop the spiritual power to break the spell. When he returned to Devīkoṭa to confront them, the worldly ḍākinīs excitedly gathered at night to devour him. He manifested the powers of the wrathful deity and subdued them with the heruka's laugh, binding them by oath to do no more harm.[72]

These affiliated worldly ḍākinīs could remain hostile to spirituality or could advance to a more profound level, depending upon their liege. A ḍākinī in service to a powerful worldly spirit could become even more powerful in performing magic, without any change in the malice of her intent. But the fortunate ḍākinī, in service to the dharma and a tantric guru, could advance to the ultimate realization. In many cases, she aroused the compassionate motivation of the awakened heart (*bodhicitta*) dedicated to others' benefit. She often became a powerful and faithful protector of the Buddhist teachings.

The subjugation of worldly ḍākinīs was accomplished in a variety of ways. Guru Rinpoche subdued them and other demons and mamos on Chu-bo-ri Mountain, where he engaged in a duel of miraculous displays. The White Ḍākinī of the glaciers deployed a thunderbolt against him, and he surrounded her with a finger, swept her into a boiling lake, and blinded her in one eye. She immediately surrendered, swearing to do no more harm, and asked to become his vassal.[73] To subdue other demons, Guru Rinpoche transformed their weapons, bound and chained them, and frightened them with displays of power. Methods of subjugation might employ relative *siddhis* such as physical acts of great power like Guru Rinpoche's, or they might employ the absolute *siddhi* of meditative realization, as Milarepa displayed.[74]

When subdued, worldly ḍākinīs became the most important of dharma protectors. After Guru Rinpoche pacified the mamos, they continued to manifest in fearsome ways to protect the integrity of the Vajrayāna teachings, enforcing the sacred outlook (*tag-nang*) of tantra practitioners. When the environment of practice deteriorates, the mamos are said to express their legendary wrath in order to repair Vajrayāna commitments (*samaya, tamtsik*) and to restore the practitioner's appropriate attitude. Their wrath arises not from personal insult or violation (*drip-pa*), as it previously did, but from the practitioner's improper relationship with Vajrayāna commitments and practice, or spiritual obscurations (also called *drip-pa*, but in the Vajrayāna sense). The mamos are invoked in this liturgy of pacification:

At the end of the five-hundred-year dark age,
When the secret mantra has strayed into Bön,
When sons do not listen to their father's words,
An evil time, when relatives quarrel,
When people dress sloppily in clothes of rags,
Eating bad, cheap food,
When there are family feuds and civil wars:
These provoke the black mamos' wrath.
These various women fill a thousand realms
Sending sickness upon man and beast.
The sky is thick with purple clouds of sickness.
They incite cosmic warfare.
They destroy by causing the age of weaponry.
Suddenly they strike men with fatal ulcerous sores.
Completely daring, they bring down hail and thunderbolts.[75]

In order to repair the spiritual obscurations and violations of vows that pollute the relationship with the mamos, the Vajrayāna practitioner makes offerings and appeasements, acknowledging the power of the mamos and begging for forgiveness:

Please change the course of evil and sickness.
I make this offering so you may be appeased. . . .
Please perform the activities we request of you.
Overcome by ignorance from beginningless time,
Clouded by stupidity due to laziness,
However we have strayed from the path of omniscience,
May the host of emanation ḍākinīs forgive us.[76]

In this capacity, the mamos are acting on behalf of their master, Guru Rinpoche, restoring the practitioner's samaya commitments and ensuring the integrity of Vajrayāna practice. They are appeased by the traditional offerings, which include those of body (meditation postures and gestures, *mudrā*), speech (liturgical recitation and music, *mantra*), and mind (confession and devotion). Other offerings are the components of the Vajrayāna feast (*tsok, gaṇacakra*) which include the blessed sacramental cakes and wine.

In one of the pantheons of yidams in the higher tantras of the Nyingma lineage, the mamo was elevated to a wisdom ḍākinī.[77] In this rank, Mamo is depicted with dark brown or black skin, a terrifying grimace, and blazing, angry eyes. She carries a drawstring bag of liquid poison bound at the mouth with the writhing body of a poisonous snake. She represents "liberating sorcery" (*mamo bötong*), which means that Mamo protects the practitioner's relationship with the sacred world, such that if one adopts a disrespectful attitude toward sacredness, poisonous results might follow. The practice of this yidam is a potent reminder to practitioners to strengthen their samaya commitments and sharpen their sense of the preciousness of life.

In order to understand contextually the contrast between worldly and wisdom ḍākinīs, it may be instructive to study the story of Milarepa and the ḍākinī Tseringma.[78] This account traces the journey of worldly ḍākinīs from their experience as local protectors and architects of destruction to their engagement with the path of dharma, in which they become loyal to their tantric guru and protectors of the dharma. In the region called the Lachi Snow Range, Milarepa was repeatedly harassed in his meditation by five worldly ḍākinīs who described themselves as "ghosts who wander in graveyards . . . who magic make."[79] They appeared in hideous forms to Milarepa while he was in retreat, each taking her own characteristic guise: one had a skeleton's grinning face, another gushed blood from her jackal face, a coal-colored one smashed the sun and moon, and the fourth was the wrathful Yamāntakā, the empress of death, juggling the sun and moon. The final ḍākinī took a particularly beguiling form, inciting uncontrollable lust.[80] They told him that they had cast dice for lots, and the divination indicated that it was Milarepa's turn to be slaughtered:

There is no way of your escaping!
You have no power, no freedom.
We have come to take your life, your soul, and spirit;
To stop your breath and take consciousness from your body,
To drink your blood and eat your flesh and skandhas.
Now your life has come to its final ending—

Your karma and all your merits are exhausted.
Now the Lord of Death will eat you,
And the black rope of Karma will bind you fast.
Tonight you leave this world.[81]

Milarepa listened carefully and responded that because of his meditation, he had neither regrets nor fear of dying. If they must, they should take his life. And saying this, he offered his body to them with great compassion. The five fierce ḍākinīs and their retinue were so impressed by the great yogin's kindness and fearlessness that they felt great remorse. Later, they returned to confess their mischief and to take refuge vows with Milarepa.

In their ensuing conversations, they appeared in increasingly charming forms, requesting more and more advanced teachings from their new master. Milarepa remained wary, giving them teachings on the condition that the ḍākinīs surrender incremental amounts of their malicious magical powers to him. First, Milarepa specifically asked them to renounce their practice of harassing meditators, saying that otherwise their vows would be a waste, like "throwing a yak cow into the abyss."[82] Then, in return for giving them bodhisattva vows, Mila demanded as gifts their worldly powers such as divining with a mirror, protecting and increasing progeny, and winning food and prosperity. Finally, in return for the Vajrayāna vows, they surrendered to him the quintessence of their very lives. In his instructions, he clearly indicated the commitments to which they were bound, which included love and respect for all beings.

Subsequently, Milarepa was outraged to learn that his five new students had caused plague to spread through a nearby region, to avenge a forest fire in their habitat. When he visited his charges, he discovered Tseringma on her deathbed, coughing and pale. As he healed her and the inhabitants of the surrounding countryside, she and her retinue of ḍākinīs were deeply grateful. Realizing that these ḍākinīs had never comprehended the dharma fully, Milarepa took the opportunity to teach them about death, impermanence, and the intermediate state:

The human body is beset with sickness,
And trying to free one's mind from grief
Often leads to more distress.
By the force of karma and the senses
All self-made confusions are created.

They are but dreams passing in a flash . . .
The whole universe is but "imagination,"
All in all, it is but a shadow-show
Of one's own mind. . . .
Only through cultivating [awakened] mind
And contemplating [emptiness]
Can karmas, troubles, hindrances, and habitual thoughts be killed.[83]

Upon hearing this, the ḍākinīs developed a deep desire for awakening and dedicated themselves to the practice of dharma, singing:

Driven by deep-rooted ignorance,
We worldly, magical ḍākinīs
Wander in saṃsāra from time without beginning.
First, we must take an earthly birth—
We have no other choice.
Then we think we can live for long,
But suddenly we hear the call of death
And our hands are tied—
We cannot escape.
Dizzy are our heads and dark our thoughts.
Without freedom from death, we must fade,
And with us all our beauty and splendor. . . .
Today you have given us the raft of [awakened] mind
On which we shall escape the witch-land of desires,
And elude the dreadful monster of the deep.
We shall arrive safely
In the [pure land of joy].
From despair and weariness
We shall revive;
With hope and guidance,
Will our wishes be fulfilled.[84]

As they swore eternal devotion to their teacher, Milarepa empowered them in the Mahāmudrā tradition, and they became dedicated practitioners of Vajrayāna meditation.[85]

It is clear from tracing the development of the ḍākinī that the worldly ḍākinī most closely resembles the ḍākinī in the early Indian tradition, and that the worldly ḍākinī of Tibet represents a remnant of her preassimilation identity from pre-Buddhist Indian culture. The other classifications of ḍākinī retain her wrath, unpredictability, and association with the charnel ground, and they take her guise in many situations in order to display their power. But in their assimilated form, their more powerful identity displays the power of realization of the truth of dharma.

THE WISDOM ḌĀKINĪ: YESHE KHANDRO

The second general classification of ḍākinīs is the more spiritually significant one for an understanding of Tibetan Vajrayāna Buddhism. The wisdom ḍākinī is fully awakened and acts to awaken others.[86] She is the essence of enlightened mind beyond any concept of gender, the preeminent symbol of the nature of mind itself, in a female form. She simultaneously realizes the ultimate nature of phenomena, embodies it through her manifestation, and acts it out in her enlightened activity. She is the supreme protector of the teachings, a tantric guru, a female buddha with her glorious retinue. The yeshe khandro is the manifestation of wisdom par excellence, the unblinking and penetrating gaze that sees phenomena just as they are. She embodies the full meaning of "sky-dancer."

As we have seen, it is often difficult to recognize the wisdom ḍākinī. She may appear in the form of a human woman or take the visionary form of a worldly demoness ḍākinī. Because of the ambiguity of her appearance, which is a central part of her lore, tāntrikas study her identifiable marks, which differ from one lineage to another. Seeing her depends upon the depth of the practitioner's realization and upon the particular circumstances of her appearance. Her characteristics closely resemble her worldly sister's, but she has distinguishing marks that are hers alone. The wisdom ḍākinī has three eyes, the third of which is placed vertically in her forehead. With her threefold gaze, she sees pure unimpeded space, unbounded emptiness.

When seen clearly, she is described by those who witness her as beautiful, but this beauty does not necessarily follow established norms. She may be tall and comely, short and broad, fair or dark. She may be gentle and melodious in her communications, or sharp and harsh. She may be sixteen years old, in the full bloom of youth, or she may be gruesome and wrathful, initially inspiring terror.[87] When she is seen clearly, her power is very definite, penetrating, and even threatening in its directness. This power comes not from conventional magic but from wisdom, and her fierceness is not emotional but is the sharp energy of wakefulness. The tāntrika is said to be entranced by her in whatever form she takes.

When the wisdom ḍākinī appears, her visionary form is classically understood to be dancing, which dynamically unfolds her wisdom, unceasingly manifesting the activities of the Buddha.[88] But she also manifests in other active forms, both visionary and embodied, that communicate her wisdom in a variety of situations. In these forms she is the *karma ḍākinī,* the "action sky-dancer." The relationship between the two ḍākinīs can be likened to the relationship between the eyes and the arms.[89] The karma ḍākinī carries out the wishes of the wisdom ḍākinī and fulfills her enlightened activity. Their realization and aspiration might be on different levels, or the karma ḍākinī may have the same realization and aspiration as her wisdom sister.

As we investigate the wisdom ḍākinī, we will see her spiritual depth, her many manifestations, forms, and activities, and her pervasion of the sacred world. Without her gifts, her counsel, and her blessing, the gates of wisdom can never open for the Vajrayāna practitioner. For this reason, she is an essential element in Tibetan Buddhist practice and realization.

The Three Bodies of Enlightened Ḍākinīs

When remarkable human yoginīs are described as wisdom ḍākinīs, they are depicted as having the three bodies of enlightenment, suggesting that they may be considered female buddhas. Most subtle is the formless, empty expanse that is the nature of mind itself (*dharmakāya, chöku*). Second is the meditational deity internalized by the tantric practitioner who manifests the dynamic wisdom inherent in the mind, expressed as the visionary form of a semiwrathful or wrathful ḍākinī (*sambhogakāya, longku*). The outer expression of the ḍākinī refers to the many forms in which the ḍākinī appears, human and visionary, peaceful or wrathful, the embodied ḍākinī herself (*nirmāṇakāya, tülku*).[90]

Yeshe Tsogyal, the great Tibetan yoginī, is supplicated in this way in her ritual from the *Longchen Nyingthik* tradition:

> *In the center of that palace,*
> *Upon the pistil of a blooming lotus*
> *On a sun-seat is the chief of the ḍākinīs,*
> *[Who is] Samantabhadrī in the vast expanse of dharmakāya,*

Yeshe Tsogyal, the Ocean of Wisdom, in human form.

Vajravārāhī in the field of saṃbhogakāya and
Yeshe Tsogyal in the form of nirmāṇakāya.[91]

On an embodied level, Yeshe Tsogyal was a historical figure, the queen of Trisong Detsen, the king of Tibet (742–776 C.E.) at the time of the introduction of Buddhism. She became one of the primary consorts of Padmasambhava, Guru Rinpoche, who began the first diffusion of Buddhism in Tibet, and she was responsible for the transmission of many early Nyingma teachings. Because she was a wisdom ḍākinī, it was recognized that her outer manifestation was closely related to these other two dimensions. In her famous biography, she is lauded shortly after her birth in this way:

HRĪ!
Nature of the dharmakāya, Samantabhadrī of great bliss,
Vajrayoginī, sambhogakāya ḍākinī,
Nirmāṇakāya, supreme mother of all Buddhas,
To you all happiness and fortune!

Dharmakāya ḍākinī, abyss of Voidness,
Sambhogakāya, Sarasvatī, mother of Buddhas in the triple time,
Nirmāṇakāya, supreme and perfectly endowed,
To you the victory!

Dharmakāya, expanse of Primal Wisdom,
Sambhogakāya, mother of exalted ones, white Tārā of the seven eyes,
Nirmāṇakāya, supreme among the living,
To you we bow![92]

In this supplication, her embodied form is acknowledged as extraordinary, for she is called Mother of Conquerors, or of buddhas, supremely qualified and supreme among humans. This signifies that she, an inherently enlightened one, surely will again become enlightened in this human birth as the woman Yeshe Tsogyal.[93]

As for her inner dimension, Yeshe Tsogyal was remarkable because she was not merely a mortal; in her dynamic nature she was a tantric Buddhist meditational deity. She is called Sarasvatī (Yangchenma), the great female bodhisattva of learning, culture, and music, the peaceful consort of Mañjuśrī, who carries a lute that serves as her symbol. Sarasvatī is also called Vākīśvarī, (Ngawang Lhamo) or "lady of speech" for her connection with seed syllables, music, utterance, and poetry. She is the ḍākinī of the mirror-like wisdom, and the "white-cloaked lady" (Kö Karmo) who is ḍākinī of inner heat in the yogic practice of *tummo.*[94] It is said that Yeshe Tsogyal was Sarasvatī in her previous life.

Yeshe Tsogyal in her visionary dimension was the radiant White Tārā (Drölma Karmo) the savior who, with her compassionate seven eyes, attends to the health and welfare of beings in all quarters. In another manifestation, she was Vajrayoginī or Vajravārāhī, who are two aspects of the most important ḍākinī in the Tibetan tantric system. Vajrayoginī is a semi-wrathful deity, depicted as red and dancing, wearing bone ornaments; she is the most expressive of the qualities of wakefulness, the personification of the wisdom-mind itself. In her alternate identity as Vajravārāhī, she is the "Vajra Sow," the manifestation of the nonconceptual quality of the mind, who severs thought with her hooked knife (see chapter 4).

In her most subtle, essential form, Yeshe Tsogyal is called "expanse of mahāsukha Küntusangmo [Samantabhadrī], the all-good queen." This deity is called the primordial Mother Buddha, source of all enlightenment. She is the consort and female counterpart of Samantabhadra (Küntusangpo), the primordial buddha of the Nyingma school, who represents the formless space of wisdom, the dharmakāya dimension of buddhahood in whom delusion and conceptual thought have never arisen. Samantabhadra is depicted as blue, the color of the sky, a reminder that his nature is limitless and formless as the sky. The feminine Samantabhadrī is depicted as white and is the primary symbol of the awareness-wisdom aspect of the mind. Both are naked and unadorned, just as the mind and awareness always are in their essence. But it is Samantabhadrī who is the expression of limitless space, the natural state that is ultimate truth.

Samantabhadrī is the expression of that which cannot be expressed in words or symbols, the ultimate nature of mind, the limitless expanse of simplicity. This is the most subtle aspect of the ḍākinī, beyond all dualities of gender, form, or expression. This aspect of the ḍākinī must be experienced directly. All meditation practices in the Vajrayāna tradition eventually point to this transformative experience. This is the secret of the power of the ḍākinī, and it is to this that she points in all of her manifestations.

Yeshe Tsogyal was also depicted as having eyes that reflect each of these aspects. She performs the three gazes (*tatang sum*) of a wisdom ḍākinī in this way:

Her middle eye [of dharmakāya] gazes [upward] into space.
Her [right] eye of sambhogakāya disciplines beings.
Her [left] eye of nirmāṇakāya summons the three worlds.
All deities of the tantra are present in her body.[95]

Her left eye sees the world of ordinary manifestation, which she summons to the path. The right eye sees the dynamic display of the visionary level, and this reminds beings of the true nature of phenomena, which disciplines them. Her central eye of wisdom, placed vertically in her forehead, marking her as a wisdom ḍākinī, gazes without allegiance or confusion into the vastness of space, the *kha* of her very being. With this threefold gaze, saṃsāra and nirvāṇa are seen as inseparable, obstacles to enlightenment are removed, and primordial wisdom arises.[96]

Four Aspects of Ḍākinī: Outer-Outer, Outer, Inner, and Secret

The paradigm of the three bodies of enlightenment used in the description of human yoginīs has limitations in fully depicting the aspects of the wisdom ḍākinī. Throughout my investigation of the sources, both oral and textual, I encountered references to the three kāyas as having a masculine bias. It was suggested that the paradigm most appropriate to ḍākinī manifestations was that of outer-outer, outer, inner, and secret ḍākinīs.[97] The two outer ḍākinīs correspond to the apparitional form (nirmāṇakāya), the inner to the visionary form (sambhogakāya), and the secret to the empty form (dharmakāya). This classification is a popular one in Vajrayāna sources, describing in mythic, symbolic, and visionary fashion the relationship between the formless expanse of the ultimate ḍākinī and the feminine forms that manifest in our experience. Upon the advice of several lamas, this is the paradigm that structures this book.

I was particularly aided by an early interview with Khenpo Tsultrim Gyamtso Rinpoche, a renowned Tibetan yogin-scholar of the Kagyü lineage whose spontaneous teachings emerged as foundational in my understanding of the ḍākinī. Unlike most incarnate Tibetan lamas who were discovered in early childhood to be emanations of previous realized teachers, Khenpo was given the title of *rinpoche* ("precious one") because of his spiritual realizations in *this* life. Born in humble circumstances, Rinpoche embraced the life of a yogin-ascetic, practicing in solitary retreat in remote caves in eastern and central Tibet, and later received scholastic training under the sixteenth Karmapa, the supreme head of the Kagyü lineage. Rinpoche is recognized equally as a great scholar (with degrees of both *khenpo* and *geshe lharampa*)[98] and a great meditator (*gomchen*) who teaches the intricacies of scholastic texts in spontaneous songs that closely resemble those of Milarepa.

When I entered Rinpoche's quarters, I found him sitting on the brocaded couch, his rough robes thrown nonchalantly over his shoulder. His eyes danced with curiosity as I began my request: Could he tell me about the ḍākinī? Before his translator or I could continue, Rinpoche immediately burst into spontaneous song, sitting upright on the edge of the couch with legs crossed, brimming with joy. He sang in the lilting rhythm of traditional yogic songs of realization. His translator and I were taken by surprise, and I hastened to capture this on tape. Later, after consulting with Rinpoche, the translator produced this English version:

Between ḍākas and ḍākinīs there's a difference
In how their bodies may seem in apparent reality,
But for Mahāmudrā, luminous clarity,
There's not an atom of difference in their essential nature.

Those with good fortune and intelligence,
Who enter into the Vajrayāna
And attain the mantric siddhis,
Are renowned as mantra-born ḍākinīs.

By attending a realized teacher and
By the power of meeting mind's natural state
They directly realize the reality that abides.
These are called coemergent ḍākinīs.

By dwelling in the fields of the twenty-four
Sacred places of body, speech, and mind,
They accomplish the benefits of others.
These are called sacred-realm ḍākinīs.[99]

Chuckling with delight, Rinpoche hummed the song to himself, his eyes blazing as I managed to ask several questions about it. Then, with an abrupt wave of his hand, the interview was over.

For years these verses seemed opaque to me. What did they mean, and how do they express the essence of the ḍākinī? The latter three stanzas list classifications that are often associated in Anuttara-yoga-yāna with types of female consorts, graded according to level of realization.[100] When choosing such a consort, the yogin is said to be able to attain a level equivalent to the consort's, and so such ḍākinīs are revered and supplicated for their blessings, for their cumulative spiritual power is great.

Yet the descriptions of which ḍākinī referred to which level of realization differed widely in the various sources I consulted. In a commentary on a Tsongkhapa text, the fourteenth Dalai Lama, His Holiness Tenzin Gyatso, ranked the three in two different ways, while an additional Tsongkhapa commentary on the *Cakrasaṃvara-tantra* presents yet a third interpretation.[101] The *Saṃvarodaya-tantra* speaks of the three kinds of ḍākinīs as well, but in a different context and without any particular ranking of their realization or power.[102] Lhalungpa gave yet a slightly different interpretation of the three, suggesting them as different orders spanning different manifestations of the ḍākinī. Most of the lamas I interviewed confessed to never having heard of these three categories.

My confusion in interpreting the Khenpo's spontaneous song was characteristic of the entire project I had undertaken. In the next several years, I returned several times to him and to his primary successor, Ven. Dzogchen Pönlop Rinpoche, for explanation. Their combined guidance gave me the following commentary, which exemplifies how the textual tradition of Tibetan Vajrayāna cannot be accessed without oral commentary. Khenpo Rinpoche helpfully remarked that this teaching related to ḍākinīs in both the subjective and objective sense—that is, it related to levels of inner realization for practitioners themselves as well as to the focused choice of a specific female consort. In instructions like these, the embodied ḍākinī is the yoginī who has developed fully in tantric practice and who has traversed the customary stages to realization. Nevertheless, even at the lower stages of development, the female practitioner becomes a ḍākinī, albeit one of lesser depth. It is also clear from Khenpo Rinpoche's commentary that the term *ḍākinī* could be applied to the male tantric practitioner as well.[103]

Much later, as I reflected on this song, I realized that Khenpo Rinpoche had given me a great gift. These four categories closely parallel what I had received elsewhere[104] and reveal a basic structure of the ḍākinī symbol. The categories are not to be understood only as levels of realization for ordinary women (for Rinpoche himself said that sacred-realm ḍākinīs are not human and were in fact invisible); they can also be understood as aspects of the ḍākinī symbol.

The four aspects of the ḍākinī are revealed in this way: (1) The secret ḍākinī shows that on the ultimate level of realization, the ḍākinī is the nature of the mind beyond any form of duality, including gender. (2) The inner aspect is the coemergent ḍākinī, the realization of wisdom at the heart of all seeming dualities of pleasure and pain, life and death, through the practice of the meditational deity. (3) The outer ḍākinī is the ruler of the sacred, energetic subtle body, mind's emanation in the physical realm, which serves as the play of wisdom. (4) The outer-outer ḍākinī is the living human ḍākinī, whose physical form is an expression of the meeting of confusion and wisdom in compassionate engagement with the world. These four aspects of the ḍākinī are interpenetrating dynamics, the inner no more sacred than the outer, revealing the relationship between form and emptiness, body and mind, gender and beyond-gender in the ḍākinī lore.[105]

Explained in classical texts, this fourfold classification is succintly presented in the *Tantra of the Secret Flame of the Ḍākinī* (*Ḍākinī-guḥya-jvala-tantra*) as follows: (1) the physically manifested ḍākinī with characteristic color and ornamentation; (2) the subtle body with its vital winds and channels; (3) the ḍākinī whose nature is coemergent joy (*lhen-chik kyepa gawa*); and (4) the most secret ḍākinī who is the self-aware primordial mind (*rang-rik yeshe*).[106] These accord with the outer-outer ḍākinī, the physically manifested ḍākinī, whose body appears with characteristic marks and qualities yet in its ultimate nature differs not at all from the physical body of the male. The outer ḍākinī is what is called the subtle body of vital winds and channels ruled by the ḍākinīs of the twenty-four sacred places, the symbolic network of yogic power. The inner ḍākinī is the creation-phase practice of a ḍākinī yidam, in which the tantric practitioner becomes the deity and realizes the emptiness and luminosity of all apparent existence through the deity's blessing. The secret ḍākinī is the realm of the natural state of mind, the vast and limitless space that is the source of all experience. The realization of this natural state is spoken of as coemergent wisdom.

Returning to Khenpo Rinpoche's song and its commentary, we see that he has presented the same four general categories, but as levels of realization, suggesting that it is possible, through direct realization of the ḍākinī, for the aspiring tantric practitioner to manifest enlightenment in four stages. The brilliance of his teaching is that he began with ambiguous categories usually associated with types of consorts, based them in the ultimate Mahāmudrā, and presented a profound reinterpretation in a fourfold classification, resonating to classical presentation. In his commentary, the meaning revealed itself as far surpassing the original set of categories.

According to this commentary, the ultimate ground of the investigation of the ḍākinī is Mahāmudrā, the vast and limitless nature of mind in which such distinctions as male and female or realized and unrealized have no footing. Ultimately, there is no distinction between male and female:

Between ḍākas and ḍākinīs there's a difference
In how their bodies may seem in apparent reality,
But for Mahāmudrā, luminous clarity,
There's not an atom of difference in their essential nature.[107]

The song's first verse presents a view in which the physical attributes of ḍākas and ḍākinīs appear different, but on the ultimate level of realization of things as they are, there is not an ounce of difference between their natures. The perceived physical embodiments of ḍākinīs and ḍākas are emanations of the more subtle qualities of their natures. For ḍākinīs the subtlest quality is pure space combined with the radiating wisdom of Mother Prajñāpāramitā. Khenpo Rinpoche was pointing out that from this perspective, perception or experience of the ḍākinī rests on the mind-transmission of the guru who empowers the disciple to see the world from a sacred perspective. Based on this transmission, the practitioner can come to see the ḍākinī in her various aspects, in oneself as a woman or in others if one is a man.

Given this context, ḍākinīs appear in the manifest world on three levels, achieved by a combination of auspicious karma, committed practice, and luminous penetrating insight. The outer-outer aspect of the embodied ḍākinī is the mantra-born ḍākinī (*dhāraṇijā, ngak-kye khandroma*).

Those with good fortune and intelligence,
Who enter into the Vajrayāna
And attain the mantric siddhis,
Are renowed as mantra-born ḍākinīs.[108]

Mantra-born ḍākinīs, or ḍākas for that matter, are practitioners of tantric ritual (*sādhana*) who have the proper motivation and circumstances to practice, such as instructions from a qualified guru. When they begin their practice, they may have quite conventional understandings concerning gender, bodies, and attainment. But through the practice of the creation stage (*utpattikrama, kyerim*), their visualization of the maṇḍala and recitation of the mantra transform conventional understandings. Of course, among these conventional understandings are concepts of body and gender, but more important, those concerning inherent existence, the nature of appearance, and effective action in the world change. These practitioners experience clear appearance (*selnang*), the union of bliss and emptiness, which is associated with the practice of inner heat. This is the mantra-born ḍākinī.[109]

The next stanza describes the inner ḍākinī. The coemergent ḍākinīs (*sahajā, lhen-kye khandroma*) have developed further in practice. Having fulfilled commitments to the guru, they have received the pointing-out instruction of the natural state of mind and have practiced accordingly. Having directly seen and realized this abiding reality, they are known as coemergent ḍākinīs:

By attending a realized teacher and
By the power of meeting mind's natural state
They directly realize the reality that abides.
These are called coemergent ḍākinīs.[110]

These ḍākinīs are not bound by any particular path; they simply realize coemergent wisdom directly and have realized the nature of mind through Mahāmudrā or Dzogchen. The experience of bliss and emptiness, or of any duality for that matter, is no longer seen dualistically. Because of the depth and power of their realization, they are considered *āryā*s, or noblewomen.

For the coemergent ḍākinī, in their essence there is no real separation between bliss and emptiness, or masculine and feminine, or penetrating insight and skillful means. Certainly, relatively speaking, there are differences in appearance. But starting with conventional duality, the practitioner recognizes that in the essence, there is union, not-two. This has been pointed out by the lama and has struck the practitioner in her heart, so that she has had a direct and naked experience of realizing coemergent wisdom, which is the coemergent ḍākinī.[111] Those ḍākinīs who have realized this aspect are said to have spontaneous style, described in the tantric twilight language as women who are "always fond of meat and spiritous liquors and forget shame and fear,"[112] which means that they are not deluded by the most intense experiences. Instead, they relish them as opportunities for practice.

The final stanza presents the outer ḍākinī, and those who have manifested the outer ḍākinī have realized the highest attainment or integration of body and mind. The sacred-realm ḍākinī (*kṣetrajā, shing-kye khandroma*) is one who has taken birth from a completely pure enlightened realm (*shing kham*), practicing purely for the benefit of others and carrying out the activities of Vajrayāna, especially as a protector of the teachings. She may have become a sacred-realm ḍākinī through emanation or through practice attainments in this life.

By dwelling in the fields of the twenty-four
Sacred places of body, speech, and mind,
They accomplish the benefit of others.
These are called sacred-realm ḍākinīs.[113]

The manifest sacred-realm ḍākinī is not human; she is a deity in her own right, dwelling in a completely pure ḍākinī land. She is always depicted joined with her consort in the maṇḍala, and in union they have entourages accompanying them. Having achieved the previous levels of the ḍākinī, the sacred-realm ḍākinī cannot be truly seen in the conventional way, for she has purified her sacred outlook so that the phenomenal world is transformed into a completely pure ḍākinī land. These ḍākinīs represent the sacred maṇḍala of the subtle yogic body, which is the foundation of meditation practice in tantra. Hence, their power is great, and they are called "the heroic female lords who hold sway over (all) the heroes."[114]

When we see these four aspects as exhibiting the way in which mind and body are synchronized and utilized for a complete realization of the nature of phenomena, we can see the ḍākinī symbol in its fullest flower. All of these aspects are apparent in the stories of ḍākinī visions from tantric literature. In exploring the activity of ḍākinīs, we began with the story of the ḍākinī servant girl, Kumarī, who confronted Guru Rinpoche near the gates of the queen ḍākinī's palace.[115] She delivered her instruction by drawing her crystal hooked knife across her torso in one sweeping flourish, revealing the vast and limitless space of her body, the ultimate nature of phenomena, which was her secret-ḍākinī essence. Within that space arose a complete maṇḍala of the peaceful and wrathful dieties, the inner ḍākinī essence. The water that she carried is associated with the subtle body, which is the outer ḍākinī, the channels and the vital breath flowing through them. She herself as the servant girl represents the outer-outer ḍākinī, initially undetected by Guru Rinpoche. The four are inseparable, and she revealed all four levels of her essence to Guru Rinpoche, completing the wisdom ḍākinī's transmission. He was awestruck at her directness. The profundity of the wisdom ḍākinī rests in her communicating all these aspects of her meaning at once, a symbolic expression of the nature of awakening in the Vajrayāna sense.

When we look at the ḍākinī in her four dimensions, we come to see her as not merely a motif in mythology and ritual or a recurring multivalence. She becomes a symbol, the emblem of all the most personal aspects of Vajrayāna practice, integrated in physical manifestation, energetic dynamism, blissful emptiness, and primordial essence in accord with the most subtle and profound teachings of Tibetan Buddhism. By understanding the wisdom ḍākinī in all her dimensions, one is introduced to the essence of the Vajrayāna path; through her various levels of manifestation, she shows the way to the ultimate realization itself, which is realizing these four aspects within the heart of personal experience.

To summarize the four levels of the ḍākinī: the outer-outer (*chi-chi*) ḍākinī is the tangible physical body of women, seen as distinct from the male body in the radiation of feminine qualities. From the perspective of outer-outer, our physical bodies are subject to the impermanence of birth, old age, and death. And yet the actual form of our bodies is a reflection of certain qualities of our minds. Women's bodies reflect the dynamic qualities of limitless space and the wisdom that knows that space. Men's bodies reflect skillful action, which enacts the wisdom of space. When we see our physical bodies in a direct and unconfused way, we see the sacred dynamics of mind literally embodied in our experiential world. From this point of view, every woman is a ḍākinī by virtue of being female.

According to Vajrayāna Buddhism, our human bodies are enlivened by subtle energetic dimensions that give the corruptible form vitality. Streams of vital breath flow through channels throughout the body, animating every aspect of physical existence. The movement of this vital breath is wisdom itself and is also called the outer (*chi*) ḍākinī. From this perspective, every human, male or female, experiences the ḍākinī as the radiant energy of the subtle body.

The inner dimension (*nang*) refers to the dynamic qualities of phenomenal experience. From the inner point of view, there is no real separation between perceiver and perceived or between subject and object. Instead, the perceptual and experiential world is understood as an energetic field that is ultimately empty of inherent existence, characterized by limitless space. Within that space, phenomena arise interdependently and fleetingly as the play of color and texture, which is experienced in a variety of ways. Perceptually, emotionally, and conceptually noumena and phenomena are simultaneously experienced in a display of intensity, or coemergence. The landscape of the inner dimension is related to communication, interchange, and the movement of energy that undergirds the conventional occurrences that we ordinarily perceive. For the ḍākinī, the inner is expressed through visionary experience.

From an inner point of view, there is no judgment, no conceptual overlay. Things are very simply what they are, but seen from a dynamic and appreciative perspective. Anger is just anger—hot, impatient, with no particular plotline or reason. There is a kind of beauty and sanity about anger just as it is, without the additional thoughts that generally arise to give anger its justification, solidification, or outward expression. Anger is completely sacred just as it is, a blazing dark red dot in space, vibrating with power. The qualities of the inner can only be expressed symbolically, ritually, or poetically.

The secret dimension (*sang*) has to do with space itself, which has no need or desire to arise as anything and is primordially pure. The secret refers to the ultimate essence of phenomena and is that moment before that dark red dot of anger has arisen. From a secret point of view, when we look deeply into the arising of emotion, we experience a pure, limitless possibility in which nothing has occurred and there is nowhere to go, nothing to do. This aspect is secret not because it is obscure or mysterious alone but because "it indicates something that must be experienced to be known."[116] It is primordial because it is the basis of all experience, all emotions, thoughts, sense perceptions, and reflections. It is the nature of mind and experience itself. All other aspects are merely ornaments on empty space. The quality of the secret cannot really be expressed in words. Among these four dimensions of the ḍākinī's manifestation, the secret level is the most important, and it is this secret dimension that the inner and outer ḍākinīs are dedicated to selectively revealing.

The wisdom ḍākinī manifests these four aspects simultaneously. Secretly she is pure space-emptiness, vast and inexpressible, which can be seen in the nonconceptual gaze of her eyes in her outer forms. Fundamentally we see "her" as inseparable from the mind, not identifiable as an object of perception, and so we do not find "her" at all. The inner ḍākinī is a visionary manifestation of the dynamic quality of the mind and phenomena, experienced in brilliant color and form, empty and vivid. In the outer aspect, this purity manifests as intense heat and desire without ego, fueling nonconceptual insight. In the outer-outer aspect, she takes whatever physical form may be of most benefit for those whom she may meet or instruct; whatever the form, her very body expresses her qualities directly and nonconceptually.

These four aspects also relate to kinds of tantric meditation practice that the practitioner experiences in different aspects simultaneously. The inner ḍākinī is expressed in the practice of the tantric sādhana, based on the sacred maṇḍala of the deity who is the symbol of the mind's coemergent wisdom. This is the creation phase of tantric practice, which entails making ritual offerings, hand gestures, visualization, and praises and invocations of the deity. There are two aspects of the completion-phase practice: subtle-body yoga and direct experience of the nature of the mind. Subtle-body yoga is the realm of the outer ḍākinī, in which the energetic body is sacralized and harmonized, creating a link between the visualized maṇḍala and the realm of physical manifestation. The secret-ḍākinī realm is that of naked awareness of the nature of mind, experienced as vast and luminous space pregnant with possibilities. When all of these are unified in the practice of everyday life, one has entered the outer-outer ḍākinī realm, in which the ordinary is extraordinary in its inherent sacredness, and all problems and conflicts are seen as the wisdom display of the nature of reality.

One of the ways in which the fourfold classification contributes to an understanding of the ḍākinī's uniqueness is how it captures her powerful dynamic. She is at once the external instructor and protector who represents the lineage of enlightened ones and empowers the practitioner in meditation. Simultaneously she is the wisdom inherent in the practitioner's body and mind. In this presentation of four levels, the ḍākinī alternates creatively between being an objectified deity or being (inner and outer-outer) and the experiential subjectivity of one's own body (outer) and mind (secret). These are interpenetrating dimensions of experience, in which the outer manifestations we encounter may generate an inner resonance that enlivens and activates our realization.

Conclusion

The ḍākinī in Tibetan Buddhism is a complex feminine symbol that developed from the Indian tradition, uniquely assimilating to Buddhist perspectives on the nature of mind and the path to realization. These aspects of the ḍākinī can only be understood in the contexts of Tibetan Buddhism; elements of Hindu tantra and Indian Buddhist tantra that have not directly passed to Tibet are peripheral to her analysis. From this point of view, the worldly ḍākinī is a lesser figure who serves the mundane goals of the practitioner, while the wisdom ḍākinī is a realized buddha. The wisdom ḍākinī derives her power from her association with the most profound insights of Vajrayāna meditation. Since she represents fundamental wisdom, the essence of mind, she guards the gates of wisdom for tantric practitioners, who supplicate her with devotion to effectuate their practice. She also guards the most private details of the practice, so that only those with the purest motivation are able to penetrate their essence.

However, the ḍākinī expresses the feminine gender in only a qualified sense, since in her absolute essence she represents the ultimate beyond gender. From this point of view, she has no allegiance to anyone; it is inaccurate to say that women alone possess the ḍākinī. When the practitioner truly understands this, liberation from gender concepts can be glimpsed. The wisdom ḍākinī can best be understood in terms of her enlightened essence, the four dimensions that depict how the limitless nature of mind can manifest in human forms dedicated to the welfare and awakening of all beings.

From a traditional point of view, the ḍākinī is not about women or gender at all, but the power of the realization of emptiness to transform worldly concerns into enlightenment. She is a symbol of the personal subjectivity of every tantric practitioner, blending devotion, renunciation, and awareness into a potent spiritual journey. Part of that journey is clarifying confusion about gender concepts, seeing all women and men as sacred emanations of the fundamental dynamic of phenomena. Full engagement in this path may clarify those very issues of identity and politics that the ḍākinī may evoke from a conventional perspective.

The ḍākinī appears in many guises. Generally in Vajrayāna literature such as tantras and hagiographies she is depicted objectively, as a presence one encounters, rather than subjectively, in a first-person account.[117] To this end, she is not usually a personality or historical figure in any conventional sense. Sometimes she is named as a specific ḍākinī, such as Vajrayoginī or Vajravārāhī, with specific symbolism and iconography. Often she is unnamed, capable of changing her shape and appearance to suit the message she wishes to deliver. She may emanate in human form, but she is boundless in her possibilities.

As for her relationship with ordinary human existence, it is understood that all humans have a ḍākinī element that is uncovered in Vajrayāna practice. And human women in particular, by virtue of the fact that their bodies are female, are emanations of the ḍākinī principle in some fashion. But people are not ḍākinīs—men and women alike are embodiments of particular aspects of the ḍākinī principle.

THREE

The Secret Dakini

THE GREAT MOTHER

Because the expanse of reality is not "I,"
It is not a "woman," not a "man."
It is completely freed from all grasping.
How could it be designated as an "I"?

In all phenomena without attachment
Neither woman, nor man are conceived.
To tame those who are blinded by desire
A "woman" and a "man" are taught.

—NĀGĀRJUNA[1]

MACHIK LAPDRÖN, THE GREAT yoginī who founded the Chö lineage in Tibet, meditated on retreat in a sanctified cave during the spring of her forty-first year. In the middle of the night, the majestic savior Tārā appeared to her, surrounded by a host of ḍākinīs, and gave detailed empowerments and blessings. As Machik bowed to thank Tārā for her kindness, she humbly questioned whether an ordinary woman like herself could benefit beings in any way. Tārā smiled and, glancing at the ḍākinīs in her retinue, said:

> Yoginī, do not feel discouraged! In the course of previous lives you have studied and mastered the meaning of the scriptures of sūtra

Yum Chenmo, the Great Mother Prajñāpāramitā.

> and tantra. . . . You are a mind emanation of the Great Mother Yum Chenmo: we are inseparable. You are the wisdom ḍākinī, the sovereign of the great expanse [*vajradhātu*][2] and the source of liberation of all phenomena. Don't lose heart. Keep your determination.

Incredulous, Machik replied:

> How could I possibly be an emanation of the Great Mother, inseparable from you? And in what way am I the source of the liberation of all phenomena? And where is the residence of the Great Mother?

Tārā answered:

> Yoginī, although in your innermost heart there is a clear knowledge about the past, listen carefully and I'll explain it to you. The one known as the primordial Mother Yum Chenmo is the ultimate nature of all phenomena, emptiness, the essence of reality [*dharmatā*] free from the two veils. She is the pure expanse of emptiness, the knowledge of the non-self. She is the matrix which gives birth to all the buddhas of the three times. However, so as to enable all sentient beings to accumulate merit, the Great Mother appears as an object of veneration through my aspirations and prayers for the sake of all beings.[3]

The secret level of the ḍākinī is the most subtle and profound and is the basis for all manifestation. Although often spoken of as feminine, she is known as simultaneously gender-inclusive (both male and female) and beyond gender altogether (neither male nor female). She is primordially vast space that accommodates everything but cannot be grasped as a thing or a person. Yet, as Tārā explained to Machik, in order for beings to venerate her and to articulate her qualities properly, she is given name and form.

In the various meditation traditions of Tibetan Vajrayāna Buddhism, the secret ḍākinī is known by different names: she is the Great Mother (Yum Chenmo);[4] she is the Dharmakāya Great Mother (Prajñāpāramitā) (Chöku Yum Chenmo);[5] she is Mother of All the Buddhas (Gyalkün Kyeyum);[6] she is the All-Creating Sovereign (Künje Gyalpo or Gyalmo).[7] Although the way in which she is described varies slightly among traditions, there is tremendous commonality in her depiction. Even while she is vast space, she is called the mother principle in Tibetan Buddhism.

This mother principle stands in some contrast to the mother goddess traditions in some other religious traditions, as we have discussed.[8] Whether they appear in prepatriarchal traditions or subsequent to them, mother goddesses generally emerge as personalized deities characterized by majesty and power, or as embodying the forces of nature, particularly the powers of creation. The most famous of these are the matriarchal deities prevailing in other South Asian traditions, in which the mother goddess appears as the primeval mother Kālī, the cosmic waters from which creation arises or the womb that gives birth to the world. There she is associated with materiality, delusion, and the fecund forces of the natural world. In her highest form as Devī-Māhātmya,[9] she is ultimate reality itself as the manifester of the great illusion (*mahāmāyā*), the subduer of obstacles, and the animating power (śakti) of the universe.

The Tibetan Buddhist understanding of the mother principle is somewhat different. The material world and forces of nature are seen as insubstantial, empty, and transparently luminous phenomena. There is no essential struggle between spiritual and temporal, for all phenomena find commonality in their unborn, pure nature, which cannot be said to exist in any independent way. Because of this, the mother principle in Buddhism is associated with emptiness (śūnyatā, tong-pa-nyi) and the wisdom that sees this fundamental truth of how things really are. Within this context the mother principle is understood allegorically as feminine, yet it is beyond gender.

The Great Mother Prajñāpāramitā

> Knowing the nature of emptiness nondualistically is liberation. Whether you call it emptiness, the absolute, or the ḍākinī makes no difference. All are liberating.
>
> —VEN. CHAGDUD TULKU RINPOCHE[10]

The Tibetan understanding of the feminine principle as mother was drawn from a variety of sources within the Buddhist tradition. The most important source was the Prajñāpāramitā-sūtras of Indian Mahāyāna, which date from the second century B.C.E. and continued their influence in Tibet until the present day. *Prajñāpāramitā* refers to wisdom or "penetrating insight" (*prajñā*) that is perfected or has "gone beyond" (*pāramitā*), which means that it has transcended concept, expectation, or conventionality of any kind. The earliest of these sūtras, the *Aṣṭasāhasrikā*, proclaimed Prajñāpāramitā to be the "mother of all the buddhas" in the following verses:

The Buddhas in the world-systems in the ten directions
Bring to mind this perfection of wisdom as their mother.
The Saviours of the world who were in the past, and also those that are in the ten directions,
Have issued from her, and so will the future ones be.
She is the one who shows the world (for what it is), she is the genetrix, the mother of the [conquerors],
And she reveals the thoughts and actions of other beings.[11]

The theme of the motherhood of Prajñāpāramitā was carried throughout the Mahāyāna sūtras, though it was not until a late date that she was personified as a deity.[12] She was lauded as the "mother of the tathāgatas," "their nurse to all-encompassing wisdom," and their "transmitter of the realization of all the buddhadharmas, and the creator of the world."[13] However, at this early date she was not particularly personalized and had no identifiable anthropomorphic form. These epithets were primarily metaphorical until roughly 400 C.E., when she began to appear as a female bodhisattva in the Buddhist pantheon.[14] Although in the early Prajñāpāramitā texts she was not personalized, from the Sanskrit conventions she was always referred to by feminine pronouns.

The epithet "Mother of All the Buddhas" became a theme in renaissance Indian Buddhism and in Tibet. How is Prajñāpāramitā the mother of all the buddhas? The answer can be found in her association with emptiness, or śūnyatā, and with penetrating insight, or prajñā. First, she is called emptiness, understood through the realization that all phenomena are unborn, unproduced and without end. There has never been an abiding essence in any phenomenon, hence no phenomena have even a fleeting existence. All phenomena (which have arisen from emptiness, the mother) are empty of any designations attributed to them or any nature or characteristics. Put differently, phenomena are completely free of concepts, and hence they are said to be completely pure. Because of this, experience is said to be dreamlike, radiantly clear and transparent; and nowhere in the dream is there any true existence.

The effect of such a realization is a transformation of the practitioner's naïve beliefs about the nature of reality. Experience is not negated; Buddhism carefully refrains from the nihilistic position that the nature of experience is delusory. Instead, assumptions concerning the ontological status of one's experience are questioned, which affects the entire framework of mental constructs. According to the Buddhist path, taking phenomena to be existent in any independent, abiding way conceals from the practitioner the true nature of things as they are (*yathā-bhūtam*). When this obscuration is removed, there is tremendous freedom, joy, and fearlessness.

When emptiness is realized in this way, all phenomena are found to be pure, just as their source, their mother, is pure. Since phenomena have arisen from emptiness, they have never actually arisen: they are considered unborn. This is akin to the analogy of the dream: although we know that dreams are merely dreams, their vividness and clarity remain. When the concept that dreams are true is abandoned, dreams are seen as they really are. Dreamlike phenomena have never been produced, and they also have no end. They are similar to all beings in that their nature is indestructible emptiness. Emptiness is the ultimate essence of all phenomena, all beings, and all buddhas.[15]

Interpreting emptiness as the unborn nature of all phenomena seems to contradict Prajñāpāramitā as the mother. But it is precisely because all phenomena are unborn that she is the mother. As Śāriputra praised her, "she does nothing about all phenomena. . . . She never produces any phenomena, because she has forsaken the residues relating to both kinds of obscurations. . . . She does not stop any phenomena. Herself unstopped and unproduced is the perfection of wisdom."[16] Because the nature of all phenomena is ultimately found to be emptiness, the Prajñāpāramitā, which is emptiness itself, is the mother.

Prajñāpāramitā is also explicitly stated to be the mother of buddhas and bodhisattvas. As the passage above continues, "she is the mother of the Bodhisattvas, because of the emptiness of her own characteristics." This is related to her second aspect, that of penetrating insight, prajñā (*sherap*). Since emptiness is not an object of knowledge—since it is not a thing—Prajñāpāramitā is associated with the dynamic way in which one directly realizes the unborn nature of phenomena. One sees or realizes emptiness through the penetrating power of insight, which carefully examines phenomena and finds no inherent essence. This prajñā is supremely excellent because it has gone beyond (*pāramitā, pharöltu chinpa*) any concept or reference point or an inherent existence of any kind. Because of this, penetrating insight is not different from that which it sees: emptiness.

Prajñāpāramitā is the symbolic mother of all those who realize this nature; that is, this insight is the beginning of the practitioner's uncovering of awakened nature. Finding no inherent essence in phenomena awakens nondual wisdom in the practitioner, and this is the seed of buddhahood. For this reason, "prajñā which has gone beyond," or Prajñāpāramitā, is an experiential discovery that becomes at that moment the Mother of All Buddhas. So, she who manifests as Prajñāpāramitā is the Great Mother of the buddhas of the past, present, and future.

In the sūtras, the Mother is called the "genetrix" or progenitor of the Tathāgatas, the one who actually gives birth to buddhas. But she is also called the "instructress in cognition" of all qualities of the Buddha. Only through penetrating insight is buddhahood achieved, and only through penetrating insight can it be perceived. For this reason, it is said that the Tathāgatas hold the Mother in their minds and work on her behalf. They feel great gratitude toward her and are said to "look well after their mother, protect her well, and hope that she will meet with no obstacle to her life, . . . make much of her and cherish her, because they are aware that she has instructed them in the ways of the world."[17]

Late in the Prajñāpāramitā tradition, in what is considered the transitional "tantric phase" of its teaching, the presentation of these sūtras was condensed into mantra (*ngak*), which expressed the central truth of the genre directly, without referential language. This reflected the movement in Vajrayāna Buddhism toward language that did not rely on inference, conventional meaning, or logic. Instead, potent reverberating sounds were used to elicit understanding directly, through a kind of transmission that bypassed the conceptual mind.

The most condensed of these sūtras, dated sometime between 600 and 1200 C.E., is the *Perfect Wisdom in One Letter,* a classical Prajñāpāramitā sūtra whose entire teaching was contained in the seed syllable A (pronounced *Ah*).[18] The Buddha said, "Ānanda, do receive, for the sake of the welfare and happiness of all beings, this perfection of wisdom in one letter: A."[19] This seed syllable continued to be of importance in Mahāyāna literature, especially in the early A-RA-PA-CHA-NA syllabary, said to express the essence of the Prajñāpāramitā. The letter A was said to be an abbreviation of the entire syllabary and symbolized emptiness; in fact, it was called the "empty letter door that displays emptiness."[20] This is important for the later Tibetan tradition, in which the seed syllable A is one of the identifying marks appearing on the tongue, hands, or other parts of the body and one of the resonant sounds heard by the parents of an incarnate ḍākinī.

In any case, the tantric Prajñāpāramitā-sūtras foretell the symbolic expressions of emptiness that appear in ritual practice in Vajrayāna Buddhism. The best examples of this can be found on three levels: on a body level, this realization is expressed in gestures and body postures, called mudrās. On a speech level, essential syllables are used that bypass intellectual interpretation and directly express the realization. On a mind level, one visualizes a fully enlightened deity in prescribed form, the vividness and details of which express realization. When these three are used simultaneously, a fully developed symbolic world is manifested that expresses nonconceptually the experience of emptiness from a luminous, enlightened perspective. All of these expressions probably developed in the late Indian tradition of the Prajñāpāramitā, pointing to the possibilities for meaningful ritual life in the Vajrayāna.

One remarkable example of the tantric expression of the Prajñāpāramitā can be seen in the development of the Chö meditation tradition of India. Chö or "cutting through grasping," is an important lineage of practice that was transmitted by Tampa Sanggye to Machik Lapdrön (1055–1154), the great Tibetan yoginī whose encounter with Tārā opened this chapter.[21] While it is unclear how the Chö tradition developed in India, its basis in the Prajñāpāramitā-sūtras is clearly indicated by the "Grand Poem on the Perfection of Wisdom," composed by Āryadeva the Brahmin (ninth century C.E.). He professed to teach "the actual meaning of the profound Prajñāpāramitā,"[22] a tantric expression in nonconceptual and direct method of the great Mahāyāna sūtras. His poem suggests that there was probably a meditation tradition associated with the Prajñāpāramitā-sūtras that was carried into the later period of Indian Buddhist tantra.

The meaning of the Prajñāpāramitā
Is not to be looked for elsewhere: it exists within yourself.
Neither real nor endowed with characteristics,
The nature [of the mind] is the great clear light.[23]

The great clear light (*ösel chenpo*) refers to the essence of the mind as emptiness, its nature as clarity or luminosity, and its manifestation as limitlessness. These are not existent qualities attributed to an existent thing, however, but attributes designed to evoke the experience of the practitioner. This tradition of describing the nature of the mind as Prajñāpāramitā became important in Tibetan tantra.

The Prajñāpāramitā-sūtras became a powerful foundation for understanding the feminine principle in late Indian and Tibetan Buddhism, and their influence is evident in a wide variety of ways. In her various forms in tantric traditions, the ḍākinī is closely associated with Prajñāpāramitā. She is often given that epithet or associated with it directly or indirectly, as we shall see.

Vajrayāna Transformation: Great Queen Prajñāpāramitā

Homage to the immaterial, immaculate, sky equilibrium.
Homage to the wordless illiterate entirety.
Homage to the utterly pure, transcendent and worldly.
Homage to the empty, absolutely everything.[24]

—UMA

In the Vajrayāna tradition, the Indian Mahāyāna understandings of Prajñāpāramitā were transformed into new expressions. While the Mahāyāna tradition described her in allegorical fashion, Vajrayāna developed symbolic forms and words to evoke her meaning. In the tantras, the Prajñāpāramitā symbols are called the Great Mother (Yum Chenmo), the source of all phenomena, expressed in new language.

The Vajrayāna transformation of the Mahāyāna teachings on emptiness can be understood in terms of the contrast between theory and practice. The Mahāyāna teachings provided the theoretical understanding and indirect indication of emptiness. In the Vajrayāna these teachings are experienced directly. As Milarepa expressed it, "I've realized that just as mere knowledge of food doesn't help a hungry man, it's not enough to understand the goal of emptiness (intellectually); one must cultivate (its direct experience) repeatedly."[25]

In Vajrayāna Prajñāpāramitā is the secret aspect of the wisdom ḍākinī. A key to understanding this can come from elucidating the meaning of wisdom in the Vajrayāna sense—*yeshe,* or *jñāna*—the quintessence of the ḍākinī. Yeshe is nondual, radiant wisdom, the spontaneous arising of awakened nature as clarity concerning things as they really are. As in the Mahāyāna tradition, everything is empty of any inherent nature, and penetrating insight is emphasized. In the Vajrayāna tradition, wisdom is nondual wakefulness applying both to phenomena and to the mind that realizes the nature of phenomena. It is a direct experience. In a spontaneous realization song addressed to his mother, the Dzogchen master Nyoshul Khen Rinpoche sang:

Look outward at the appearing objects,
And like the water in a mirage,
They are more delusive than delusion.
Unreal like dreams and illusions,
They resemble a reflected moon and rainbows.

Look inward at your own mind!
It seems quite exciting, when not examined.
But when examined, there is nothing to it.
Appearing without being, it is nothing but empty.
It cannot be identified saying, "That's it!"
But is evanescent and elusive like mist.[26]

In Vajrayāna meditation, the practitioner becomes accustomed to the vast openness of this experience of the ultimate nature.

This is the true meaning of *kha* in *khandro.* The wisdom ḍākinī is of the essence of emptiness, understood in Vajrayāna language to be pure space. The images used to express this ungraspable experience are, in the inner tantras, those of sky (*namkha*) or space *(kha).* This is not ordinary space; it is *ying (dhātu),* which is the unconditioned, ineffable ground of all experience. *Ying* does not refer to a philosophically derived conclusion concerning the lack of inherent existence of all phenomena, as one might find in the Madhyamaka schools of Mahāyāna. Instead, it refers to a direct experience of primordial vastness out of which all other experiences arise. While this vastness is in the realm of experience, it is not accessed by any method or experience of anything other than itself, for it is inherent in the nature of mind.

One can understand ying through the analogy of a cloudless sky, but one realizes ying through the practice of actually contemplating the cloudless sky. Such a sky is ideal for practice because it has no support and contains nothing upon which to fixate. When one gazes deeply into a cloudless sky there is tremendous capacity to experience the nature of mind, the inner ying. Perceiving the simultaneity of the cloudless sky and the nature of mind is the real discovery of space. There is no arising, dwelling, or ceasing in what one observes; neither can these be found in the mind that observes.[27] When the practitioner receives transmission from the guru, the inseparability of ying and yeshe is recognized experientially as nondual awareness.

From this point of view, the quintessential ḍākinī is not merely space itself, but simultaneously wakefulness that realizes space. Calling this the mind is too narrow, for its nature transcends the mind, yet because it is an experience we speak of space and wakefulness as the ultimate nature of the mind. Because there is space, an all-pervading vastness; it is possible for nondual, self-existing wakefulness to arise, which is yeshe.[28] If knowing were separate from what it knows, we could not know. The moment space is known in our experience, yeshe is there. They cannot be separate. Space is likened to water, wakefulness to wetness; space is the flame, wakefulness the heat of the flame. There is no space without wakefulness, no wakefulness without space.[29]

Wakefulness radiates uninterruptedly and illuminates all experience. For this reason, a favorite image of yeshe is the dawn, the rising sun that illumines ignorance and confusion. The ultimate feminine principle is this inseparable space-wakefulness, *ying-yeshe.* Wakefulness and space are also the secret nature of the Great Mother in the Chö tradition. The great guru Machik describes it in this way:

> The birth of all the buddhas of the three times from this utterly pure realm [of] mind itself is this. The basis of the generation of all the sugata's power, fearless miracles and qualities is also this. The source of all the holy dharma is also this. Therefore, it is the absolute Great Mother.[30]

The Mother is also known in the Vajrayāna as the Queen of Ḍākinīs (*ḍākki jemo*),[31] for she rules the realm of space. She is supreme among the ḍākinīs because she is beyond attributes, beyond relative reference points. There is an irony to this name because, being beyond all dualities, all conventions, all limiting qualities, "she" is beyond gender.[32] Yet, because of her generative powers, giving birth to all buddhas and tathāgatas, "she" is called the mother. More will be said about this later.

The primary quality of all realization is coming to know the nature of mind itself. This intelligent and cognitive aspect relates to the second part of *khandro;* that is, *dro* refers not just to movement but to understanding.[33] Having understood, the ḍākinī becomes the embodiment of understanding itself, the emblem of awakening. This again highlights the sheer intelligence of space, the wisdom qualities of the feminine.

Vajrayāna literature sometimes uses "insider's" humor to express Mahāyāna's emptiness aspects of the ḍākinī. Nāropa, the great scholar who mastered all the philosophical schools of the Mahāyāna in India, spoke of the ḍākinī using many of the paradoxical, self-contradictory images traditionally used to depict emptiness:

The flower ḍākinī of the sky
Rides on the horse of the barren hearing lineage
Which is reined with the inexpressible turtle's hair.
With the horn of an unborn hare
She kills the preconception of the expanse of reality [dharmatā].[34]

In the Madhyamaka literature of India, all phenomena have no more intrinsic existence than the flower that grows in the sky, the offspring of a barren woman, the hair of a turtle, or the horns of a hare. In this song, the ḍākinī is the nonexistent flower riding on the nonexistent horse, reined with the nonexistent turtle's hair. And with the nonexistent horn she kills concepts in the midst of dharmatā. From this, the ḍākinī flies and acts in the realm beyond conventional ideas of existence and nonexistence. The ḍākinī is the quintessential symbol of emptiness.

All confusion comes from not understanding our fundamental nature, inseparable wakefulness and space. Beings fall into the erroneous view that the self and phenomena are truly existent, and painful emotionality arises from this view. We yearn for friends and lovers, grieve for our losses, hate our enemies, and groom our reputations all because we do not understand the vast and wakeful ground of experience.

Accessed through meditation practice, this ground becomes the basis for "a new sensibility about subjectivity,"[35] as Anne Klein called it. Subjectivity in this case becomes the mind's experience of its own nature, rather than a centralizing activity of the self to confirm itself. Meditation practice begins by focusing attention on the mundane thoughts, emotions, and sense perceptions that make up moment-to-moment experience. With time and discipline, these are seen to be constantly changing components of experience, each of them fleeting, vivid, and transparent. The notions one has about personal identity change under the scrutiny of mindfulness.[36]

Eventually, rather than focusing on the dualistic tendencies of the mind, which allow no escape from pain, meditation practice moves the practitioner from normal preoccupation with conceptual topics, sense perceptions, and emotional states to unnoticed aspects of experience. What dawns is a new kind of subjectivity, a capacity to know nonconceptually the actual knowing process itself, which is nondual awakened awareness. Such an experience has no objective content; no matter how much one looks, the specific content of our discoveries remains elusive and unimportant. Instead, this subjectivity is the direct realization of the natural qualities of the mind, the experience of an inherent clarity that relieves the practitioner of narrow definitions of identity. Klein calls this "subjectivity not anchored in either language or oppositionality."[37] It is also not anchored in the experiencer, and so we might call it subjectless subjectivity.

The quintessential quality of this newfound subjectivity is subtle and intangible, yet clear and radiant. It is the basic wakefulness inherent in mind that liberates dualistic confusion. Whatever arises in experience, whether joy or sadness, fear or contentment, it is seen as an expression of the play of the mind. This awareness can only be accessed through the practice of meditation under the guidance of an authentic teacher. And while the tantric teacher introduces the student to a variety of methods to uncover this inherent wakefulness, the fundamental simplicity of the natural state of mind remains the same. Within the esoteric traditions of Tibetan Vajrayāna, this natural state is often called the Mother.

In the context of our discussion, the Mother is the spiritual subjectivity of the tantric practitioner, whether male or female. It is experienced personally as the penetrating realization of nonduality. At the same time, it is recognized as not only one's personal experience. It is the treasure of the oral instructions of the lineages of enlightened teachers tracing back to the Buddha. When this realization dawns, as the yogin Mikyö Dorje the eighth Karmapa said, "rock meets bone in insight."[38] Spiritual subjectivity is experienced simultaneously as personal realization and as spontaneous devotion to those lineages and to the tantric guru who embodies those teachings.

Evoking the Secret Ḍākinī: Practicing the Guru's Instructions

The Great Queen Prajñāpāramitā is above all an experience that cannot be accessed through intellectual understanding, artifice, or intention alone. As the practitioner searches for that experience, the habitual patterns of ego-clinging and conceptual construction are so strong that he or she easily becomes enmeshed in obstacles. These obstacles manifest as arrogance, discouragement, aggression, grasping, fixed ideas, and so forth. Worst of all, the confused practitioner may think she or he has actually understood the Great Queen Prajñāpāramitā accurately. This leads to great delusion and suffering.

In order to discover the way, it is important to rely on the guidance of an authentic tantric guru who has realized these teachings and is authorized to transmit them to others. The extraordinary means necessary for removing the obstacles of conventional striving are in the hands of the guru, who is not confused by worldly motivations. The guru is the actual, living link to a tradition of oral instruction carried by the enlightened lineages of Vajrayāna Buddhism. As Jetsün Rangrik Repa said:

Wishing for primal wisdom beyond intellect to dawn
Without praying to the teacher
Is like waiting for sunshine in a north-facing cave.
Mind and appearances will never merge.[39]

For this reason, the living human guru with whom one may develop a personal relationship is considered the embodiment of all authority and power in the practice of Vajrayāna. The guru is considered the Buddha, dharma, and saṅgha of the threefold refuge, the source of all meritorious purification, and the embodiment of all gurus of the past, present, and future. The teacher surpasses all of them in one specific way—his or her kindness.

Why? It is because the human communication with a realized teacher and the direct experience of his or her mind are more powerful and transformative than all the study, practice, or virtuous deeds one may perform. The relationship with the guru can activate knowledge of the essence of reality such that these other activities may bear fruit. As the yogin Saraha said:

> *When the teacher's words enter your heart*
> *It is like finding a treasure in the palm of your hand.*[40]

A personal guru is always necessary. Only the tantric guru can introduce the student directly to the ḍākinī, the Mother who is the nature of the mind, one's own spiritual subjectivity. Finding an authentic Vajrayāna guru who is authorized to transmit the tantric teachings and with whom one has a genuine connection is the foundation of the path of Tibetan Vajrayāna. There is a great deal of literature devoted to the determination of whether the teacher is a lineage holder, pure in discipline, or someone with whom one may have a karmic connection. But the teacher's gender plays a minor role and ultimately has no spiritual importance.[41]

A student opens to the guru's instruction through devotion. Intellectual understanding, striving, and merit alone can never open the gates of wisdom in the Vajrayāna sense. Only devotion has the power to activate the path and to awaken the student's nonconceptual realization. Devotion is described in Vajrayāna Buddhism as the unmediated encounter between guru and student, so that the mind of the guru and the mind of the student meet as one. This encounter is experienced as an unfabricated nakedness, such that all strategies for masking or achieving are exposed and the fundamental awakened mind is seen as it is. Such an encounter is immediately and undeniably transformative and evokes longing and respect (*mögü*) in the heart of the student.

Having met the guru, the student acknowledges his or her realization and kindness and relies unerringly on the guru's guidance on the spiritual path, keeping the commitments (tamtsik, samaya) of that relationship. The guru is also bound to these commitments, partnering with the student to cut through obscurations and activate realization. The guru introduces the student to a sacred outlook (*tag-nang*), a basic perception of the fundamental purity, wakefulness, and power of all aspects of the world, no matter how threatening or foreign they may appear. The tools and perspectives offered by the guru are extensions of the guru's realization and the blessing of his or her lineage.

One of the cornerstones of sacred outlook is the ḍākinī in all of her aspects. The ḍākinī is a traditional Vajrayāna symbol of the profundity of seeing phenomena and the mind as they really are, an expression of the realization of the tantric guru and the lineage. When the guru points out the nature of mind in an unmediated encounter with the student, he or she points out the secret ḍākinī, the feminine principle. As Tilopa repeatedly said to Nāropa when giving tantric transmission:

Look into the mirror of your mind,
which is Mahāmudrā,
the mysterious home of the ḍākinī.[42]

Having received this transmission, the student recognizes the Great Mother as the nature of reality. As Milarepa's female student Sahle Aui sang to her guru, demonstrating her understanding and devotion:

You ripened the unripened,
You emancipated those who were not free.
You made me realize that all
Manifestations in the outer world
Are unreal and magic-like.
I have thus seen the Mother
Of the illuminating [nature of phenomena].[43]

By introducing the student to the ḍākinī, the guru is introducing his or her own realization and the treasury of the lineage's realization as no different from the student's. And the student's response is spontaneous devotion and appreciation of the guru's kindness.

In the process of transmission, the guru also introduces the student to the masculine principle, the skillful means to apply wisdom in the world. This transmission is also fundamental to the path, for wisdom without skillful means cannot manifest in compassionate or effective action in any meaningful way. Both feminine and masculine aspects are necessary for full development and completion of the path. But these aspects are elaborations of the fundamental ground, the infinite expanse, which precedes gender entirely.

Vajrayāna Meditation Practice: Creation and Completion

The guru instructs the student in the fundamentals of Vajrayāna meditation, based on two complementary aspects or styles, the creation and completion. The fundamental space or emptiness of mind and phenomena, the pristine awareness, is associated with completion-phase practice (sampannakrama, dzog-rim), which is the nondual basis of all. Because of the habitual patterns of mind that conceptualize a subject and an object, it is difficult to experience the nondual ground directly. For this reason, the creation-phase practice (utpattikrama, kyerim) is taught.

Creation-phase practice skillfully uses the dualistic tendencies of mind to point out the nondual ground of awareness. These tendencies, which are based on forgetfulness of the pristine awareness, give rise in all beings to habitual sense perceptions, emotions, and thoughts. These engender a complete, dramatic world in which the starring figure, the self, enacts story lines of jealousy, shame, ecstasy, and rage that exaggerate the fundamental duality. In the ritual practices of sacred mantra, these proclivities are given a protected and pure environment in which to play out. Intense emotions and their associated thoughts are immediately visualized through the senses as deities that vividly express their contours. Yet the deities also manifest, with their prescribed traditional forms, the forgotten wakefulness inherent in each of these emotional constructs.

In creation-phase practice, every aspect of the liturgy, iconography, and symbols points out the emptiness and the inherent wakefulness of the ritual forms. The purity of the forms carries none of the conventional attachment associated with habitual patterns. When attachments arise in the practice, they are to be experienced and relinquished. The deity and the environment must be visualized with sustained precision, held clearly in mind while remaining dreamlike and empty. There must also be a continued recollection of the purity of the visualization, a reminder that it is a manifestation of the fundamental purity of the nature of the mind.

The result of creation-phase practice is the purification of habitual patterns to some degree. The tāntrika begins to understand how personal prejudices and proclivities shape her or his entire experience and how damaging those perspectives can be to others and oneself. The tāntrika also begins to see the pristine awareness inherent in those proclivities, and appropriate renunciation arises. Ordinary fixations are liberated, and confidence in the basic awareness begins to dawn. As Jamgön Kongtrül said, "Creation stage is mainly for undermining the deluded appearance of ordinary reality."[44]

Completion-phase practice is a different kind of practice, free of fabrication. Here the tāntrika looks directly at the nature of mind and finds no object that can be called the mind. Because none is found, eventually the pristine awareness dawns. Jamgön Kongtrül explained, "[The] completion stage [is] for undermining attachment to the reality of that creation stage itself."[45] Since this phase gives up preoccupation with dualistic tendencies, it is without form, and its profundity is inexpressible. Having seen through the dualistic creations of the mind, one rests in the basic nature, the pristine awareness. It is completely natural, without thinking or striving of any kind, hence there is obviously no object. It may accord with the term *subjectivity* in the sense that it can be experienced, but since there is no experiencer or separate experience, it is also subjectless. Words cannot adequately express the completion phase. Yet, because of this profundity, it can be said that there is deep spirituality in Tibetan religion.

There is another, "not profound" completion practice that is used to enhance nonconceptual awareness. It is a subtle-body yoga practice called *tsa-lung,* the topic of chapter 5, which generates internal heat, bringing the movement of the vital winds into the subtle central channel of the body. This yoga clears away obstacles to resting in the nature of mind and accentuates the basic experience of completion-phase practice.

The Mother Prajñāpāramitā is accessed through completion-phase practice, but "she" is also not averse to forms or expressions of her nonconceptuality, which point the tāntrika back to her basic nature. In tantric practice, identifiable forms have arisen that express her inexpressibility, and these forms arise from the space of the Mother.

The Mother as Birth-Giver: Symbols Arising from Space

After transmitting the nature of mind and phenomena as the secret ḍākinī, the guru introduces the student to ritual practices that deepen and stabilize the understanding of this experience. The most important practices that cultivate this view are sādhanas (*drup-thap*), or ritual invocations of a symbolic sacred world. Through the evolution of the ritual, the practitioner rehearses the actual arising of all phenomena from the tantric point of view, forms arising from limitless space.

The ritual elements of these practices are symbolic forms that express the fundamental unfabricated nature of reality. The Vajrayāna use of symbols is somewhat different from the usual understanding of symbols. In customary usage, symbols point to something else, which is the true meaning or reality. But in Buddhism, the ultimate nature of reality is emptiness, the unfabricated vast expanse. All symbols in Vajrayāna ritual point to that ultimate nature, but that nature is never separate from ordinary appearance. Since the meaning "behind" appearances is empty, this means that appearances are just what they are:

> The Vajrayāna has sometimes been misinterpreted as a highly symbolic system. For example, one often says that the *vajra* scepter *symbolizes* skillful means or that the *ghaṇṭā symbolizes* wisdom. When it is said that the vajra is a symbol of skillful means or of indestructibility, that is true; but, in the genuine Vajrayāna sense, it is not simply that the vajra is used to represent or symbolize skillful means, because skillful means is too abstract a concept to be dealt with, or shown, directly. The *vajra* scepter *is* skillful means; it actually communicates and transmits skillful action directly if one understands the literalness of the Vajrayāna.[46]

This is the Vajrayāna expression of the Prajñāpāramitā teaching from the *Heart Sūtra,* "Form is emptiness, emptiness itself is form, emptiness is not other than form, form is not other than emptiness."[47]

In this view, the conventional world, just as it is, has tremendous power and vividness that can stimulate understanding and awakening. Every single phenomenon encountered is refreshing, beyond concept, and beyond compare. The rose of Sharon bush in my front yard catches my eye as a completely unique experience, brand-new every time I gaze on it, changing from season to season, day to day, moment to moment. And in that uniqueness, the lavender-pink blossom, the magenta throat with fuzzy yellow stamen can stop my mind as surely as meeting a great teacher.

> As experience, first of all you clear out the confusion of duality. Then, having cleared that out, you appreciate the absence of the blindfold in terms of appreciating colors and energies and light and everything. You don't get fascinated by it all, but you begin to see that it is some kind of pattern. . . . The pattern of life is a pattern. It is a definite pattern, a definite path, and you learn how to walk on it.[48]

Every part of our world, then, stands as mudrā, or *chag-gya* in Tibetan. *Chag* is an honorific word for *hand,* which in tantra became the code word for emptiness and the transparency of mind and phenomena, and specifically the direct experience of that transparency. *Gya* conventionally is the seal of a document, and in this case refers to the imprint that ultimate reality leaves on all phenomena, whether it is perceived as confused or as awakened. The words *seal* and *imprint* are used dramatically here, for the ultimate nature is empty, clear, and unimpeded, and it "gathers everything under one heading and seals it in its embrace."[49] Or, to put it differently, mudrā might be understood as "a tremendous encounter in which two forces come together and make a very deep impression."[50]

Mudrā can also be translated as *symbol,* which refers to the realization of the emptiness and clarity of all phenomena. "When reality is realized to be empty and free from saṃsāric confusion, it becomes the greatest symbol of all, a self-existing symbol of enlightened nature."[51] This means that phenomena become symbols for themselves and that there is no reference point for reality separate from our nonconceptual, nondual experience. In this sense, mudrā refers to the vividness and display of apparent phenomena. When *mudrā* is translated as *gesture,* it refers literally to the ritual expression of this understanding of reality, in which one displays through prescribed physical gestures or postures the utterly unique quality of each moment of experience. Through these gestures, the practitioner manifests the complete quality of experience, inexpressibly profound. The gesture is not a substitute for other phenomena; it is an expression of the quality of complete sacredness experienced. In fact, all phenomena are seen to be gesture, fraught with meaning. The profundity of this meaning is that it is none other than the vivid, unparalleled quality of ordinary experience itself.[52]

The details of Vajrayāna ritual express this sense of symbol. Sometimes even great tantric practitioners fall into the error of considering rituals "merely symbolic" and neglect the details of ritual expression. For example, the great meditation master Longchenpa prepared an important ritual empowerment of his disciples. Immediately a wrathful ḍākinī appeared to him, asking why the shrine did not have the requisite peacock quill. When Longchenpa assured her that he had visualized it mentally, the ḍākinī replied, "In this symbolic doctrine, what has that got to do with it?" She then corrected the arrangement and allowed him to proceed.[53]

Vajrayāna ritual practices begin with formless awareness of the unfabricated ground of experience, the Great Mother Prajñāpāramitā. Then ritually the Mother gives birth to all aspects of experience through the visualization of phenomena, from elemental to intricate. The secret ḍākinī encompasses the transition from space to elemental form in a ritual act of tantric birth of seed syllables. When the tantric practitioner experientially learns the relationship between space and form, the foundation of Vajrayāna practice has been laid and the secret ḍākinī as Mother has been expressed.

In practice, the feminine as Prajñāpāramitā is evoked by a mantra, a ritual utterance that opens the visualization section of sādhana. The utterance, which varies slightly from one ritual text to another, reminds the practitioner that all of our practice mimics the nature of phenomena itself; it arises out of vast space. A typical mantra used in Vajrayāna ritual texts is *Oṃ svabhāva śuddha sarvadharma svabhāva śuddho 'ham.* It is translated, "Oṃ, the inherent nature of all phenomena is pure; my own nature is also pure." Ven. Trungpa Rinpoche commented on the mantra in this way:

> It proclaims inherent purity or the immaculate space of basic sanity, which means space uncorrupted by dualistic confusions. This space is the mother principle, which safeguards against the development of ego's impulses. But perception without perceiver or visualization without visualizer is impossible. The mother, having occupied the space with purity, gives birth spontaneously to the visualization.[54]

Having evoked the unconditioned space of the Mother, the practitioner is ready to generate the practice of the completely pure visionary realm in tantric ritual beginning with the arising of a seed syllable (*sabön, bīja*).

Mantras are more elaborate expressions of tantric seed syllables, seminal utterances that carry the essence of a particular Buddhist deity in a nonconceptual manner. In Vajrayāna ritual, the practitioner always begins with space, out of which arises a seed syllable, from which arise mantras and the central visualizations of the practice. The seed syllable A that expresses the essence of the Mother Prajñāpāramitā is derived from the shortest Prajñāpāramitā-sūtra, in which A expresses the entire teaching of the sūtra. The syllable A is the primordial sound of the Sanskrit alphabet, the root of all vowel sounds, and the sound implicit in every consonant.[55] From this, the Tibetan tradition speaks of A as the most basic sound of experience, the utterance of dharmatā, the pure space from which everything has arisen. All mantras have A as their undertone, and its sound echoes unceasingly in our bodies and hearts. In the Dzogchen tradition of Tibetan meditation, it is instructed that if we close our ears and listen to the silence, we hear the echo of A. As the *Lam-rim Yeshe Nyingpo* quotes from the Prajñāpāramitā, "Subhūti, syllables are in the ultimate sense unborn and thus the nature of A. That which is the nature of A is the nature of mind and thus completely transcends everything concrete and inconcrete."[56] The syllable A is a quintessential expression of the Prajñāpāramitā in its Vajrayāna form as Mother of All the Buddhas, and it commonly appears as a part of longer mantras in tantric ritual.

More commonly in Anuttara-yoga-tantra, the seed syllable that generates the full practice of the ritual of the deity is EVAṂ, the seminal ground signifying the arising of feminine and masculine principles in the practice. These correlating principles arise from the nondual Mother, the unconditioned space that is the secret ḍākinī. Let us describe the ritual transition between space and the arising of the seed syllable.

From the space of the primordial mind, the Mother Prajñāpāramitā, something occurs; the very vastness of space invites something to occur. Trungpa Rinpoche spoke of this as outer space in which there is no reference point, only deep, dark, weightless vastness.[57] If there is only vastness, there is nothing with which to measure it. And so vastness invites the possibility of appearance. This is called the E principle, the essence of the Mother Prajñāpāramitā and the essence of ying, or space.

From vastness's invitation, "some kind of clear perception begins to dawn in the midst of that gigantic vast space."[58] This is the dawn of the possibility of appearance, of action, of form arising. It is analogous to the first stirrings that preceded cell division in the swamps, which are thought of in Western culture as the beginning of life. However, we are not referring here to the first cell divisions but to the shift in possibilities that made such a change possible. In Vajrayāna Buddhism this is called the VAṂ principle, the masculine. Trungpa Rinpoche called this the unconditional question.

> Unconditional space gives birth to unconditional question, what? It is like a traditional idea of *mantra*, the first utterance. There is a *vajra* carved out of a diamond floating in this gigantic space, outer space, glinting lights all over. Or, for that matter you could say, question mark carved out of a diamond floating in the midst of space.[59]

The seed syllable EVAṂ is a generative one in Vajrayāna,[60] for it signals the foundations of the mind and all phenomena. Space must come first, but it does not stand alone; "she" gives birth to and invites the genuine possibilities. The feminine is the mother of all realization, but she cannot be the only parent. The EVAṂ principle expresses both the feminine and the masculine in an essence form and becomes the ground of all experience. The foundation of all life, the body and mind, is the seed syllable EVAṂ, which resides at the center of the body, manifesting penetrating insight (prajñā) as the feminine and skillful means (upāya) as the masculine.

The Sanskrit word EVAṂ has an interesting origin in Buddhism. As an ordinary indeclinable particle used as a conjunction, it has been translated as "thus, in this way, in such a manner." In the Indian tradition, EVAṂ was the opening word in the phrase that began every sūtra, *EVAṂ mayā śrutam,* "Thus have I heard." This was said to be the hallmark of Ānanda, the Buddha's cousin, who was the holder of the memorized teachings that the Buddha transmitted in his discourses. This phrase indicated that Ānanda had heard these teachings with his own ears and was passing on the authentic record of them with this recitation. All sūtras of any Buddhist tradition are to begin with these words.

In the tantras, EVAṂ was elevated to a seed syllable, with esoteric meaning. The *Hevajra-tantra* speaks of EVAṂ as the union, the two-in-one, of all the buddhas and ḍākinīs,[61] the great bliss. The letter E, when it is adorned at its center by the syllable VAṂ, is the abode of bliss and the receptacle of the wealth of all the buddhas, especially the enlightened beings of the maṇḍala.[62] In this vein, the *Hevajra-tantra* opens with the words, "Thus have I heard: At one time the Lord dwelt in the vaginas of the vajra maidens who are the body, speech, and mind of all the Buddhas." A commentary explains this opening with a tantric interpretation, saying that *EVAṂ mayā śrutaṃ* expresses the essence of tantra. "E is *bhaga* (the female sexual organ), VAṂ is *kulisā* (the male sexual organ), *mayā* is the activation, and *śrutaṃ*, what was heard, is said to be two-fold."[63] The commentary also notes that the Buddha is given the epithet *bhagavan,* or blessed one, because he is blessed with union with the *bhaga,* the vagina.[64] This means that he has been blessed with the vast and limitless mind of the feminine principle, without which enlightenment is impossible.

Jamgön Kongtrül Lodrö Thaye taught that EVAṂ expresses the essence of the profound meaning of all the sūtras and tantras.[65] This is because all of the profound teachings of all the buddhas of the three times are summarized as the union of penetrating insight and skillful means. When they are joined, realization arises spontaneously. The *Exposition Tantra of Guhyasamāja* says:

Since omniscience abides
In the magical display of the two letters E *and* VAṂ,
E *and* VAṂ *are fully explained*
At the beginning of teaching the sacred dharma.[66]

The Vajra Garland adds:

E *is emptiness, it is taught.*
Likewise, VAṂ *is compassion.*
The bindu results from their union.
This union is the supreme marvel
Embracing the 84,000 dharma teachings.
In short, it is the seal of the dharma.[67]

With the seed syllable of EVAṂ there is a shift for the feminine principle from nondual wisdom to penetrating insight-wisdom.[68] The first, yeshe, is wisdom without any split between subject and object—or between wisdom and anything else, for that matter. But penetrating insight-wisdom has a dynamic dance, a vector placed in counterpoint with what it sees. *Sherap* is the expression for wisdom when it is paired with skillful means or compassion, its eternal consort. Hence, whenever wisdom is juxtaposed in this way, it is always expressed in the dynamic form of the interplay between feminine and masculine principles.

The foundations for this understanding come from the Mahāyāna sūtra tradition of Indian Buddhism, in which prajñā (sherap) and upāya (*thap*) are paired as necessary components of the bodhisattva's path, as two wings of the flying bird. Sūtra teachings are an extremely important ground for tantric practice, for without the proper motivation and conceptual understanding, meditation cannot succeed. For this reason, sūtra teachings are essential for beginners and continue to be important throughout the training of monastics and yogins or yoginīs alike.

For a developing bodhisattva, one who is personally dedicated to enlightenment, sūtra teachings first emphasize a proper understanding of emptiness. Without a direct, experiential, and penetrating understanding of emptiness, any activity for the benefit of others or any tantric practices are probably fruitless and in the case of tantra extremely dangerous. Because of this, prajñā teachings are particularly prominent in sūtra discourses. Whenever upāya is presented, it is paired with prajñā, for the two together ensure the proper understanding of emptiness.

Prajñā is defined as penetrating insight, and in the bodhisattva context it always suggests a transcending function, the ability to go beyond (pāramitā, pharöltu-chinpa) the limits of our ordinary understanding. What penetrating insight sees is, of course, things as they are, ultimately empty of any self-nature, without origination, basis, or foundation. Upāya is described as means; it relates to the way in which the ultimately empty practitioner interacts with ultimately empty phenomena. Skillful means always centers on compassion, the ultimate motivation for any bodhisattva activity. When paired with penetrating insight, means becomes skillful activity (*upāya-kauśalya, thabla khepa*).

Ven. Khenchen Thrangu Rinpoche explained that upāya (thap) denotes merely means, the way something is done. There is no implicit assumption of skill in thap. But in conjunction with penetrating insight, thap becomes skillful. The term *thabla khepa* refers to one who has become skilled in means through the cultivation of insight.[69] Skillful means focuses upon the cultivation and expression of compassion (*karuna, nyingje*) toward others. The centrality of skillful means suggests that a proper manifestation in the world is an essential part of the practice. In fact, an authentic initial experience of emptiness is signified in Tibetan practice by the blooming of genuine compassion for other beings.

Classic Tibetan texts that outline the fundamental approach to meditation practice in the bodhisattva tradition emphasize the linkage of prajñā and upāya. It is considered necessary for these two to interact in order to catalyze one's entire practice. Gampopa, the great eleventh-century meditation master, drew on popular Indian imagery in his famous description of the stages of the bodhisattva path: "When we walk, our eyes and feet must cooperate if we are to reach the city of our choice. In the same way, the eyes of prajñā and the feet of upāya must work together when we want to go to the citadel of highest enlightenment."[70]

If we cultivate skillful means without cultivating penetrating insight, we will stumble blindly and never discover the desired city; if we have penetrating insight without skillful means, we have no way of actually traveling there. For this reason, the bodhisattva who resorts to penetrating insight without skillful means is said to become fettered by one-sided enlightenment; those who resort to skillful means without insight remain bound by the chains of cyclic existence.[71] Such a lopsided experience is considered so deleterious that to persist in this is said to be tantamount to working for Māra, or evil. As Thrangu Rinpoche taught, mothers are essential for birth; without them, there would be very few people in the world. But fathers, the skillful-means principle, are equally invaluable. Joined, there is the possibility for the birth of enlightenment.[72]

While it is true that Mahāyāna sūtra teachings present these two as linked, insight always seems the dominant partner, and skillful means, while lauded in a general way, always seems to play a secondary role. Direct insight into emptiness is important for the bodhisattva path, and the practice of skillful means is presented as a way to uncover wholesome roots so that one might cultivate insight, rather than as a virtue in its own right. It is in tantra that skillful means emerges as a central force in Buddhist practice.

The seed syllable EVAṂ expresses the balanced interdependence of penetrating insight and skillful means on the path of Tibetan Buddhist tantra. Certainly the nondual Mother comes first, as radiant space, the vastness out of which all phenomena arise. Out of that space arise the syllables, first the feminine and then the masculine. In the *Cakrasaṃvara-tantra,* in the sādhanas of both Vajrayoginī and Cakrasaṃvara, E arises first, the seed syllable of openness. Then, within that space, VAṂ arises, the energetic activity. We might say that the utterance of EVAṂ is the emergent masculine already joined with the feminine. But in any case, Vajrayāna practice is always a dance between the feminine and masculine dynamics.

Aniconic Representations of the Mother

In Vajrayāna practice, there are two phases, each indicating some aspect of our experience of the world. The first, utpattikrama, or kyerim, is the creation phase of practice, in which we acknowledge that all phenomena arise from vast space. In order to understand this more directly, the practitioner uses visualizations that construct the entire universe in a particular sequence. The creation phase is like a reenactment of our moment-to-moment experience in which all phenomena arise from vastness. All brush strokes begin with a dot of ink on paper; all speech issues forth from basic utterance projected from the voice box through the mouth via the breath.

The creation-phase visualization arises first as seed syllables such as EVAṂ, then as aniconic (abstract, nonimaged symbol) forms, and then as iconographic representations in anthropomorphic forms. This process reconfirms the practitioner's basic transmission concerning the nature of the mind and phenomena. With every practice session, this experience becomes more certain and clear. At the end of the creation phase, the entire visualization is dissolved back into primordial space, and the completion phase is practiced.

The Mother Prajñāpāramitā in Vajrayāna practice is expressed in the creation phase as the seed syllable EVAṂ giving rise to the yantra symbol of the "source of phenomena" (*dharmodaya, chöjung*).[73] The secret ḍākinī, which cannot be grasped or named, is signified in a symbolic diagram of crossed triangles. The fathomless awareness-space that undergirds and permeates all experience and phenomena can only be symbolically expressed; "it is absolute space with a boundary or frame."[74] The source of dharmas is visualized two-dimensionally[75] by two juxtaposed triangular shapes, forming a symbol reminiscent of the Star of David. The triangle is to be understood in Vajrayāna as the centerless "cosmic cervix" that has given birth to all phenomena; it is the preeminent symbol for the mother. The triangle is the most economical bounded space, sharp and penetrating, the most appropriate representation of that which cannot be represented. When we understand this triangular form, we understand something about the Great Mother Prajñāpāramitā.

In the oral tradition, each of the three corners of the triangle expresses an aspect of the Mother.[76] Her three primary qualities are unborn, nondwelling, and unceasing. In this Vajrayāna expression, the traditional categories common to the early Buddhist traditions, most characteristically in the Vaibhaṣika abhidharma,[77] are reversed. In those traditions, all phenomena, understood to be impermanent, are defined as having a beginning or an arising, a middle or a dwelling, and an end or a cessation. This was the definition of conventional views of existence, a refutation of habitual belief in permanence. In Vajrayāna Buddhism, however, our attention is turned to the source from which all phenomena have arisen, which is pure space itself. The source of phenomena stands outside the conditioned realm altogether, and, from a Vajrayāna perspective, when we understand the source of phenomena we understand the whole of phenomena more clearly.

First, the tantric Mother Prajñāpāramitā is unborn. Unborn does not refer to sequential time, before birth could happen. Rather, it refers to

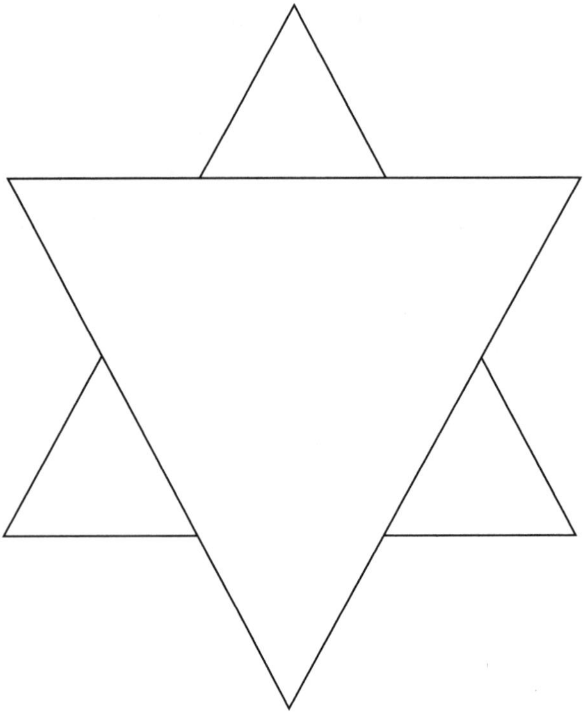

Source of phenomena, the chöjung.

freedom from any notion of being born or not being born. Ven. Chögyam Trungpa Rinpoche, in speaking of this, referred to "unborn" as "not having desire to be born, not willing to play with sophistries of all kinds, . . . self-existing, transcendent arrogance."[78] The unborn quality of basic space is free of any dualities, conceptualities, or notions of existence or nonexistence altogether. The space is indestructible and primordial.

One of the traditional Vajrayāna images used to express the qualities of space is the sky. Usually we think of sky as a relative notion, contrasted with earth. But if we imagine ourselves floating in outer space, with no space suit, no real sense of our physical bodies at all, just floating in deep, dark space, with no distant planets or stars as reference points, we have a sense of the ultimate quality of space.[79] The sky is like that; there are no limits or boundaries to the sky. This evokes the quality of unborn that describes the Mother.

The next corner of the triangle expresses the quality of nondwelling.[80] This quality is an embellishment of the first, for the Prajñāpāramitā not only has never been born, but she has never dwelt anywhere. This refers to her unconditionality, which means that we cannot ever really understand or grasp that space. The nondwelling quality of the Mother is beyond the extremes of eternalism and nihilism, and so it is the middle way, the essence of space, beyond thought or memory.[81]

Finally, the Prajñāpāramitā is unceasing, "because it can't be obstructed or prevented."[82] Space is very powerful, for it cannot be manipulated, moved, or shaped. Every situation is affected by space, and even the most elaborate structures, administrations, and bureaucracies are built on nothing. Śūnyatā in its Vajrayāna formulation as space has the power to undermine ambitions and delusions of grandeur. Chögyam Trungpa Rinpoche refers to it as "the black market of the mother," a kind of

> spiritual atomic bomb that's been manufactured in the basement. The idea of unceasing is not so much unceasing as a resigned, passive thing—but it is unable to be controlled by any efficient organization of anything. The overlay of reality is unable to detect the underlayer of reality anymore. The surface may go quite nonchalantly, it usually does, but the undercurrent is extraordinarily powerful. It begins to manufacture a world of its own, in the feminine principle of potentiality, embryonic and resourceful and glamorous at the same time.[83]

In this case, the Vajrayāna feminine becomes representative of what is spoken of in early Buddhist traditions as impermanence. Whatever arises eventually falls apart. This very fact is evidence of the indestructibility of the source of phenomena, the vast space that pervades all existence. The power of the Prajñāpāramitā space cannot be undermined or resisted. Impermanence becomes self-luminosity, and therefore it is unceasing.[84]

When these three qualities come together in the form of a triangle, they create a boundaried space that is the expanse of reality (*dharmadhātu*). This space is not random or arbitrary; it has definite boundaries and a kind of sharpness that is associated with the wisdom of the feminine principle. "The more spaciousness there is, the more there are restrictions to it. That space becomes very sensitive and very discriminating, but at the same time very openminded equally."[85] The triangular form of the source of phenomena expresses these unyielding qualities of the secret ḍākinī quite directly.

Iconographic Depictions of the Great Mother

The Mother Prajñāpāramitā is also given various names that express in relative terms those aspects that are utterly beyond the relative. Sometimes she is depicted in human form, yet emphasizing the vast and limitless qualities represented by the source of phenomena. These forms are peaceful or wrathful and sometimes naked in order to highlight the qualities of uncloaked reality. Lady Tārā explained to Machik that, in order "to enable sentient beings to accumulate merit, the Great Mother appears as an object of veneration."[86] She also described how, from the vast realm of reality, there appeared a brilliant orange dot out of which emanated a luminous deity, the Great Mother, with one face and four arms, beautiful and golden, wearing silks and jewels. She sits with legs crossed, with a peaceful expression and all the auspicious marks of an enlightened being. Surrounded by her princely sons, the buddhas and bodhisattvas of every realm, she resides in a celestial palace inseparable from our minds.[87] (See page 82.) While she has form, she is merely a representation of the ungraspable ultimate feminine principle.

Another secret form of the Great Mother is the visualized Samantabhadrī, or Küngtusangmo, the "all-good woman." As discussed previously, Samantabhadrī is the primordial feminine buddha of the Nyingma lineage, the counterpart of Samantabhadra. She is depicted as white, completely naked, and unadorned, as mind itself is in its essence. Seeing her strips away the fabrications of emotions, conceptions, and sense perceptions that make up our conventional world. She is the source of luminous, nondual wisdom, and her iconographic representations evoke that in the practitioner.

The Mother is also known as Nairātmyā (in Tibetan, Dagmema), "egoless woman." In the *Hevajra-tantra,* Nairātmyā is the consort of the central yidam heruka Hevajra, but she has other roles as well. As Snellgrove explains:

> In this union, Wisdom, although unrealizable apart from Means, yet predominates. It has behind it the whole tradition of the Perfection of Wisdom, already actually symbolized in a feminine divinity, the Goddess Prajñāpāramitā. She is therefore herself the supreme truth of . . . [śūnyatā] which is the Perfection of Wisdom; in the Hevajra-tantra she is Nairātmyā, "absence of the notion of selfhood," and it is in her that the yogin, as Means, is consubstantiated.[88]

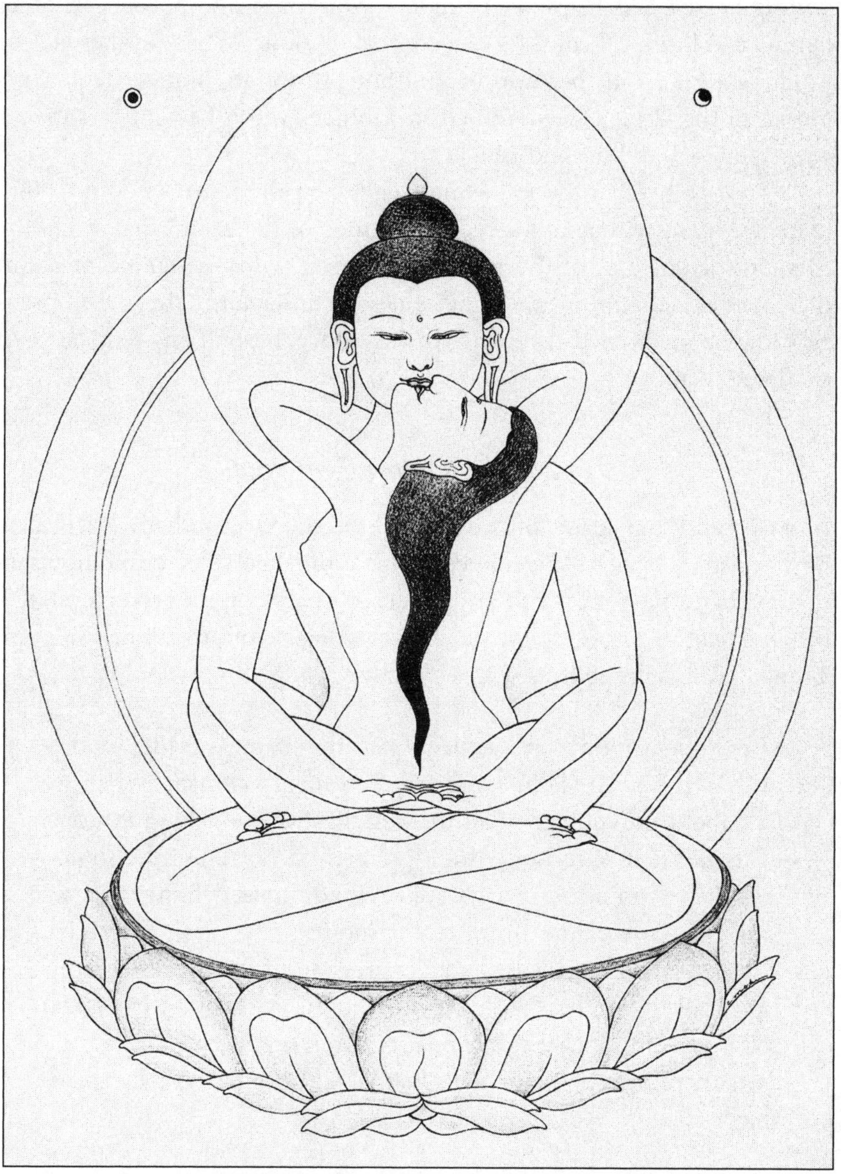

Samantabhadrī, the ultimate female buddha, in union with her consort Samantabhadra.

Sometimes in depictions she appears alone, completely wrathful, representing herself and Hevajra in union.[89] Nairātmyā also appears in other tantras and liturgical contexts as a consort or alone. Whenever her face or profile appears, with her eyes of nonthought, we are immediately transported to the Great Queen, the Great Mother, who is beyond person, beyond qualities, and beyond gender.

As we will see in the following chapter on the inner wisdom ḍākinī, there are many iconographic representations of the ḍākinī that signal the coemergent qualities of the Mother. However, what is significant about these deities is that, while they have quasi-feminine form, they are messengers for the meditative experience of vast space, beyond any semblance of gendered form.

How Is the Mother Feminine?

In what sense can space, thus described, be called a mother? Specifically, how can space be given a gendered designation? The Tibetan tradition says that *mother* does not refer to any gendered quality on the secret level; it is beyond relative terminology, duality, or concept of any kind. Chögyam Trungpa Rinpoche addressed this directly:

> The Prajñāpāramitā is actually *not* the name of the mother principle. . . . [It] is in some sense an incorrect term. When we talk about the mother of all the buddhas we are talking in terms of its *function:* somebody produced a child, therefore she should be called "mother." That is still a conditional definition. If we look back, we cannot even call it mother. . . . Prajñāpāramitā, transcendental knowledge, is an expression of that feminine principle, called "mother." Mother is one of its attributes. Maybe that attribute is just a cliché; maybe it is purely a concept. But beyond that, there is nothing actually namable, nothing actually workable.[90]

This point expresses an essential aspect of the feminine principle in Tibetan Buddhism: At its most profound level, it is beyond gender.

Yet, because all insight and understanding arise from this experience, space or the sky is said to be the source of all. For this reason, there is great devotion for the source, which is called the Mother. This devotion arises from understanding the genderless, vast nature of the Mother, the mind itself. Because it is the source, when we speak of it in relative language we call it Mother. Herbert Guenther explains it somewhat opaquely this way:

> Saraha images this energy as "feminine"—the yoginī, the Mother—not so much in the sense of a doctrinally prescribed content of this image, but as the intensity with which this image affects us and which as such mediates between the human level of our experience and the divine realm of our beingness, between the part and the whole that is needed to give meaning to the part(s) that constitute it. Particularly, it is through the image of the feminine that a man can relate to a woman in the physical world and to the realm that is much larger.[91]

Another, perhaps less psychological or androcentric interpretation can be found in descriptions of spiritual experience in Buddhism in which the direct realization of emptiness is a kind of epiphany. Naked seeing of the nature of reality, free of confusion and conceptuality, has tremendous power to transform human experience and to evoke devotion for the experience itself. Attributing to this experience the name *mother* is a natural expression of its primal quality without projecting onto it an anthropomorphic gendered identity. Since spiritual power begins with wisdom, the Mother is considered primary in Vajrayāna practice.[92]

Feminist scholarship in Tibetan Buddhism has critiqued notions of a nongendered Mother, saying that the Mother is a monastically coopted version of Indian goddess traditions that have their roots in prepatriarchal prehistory.[93] Miranda Shaw has developed a "gynocentric" interpretation of early Indian tantric Buddhism, stating that "consistent with its Hindu counterparts, Tantric Buddhism displays the conviction that all the powers of the universe flow through and from women."[94] Shaw wrote that for the tantric Buddhist, the feminine is preeminent as progenitor of the universe; femaleness is considered "ontologically primary," while maleness is "derivative and dependent."[95] This is the reason, she continued, that "worship of women (*strīpūjā*)" is shared by tantric Hindus and Buddhists. The theoretical basis of this is that "women are embodiments of goddesses and that worship of women is a form of devotion explicitly required by female deities."[96] In this, Shaw recoiled from considering femaleness a principle or a symbolic designation, insisting that only fully embodied, living women are the paradigm about which the tantras speak.[97] She read the tantras with a simplistic gynocentric bias, conflating women and the feminine symbolic, ignoring the subtlety of Tibetan Buddhist symbol and ritual.

In Tibetan interpretations of Anuttara-yoga-yāna dating back to Indian sources, a gendered absolute would be a contradiction of the most precious aspects of dharma teaching. The Mother is considered primary because she is the ultimate power of the tantric path. As the nature of the mind and phenomena, she is a genderless principle pervading all existence, a principle of emptiness and space. Like her, women, men, and all phenomena are ultimately empty of gender. As Ven. Khenpo Tsultrim Gyamtso Rinpoche, spontaneously sang:

Between ḍākas and ḍākinīs there's a difference
In how their bodies may seem in apparent reality,
But for Mahāmudrā, luminous clarity,
There's not an atom of difference in their essential nature.[98]

Yet there is another, fascinating perspective on Shaw's analyses that points to the special difficulties of interpreting religious symbols, especially in tantric sources. The genderless ultimate Mother manifests in a variety of ways, some of them also genderless or representing both genders. However, an important, conspicuous way in which the Mother manifests is as a ḍākinī: as the female yidam deity, as human women, and as those aspects of conventional reality most associated with women's domain—embodiment, procreation, nurture and sustenance, and relationship.[99] Yet, even while seemingly valorizing those culturally determined female roles, the Mother's manifestation radically reinterprets those roles in a new transcultural sense, transmitting her basic nature. While smiling, dancing, nurturing through the hollow, radiant bodies of ḍākinīs, the Mother shows in her gaze the radical emptiness of all such manifestation. "She" is not female, yet female is the shape "she" takes when manifesting in the world of duality. And from the female symbolic world, "she" has tremendous power to communicate an experience and perspective associated not with "female" but with "feminine" in the sense of the secret ḍākinī. This experience is associated with the "in-between" (pardo), in which conventional reference points become fluid and the power of the liminal, marginal aspects of human life is unleashed. When one understands the Mother in this way, there is tremendous power in feminine symbol and ritual.

Are we to follow Shaw in interpreting certain of the Indian tantras literally, in a gynocentric manner? Does the Mother require that men worship women, the source of all power? It is important to interpret tantric sources with precision and subtlety, in order to capture their profundity beyond any politics of gender. The gendered symbols associated with the Mother communicate truths that are not directly related to gender. Certainly feminine symbols can have a positive effect on the respect or standing of women in a patriarchal society, but there is often evidence to the contrary in research.[100] Liberation in Tibetan Buddhism is based on a more profound understanding of the Mother. In the realm of mind, she is vast awareness; in speech, the dynamic play of seed syllables becoming deities; in the realm of form, the subtle yogic body; and in daily life, human women. In Vajrayāna the Mother is said to be powerful because of her unique abilities to express the vast, awesome, limitless (and genderless) nature of emptiness. And ḍākinīs are the transmitters of the radical realization of emptiness in all levels of manifestation.

This interpretation favors the feminine without denigrating the masculine, which is also important in the world of duality. The masculine manifests in the conventional domains of men such as culture, organization, strategic action, and protection.[101] It also manifests in the bodies of human men that uniquely radiate the qualities of skillful means, compassion, and effective action necessary to carry the wisdom of space into the world. Certainly, the enlightened masculine also radically reinterprets those roles in a new transcultural sense, as can be seen in the heruka of indestructible wakefulness.[102] Sacred outlook requires that both feminine and masculine be revered in ritual practice. But spiritually in Vajrayāna, the realization of the feminine must come first; one needs wisdom in order to enact skillful means.

Finally, the Mother is primary because of the dynamics of the yogic path. If the practitioner does not begin with a personal experience of emptiness, given and activated by transmission from a tantric guru, the path of meditation is nothing but entertainment at the very least and a dangerous charade at worst. This realization, which is described as prajñāpāramitā, is the foundation of all genuineness and power in Vajrayāna Buddhist practice. The Mother is not ontologically primary; she is soteriologically primary. Without her, there is no enlightenment. With her, the next stage on the tantric path is possible, that of uniting wisdom and skillful means. Without the masculine principle in union with the feminine principle, there is no enlightenment.

FOUR

The Inner Dakini

THE VISIONARY QUEEN

Regard the vajra master as precious as your head.
Possess the yidam deity like the heart in your chest.
Keep constant company with ḍākinīs as protectors
like the shadow of your body.
Guard the Profound Secret Mantra like your eyes.
Retain the profound essence mantra like your breath.
Value the profound creation and completion as dearly
as your body and life.[1]

—GURU RINPOCHE'S ADVICE TO PRACTITIONERS OF VAJRAYĀNA

THE YOUNG YOGIN VIRŪPA WAS given the yidam practice of the Sow-Faced Ḍākinī Vajravārāhī. He threw himself into his practice for twelve years, completing twenty million recitations of her mantra, but no signs of progress arose, not even an auspicious dream. He fell into a deep depression and broke his rosary (*mālā*), throwing its beads into a latrine in disgust. At the time of evening practice he realized he had no rosary. Suddenly the ḍākinī appeared, slipping the repaired rosary into his hand and saying, "Most fortunate child, do not be troubled. With my blessing continue your practice. Rid your mind of the habit of thinking of things as either this or that, and abandon all wandering and critical thought. Strip your mind of mental fiction." Then she sang this song of instruction:

The innate purity that is the nature of mind
That *is the essential Vajravārāhī.*
She exists within,
So do not look elsewhere.
That *is foolish and childish.*
The nature of mind, a wish-fulfilling gem,
Stripped of all mental fiction,
That *is the most satisfying achievement.*[2]

Heartened, Virūpa returned to his practice and in another twelve years attained realization.

Virūpa had experienced many obstacles because he viewed the Sow-Faced Ḍākinī as an external being whom he should supplicate. Occupied by thoughts of achievement and failure, numbers of mantra recitations, and signs of success, he relied on external help and approval. Done with this attitude, his practice was no different from any worldly project, and no personal transformation was possible. This could change only when he became completely disgusted and depressed. Only then could the gates of wisdom open and could he understand the ḍākinī as the intimate meeting of his own understanding, the deity, and the lineage of realization.

On the level of the inner ḍākinī, the tāntrika engages in ritual practice that has been transmitted from the tantric guru. This practice is designed to introduce the unavoidable reality of the awakened mind in inventive ways, demonstrating the inseparability of emptiness and form in a completely sacred realm known in Tibetan Vajrayāna as the *maṇḍala*, the pre-eminent symbolic world of tantra. Through performing the ritual, the tāntrika gradually comes to intuitively understand the immanence of wisdom in all dimensions of everyday life.

Maṇḍala Principle

The inner wisdom ḍākinī manifests in the maṇḍala, the representation of the complete environment of the universe as it is, physically, psychologically, and spiritually, for the practitioner who has been introduced to wakefulness. As a symbol, the maṇḍala expresses a method for transforming a confused, defiled understanding into a view based on understanding things as they really are: ultimately empty of inherent existence and full of the qualities of complete wakefulness.

In Tibetan tantra, when the world is understood from the perspective of emptiness and luminosity, it is seen as inherently awake and sacred. This means that no matter how confused and painful existence might be, from an awakened perspective, all pain and confusion are merely the play of wisdom. And that play has a recognizable pattern called the maṇḍala principle. If one can identify difficult situations as maṇḍalas, then transformation of painful circumstances is possible. The maṇḍala principle lies at the heart of Vajrayāna Buddhism and is the sacred realm of the inner ḍākinī.

A maṇḍala (*kyil-khor*) is iconographically depicted in Tibet as a two-dimensional diagram or three-dimensional reproduction of a prescribed universe, represented by a palace, throne, or pedestal in the midst of dramatic beauty. The features of the maṇḍala are based on a central focal point (*kyil*) surrounded by (khor) boundary walls, perimeters, or realms. The center and perimeter are seen as interdependent, and that is the key to the power of the maṇḍala. Narrowly interpreted, a maṇḍala is a representation of a tantric deity's realm of existence, for a deity occupies its central seat.

In a broader context, the maṇḍala is a paradigm of the natural functioning of phenomena. Maṇḍalas are like Vajrayāna "systems theory,"[3] and from this view every situation operates on the dynamic of the maṇḍala principle. A city, for example, has a center of power—its business districts—and its suburbs, linked with expressways. Communication networks have a common vision and organizing principles. Swarms of bees decide collectively about the suitability of new sites for hives. Families have intricate patterns of activity and communication, with interconnecting roles. When one understands the dynamic relationships in these maṇḍalas, it is possible to glimpse the meaning of sacredness in Vajrayāna Buddhism.

Conventionally, naturally existing maṇḍalas cannot acknowledge that they are maṇḍalas or systems with their own dynamics and parameters. It is especially difficult for maṇḍalas to acknowledge the power radiated between the center and the perimeter. The center would like to manipulate its boundary, or the perimeter would like to overthrow the center. From a conventional point of view, the maṇḍala may be a dictatorship, in which the central figure does not acknowledge or respect the perimeter, and so it imposes its tyranny. Conversely, perhaps the perimeter does not acknowledge or respect the central power, and so it undermines and overthrows the center, creating rebellion, chaos, or anarchy. When this happens, everything is reduced to the lowest common denominator, and sacred outlook is impossible to maintain. Pain, fear, and self-serving preoccupation overtake the power dynamic, and no one can thrive. This dynamic can be seen in organizations, in the flow between the extreme of too much power centralized in one or two leaders and the extreme of no centralized leadership, with power struggles erupting between factions. When we do not see the maṇḍala principle at work, we constantly reject, grasp, or attempt to manipulate the world around us to make it into something other than what it is. We find it difficult to experience the richness of our environment.

From a Vajrayāna perspective, we live in many maṇḍalas at the same time: our career or livelihood, our leisure activities, our family, our spiritual community, our neighborhood, town, city, country. In Vajrayāna, as in feminist studies, there is no real boundary between the personal and the rest of our lives; the most intimate maṇḍala in which we live is our own personal one, in which all of these parts play a role, adding the dimensions of our physical bodies, health, and state of mind. In each of these maṇḍalas, there is a similar dynamic in which we do not customarily acknowledge the sacredness of every part of our circumstances, and because of this we experience constant struggle and pain. This is the Vajrayāna description of the Buddha's First Noble Truth of suffering.

The only transformative choice that remains, according to the Vajrayāna, is to take our seat in whatever world we find ourselves in and acknowledge it as a maṇḍala. This means settling into our jobs, our intimate relationships, and our communities, and committing to all of their difficult parts. Our lives can only be seen as a maṇḍala if we include everything, all the positive qualities as well as all that we would like to ignore, reject, or distance ourselves from.[4]

Once we open to our circumstances and accept them as they are, inescapably, we take our seat in the center of a maṇḍala and establish boundaries by identifying the natural physical and mental limits for this particular system to operate. It then becomes possible to work with our situation and to develop a relationship with our circumstances. Each part of the system can communicate with every other part, and a sense of totality begins to emerge. It is then possible to realize the role each part plays in our lives and how the totality works or does not. The maṇḍala view allows us to experience the natural goodness and workability inherent in our lives.

In Vajrayāna this view is called sacred outlook (tag-nang): seeing the world as sacred in a self-existing way.

This shift in the working paradigm of how we think and relate is the transformative power of the maṇḍala, and it is the foundation of tantra as a powerful method in Buddhist meditation. Seeing the world as maṇḍala makes it possible for Vajrayāna practitioners to drop their habitual ways of relating to events and aspects of life and to engage directly. When this is done everything is accentuated, whether it is pleasurable or painful, and there is nowhere to go. The central seat of the maṇḍala may be a throne, but it may also be a prison cell. When we feel the inescapability of our life circumstances true practice is finally possible.

The strategy of Vajrayāna practice is to accentuate our state of mind and context of experience and to seal the boundaries to allow no possibility of escape, so that we relate to everything fully. Usually we are very cunning and do everything possible to escape the experience of suffering of which the Buddha spoke so eloquently. When our ruse succeeds and we hold suffering at bay, it returns in a new form to haunt us. In Tibetan tantra, all these ruses are willingly given up in the commitment to a teacher and a path of practice. The power of Vajrayāna practice comes from this simple technology of claustrophobia, in which the practitioner commits to the maṇḍala perspective. When we experience our suffering directly, without the dilution of habitual patterns of avoidance, insight naturally arises. We can begin to experience the heart of our suffering, which is self-existing wisdom. The spiritual secret is that giving up any hope of escape actually opens the door to compassion and skillful action.

In the sacred maṇḍala of the Vajrayāna, the dynamic between center and fringe is not based on struggle or competition. The central deity of the tantric maṇḍala is not a supreme being or even an existent being of any kind. The boundaries are as important and powerful as the center, and they are not existent either. Instead, the maṇḍala is an expression of the dynamics of the world once the profound understanding of space, of emptiness, is realized. With no supreme being or god, everything in the world is a transparent emanation, a play of empty space.

In the maṇḍala principle, everything in one's experience is understood to have the four dimensions discussed in chapter 3, outer-outer, outer, inner, and secret. All these levels manifest at the same time in an interpenetrating way, and the haunting qualities of the unseen impart a kind of magic to experience. When we speak of the inner ḍākinī, we are speaking of the landscape of the maṇḍala principle as a powerful visualization that allows one to experience all four levels at once and to experience the sacredness of the totality of one's life.

Ḍākinīs are important inhabitants of maṇḍalas in classical Tibetan iconography. The wisdom ḍākinī occupies the central seat as a meditational deity either alone or with her consort, and she is accompanied by retinue ḍākinīs who are aspects of her complete, enlightened wisdom. The central deity is also supported and encouraged by the deities of the perimeter, protectors of all kinds, including the protector ḍākinīs. But in order to understand the power and appearance of the inner ḍākinī, it is important to experience the landscape in which she appears, the charnel ground.

The Charnel Ground

The charnel ground is, in Tibetan tantric maṇḍalas, the location and medium of sacredness. Symbolically, it is the landscape or the psychological environment in which one can commit to things as they are. The classical iconographic maṇḍala is visualized as a transformed charnel ground, with the corpses and bones of everything that has perished. The maṇḍala is ringed by charnel grounds, and the deities of the maṇḍala wear charnel ground ornaments. This imagery is key to understanding the maṇḍala and its deities, especially the ḍākinī.

In ancient India, cremation grounds were unclean places of terror and anguish. In portions of the field, bodies wrapped in cloth shrouds were burned in large bonfires and reduced to a tangled pile of charred bones. In other portions, called *śmaśāna*, or the charnel ground, uncremated (*āma*) bodies were simply left to rot.[5] The cremation grounds were full of the foul odors (*āmagandha*) of the partially burned, rotting corpses, but it was the charnel ground area that was particularly frightful, because of the stench of the fresh bodies rotting in the Indian heat, uncovered corpses in various states of decomposition. These charnel fields were also full of many kinds of beasts of prey and wild and roving demons looking for human remains to devour.

In the early tradition, the Buddha emphasized meditation on impermanence as foundational for the spiritual path. The mark of impermanence was essential in the teachings of the Four Noble Truths, and contemplating the fact that change pervades the outer world, all beings, and one's own life has always served as inspiration on the Buddhist path. The most direct of these contemplations is to reflect on the imminence of one's own death. As is said in the Tibetan tradition, there are two certainties regarding death: first, that we will die, and second, that we do not know the moment or means of our death. Contemplating this makes worldly concerns and self-centered agendas unimportant and opens the practitioner to the cultivation of spiritual freedom. It is said that by deeply contemplating impermanence alone, one can be fully liberated.

There is no greater lesson in impermanence than contemplation of the body, either one's own or that of someone who has died.[6] In the early tradition, the Buddha encouraged those particularly bound by lustful desire to meditate on decaying corpses in the charnel grounds. This practice, incumbent upon monks and nuns, was called *śmāśānika,* or the frequenting of charnel grounds. But when such meditations produced aversion so strong that monks committed suicide, the Buddha made this literal contemplation of the unlovely (*asubha-bhāvanā*) optional.[7] However, the charnel ground maintained a central role in some Buddhist meditation traditions as a place that fostered renunciation.

Drawing on this tradition, Tibetan Buddhism viewed the charnel grounds (*turtrö*) as most sacred and used charnel ground symbolism in ritual texts and hagiographies to highlight a distinctively tantric spirituality. These Vajrayāna texts depict charnel grounds as terrifying places containing countless bodies in various stages of decomposition as well as crows, vultures, and other carnivores such as tigers, lions, and wolves:

> *Now the bird of the tombs, the swine of the tombs, the*
> *poisonous snake,*
> *and jackals of many different colors,*
> *and wolves and crows and other beasts of this kind,*
> *devour the corpses without number, fresh and decomposed,*
> *the bloody sea of flesh and bones,*
> *and the men's dried-out heads, with others still humid or*
> *broken down.*
> *Beasts of prey tear the remains, while others devour them;*
> *some fling themselves on the flesh, while others moan,*
> *some tear out the eyes, while others gnaw the feet,*
> *some pulverize the bones, seize the flesh, and tear out the*
> *entrails.*[8]

No attempt is made to mask the horrors of decay and effluvia in the charnel ground.[9] Spirits of the departed roam there, searching for their missing bodies. Those that were not properly propitiated remain stranded in demonic forms for lifetimes, haunting all who linger in the charnel ground. In Vajrayāna, these male and female spirits included rākṣasas, piśācas, and yakṣas, beings with varying demonic powers associated with possession, illness, and calamity.

But these charnel grounds were also depicted in tantric texts as places of great peace and simplicity. Since all that was once craved in life was now lost, the charnel ground was a place of release from self-cherishing tendencies. Thus the disturbing aspects of the cemetery were frightening only from the conventional, saṃsāric view of those who wish to ignore and deny death. In the view of the Vajrayāna practitioner who had achieved some degree of awakening, the charnel ground was beautiful, a place of energy and power. Tulku Thondup explained it this way:

> But they are also enjoyable places of peaceful solitude, delightful groves, blossoming flowers, abundant fruit, flocks of singing birds, tame lions and tigers, vast open sky, as high as among the sun, moon, and stars, with no systems or norms to be shaped by, free from distractions or restrictions. It is a place where oceans of ḍākas and ḍākinīs celebrate with ceremonial "feasts." The roar of Dharma discourses is sounding everywhere, and lights from inner joy of bliss and openness are radiating. Thus, these charnel grounds are places of energy, power, and spirit both positive and negative, which it is important for an esoteric trainee to transform into esoteric power and energy of enlightenment.[10]

In the hagiographic lore of tantric adepts, the charnel ground became the ideal setting for realization. When Guru Rinpoche was a young prince and was exiled from the palace in disgrace, he was escorted to a famous charnel ground in the eastern part of Uḍḍiyāṇa, called Cool Grove. There he settled himself, fashioning clothing from shrouds and eating food offerings left for the dead:

> He remained in the samādhi called Unshakable [*acala*] and thus stayed in great happiness. After some time, a widespread famine broke out in that area. Most of the people died. The numerous corpses were carried in without the [customary] sheet of cloth and without the [usual] provision of rice-pap. Therefore the prince flayed human skin for clothes and ate the corpses for food. Through this he brought all the *mamo ḍākinīs* dwelling in the

> charnel ground under his command and remained practicing the actions of a yogic discipline.[11]

Guru Rinpoche, the gentle young prince, had been accustomed to life in the palace, but he lived in the charnel ground and made no distinction between the two, showing his profound understanding of impermanence and death. Throughout his life, he considered the charnel ground his home and returned to its ḍākinīs again and again to receive teachings, to celebrate and play, and to transmit his own teachings. As he remarked to his ḍākinī consort Maṇḍāravā:

> a frightful environment such as this is the catalyst for a practitioner's true practice to emerge. Adverse conditions are the true wealth of a practitioner. . . . A frightening, uncomfortable place is the knife that severs discursive thought. The wrathful charnel ground is the environment through which the deceptive view of eternalism is exposed.[12]

The charnel ground is the most suitable place of practice for the tantric adept.

Eight main charnel grounds figure in the key events of Guru Rinpoche's life, and they remain the ring of charnel grounds around the maṇḍalas of wrathful deities.[13] Each has its own reliquary (*stūpa*), protectors (*kṣetrapāla, dikpāla,* nāga), mountain, river, cloud, and yogi meditating under a tree.[14] These charnel grounds were linked to the accomplished yogins and yoginīs (siddhas) of the Indian tradition and became the emblem of their practice and realization.

The charnel ground is a powerful landscape for Vajrayāna practice because it transforms terror and fear of death into awakening. Many tantric adepts began by facing the terrors of the charnel ground, sitting in the midst of fear without denying or avoiding it. Death can become a great teacher, a great liberator. As Padampa Sangye, the master of Chö practice and the guru of Machik Lapdrön, said, "At first, to be fully convinced of impermanence makes you take up the dharma; in the middle it whips up your diligence; and in the end it brings you to the radiant dharmakāya."[15]

When Milarepa was surrounded in his cave by the horrific worldly ḍākinīs thirsty for his blood, he met them without flinching. He acknowledged that he would die one day anyway; why not give them what they asked for and make a worthy offering?

This human body, composed of skandhas,
In transient, mortal, and delusory.
Since in time I must discard it,
He who would, may take it now.
May the offering of my body serve as ransom
For all mankind and sentient beings. . . .
Since I have offered this, my body,
With sincerest dedication,
May you all be satisfied and happy.[16]

He did not strategize, manipulate, or engage in battle; he merely offered his body to Tseringma and her hordes.

In Vajrayāna practice, it is essential to personalize the charnel ground in order to absorb the power of maṇḍala principle. When asked how to see the charnel ground in personal experience, Trungpa Rinpoche responded:

> It is a sense of threat that most people experience. You feel that you are on the verge of a freakout and are losing ground in terms of keeping a grip on who are your enemies and who are your friends. You want to make sure that they are enemies and friends and don't want to confuse the two. You want to make the whole thing definite. That in itself becomes very painful and uninviting. As Buddhists, the whole thing that we are trying to do is approach an area that nobody wants to get into. People try to run away from it all the time and in that way have created saṃsāra. As long as we are on the path and practicing and developing, we are doing this impossible thing, approaching that thing that people have been rejecting for millions of years. We find it extremely discomfiting, and we are going toward it, exploring it. That is why it is so painful to give and open. That kind of unwanted place is like the charnel ground. It haunts us all over the place, not just one place.[17]

Acknowledging this experience of constant threat creates tremendous possibility for transformation. Then the charnel ground becomes a place of openness in which one can relax the struggle of cyclic existence and celebrate freedom of clarity. The corpses rotting there are the concepts and schemes that have perished, especially the notions of self whose veins have been cut. These corpses still stink, but the odor awakens the practitioner to the impossibility of fulfilling his or her ambitions and plans.

In Vajrayāna Buddhism, the charnel ground became the emblem of renunciation and retreat, in which the eight worldly concerns[18] would cease and the craving and attachment that fuel suffering would abate. The charnel ground experience may arise in environments of solitude, and this is why solitary retreat is so emphasized in Tibetan Buddhism. Traditionally, retreats were performed in the rugged mountains, in caves and under rocky outcroppings.[19] The practitioner who goes on retreat relives the experience of the Buddha under the *bodhi* tree: sitting still, resolving not to leave, inviting the demons of one's own mind to haunt every moment. Dwelling there is an act of renunciation, removed from worldly preoccupations and committed to clearly seeing all aspects of life. However, it is important that the place of retreat not be too idyllic or pleasant. As Tashi Namgyal, the great sixteenth-century master of Mahāmudrā meditation, observed:

> monasteries and cities are too relaxing and too pleasant, and thus lack the external and internal conditions crucial to sublimating the afflicted consciousness. These places cannot easily arouse deluded thoughts and coarse passions in the meditator. And without this kind of deluded thinking and passions rapid progress in elevating the mind to the path of mahāmudrā is not possible. Progress can be achieved more rapidly during a single month of self-transformation through terrifying conditions in rough terrain and in "the abode of harmful forces" than through meditating for a period of three years in towns and monasteries.[20]

On a Vajrayāna practice retreat, the charnel ground is recreated in dramatic detail through the visualization of the maṇḍala of one's meditational deity. In this practice, corpses of thought and emotion fall on all sides, only to rise again. When the practitioner maintains discipline and decorates herself or himself with the ornaments of perished emotions and thoughts, the experience of the inner ḍākinī is accessible. Milarepa said of retreat, "abiding in this cave, alone, is the noblest service to the ḍākinīs!"[21]

When the practitioner is in retreat, relating to demons and keeping her or his meditation seat, the ḍākinīs are said to provide nourishment and support. This is because ḍākinīs themselves are manifestations of retreat realization, and they inspire the practitioner to deeper insight. When Milarepa was stranded by snow on retreat, he was asked how he was able to get food. He responded, "Most of the time, I was in the state of samādhi and hence required no food. On feast days, many ḍākinīs offered me food in their tantric feast gatherings."[22]

The charnel ground is not merely the hermitage; it can also be discovered or revealed in completely terrifying mundane environments where practitioners find themselves desperate and depressed, where conventional worldly aspirations have become devastated by grim reality. This is demonstrated in the sacred biographies of the great siddhas of the Vajrayāna tradition. Tilopa attained realization as a grinder of sesame seeds and a procurer for a prominent prostitute. Sarvabhakṣa was an extremely obese glutton, Gorakṣa was a cowherd in remote climes, Taṅtepa was addicted to gambling, and Kumbharipa was a destitute potter. These circumstances were charnel grounds because they were despised in Indian society and the siddhas were viewed as failures, marginal and defiled.

In contemporary Western society, the charnel ground might be a prison, a homeless shelter, the welfare roll, or a factory assembly line. The key to its successful support of practice is its desperate, hopeless, or terrifying quality. For that matter, there are environments that appear prosperous and privileged to others but are charnel grounds for their inhabitants—Hollywood, Madison Avenue, Wall Street, Washington, D.C. These are worlds in which extreme competitiveness, speed, and power rule, and the actors in their dramas experience intense emotion, ambition, and fear. The intensity of their dynamics makes all of these situations ripe for the Vajrayāna practice of the charnel ground.

The Ḍākinī in the Charnel Ground

If the charnel ground is adopted home for the yogin, in tantric lore it is especially the traditional abode of the ḍākinī. While tantric adepts are attracted to the charnel ground for its great peace and simplicity, it is the ḍākinīs who live there who authorize yogins in their practice, join them in sexual yoga as copractitioners, and serve in the propagation of their teachings. When the yoginī Yeshe Tsogyal visited the land of the ḍākinīs (*orgyen khandro ling*) in a visionary journey, she found a land in which

> the fruit trees there had leaves like razors, and the ground was a mass of corpse-flesh. The hills and cliffs were heaps of bristling skeletons, and for earth and rock there were but scattered fragments of bone. In the middle of this place there was a castle keep,

> its walls fashioned of three layers of human heads, some freshly cut, some dry, some putrescent, its roof and doors contrived of human skins. . . . Within this enclosed space I saw flesh-devouring birds and wild, blood-drinking beasts, and I was surrounded by ogres and ogresses and a host of other terrors. They were a fearful sight and yet proved neither hostile nor friendly.[23]

In order to understand the inner wisdom ḍākinī, it is important to understand her connection with the charnel ground.

In the early Indian Buddhist tradition, cemetery contemplations were primarily focused on the corpses of women.[24] Since lust was such a strong temptation for the ordained monk, contemplation of the once-exquisite decaying body of a woman was a successful "aversion therapy" to wean his mind from desire. Contemplation of a recently deceased woman could arouse such desire that necrophilia was sometimes a problem in the early saṅgha. But as the body's decomposition was observed, a profound renunciation arose that led to accelerated levels of realization.

This contemplation was powerful because a woman's body was an object of great desire and attachment, objectified in a way consistent with patriarchal values and culture. Sexual desire was the most compelling and disturbing of attachments for a man, drawing him into an ever-deepening entrapment in saṃsāra, for sexual desire led to marriage, family, and household encumbrances. Women, therefore, were seen in the early tradition as embodiments of the snares or traps of Māra, the tempter.[25] And when fathers like Śuddhodana wished to keep their sons from the life of renunciation, they constructed elaborate harems to distract them from understanding impermanence.

For noble laymen and husbands who were drawn to spiritual pursuits, these distractions proved insufficient. Even the bedrooms of the home or the courtly harem, filled with the graceful beauties of the kingdom, came to be seen as a charnel ground. On his final night in the palace, the young prince Siddhārtha witnessed the bodies of his courtesans in sleep and was disgusted by their tangled and disreputable appearance. As he gazed, the gods of the Akaniṣṭha heavens conjured images of the charnel ground.

> Another too had her hair loose and dishevelled, and with the ornaments and clothes fallen from her hips and her necklaces scattered she lay like an image of a woman broken by an elephant. . . .

> Others looked ugly, lying unconscious like corpses, with their ornaments and garlands cast aside, the fastening knots of their dresses undone, and eyes moveless with the whites showing.
>
> Another lay as if sprawling in intoxication, with her mouth gaping wide, so that the saliva oozed forth, and with her limbs spread out so as to show what should have been hid. Her beauty was gone, her form distorted.[26]

For the young prince and other renunciant practitioners of pre-Vajrayāna depictions, the bodies of women came to represent the deceptiveness of saṃsāra. Although clothed in silks, ornamented with jewels, and colored with the most delicate of cosmetics, these bodies were actually "boils with nine openings."[27] The disgusting quality of their naked form was disguised by a facade of loveliness. A truly dedicated practitioner was encouraged to contemplate this quality, either in others or in herself, and renounce attachment to that which is inherently impermanent, repulsive, selfless, and full of suffering.[28]

In Vajrayāna Buddhism, just as the charnel ground was transformed from a place of horror to a symbol of meditation practice, the ḍākinī was transformed into a symbol of the transmutation of painful emotions such as desire into wisdom. As we have discussed, the ḍākinī in the pre-Buddhist traditions of India resided in the charnel ground, feasting on the bodies and sucking the blood of the dead as a kind of ghoul or witch. As the ḍākinī became assimilated into Tibetan Buddhism, she brought with her the imagery of the cemetery contemplations, cast in a different context in which her beautiful female body expressed the essence of the Vajrayāna teachings. She arose in the charnel ground as a new, completely Vajrayāna symbol expressing the dynamics of tantric meditation and realization.

The discrepancy between the desirability of beautiful young women's bodies and the decay and death of the charnel ground is used and transformed in characteristically tantric ways.[29] The naked, dancing wisdom ḍākinī represents the wisdom and freedom from attachment of one who has given up self-cherishing. Rather than serving as the passive object of cemetery meditations, she is active and dynamic, a teacher in her own right. Rather than arousing only revulsion and disgust in the practitioner, she joins the quality of sensuous, vibrant womanliness with the reminders of death from the charnel ground. She sees all the realities of life and death, youth and aging, attraction and revulsion, without being seduced into duality. In her inner form, she is the observed and desired one, but her devotees are attracted not only to her body and sensuality. They are dazzled by her wisdom.

An example of this can be seen in the life of King Lalitacandra of Bengal, disciple of the great master Kānhapa. Lalitacandra became inspired to practice tantra and went secretly to the charnel ground at night to make offerings.[30] There he found the complete skeleton of a woman, picked clean by vultures. He bowed in reverence before her, making offerings, and the skeleton tried to stand. Realizing immediately that she was the great wrathful ḍākinī Vajravārāhī, the young king recited mantras. In response the wisdom ḍākinī danced and gave him a special dharma teaching called Tāraṇa, which means "safe crossing." The king remained and practiced with her, attaining great realization.

It is important to note that the ḍākinī is native to the charnel ground. According to tantric lore, some ḍākinīs were born there and many were reared there. In the Indian tradition, when women died in childbirth their baby daughters were also given up as undesirable, since girl children were considered burdens on the family resources. Sometimes the infant girl was delivered in the charnel ground from her dead mother's womb; at other times, the newborn girl was left there with her mother's body. For example, a weaver's wife died in childbirth, and the distraught father, thinking that the child would not survive, took the baby girl and her mother's corpse to the charnel ground. There the yoginī Maṇḍāravā,[31] in her guise as a tigress, found the baby sucking on her dead mother's breast. Feeling infinite compassion, Maṇḍāravā suckled the child with her own milk. Each day, the tigress ate of the mother's corpse for nourishment, and eventually she gave bits of the mother's flesh to the baby. As the girl grew, she learned to spin wool into thread and weave it on a loom. Her beauty was evident to all, and at age sixteen she was recognized as a ḍākinī and was initiated into the maṇḍala of Vajrasattva. She was given the name Kālasiddhi and became a famous consort of Guru Rinpoche's.[32]

Because the wisdom ḍākinī is native to the charnel ground, she has special powers to tame the raw and terrifying spirits who dwell there. Princess Maṇḍāravā was especially known for her abilities to tame the charnel ground beings. In her first encounter, she was daunted by the horrific appearances, screams, and behaviors of the demons there. But Guru Rinpoche explained that she alone could do this, having in previous lifetimes made the aspiration to compassionately bring them to the dharma. Reassured, she confronted them and insisted upon bathing them with her loving-kindness. In return, they assaulted her, raped her, and began to tear her body to pieces. First she remained in wrathful meditative absorption; then she arose as a fierce ḍākinī terrifying in her brilliant wakefulness, overwhelmed the worldly demons, and demanded that they surrender their life essence to her. Blinded by her brilliance, they became her devoted students.[33]

The ḍākinī dances in the charnel ground, reminding the practitioner of the destruction of all that the self holds dear. Unlike conventional women who cover their "repulsiveness" with ornaments and cosmetics, she is naked, the quality of awareness itself. Rather than deceptively posing as what she is not,[34] the ḍākinī has nothing to hide and displays her secrets for all who have the realization to see. Still, she wears a few beautiful garments and pieces of jewelry gleaned from the charnel existence, chosen to ornament and accentuate her nakedness and yet to remind the practitioner of the devastated setting. Her bone jewelry includes a crown of five dry skulls, and carved earrings, necklace, anklets, and bracelets fashioned of bleached human bone. Her skirt is a dazzling lattice of bone fragments, and it swings and clatters as she dances.[35]

She carries two customary implements. The skull-cup of fresh blood in her left hand, normally considered repulsive, is for her the nectar of deathlessness (*amṛta, dütsi*). The knife in her right hand has a long convex blade suitable for slicing; it ends in a curved hook useful for tearing, the classic implement of the charnel ground. Both are symbols of wisdom, showing the cutting-through quality and the intoxicating quality.

In her various forms, she has two standard poses when she appears alone. When she is in dancing pose (*kartap*), she stands on her slightly bent left leg, stamping on the corpse of self-cherishing. She raises her right leg high in a dance step, heel pointing to her secret center.[36] She raises the hooked knife above her shoulder in a flourish and embraces the skull-cup in the left, near her heart. She dances in a ring of flames and embodies fiery passion, joy, and freedom, no matter what her color.[37] In an alternate pose, she stands on both feet in heruka posture, left leg bent standing on the male corpse, while the right leg extends, pressing down the female corpse. She holds her hooked knife low in the right hand, and with her left raised, pours blood from the skull-cup into her upturned mouth.[38] She is also depicted in flight, with her ornaments and hair streaming around her.

When the wisdom ḍākinī skillfully joins the extremes and dualities of life, she holds power at once ambiguous and dangerous. Her female body might conventionally be seen as an object of desire and as a birth-giver, which ties her to the powerful forces of nature. In keeping with early Buddhism, she might be viewed as a temptress unintimidated by cultural norms that would hide her away in chaste appearance. When she is a woman unencumbered by societal demands, she holds power enough. But she also dances joyfully in the charnel ground, wearing ornaments made of funerary remains. For her, death and destruction are not fearful; she understands them clearly. Holding these dualities of birth and death, she manifests a primal power.[39] Her female body arouses lust in the virile, and fear and caution in the monk. She is auspicious when chaste, dangerous when sexually available, and a threatening omen when a crone.

But the Vajrayāna understanding of the ḍākinī's power goes further. Her highest power has only nominal relationship to her ties with the natural world. She gazes into unfathomable space, and her body itself is luminous, empty of solidity. She embodies the teachings of emptiness in a uniquely Vajrayāna way: she is the manifestation of coemergent wisdom, the all-inclusive wisdom generated in meditation. She captures the totality of the minds of the yogis and yoginīs, bringing both poles of attraction and revulsion directly to the path of realization. She cannot be conceptualized or categorized. She stops the mind.

The ḍākinī refuses to accept the logic of life versus death, gain versus loss, and pain versus pleasure. This logic is the reasoning of the endless cycle of suffering in which we are trapped, and when we perpetuate this approach, we are trapped in a saṃsāric prison. The ḍākinī shows the landscape in which this hopeless logic disintegrates and we directly experience the world as it is, infused with intensity and natural power. In this charnel ground, beauty has no rival in ugliness. The polarities have collapsed, and great joy is found in the greatest devastation. This is the power of the dancing ḍākinī.

Coemergence, Heat, and the Charnel Ground

In the higher tantra tradition, especially in the meditation tradition of Mahāmudrā, the charnel ground is the primordial expression of coemergent wisdom (*lhen-chik kye pe yeshe*), literally, the "wisdom born within," experiential wisdom that arises naturally in our practice and our everyday life. This wisdom is inherently present within normal confusion; it is the sanity within neurosis. Often wisdom arises in our experience in the midst of our emotional turmoil. The realization of coemergent wisdom requires that we give up the struggle to reject our suffering and confusion and awaken to the wisdom inherent in painful experiences.

The teachings on coemergent wisdom are central to the Mahāmudrā tradition of meditation but have their roots in the Mahāyāna tradition. They are based on the teachings concerning emptiness, in which the nature of all phenomena, thought, and experience is unborn, nondwelling, and unceasing. In the Mahāmudrā sense, this nature is without limit and cannot be understood conceptually.

Coemergent wisdom is associated with the ḍākinī principle in intimate ways. First, if the vast and luminous space of the Mother is the source of all phenomena, then all her offspring are also of her nature. This means that all phenomena in our experience are empty, luminous, and vast as well. The prolific dynamic of the Prajñāpāramitā constantly gives birth to the richness of confusion and wisdom. This quality of wisdom is the nonconceptual experience of the source of all. Since the Mother is empty, all children are empty as well, and at the very moment of arising, the wisdom that knows this is fully present.

Milarepa taught his student Rechungpa about this quality of coemergence by creating for him a spectacle of a succession of mountain she-goats giving birth to kids, which gave birth to more kids, until eventually there were two hundred of them frolicking on a mountain plain. When Rechungpa became fascinated by them, Milarepa reminded him that they were nothing other than "a spontaneous play of non-arising reality."[40] Since the first goat had no mother and the last goat had no kid, it must constantly be remembered that all the goats are of the essence of śūnyatā. Since the nature of the mother is unborn, all offspring of the mother—that is, all phenomena—are also unborn.[41]

But phenomena are not only empty, luminous, and vast; they bear a kind of intensity associated with the inextricability of confusion and wisdom. The tantric understanding of coemergent wisdom completely stupefies the conventional understandings of the duality of saṃsāra and nirvāṇa described in the sūtras. This wisdom is called coemergent because of the recognition that when deep confusion or turmoil arises, with it arises the clarity that can cut through that confusion and turmoil. Whenever our minds open, whether in intense emotion or in extreme physical sensations, there is tremendous clarity and radiance that sees and understands the intensity in a nondual, nonjudgmental fashion. With the guru's help, Vajrayāna practitioners learn to embrace all of experience as a manifestation of unconditional mind.

Vajrayāna meditation training is based on two aspects. First, it is essential to recognize the unborn, nondwelling, and unceasing nature of our experience. We must personally experience the transparency and dreamlike nature of ourselves and our world and the nature of our projections that imbue these phenomena with reality. Then, we must recognize the naturally arising wisdom and develop an allegiance to the brilliant aspects of our experience. When we do this, we can liberate confusion on the spot.

The inner ḍākinī is the messenger of coemergent wisdom, for she aids us in both of these areas. First, she is a representative of the secret ḍākinī, the Mother, for she embodies the vast, spacious, and luminous qualities of our minds and of phenomena. Second, she introduces us to the nature of coemergent wisdom through her manifestation, which is blazing heat. Attachment and suffering in our lives have generated tremendous turmoil and obsession, which we experience as a burning sensation in the mind. This is aptly described in the early tradition, in which fire is a favorite image to describe mental anguish. It is said that as the Buddha sat under the tree of awakening, he surveyed the world around him and saw that it was burning with the fires of lust, hatred, and delusion. As he taught this in the famous "Fire Sermon," he recited a litany detailing the psychological experience of suffering:

> Bhikkhus, all is burning. And what is the all that is burning? Bhikkhus, the eye is burning, visible forms are burning, visual consciousness is burning. . . . Burning with what? Burning with the fire of lust, with the fire of hate, with the fire of delusion; I say it is burning with birth, aging and death, with sorrows and lamentations, with pains, with griefs, with despairs.[42]

As his litany continued, also burning are the ear, nose, tongue, body, and mind—all of experience. The goal, he suggested in his first teachings, was to extinguish (*nirodha*) those flames. The practice in the early tradition, best preserved in Theravāda Buddhism, is to extinguish the flame by removing desire (*tṛṣṇā*) and ignorance (*avidyā*), thus cutting the continuity of saṃsāra. This required scrupulous mindfulness over lifetimes of practice governed by strict vows and retreat from worldly concerns.[43]

This approach to the intensity of suffering is a necessary foundation for developing sufficient stability and merit to go further. But merely retreating from saṃsāra might be seen from a Mahāyāna perspective as turning one's back on the sufferings of the world. Tibetan Buddhism cultivated a foundation of renunciation upon which is built the motivation to benefit others, and this compassionate inspiration serves as the central impetus for meditation practice.

Tibetan Vajrayāna practice is based on three levels of vows, all of which must be observed in order to progress along the path. The *prātimokṣa* vow is foundational, emphasizing physical discipline in one's behavior to avoid harming others or oneself. It is based on refraining from impulse and emotionalism as the cause of negative actions. The bodhisattva vow builds on this vow. It is a commitment to benefiting others directly, serving them through the cultivation of compassion and placing their needs before one's own. The tantric vow is based upon the first two but intensifies their actual accomplishment by introducing the samaya vow: commitment to the tantric guru and to practicing his or her oral instructions and fulfilling his or her intentions. This vow deems it imperative to embrace the intensity of suffering; one commits to seeing wisdom within what is usually considered confusion and to experiencing one's world as a sacred maṇḍala. The motivation for this is based on a commitment to liberate oneself and others in one lifetime.[44]

Examining the understanding of heat in Vajrayāna gives insight into tantra's somewhat different embrace of classical Buddhist imagery. From this perspective, the experience of mental burning is indeed the central suffering of our lives. It is the experiential dimension of the intensity of our obscurations, whether emotional, conceptual, or habitual. But rather than attempting to put out the flames with meditation methods, it is important to allow the burning to occur during practice. Certainly in the foundational stages of the path we must learn not to become engulfed in the flames, to tame the wild mind and emotions, and to train ourselves to open further to experience. Finally, however, through Vajrayāna practice under the guidance of a guru, the burning we experience becomes a great teacher and a great blessing.

This means that when intensity arises, we resist the temptation to reject it; instead, we open to it and allow it to scorch us, waking us up further and further. Whenever there is heat, there is pain and confusion, but there is also wisdom present. The sheer intensity of this unbearable situation cuts through all our denial and defenses, and confusion clears up on its own. Nāropa used the analogy of a huge snake tangled in a knot. It is useless to try to uncoil the snake ourselves—it will only tighten itself against our attempts. If we throw the snake into the air, it will uncoil naturally. Emotional suffering, which thrives on avoidance, burns up in the fire if we can remain in the flames. And we discover the clear, selfless wisdom inherent in that moment.

This is the kind of training undertaken by the great adepts of the past. When Kucipa was tortured with the pain from a large goiter, his guru Nāgārjuna instructed him in two stages. First, he was to meditate that the goiter was growing larger, as an expression of creation-phase meditation. This practice only increased Kucipa's agony. Then he was to meditate that the entire world was contained in his goiter, the completion phase. When Kucipa did this, the goiter disappeared, and he was relieved and happy. Then Nāgārjuna appeared and sang this song:

Pleasure and pain come from assertion and negation.
Free yourself from these extreme concepts
And what is the difference between pleasure and pain?
Experience the emptiness of every separate situation.[45]

Hearing this, Kucipa attained realization and became a great teacher.

A simple way to experience this is to work with an intense and burning emotion such as desire.[46] The instruction when one feels intense lust is to experience the power of the desire itself. Identify the object of desire and the plotline surrounding it. If one is attracted to a gorgeous man and constructs an elaborate fantasy about him, the instruction is to let go of the fantasy, let go of the vision of the man, and contemplate the lust or desire itself. Whenever the fantasy returns, let it go, and return to the feeling of desire. Then the nature of desire will be experienced directly. This practice is described briefly by the great nonsectarian meditation master of the nineteenth century, Jamgön Kongtrül Lodrö Thaye. He wrote that the exceptional approach from the Mahāmudrā tradition is based upon relating directly to desire:

When desirous thoughts arise vividly,
looking directly at their essence, they subside in themselves.
This is the dawning of the Great Seal, bliss and emptiness
inseparable.

> *It is also called the pristine wisdom of discernment.*
> *There has never been anything to reject, nor to accept,*
> *nor to transform; everything is contained within mind.*
> *Know that there is no other intention of buddha*
> *than simply the uncontrived mind itself.*[47]

The inner ḍākinī embodies the intense heat of emotional suffering in the coemergent sense. While she represents ultimate selflessness or emptiness, she also symbolizes the unbearability of confusion against the backdrop of emptiness. She arises from space very hot, exposing any attempt to barricade ourselves into the cozy fortress of self-cherishing. She exposes the heat inherent in our experience, accentuates it, and heightens it. She is said to "dwell in the heart of saṃsāric chaos,"[48] expressing the intensity directly and powerfully in her dance, shocking the practitioner into seeing coemergence constantly.

In this context, the ḍākinī is depicted as the trickster who appears as an embodiment of the practitioner's emotional life and mind, teasing and harassing and showing the way to liberation:

> The playful maiden is all-present. She loves you. She hates you. Without her your life would be continual boredom. But she continually plays tricks on you. When you want to get rid of her, she clings. To get rid of her is to get rid of your own body—she is that close. In Tantric literature this is referred to as the ḍākinī principle. The ḍākinī is playful. She gambles with your life.[49]

In this way, through coemergent wisdom the practitioner recognizes the Great Mother Prajñāpāramitā directly in the gaze and dance of the ḍākinī. Even while she expresses furiously the heat and intensity of the emotional and physical world, the nonconceptual quality of space reigns everywhere.

Vajrayoginī, the Coemergent Mother

The queen of all ḍākinīs in the Tibetan Buddhist pantheon is Vajrayoginī (Dorje Naljorma), the preeminent tantric form of the female buddha. She is important in all the tantric lineages of Tibet and is said to have directly transmitted her teachings through the siddhas Nāropa, Maitripa, and Indrabhuti.[50] Her practice is considered a vanguard of all the tantras, but she is particularly connected in the new translation school (Sarma) with

Vajrayoginī, the Coemergent Mother, dances in a circle of flames.

Anuttara-yoga-tantra, the Unsurpassable Meditation approach that is the highest of the four orders of tantra.

Vajrayoginī's most important manifestation is as a meditational deity (yidam), in which she appears in the classical dancing (kartap) ḍākinī form. In order to accomplish her realization, the meditator must complete special yogic preliminaries and receive empowerment from an authorized tantric guru. To understand the context of her maṇḍala, it is important to lay a foundation of Vajrayāna and the Three Roots.

The ḍākinī is no mere historical artifact of the Vajrayāna Buddhist tradition. She is an active player in the practice of the yogin or yoginī of all times in her roles as one of the Three Roots, the dynamic energy cells of tantric practice. In Tibetan tantra, the Three Roots (*tsasum*) are the sources of all power in practice; they surpass in importance even the Three Jewels (*könchok sum, triratna*) of Buddha, dharma, and saṅgha.[51] The Three Roots are the umbilical cord for the practice of tantra, nourishing the essential points of practice and leading to the goal of enlightenment. As Patrul Rinpoche wrote in *The Way of Great Perfection:*

> *Crowned with the three jewels of the outer refuge*
> *You have truly realized the three roots, the inner refuge;*
> *You have made manifest the three kāyas, the ultimate refuge.*
> *Peerless teacher, at your feet I bow.*[52]

The Three Roots are guru, yidam, and protector. Of these three, the guru is the most important, for the actual teacher is the living, earthy embodiment of awakening itself. It might be possible to idealize or romanticize the Buddha, keeping the actuality of realization at arm's length. The living teacher proclaims to the student through his or her very existence that awakening is not only possible but immediate for every living being. The guru transmits the specific instructions that uncover and display this awakening. In so doing, the guru personally concentrates all the blessings of the lineage of realized teachers, who act as supports and sponsors of their spiritual descendants. Beginning Vajrayāna practitioners visualize a huge tree with spreading branches in which are seated the figures of the lineage gurus, all of whom are facing the student, witnessing and supporting the practices they have passed on. Enthroned at the base of the branches, at the crest of the trunk, is the root guru who channels the blessings of the lineage to the student. Hence, the root guru (*tsawe lama*) is considered the root of blessings, the creator of an immediate environment soaked with direct awakening. These blessings are accessed through the practitioner's devotion.

The second root, the meditational deity or yidam visualized in Vajrayāna practice, represents awakening, in peaceful or wrathful form corresponding to the practitioner's nature. Initiation to the sacred maṇḍala of the yidam is given by the guru, and so the yidam is an extension of the guru's mind. This means that the essence of the guru's mind is embodied in the yidam practice, and through propitiating the yidam the practitioner strengthens her or his relationship with the enlightened guru. The yidam is considered the root of accomplishment or success in one's practice. More will be said about the yidam later.

The protector is the third root of Vajrayāna practice. Protectors are the root of all action, which means that they fulfill the enlightened activity of the lineage of realized ones. In the Nyingma tradition, the specific protector is the ḍākinī, for it is she who specifically protects the secret oral transmission of the lineage of gurus; in the Sarma traditions, the protectors are many, including the ḍākinī and all the variety of spirits bound by oath by great yogis and yoginīs to protect the dharma. There are many dharma protectors in the Tibetan pantheon who guard the growth and success of the sūtra teachings or aid the practitioner in specific meditation practices.

The ḍākinī, in her various guises, serves as each of the Three Roots. She may be a human guru, a vajra master who transmits the Vajrayāna teachings to her disciples and joins them in samaya commitments. The wisdom ḍākinī may be a yidam, a meditational deity; female deity yogas such as Vajrayoginī are common in Tibetan Buddhism. Or she may be a protector; the wisdom ḍākinīs have the special power and responsibility to protect the integrity of oral transmissions.

Criticisms of the guru tradition in Tibetan Buddhism often target the preponderance of males in the lineage. In my years as a meditation instructor, I have often seen women tāntrikās in distress about the difficulty of accomplishing the practice when the message conveyed by the lineage tree is that only men become enlightened. But this is not insurmountable. With a deep understanding of gender in Tibetan tantra, the guru is seen in a new way. When one understands the human guru—whether male or female—to be inseparable from the ḍākinī, then one is closest to the qualities of the inseparable Three Roots.

Certainly, Tibet's tülku tradition is patriarchal in the sense that women tülkus and lineage holders are rare. However, patriarchal institutional patterns in Tibet[53] are undergirded by a spirituality that places great emphasis upon the feminine as a source of wisdom and power. In my experience, patriarchy is a conditional and circumstantial cultural pattern that is not embedded in the essence of Tibetan Buddhist spirituality. It is important to cultivate a spirituality that draws from the inseparability of the guru and ḍākinī and to eventually transcend any fixation upon gender whatsoever.

Personal experience of the ḍākinī principle is most available to the practitioner when the ḍākinī serves as a yidam, for a long-term relationship is established in which the instruction of the ḍākinī becomes deep and abiding. As the adept Kaṅkāripa sang to his yidam:

My ḍākinī-woman, my queen, my lady!
The visible form of my pure awareness,
Form not separate from me, nor yet a part of me,
The phenomenal appearance of empty space;
She is beyond compare and beyond words.[54]

The ḍākinī as yidam is the projected form of the pure wisdom of the practitioner's own mind, identical with the mind of the guru, and can be said to be part of her or him, yet separate.

The supreme wisdom ḍākinī who serves as a yidam (*iṣṭa-devatā*) of the higher tantras is Vajrayoginī, "the personification of vajra emptiness."[55] *Yidam* is a shortened form of *yid-kyi-damtsik,* or sacred bondage of the mind. The practice of the yidam deity in her or his maṇḍala is what binds the practitioner irrevocably to the enlightened sanity within.[56] The yidam is given to the practitioner by the guru in an empowerment (abhiṣeka, *wang*) and serves as the constant presence and reminder of the guru's mind and instructions.

It is said that the guru and the yidam are inseparable and that the sacred bondage of Vajrayāna practice is the choiceless commitment to the guru and yidam simultaneously, which is another way of saying commitment to one's own indestructible nature or inherent wakefulness. Vajrayoginī deity yoga practice comes from the Mother Tantra cycle of Anuttara-yoga-tantras, a body of teachings that place special emphasis upon devotion as the foundation of tantric practice. For this reason, the deity yoga practice of Vajrayoginī depends upon one-pointed devotion to the guru, the vajra master, who has completely realized the vajra nature of all phenomena and is empowered to transmit this understanding to others. Because the guru has realized indestructible truth, he or she has fully uncovered the feminine principle (and the masculine principle, for that matter) in personal experience. In giving the student a ḍākinī or heruka as yidam, the guru is giving the student an aspect of the guru's own mind (which is also already an aspect of the student's mind), empowering the student to join fully with the practice.

The common theme in these higher tantras is that the inner wisdom ḍākinī always signifies the wisdom-mind, the pure and radiant space that is the nature of mind itself, as well as the wisdom that knows the complete nature of that space in a nondual way. Because of her wisdom orientation, the practice of the feminine yidam is said to yield quick results.[57] The specific way in which the ḍākinī manifests wisdom varies from tantra to tantra, but in the *Cakrasaṃvara-tantra* Vajrayoginī's meaning can be seen in her iconography.

The yidam Vajrayoginī is visualized in semiwrathful style, fiery red in color because red is the color of Mother Prajñāpāramitā. She is naked, with charnel ground ornaments, because she is "untouched by the neurosis of kleśas, with no armour of ego to clothe her."[58] Since she dwells in the charnel ground of egocentrism, she stands on the chest and lower face of a decaying corpse.

As a wisdom ḍākinī, Vajrayoginī carries a hooked knife (*kartari, triguk*) known as the hook of mercy,[59] the weapon of nonthought that cuts the deceptions of self-cherishing. Nonthought (*togme*) is the most basic expression of Vajrayoginī, for her mind is completely free from subconscious chatter and from the habitual patterns that give rise to obsessive thought patterns. Nonthought is a purified form of ignorance or bewilderment, traditionally symbolized in Buddhism by a pig. In this sādhana, the ḍākinī is secretly known as the Vajra Sow, or Vajravārāhī, for her ignorance is completely transformed into freedom, the wisdom of limitless space. As the sādhana praises her, "Your sow's face shows nonthought, the unchanging dharmakāya."[60] To remind us of this, Vajrayoginī's loosed and flowing hair partially conceals the head of a sow rising from near her right ear. The nonthought qualities of Vajrayoginī harken to her secret dimensions of nondual wisdom and space, for she has no allegiance to emotional upheavals, interpretations, or habits of any kind. She is completely concentrated on the source of everything (chöjung), the vast space that is her basic nature, the rootless root of thoughts and emotions. Her three eyes radiate unbiased clarity. In this aspect, she is the vast and limitless mind of the Buddha.

The other most important quality of Vajrayoginī is her intense heat. She blazes in two ways: she is wrathful and she is passionate. Her most obvious manifestation is threatening. She is brilliant red in color because she is "enraged against the hordes of māras," the forces that would draw us into worldly concerns. When she defeats the māras, she is defeating tendencies toward self-cherishing. Her fangs are clenched in rage as she bites her lower lip, and her hair streams upward. As a semiwrathful deity, she has the power to immediately cut off emotional and conceptual obscurations using her hooked knife. Her wakefulness is so sharp and penetrating that it is perceived as threatening to habitual patterns.

Vajrayoginī is also associated with passion, "the wrath of passion," which fiercely burns the fuel of emotional obscurations. Hers is passion in the coemergent wisdom sense—it is unconditional freedom from lust. With her passionate appearance, she magnetizes the practitioner and intoxicates while she consumes; in her left hand she carries a skull-cup holding liquor that intoxicates concepts into nonthought. Around her neck she wears two seductive garlands, one of fresh red flowers, signifying nonattachment, and one of fifty-one freshly severed heads, each exhibiting a different expression, representing the fifty-one emotional obscurations, which she has cut off before they arise.[61]

In her wild dance, she warmly cradles in the crook of her left arm a beautifully fashioned full-length staff (*tse-sum, khaṭvāṅga*) with an eight-sided shaft, the hidden representation of her consort Cakrasaṃvara. Without this staff, she is not complete, for the feminine principle is merely one aspect of the realized mind.[62] In her form as wisdom ḍākinī, she is never without her staff, which is adorned with an elaborate scarf with two furls, representing the inseparability of the Mahāyāna and Vajrayāna teachings. At the top of the staff is a double vajra scepter, below which are impaled three skulls. The bleached skull on top expresses the dharmakāya, the rotting head below it the sambhogakāya, and the freshly severed head the nirmāṇakāya, showing the inseparability of the three.

Vajrayoginī has three eyes that know the past, present, and future, signifying omniscience. The appearance of these eyes is associated with Prajñāpāramitā, for wisdom is associated iconographically with eyes. But in her case, as "knower of the past, present and future, she rolls her three furious bloodshot eyes."[63] The eyes of the yoginī are said to gaze into fathomless space and to exhibit the qualities of nonthought. In the creation of Tibetan painted scrolls (*tangkas*), the detail of the deity's gaze is left until the final moment and is completed by a guru, who blesses it with the subtle flourish of the brush.

Vajrayoginī completely manifests the qualities of the secret ḍākinī, even as she embodies the inner ḍākinī. She is known as Prajñāpāramitā in her Vajrayāna aspect. The limitless wisdom nature of the mind cannot be explained in conventional language. It can only be expressed evocatively, through praise, ritual, and iconography, which in this case is the practice of Vajrayoginī. It can be experienced, however, and this experience gives rise to devotion.

Alternate Forms of Vajrayoginī

In addition to various epithets that describe her multifaceted nature, Vajrayoginī also has alternate forms. The continuity among these forms is her personification of Prajñāpāramitā as a wisdom ḍākinī. In each of these manifestations, she embodies the realization of phenomena's ultimate emptiness of inherent existence expressed in the passionate and wrathful form of a feminine yidam.

In the Cakrasaṃvara tradition, the form closest to Vajrayoginī is Vajravārāhī, the Vajra Sow. Vajravārāhī is the more wrathful aspect of the wisdom ḍākinī and is often depicted in union with the heruka Cakrasaṃvara. In Indian Buddhism, the sow symbolized the defilement of ignorance that blinded the practitioner to the nature of reality. In her manifestation as the Vajra Sow, Vajravārāhī's ignorance is completely transformed into freedom, the wisdom of limitless space that instantly liberates all defilements. Vajravārāhī's iconography is very similar to that of Vajrayoginī, but she often has more prominent fangs and a more wrathful expression, and she prominently displays a sow's head above her right ear. In other forms of Vajravārāhī, the ḍākinī is depicted in an even more overtly wrathful manner associated with the Hindu and Newari Buddhist forms of Chinnamastā, who severs her own head as blessing.[64]

Another distinctive form related closely to Vajrayoginī is Nairātmyā, together with Hevajra the central deities of the *Hevajra-tantra.* Her name means "selflessness in feminine form." As the *Hevajra-tantra* says of her, "No form may one apply to her, neither tall nor short, neither square nor round. She transcends all taste and smell and flavour, and it is she who

Passionate Kurukullā draws her bow.

brings (coemergent joy)."[65] Nairātmya is also considered a representation of Prajñāpāramitā, and as a wisdom ḍākinī she is depicted with charnel ground ornaments, wrathful demeanor, and third eye. Her distinctive iconographic qualities are her blazing red hair and her sky-blue color.

Kurukullā is yet another form of Vajrayoginī, one that especially magnetizes passion and transforms it into wisdom. Like Vajayoginī she is depicted as red and blazing with flames, in dancing posture, holding in her hands the emblematic hooked knife and skull-cup of amṛta, together representing the union of bliss and emptiness. Her ornaments of bone and jewels are similar to Vajrayoginī's, but she does not hold the khaṭvāṅga trident staff. In additional hands she draws a flower-bedecked bow set with an arrow and holds other weapons that indicate her unique identity. She shoots her victims with the arrow in order to infect them with passion, thereby subduing discursive thought; with the hook in her lower right hand she draws the practitioner close; the lasso in her lower left hand trusses the practitioner's passion, transforming it into wisdom. She dances on the corpse of the self, signifying her selfless activity.[66]

The most wrathful form of the yidam Vajrayoginī is Tröma Nagmo, (Kālikā, Wrathful Black Lady). She is particularly associated with the Chö practice, a tantric meditation discipline based on the Prajñāpāramitā that is particularly effective in cutting through (*chö*) self-cherishing and emotional obscurations. These teachings have diverse strands traced back to Indian Buddhism, but the founder of the Tibetan tradition was the great yoginī Machik Lapdrön (1055–1153 C.E.).[67] Tröma Nagmo is the supremely wrathful manifestation of Vajravārāhī, with the large and grunting head of a black sow protruding from just behind her right ear, amid brilliant orange hair that streams upward. She is blue-black, with one face and two hands holding a hooked knife and a skull-cup of blood. Her mouth is open and her tongue curled, and her three eyes blaze. She wears a tiger skin around her waist and dances in the posture of Vajrayoginī, holding a khaṭvāṅga in the crook of her arm and wearing charnel ground ornaments in a blazing mass of fire. Tröma Nagmo herself is called the "innate energy of compassion," the "great sovereign mother of basic space."[68]

She is depicted with a vast and colorful retinue of ḍākinīs who express her manifold activities and yogic accomplishments.[69] Specifically, practice of her ritual destroys attachment to one's body, emotions, and identity through the visualized offering of one's own body in the charnel ground.

Is Vajrayoginī a Goddess?

Western interpreters have called Vajrayoginī and other major ḍākinīs of the Tibetan tradition goddesses. Certainly there are ways in which this label may be applicable, but it is important to identify the perils of some interpretations.

The Western feminist spirituality movement has centered on the experience of what is called "the goddess," but there appears to be a broad spectrum of understanding about just what that term means. Literature on the subject ranges from assertion of one central goddess who manifests in different forms, to a bevy of goddesses who may or may not be related. Generally, however, the goddess in whatever form symbolizes those feminine values that have been objectified by patriarchal culture, including the sanctity of nature and the earth, embodiment and sexuality, birthing and nurturing. "What gets soiled, rots, and dies (and is also born anew), what is female and fleshly, is precisely what is most valued in feminist spirituality."[70] Most of all, the goddess is every woman with all the varieties and complexities in which women abide.[71]

Spurred by broader interest in goddess traditions, scholarly study of goddesses in the history of religions and gender studies has flourished.[72] But in these studies, goddesses are understood as culturally constructed religious symbols with multivalent meanings that adorn a variety of religious rituals. These goddesses can be understood primarily within the cultures in which they are worshipped, and there is a tremendous range in their characteristics; that is, they represent qualities that do not fall within a narrow cultural stereotype of "feminine" traits. David Kinsley wrote, "Some goddesses have nothing to do with motherhood, fertility or the earth. Others play traditionally male roles and often seem to take delight in violating roles that are associated with women in the cultures in which they are revered. Some goddesses . . . provide paradigms for female subordination to males."[73]

Many times it is assumed that if a deity is female, her gender is the dominant factor in how she appears and how she is revered. But gender studies have shown that goddesses have relevance in the religious lives of both women and men, not necessarily counteracting the effects of patriarchy in an overt way. However, in patriarchal societies, men and women may use and understand goddesses and feminine symbols somewhat differently. When a man reveres a goddess, his practice may require his taking on her gender and giving up his male identity, privilege, and perspective; needing to make no such imaginative jump, women may have a simpler, more direct access to the goddess.[74]

The influences of the feminist spirituality movement are clear in the work of Miranda Shaw, who spoke of Vajrayoginī as a tantric Buddhist goddess in a gynocentric cult in which "proper homage to women is a prerequisite to [a man's] enlightenment."[75] Shaw accorded Vajrayoginī a divine femaleness that appears ontologically based and that favors women and threatens men who do not defer to her. And into the mouth of Vajrayoginī she places the command to worship women exclusively.[76] This interpretation bears little resemblance to the Vajrayoginī of Anuttara-yoga-yāna.

In an opposite assessment, Adelheid Herrmann-Pfandt considered whether the ḍākinī was a goddess in a way that privileged women, concluding that in the early tradition in Tibet female yidams uniquely empowered women. She and June Campbell concluded that eventually ḍākinīs like Vajrayoginī were subverted within the patriarchy of Tibetan Buddhism.[77] For them, Vajrayoginī became a creation of patriarchal oppression that idealized and objectified women's bodies and energies in a form that served male spirituality. From this perspective, Campbell argued that practices like Vajrayoginī are actually dangerous for women, deepening the exploitation and disempowerment wrought by patriarchal structures. The only alternative could be a "female-centred symbolic, articulated in the context of a *female* subjective"[78]—the creation of goddess symbols by women for women. That too is a departure from the Tibetan Vajrayoginī tradition.

If we are to consider Vajrayoginī a goddess, the methods of the history of religions and gender studies may aid in describing her meaning more accurately in a Tibetan context than those of feminist spirituality. In Anuttara-yoga-yāna, Vajrayoginī appears in feminine form in order to point out an inherent quality of the mind beyond gender; both men and women are to do the practice in order to realize this quality. She is Prajñāpāramita, the feminine manifestation of wisdom who has the power to transmit this understanding to her devotees.

There are, however, other problems in depicting Vajrayoginī as a goddess, and these have been addressed by other scholars. Rita Gross, carefully laying theological ground, suggested that in Buddhism the concept of goddess appears against a background of nontheism, which means that there is no external supreme being, and further that "religious symbols and doctrines have utility rather than truth."[79] Giving the background of the three interpenetrating bodies of enlightenment (*kāya*s), she explains the goddess as a "mythic manifestation" on the sambhogakāya level. Within these qualifications, Gross asserted that the term *goddess* may properly refer to Vajrayoginī. Taking a more cautious route, Anne Klein argued that the femaleness of Yeshe Tsogyal (manifesting as Vajrayoginī) arose from a particular cultural setting with perhaps little relevance for Western understandings of gender. In fact, there may not be anything distinctly and meaningfully "feminine" about her from any single cultural perspective. Because of this, Klein hesitated to offer her as an example of a "goddess" of any kind.[80]

Within Tibetan Buddhism there is no real equivalent to "gods" and "goddesses" as existent beings with salvific power. Instead, Vajrayoginī is understood to be a yidam, a personal meditational deity, a potent ritual symbol simultaneously representing the mind of the guru and lineage of enlightened teachers, and the enlightened mind of the tantric practitioner. Recognizing the inseparability of these two is the ground of tantric practice.

Deity yoga, or yidam practice, works in a direct, pragmatic way to challenge the practitioner's conventional dualistic tendencies in relating with phenomena. Habitually, humans centralize their dreams and desires into a constructed personality and operate a campaign to fulfill those wishes from within that habit of self-cherishing. This campaign is built on a duality in which the habit of self-cherishing fashions a centralized subjectivity that thrives on objectifying everything else and manipulating its relationship with those objects. According to Buddhism, once the scenario is set, the subject wishes to possess the object, expel it, ignore it, or some combination of these extreme tendencies.[81] This kind of subjectivity creates constant suffering, for the split between subject and object is intractable as the subject's constant yearning for a particular relationship with the object is frustrated.[82]

In Anuttara-yoga-tantra and the higher tantras, deity yogas in the creation phase are self-visualization practices, in which the practitioner visualizes herself or himself as the central diety of an elaborate, elegant maṇḍala.[83] The yidam, however, can be visualized precisely because she does not exist inherently. This practice develops an experience of subjectless subjectivity in a ritual form, using the dualistic tendencies of mind in a way that highlights and purifies them, laying the ground for more nonreferential forms of subjectivity.

Vajrayoginī-sādhana is just such a self-visualization practice for empowered, authorized practitioners. The ritual is conducted in the traditional way of a complete Vajrayāna sādhana. It opens with the invocation of space, or experiential emptiness, through an appropriate mantra. The recitation of the mantra is correlated with the inner practice of letting go of preconceptions and expectations about oneself or the practice, as well as stray thoughts and distractions brought to the meditation session. Then the practitioner establishes the boundaries of the prescribed maṇḍala, visually constructs the seat of the yidam, and propitiates the yidam through the classic preliminaries of refuge and bodhisattva vows and the four foundation (*ngöndro*) practices.

Eventually, the practitioner makes the radical shift to becoming the yidam, which means visualizing himself or herself as the central deity of the maṇḍala. The term *visualize* is the translation of the Tibetan *mikpa,* which means to contemplate, focus, or meditate upon. In a Western cultural context, this can be difficult at first because there are so few analogs in our religious and mythic traditions. But with practice, visualization becomes a spontaneous and powerful experience of overcoming duality.[84] It entails a major shift in one's habitual way of understanding a deity as external.

Deity yoga is based upon the message of maṇḍala principle: the fundamental insight of tantra is that the nature of our minds and of all phenomena in our experience is completely empty, pure, and awakened. Of course, we do not necessarily see this very often, and so the creation-phase practice of deity yoga reminds us directly and experientially. In this case, we might yearn for a deity or savior to confirm us or bless us, helping us overcome our sense of pain, oppression, and inadequacy. And if we are women who feel deprived of subjectivity, we might yearn for a female goddess whom we could emulate or who could model an experience of female being, albeit in a divine form.

Deity yoga bursts this yearning by requiring us to become the deity, overcoming the conventional subject-object duality. We cannot hold the full bloom of enlightenment at bay. We must acknowledge the inherent enlightenment in ourselves, at this very moment, and we must acknowledge it literally, by taking on the prescribed purified form of the meditational deity. Of course, there are tremendous dangers in doing this. The self-cherishing tendencies that we have cultivated so consistently in our lives would love nothing more than to be deified. Perhaps my deeply invested femaleness cultivated through feminist sensibilities might like being a liberated, dancing, naked ḍākinī. But the ritual of Vajrayoginī has safeguards and antidotes for this misguided motivation.

The most important antidote to using the practice to fortify self-cherishing tendencies is the traditional instruction to cultivate the pride of the deity (*lhe ngagyal*). This means that, having properly invoked the experience of emptiness and having earnestly and humbly venerated the deity in the preliminaries of the practice, one has ritually divested oneself of the habitual patterns of self-cherishing. Then, in the self-visualization, the practitioner must completely maintain the profound sense of actually being the deity, with full confidence in the utterly pure nature of one's mind and experience. This is quite different from ordinary pride, in which one "fakes" one's greatness in the manner of taking on a role or costume.[85] The power of the ritual and the intensity of the visualization practice embarrass the habitual self into yielding to the more fundamental experience of inherent enlightenment. And it is this aspect of the practitioner that becomes the deity.

But the most direct experience of deity yoga is that of subjectless subjectivity, a purified subjectivity that ritually builds an alternative to the mind's dualistic tendencies. From the point of view of ordinary subjectivity, self-visualization as the deity radically subjectivizes the experience of the divine in the Buddhist sense. This means that Vajrayoginī's wrathful passion, her blazing wisdom, her joining of seeming opposites, and her fearlessness are not "hers" in an external sense. They are the practitioner's. When aggression arises, it becomes a jeweled ornament; when concepts arise, they become a hooked knife of nonthought, cutting concepts at their root. Deity yoga is a direct method of overcoming the conventional duality of subject and object with relation to concepts of deity, and transmuting the practitioner's emotional obscurations and thoughts into coemergent wisdom.

Self-visualization practice has special power in overcoming misconceptions regarding gender.[86] When the Vajrayoginī practitioner becomes the deity fully and completely, the experience of his or her body is transformed. Before receiving the empowerment, one might be fascinated or horrified by self-visualization. For women, the fascination might be at finally becoming a divine woman; for a man, it might be at becoming the "other," the objectified female body upon which he is accustomed to projecting. The empty, luminous form of the deity is not an existent female body, yet it appears in vivid and dynamic female form. We realize that all women, all beings for that matter, appear in their bodies as emanations: "while they are not women in reality, they appear in the form of women."[87]

On the first level of transformation, the subjectivity of the practitioner is transformed by the simple act of becoming the "other" of one's projected emotions, thoughts, and sense perceptions. Usually, our thought patterns are reinforced by our tendency to project onto the other. Desire is fueled by thoughts concerning the desirability of the object; aggression becomes palpable when the mind holds the object of hatred. But this time the object is a deity whose nature is obviously empty of inherent existence, a hollow body of light like a rainbow. The practitioner is instructed to let go of self-preoccupation and become the deity, dissolving conventional subject-object distinctions. It is liberating to conventional views of gender to experience oneself in the empty and luminous body of a tantric female (or male) buddha.

The experience of the subjectivity of the deity becoming one's own subjectivity shifts the emphasis away from the contents of one's experience to their source or ground. But one cannot become Vajrayoginī fully and completely without experiencing her in her nature. She is called "the personification of vajra emptiness"[88]—empty of inherent nature, limitless space, iconographically represented by the source of phenomena (chöjung). But this space is not merely empty; it is radiant luminosity, the natural clarity of the mind. This next level of nondual subjectivity is generated in deity yoga by dissolving the self-visualization.

At the end of the creation phase, the practitioner dissolves the visualization of Vajrayoginī back into space. This is the completion phase which is said to undermine the practitioner's clinging to the visualized deity. The maṇḍala of Vajrayoginī is understood to be a skillful means that leads the practitioner from a conventional view to a more direct experience of the ultimate nature. At this point the practitioner realizes what Jamgön Kongtrül Lodrö Thaye taught:

In general, creation stage is a contrivance,
but the path of contrivance leads to the authentic natural state.
With the mental conviction of the lack of reality in the root or
ground of deluded grasping to deluded appearance,
resting in a pristine state is completion stage itself, the actual
natural state.[89]

The essence of wisdom in the Vajrayāna sense is that both the nature of the mind and the objects of our experience are transparently luminous, and direct experience of this clear nature liberates one from all suffering.

Through her ritual, the practitioner discovers that the ḍākinī, especially in her form as the Coemergent Mother Vajrayoginī, is the spiritual subjectivity of all beings, whether female or male. In her sādhana, she is called "self-born great bliss, the ultimate Mahāmudrā."[90] She is the realization of nonduality, the inseparability of subject and object, which is great joy. In commenting on her translations of the secret autobiography of Jigme Lingpa, Janet Gyatso quoted the great meditation master His Holiness Dilgo Khyentse Rinpoche in saying that the ḍākinī is actually the autobiographer and that "everything told in secret autobiography, generically, is the ḍākinī's words. The secret life takes place in her domains, and it partakes of her nature."[91] This means that the subjective experience of the spiritual path is always the subjectless experience of the ḍākinī. He went on to suggest that the ḍākinī is the visionary dimension of experience, relating to such elusive aspects of experience as "prophecy, mythic history, past lives, experiences in the central channel, experiences of the ground-of-all."[92] The ḍākinī represents to the practitioner the inner experience of the true nature of the mind and phenomena.

To view Vajrayoginī as an external savior figure is to misinterpret her and to diminish her significance for the Vajrayāna practitioner. Even by attempting to visualize oneself as Vajrayoginī in order to identify with a female divine being, one can never reach her. The practitioner eventually discovers the inherent emptiness and radiant luminosity of the female gender and all concepts, emotional obscurations, and sense perceptions. The significance and power of the ḍākinī far surpasses this; through her, the practitioner discovers the visionary aspect of spiritual experience. Through Vajrayoginī's maṇḍala, the practitioner discovers subjectivity, which, on a secret level, is the vast, limitless space of nonduality. On an inner level, spiritual subjectivity is the coemergent heat of the intense and dynamic play of emotions, perceptions, and thoughts in the vastness of awareness. Cultivating the inseparable ḍākinī is the essence of the spiritual life of the Vajrayāna practitioner.

The Maṇḍala of the Heruka and Ḍākinī: Cakrasaṃvara and Vajrayoginī

The feminine wisdom ḍākinī, signifying emptiness and space, cannot be fully realized unless she is joined with the masculine principle of skillful means, compassion, and great bliss. This is called the union of bliss and emptiness, and it is represented iconographically as the sexual union of male and female consorts. Together they form an inseparable pair, "not two and not one." They can never truly be apart, for penetrating insight and skillful means are interdependent and complete in a Vajrayāna world. In this case, Vajrayoginī is not complete unless she is with her consort, the heruka Cakrasaṃvara. When they appear together, they are symbolically joined in sexual embrace, the "father-mother" *yab-yum.*

Wherever Vajrayoginī appears alone, she carries the full-length staff, the khaṭvāṅga, that represents her consort, Cakrasaṃvara. In the heruka maṇḍala, they are both physically present in union. It is important to understand that in Tibetan Vajrayāna, the feminine is only one side of the dynamic of phenomena. Always, the feminine carries with her the consort, the masculine; conversely, the masculine carries with him the feminine consort. Together they explicitly represent nondual subjectivity. On the inner level, the visualized consorts signify the fundamental nature that arises from the EVAṂ principle described in chapter 3.

The heruka is a completely perfected form because "he" is actually the inseparable pair of "she and he." The heruka is, by definition, in union with the bliss-bestowing consort, and their joined power is expressed in a single manifestation. Chapter 3 discussed the importance of Mahāyāna Buddhism of the union of penetrating insight (sherap, prajñā) and skillful means (thap, upāya). These two are compared to the two wings of a bird, both of which are necessary if spiritual heights are to be experienced. The full meaning of this discussion can be seen in yab-yum iconography. Insight without means is like eyes that see but no legs to carry them to their destination; means without insight is likened to legs that wander aimlessly, knowing not where they go. Means is not skillful unless it is paired with insight; then it becomes a fully empowered skillful means (thabla khepa, upāya-kauśalya), utilizing the vision and the ability together in one unified activity. This is the meaning of the heruka and consort in union as yab-yum.[93]

The yab-heruka, the father Cakrasaṃvara, is semiwrathful and indestrucibly confident, a completely grounded and penetratingly gentle presence. The heruka (trak-thung) is a masculine deity, wrathful or semiwrathful, who represents the dynamic of compassion and skillful means in Tibetan tantra. The heruka traces its origin to the same pre-Buddhist traditions of India as the ḍākinī, in the retinues of wrathful Śiva or Mahākāla

Heruka and Ḍākinī, Cakrasaṃvara and Vajrayoginī, in union.

in which he served as terrifying demon. Heruka literally means "blood-drinker," and in a tantric Buddhist setting this refers to drinking the blood of self-cherishing, doubt, and dualistic confusion.[94] The tantric interpretation of the term *heruka* derives a further meaning: his nature is beyond conventional cause and effect, existence, and duality. He is the ultimate expression of the radiantly selfless qualities of the mind. Having drunk the blood, the heruka experiences bliss. He is fearlessly at home in the charnel ground, and under his gaze it is no longer merely charnel—it is a palace.

The heruka is depicted with nine classical moods (*kartap gu, navarasa*) which gives clues about his manifestation. He is said to be charming, with dazzling ornaments; brave, posing and strutting; threatening, with rolling eyes and a wrathful grimace; laughing, a raucous "*ha, ha*"; fierce, with laughter that mocks, "*hi, hi, hūṃ, phaṭ*"; fearsome, grinding his teeth and brandishing a weapon; compassionate; with bloodshot eyes and radiant skin; outrageous, with gaping mouth and clicking tongue; and peaceful, gently gazing at the tip of his nose.[95] The heruka embodies the mountain-like presence of the enlightened masculine principle in Vajrayāna Buddhism, with its range of fierce, hearty, and gentle qualities.

The heruka and consort are the symbol of the indestructible union of wisdom and skillful means, joining the incisiveness of insight with the expansive radiation of compassion, committed to spontaneously benefiting beings. In joining these two qualities, they are the quintessential hero (*pawo, vīra*), a selfless bodhisattva warrior of compassion. As is said in the *Hevajra-tantra,* "The yogin is the upāya and compassion, the yoginī is [wisdom and śūnyatā], the freedom from cause and effect. The absence of distinction between śūnyatā and compassion is known as bodhicitta."[96] The heruka and consort in union are the Vajrayāna expression of awakened heart, bodhicitta.

The heruka par excellence is Cakrasaṃvara. Ironographically, he occupies the center of an elaborate, ornate palace maṇḍala constructed upon a thousand-petaled multicolored lotus.[97] The palace is an expression of the completely transmuted charnel ground, decorated with precious jewels, exquisite carvings, and ropes of pearls. Cakrasaṃvara himself is depicted as brilliant blue, with one face and three eyes, like his consort able to see the past, present, and future. He wears the charnel ground ornaments of a heruka, including the crown of five dry skulls, a garland of fifty-one freshly severed heads, and human bone ornaments including earrings, a necklace, a crossed sash, armlets, bracelets, and anklets. He wears a tiger skin loosely knotted at his waist, representing the conquest of emotional obscurations. His hair is arranged in a yogic topknot decorated with bone and jewels. He exhibits threatening, wrathful qualities, rolling his eyes and clenching his four fangs in a grimace. But he is also radiant and laughing, exuding charm and playfulness. And he embodies peace and gentleness in a powerful, confident manner.

Cakrasaṃvara stands in heruka posture,[98] with his left leg firmly planted under him, his foot holding down the head of a black demon, who represents the extreme of eternalism. His right leg is extended, with the foot standing between the breasts of a red demoness, who represents the extreme of nihilism. In his right hand he holds a five-pointed vajra scepter and in his left a bell,[99] and they are crossed in embrace around his wisdom consort, Vajrayoginī, who is in his lap with her customary ornaments. Her stance mirrors his, and she embraces him with her head thrown back, holding her hooked knife with the threatening gesture (mudrā, chag-gya). As she gazes up into his face with her head thrown back, they radiate the intense heat of passion, wrath, and utter harmony. They are complete.

The yab-yum, the father and mother in sexual union, is the inner wisdom ḍākinī in her element and also the inner heruka or ḍāka in his element. In tantric terms, she signifies coemergent wisdom and he signifies great bliss (*mahāsukha, dewa chenpo*). When the two are joined together, there is a dynamic vitality to the spiritual practice expressing realization.

In Hindu tantra, this type of iconography of sexual union does not generally appear. Instead, the feminine is usually designated as active and the masculine as passive. Iconographic depictions of divine union have the ferocious feminine deity standing over the supine masculine, frozen in stasis. But in Tibetan Buddhist iconography, the feminine and masculine are not polarized into active and passive.[100] Each has both aspects in different representation. And "stasis lies in separation and alienation (failure to recognize union), while dynamic energy . . . is the result of union."[101] The complementary qualities of the pair are paramount. As not two and not one, they represent aspects of totality that are nondual and reflective of each.

The yab-yum reflects the practitioner's own mind, the perfect joining in intimate embrace of the penetrating insight into emptiness and the compassionate engagement of skillful action. The ḍākinī is spontaneously expressing coemergent wisdom, which sees beyond dualities. The heruka displays the indestructible qualities of great bliss. Just as the passionate couple have surrendered to each other, these aspects of mind have surrendered; just as their self-involvement has dropped away, so has the practitioner's. The insular emotional obscurations have been intoxicated with Vajrayāna passion, and the conceptual mind has vanished. The yab-yum expresses on the inner level the intertwined aspects of the secret EVAṂ and, as we will see in the next chapter, the outer aspects of subtle-body yoga and of karmamudrā, the practice of sexual yoga.

Yab-Yum and Subjectivity

Most iconography of the yab-yum depicts the male consort facing forward while the female's back is seen, with her face in profile. This is true of Cakrasaṃvara and Vajrayoginī. Herrmann-Pfandt cited this as an example of the patriarchal bias of Tibetan Buddhism, suggesting that such a convention elevates the yab to primary status, with the yum often an anonymous counterpart. She claimed that this is also indicated iconographically when the ḍākinī consort is the smaller figure, with fewer heads and arms and less adornment.[102] She suggested that consistently giving preference to the male perspective is not merely a convention but an indication that the deity yoga practices were designed for the male practitioner. Further, she noted that the feminine yidam is given prominence iconographically only when she is depicted alone, without consort.

If Herrmann-Pfandt is right, these aspects of the ritual of deity yoga may again raise questions about the extent to which Tibetan Buddhist practice has been influenced by patriarchy. When men practice the ritual of yab-yum deities, are they enacting a patriarchal dominance of the feminine even while they aspire to overcome conceptuality and bias? Are women who practice the ritual able to establish the spiritual subjectivity necessary to progress in their practice, and if so, how do they do this? And is performing a ritual purportedly tainted with patriarchal bias damaging to women, as feminist critics have suggested?[103]

Certainly, the fact that most Tibetan practitioners of these rituals were men is reflected in many of the extant ritual texts and commentaries. As discussed previously, insofar as these rituals were transmitted and taught within monastic settings, male monks were the anticipated practitioners. However, it is known that nuns, yoginīs, and occasional laywomen practiced them as well, but there is a dearth of supporting commentary reflecting gender differences. Yet even in this context, the male yab was not always the central deity. The central figures are reversed when the ritual demands it.[104] There are also instances in which the positions of the central figures may be exchangeable depending on a variety of circumstances.[105]

Herrmann-Pfandt noted that the yidam Vajravārāhī (the wrathful form of Vajrayoginī) is considered an exception to the patriarchal convention of the male deity taking precedence. In several texts,[106] Vajravārāhī assumes the prominent place as the central deity in *yum-yab* union, with her consort prescribed as yab or thap in her lap but otherwise neither named nor described.[107] In one text, six-armed Vajravārāhī and consort are depicted seated with retinues of reversed yum-yab deities like the principal deities. In a second text, two-armed Vajravārāhī and consort are depicted in *ālīḍha,* or heruka, posture with a stance that mirrors their reversed positions: Vajravārāhī has extended her right leg and wraps her left around the waist of her consort, whose right leg is bent and left leg is extended. Both deities hold hooked knives, and Vajravārāhī also holds a skull-cup, as is customary. The *yab* has only two eyes, just as the *yum* is often depicted as two-eyed.[108]

These practices were probably well known during earlier periods of tantric Buddhism in Tibet. In the Nyingma biography of Yeshe Tsogyal, retinue ḍākinīs offered parts of their own bodies to Vajrayoginī in yum-yab union with her consort, and facing them she snapped her fingers as she accepted these offerings.[109] Tāranātha described the empowerment of the reversed Cakrasaṃvara in the case of the yogin Thakki-nagna-pa, who devotedly practiced the ritual of Hevajra in solitary retreat without success. Despondent, the yogin aspired for a more fortunate birth and threw himself off a cliff. Finding himself unharmed, he suddenly experienced a vision of the lord Nāropa, who told him that since he had not the disposition to realize Hevajra, he should practice the ritual of Cakrasaṃvara. The yogin protested that the Cakrasaṃvara ritual required such elaborate offerings and ritual implements and such refined intellect that he was unable to perform it. In response, Nāropa instead gave him the rituals of Tārā and the "Śaṃvara in union reversed."[110]

The evidence of such rituals shows there is nothing inherent in the convention of yab-yum deity rituals, even if yum-yab rituals never prevailed. Further, if we examine the actual contexts of the rituals, their purposes and intents, we may have a clearer sense of the role of gender in the practice of deity yoga. First, in the Anuttara-yoga-yāna cycle, the self-visualization practice of the yab-yum form of Cakrasaṃvara and Vajrayoginī follows the completion of Vajrayoginī practice. This means that the practitioner first fulfills the ritual commitment of completely identifying with the wisdom ḍākinī Vajrayoginī, sealing this practice with the fire offering. Only then does one practice the yab-yum deity ritual. Because of this sequence, it seems impossible to visualize oneself as Cakrasaṃvara with Vajrayoginī in one's lap as a different being. Because the practitioner has fully identified first with Vajrayoginī in her sādhana, the practice of the deity yoga of the two seems to be two aspects of the same subjectivity described earlier. This is why the yab-yum formulation is spoken of as "not two, not one."

The primary instruction for the practice of the yab-yum yidams is to visualize oneself as both consorts inseparable.[111] The specific instructions vary depending upon the tantra, the lineage of transmission, and the guru. However, if the practitioner becomes too focused on whether to identify with the male or the female figure, the practice becomes far too conceptual to be effective. A typical instruction on this point was given by Ven. Tsoknyi Rinpoche: "You are not male, you are not female; both female and male are visualized together. If you think you're male or if you think you're female, you've completely missed the point because you have lost half of the visualization already."[112] On the inner level, the gender of the deities is transitional, a display without any substance or weight. Through this practice, the practitioner moves to subtler and subtler levels where there is no such thing as male or female, the level of the secret ḍākinī.

When the yab-yum iconography is analyzed only politically, as an expression of male and female power, most of its significance is lost. The central point of the practice is to give up the usual habit of subjectifying or objectifying gender or any other concepts of self and other, and to realize the interdependent play of phenomena as expressions of the natural state. As Jetsünma Chimme Luding, the prominent Sakya woman lama, commented: "When you purify with emptiness, there is no body, not even a world. Then, out of that, you visualize. Whether you have a female or a male deity practice depends on your karma."[113] The value of masculine or feminine yidams has less to do with one's own gender identity and more to do with the power of each individually and together to liberate the practitioner from habitual patterns and self-involvement.

FIVE

The Outer Dakini

THE SUBTLE BODY OF BLISS

From the first, the breaths and channels are the paths
of the ḍākinīs,
Whatever they may do with them,
I trust myself to you.

—YESHE TSOGYAL TO GURU RINPOCHE[1]

AS WE TURN TO the outer ḍākinī, we come to the crux of Vajrayāna, in which the specific physical form and vast, limitless mind are inseparable. The feminine or ḍākinī principle is never merely an abstraction. It manifests in the physical bodies of women and, for that matter, of men. Women are literally embodiments of a fundamental quality of wisdom and are intrinsically sacred. Men likewise embody the basic qualities of compassion and skillful means and are equally sacred. And yet, in their physical embodiment, both men and women share subtle masculine and feminine qualities of phenomena.

This means that all ordinary women are manifestations of the ḍākinī principle by virtue of the fact that they have physical female bodies. The female body has a unique ability to radiate the energy of the ḍākinī, whether or not there is any awareness of this on the part of the woman. On the subtle energetic body level, however, the feminine principle is manifest in the bodies of both men and women, as we shall see. In the sacred outlook of Vajrayāna, physical forms in the world are not merely material objects. They are emanations from pure awareness/space that are the dances of wisdom. And so ordinary women and men are understood by the Vajrayāna practitioner to be displays of awareness arising from the vast and limitless mind.

Tantra and Embodiment

The view of the body and embodiment in Tibetan Buddhism differs in important ways from those found in the current debates in biology, social science, and feminism in the West. Underlying these disciplines is a long tradition of complex and conflicting issues revolving around the materiality of the body. In discourse on the body from Christian medieval theology to the present, the construction of personal identity has an ambivalent relationship with the physical body, which is linked with the divine when animate but degraded when dismembered, decaying, or dead. In Christian theology, the promise of resurrection offered eternal preservation of the body in glory as the believer's spiritual reward. This current in medieval spirituality created theological issues that are still found in contemporary debates concerning the body.[2]

When we understand the body to be incarnate, we cannot imagine who we are separate from our current physical bodies, and spiritual seeking fully engages bodily experience. But when the body is experienced as merely corruptible, subject to decay and death, spiritual yearning entails discarding the decaying body and joining with the transcendent divine. Both of these strains are still evident in the ambivalence with which we in Western culture regard the body. To make these issues more complicated, Christianity also drew on the Augustinian tradition of dualism between body and mind. Later, scientific materialism built on Cartesian splits between mind and body, objectifying the body in a way that made indentification with physical experience difficult. From these dualistic views, physical bodies are seen as inert objects that must be manipulated, replumbed, and repaired when sick, much as one would remodel a house.[3] As a result of this complexity, Western spiritual teachings related to the body vacillate between asceticism and libertinism.

Tibetan Buddhism has its own complex issues with relation to the body, but they revolve around a somewhat different axis. Body permanence is nowhere held up as a spiritual ideal,[4] and while the beautiful and youthful body is admired and the diseased, aged, or deceased body is feared, the universal facts of illness, aging, and death became in Buddhism the most important foundation of spiritual contemplation. It was his encounter with these facts that sent the young prince into his famous renunciation, and their contemplation led to his enlightenment under the branches of a fig tree. When he began to teach as the Buddha, the foundation stone of his teaching was the truth of suffering, its most tangible forms being old age, sickness, and death. Corruptibility of the body was not resisted in Buddhism; rather, its very inescapability became an inspiration, as we discussed in chapter 4 in connection with the charnel ground.

From this tradition, contemplation of the body became a strong theme in Tibetan Buddhism, and such contemplations always involved mentally dissecting the body, seeing its impermanence, and looking for an enduring essence. Retreats in charnel grounds were revived in Tibet and were considered powerful enhancements for practice.[5] But contemplations also focused on one's own body's impermanence, insubstantiality, and lack of inherent existence. When the shepherd boy Sanggye Jhap came to Milarepa with questions concerning the nature of body and mind, the yogin sent him away to contemplate his experience. In reciting the refuge prayer, the yogin asked which takes refuge, the mind or the body? When the boy returned, he observed that neither of them did. When he contemplated the body, he observed:

> Each part, from the head down to the toes, has a name. I asked myself, "Is it the body as a whole which takes refuge?" It cannot be so, for when the mind leaves the body, the latter no longer exists. People then call it a "corpse," and certainly it cannot be called a "refuge-seeker." Furthermore, when it disintegrates, it ceases to be a corpse; therefore it cannot be the body which takes refuge in Buddha. . . .
>
> [Milarepa responded,] When you sought the "I" [last night] you could not find it. This is the practice of non-ego of personality.[6]

In these contemplations, the shepherd discovered that there is no single entity that is the body. For this reason, body (*kāya, ku*) in Tibetan Buddhism is never understood as corporeality, but instead as a collection or aggregate of constituent parts.

The two certainties in human life—that we will die and that we cannot know when or how—personalize the contemplation of impermanence that is at the heart of Buddhist practice.[7] At the same time, the body is said to be precious, for it is only with a human body that enlightenment is possible. Beings take form in a variety of ways, as animals or as denizens of blissful or horrific realms. According to Tibetan traditions, the psychological experiences of these beings allow no respite from anger, bewilderment, jealousy, or bliss. The sheer pervasiveness and constancy of such states of mind block any possibility of awakening. But we human beings experience desire and empathy and can resonate to the intense emotional experiences of all other life realms, and thus have the capacity for compassion. This capacity and its accompanying wisdom yield a more profound perspective on suffering and impermanence, which serves as the seed of awakening. All beings are caught in an endless cycle of extreme emotional states that continue uninterruptedly. Only a penetrating experience of its hopelessness can yield the necessary renunciation, empathy, and confidence to break the cycle. From this point of view, the certain corruptibility of the body provides the necessary incentive for enlightenment.

The human body is precious precisely because it is impermanent, subject to decay and death. It is also the vehicle for the practice of meditation, which provides enough stability and discipline to allow the necessary insight to arise.[8] In Tibet's understanding of embodiment, the physical form does not entail divine incarnation. All phenomena, including the body and mind, are empty of inherent nature and arise interdependently.

Yet the view of embodiment in Tibetan tantra sets it apart from Mahāyāna philosophy. The body and mind are intimately connected, pervading and mirroring each other. Meditation practice is efficacious because the body directly influences the mind, and the mind directly influences the body; the body expresses the mind, and the mind expresses the body. There is no identifiable boundary between body and mind. Their synchronization joins awareness with physicality, transforming both body and mind in awakening. As is said in the *Hevajra-tantra*, awakening is impossible without the body:

> Without bodily form how should there be bliss? Of bliss one could not speak. The world is pervaded by bliss, which pervades and is itself pervaded. Just as the perfume of a flower depends upon the flower, and without the flower becomes impossible, likewise without form and so on, bliss would not perceived.[9]

Experiences of bliss and so forth are integral to realization, and so the body is the essential basis of enlightenment. In tantra, certain physical yogas affect the experiences of the mind, and mental yogas such as visualization affect the body.

Nevertheless, in this interpenetrating display of synchronized body and mind, the mind is primary. It is the mind that binds one to suffering; it is the mind that liberates one from the repetitive pattern of suffering. As Milarepa instructed the shepherd boy:

The body is between the conscious and unconscious state,
while the mind is the crucial and decisive factor!
He who feels sufferings in the lower realms,
is the prisoner of saṃsāra,
yet it is the mind that can free you from saṃsāra.
Surely you want to reach the other shore?
Surely you long for the city of well-being and liberation?
If you desire to go, dear child, I can show
the way to you and give the instructions.[10]

When tantric yoga is performed properly under the guidance of an authentic guru, meditation and wisdom can be activated and the patterns of confusion can be dispelled.

Tantric practice, then, joins body and mind in a way that expresses the fundamental dynamics of embodiment. This experience, however, demands a proper understanding of the nature of our bodies and of embodiment. Misunderstanding the nature of our bodies causes tremendous suffering and confusion, which in turn gives rise to impulsive activities, creating greater harm for ourselves and others. Milarepa gave advice in one of his realization songs concerning proper understanding of the body.[11] This view is presented in three phases: first, the confused person naïvely regards objects as existent; second, the realized person sees objects as dreamlike appearances; but on the ultimate level, all things are seen to be uncreated and pure, having never existed in any way. The first three lines refer to the merely conventional view of the body:

This skandha of form, which is brought about compulsively,[12]
When there is no realization, is a body of the four elements;
Sickness and suffering arise from it.

When we objectify the body in this way, our experience is profoundly affected. Viewing our bodies naïvely, seeing blood, bones, organs, and flesh as in some way permanent or existent, we experience great suffering. When we age or get ill, we become anxious and worried, thinking that this solidly existent, material self is changing and deteriorating, and we are swept into the vortex of hope and fear regarding our bodies and everything physical. This manifests in our society as preoccupation with youth, attractiveness, health, body image, and gender. We become fixated on being men or being women, and we use this preoccupation to engage in a struggle, using sexuality, power, wealth, avoidance, or intelligence to establish an identity. These are all styles of imprisonment, according to Milarepa, and will only culminate in increased anxiety with physical suffering and sickness. The antidote is found in contemplating the insubstantiality of the body, beginning to see how our expectations and concepts of our bodies do not match what we actually experience.

Milarepa suggested a deeper realization of the nature of our bodies as transformed into a visualized meditational deity, the yidam. In this view, we begin to see our physical bodies in a more vital and dynamic way.

> *When there is realization,*
> *it is the form of the deity, which is union.*[13]
> *This reverses ordinary clinging*

In our previous investigations, we saw that the body has shape, form, and impermanent constituent parts, but no inherent existence. Perhaps we then conclude that the body is merely nothing, a view that could lead to discounting the preciousness and power of our human life. Deity yoga in Tibetan Buddhism gives traditional expression to the fundamental sacredness of human life, our enlightened natures. This inherently awake nature has no conditioned existence, but it arises in radiant forms ceaselessly throughout our lives. Tantric meditation practice trains us to see radiant emanations of this kind through creation-phase practice, in which we visualize our physical forms as a yidam. In this practice we typically see our bodies as hollow bodies of light, radiant with shape, color, and posture, clothed in stylistic ways, holding prescribed implements, and ornamented with crowns and jewelry. At the same time, we understand these forms to be insubstantial, like a dream, a rainbow, or a mirage. Through this practice we begin to experience our physical bodies as emanations from space, dreamlike and vivid, yet empty. From this perspective, the physical body is an outer emanation of an inner energetic expression based upon a vast, limitless mind. Then, the clinging associated with an objectified body is transformed, and "this reverses ordinary clinging."

When the great yogins and yoginīs of Tibet understood the body in this way, they displayed their understanding through use of charnel ground ornaments. In iconographic representations they sat on human skin seats, drank from skull-cups of blood, and wore garlands of freshly severed heads. This demonstrated that they had mastered the conventional view of the body through their meditations, and that they knew the single-taste experience (*ekarāsa, ro-chik*) of regarding the body, whether decaying or lovely, as empty and radiant. This is the meaning of charnel ground iconography, as described in chapter 4.[14]

In the final lines of Milarepa's song about the physical body, he proclaimed that the ultimate nature of the body is without inherent existence:

Ultimately there is no body;
It is pure, like the cloudless sky.

The body is free from constructs of male or female, young or old, ugly or beautiful, large or small. It is free from any concept we may have about it.

We can look at any part of the body, such as the hand, and see that the naïve scientific materialistic view is entirely fictitious. This is seen in stages. First, we see that the hand is composite, made up of palm, fingers, joints, nails, and skin. When we look further, we see that every part has many parts as well. The root of the ring finger is made up of epidermis, fatty tissue, bones meeting bones, ligaments, and tendons. And each of those is made up of many parts: cells, molecules, atoms, and so forth. We no longer grasp what the root of the ring finger might be—it is a phenomenon made up of parts, each of which is made up of many more parts.

But this analysis does not express our experience, in which there is exquisite, radiating sensation that can detect heat, proximity, pressure, and weight. When we contemplate in this kind of analytic manner, we are merely deconstructing a scientific materialistic view, and we see the naïve assumptions involved in the experience of the hand. Life radiates from this area of our finger in the same way that a deity arises in a visualization. The living, sensing quality of the hand is a magical emanation, empty but radiant.

Finally, the vibrant vitality of the hand does not change one whit the hand's lack of inherent existence. The experiential quality is unimpeded; my hand is vividly alive, responsive, and unparalleled. Its power to wave, tinker, recoil, or fondle vibrates in every moment. But the ultimate quality of my hand is empty, pure, like a cloudless sky; there is no *thingness* in it to be grasped. It is impossible to cling to that which has no solid existence. In other words, we cannot actually conceptualize what our bodies are. This is not a negation of the physical body; rather it is an affirmation of the phenomenon without any assumptions or conclusions about the nature of our physicality. We understand the nature of our physical bodies to be akin to space, pure and unobstructed. When we develop an unmistaken view of the nature of the physical body, we will also have an unmistaken view of gender, of masculine and feminine, and we will be able to bring our gender preoccupations effectively to the path. For this reason, it is important to deeply understand the nature of embodiment.

The Subtle Body in Tibetan Buddhism

How is the body understood in Tibetan Buddhism? The tradition distinguishes two levels, as described by Milarepa in the previous section. The "gross body" (*lü*)[15] conforms to what is conventionally considered the body; this gross body is undergirded by an energetic body, or the subtle, illusory body (māyadeha, *gyu-lü*), an invisible network through which the consciousness moves in patterns of sensitivity. The patterns of the subtle body reflect feminine and masculine aspects, shared equally by men and women, understood as a continuous dance or interchange of the feminine and masculine principles. This dance can best be understood through Buddhist meditation practice.

Buddhism as a tradition of transformation was built on the foundation of the sitting practice of meditation. When Buddha Śākyamuni took his seat on a mound of fresh *kusá* grass on the east side of a fig tree, he vowed not to rise until he became fully enlightened, free of confusion. There he sat very still, with upright posture, and synchronized his body and mind by bringing his awareness to his physical presence and following the movement of breath in and out of his nostrils. His discursive mind, accustomed to wandering, returned to the presence of simple awareness and dissolved into the present moment of body and mind joined together.

How can body and mind, so seemingly different, be synchronized? The essential link here is what is called the subtle body, sometimes called the mind-body or "body made of mind" (*manomaya-kāya*) in Vajrayāna Buddhism. As the linking factor between the gross physical body and the mind, it is a major vehicle in meditation practice. Synchronization of body and mind is practiced in sitting meditation, and in Vajrayāna it is cultivated through yogic methods that are passed on from guru to disciple.

The subtle body is not really a body; it is much more like the mind. Its fluidity is seen in the way one clings to concepts and emotions and the way one can let them go. Unlike the usual conventions of language, the subtle-body vocabulary expresses a unified understanding of the body-mind complex.[16] The dynamics of the subtle body are liquid, in constantly flowing patterns, impossible to conceptualize. Views of the physical body are transformed by creation-phase practice, leading the practitioner to an experience of the subtle body in completion-phase practice. That subtle body, made of mind, links with an actual state of mind. The lore surrounding the subtle body is abundant, and from lineage to lineage it has sometimes contradictory descriptions associated with a variety of yogic practices. This discussion will explore only the most general sketches of the lore of the subtle body, drawn from the Anuttara-yoga-yāna.

The subtle, illusory body is a supple network of energy channels (*tsa, nāḍī*) that are like invisible pathways radiating from a vertical channel in the spinal area, interlinking the entire body-mind complex. Winds or subtle breath (*lung, prāṇa*)[17] move through the unseen channels, invigorating the entire body. While there are many breaths of the subtle body, the vital breath (*sog-lung*) is considered the most basic and the source for all breath; it is the essence of life itself that animates and sustains all living beings.[18] The movement of subtle breath allows sense perceptions to function, emotions to be felt, and speech to be uttered. The proper circulation of the subtle breaths through the channels ensures excellent health, emotional balance, and mental clarity; the blockage of breaths creates emotional eruptions, health problems, and general confusion. On an outer level, the breath of the subtle body relates to the physical inhalation and exhalation of breath through the nostrils. In our everyday experience of emotions and thought, the gross and subtle breaths move aimlessly through the channels, which are knotted and blocked, causing an experience of great turmoil.

Although the mind and the breath are different in function, they are of identical nature: neither has concrete substance. In yogic practice, it is crucial that the mind consciousness be trained to follow, even ride, the movement of the breath. In a traditional metaphor, the breath is likened to a horse, which when recognized properly can be ridden by the natural, undisturbed mind (*nyug me sem*) in meditation practice. When the mind rides the breath with careful attention, the turbulence of an unsettled mind is dispelled and awareness may eventually dawn in the mind as a kind of radiant clarity. This is the essence of calm-abiding (*śámatha, shi-ne*) meditation practice.

When awareness dawns in calm-abiding, its power may generate a concentrated energy point of energized awareness (*bindu, thigle*) in the subtle body.[19] This concentrated energy, also called bodhicitta (*changchup sem*), comes from an indestructible sphere of awareness at the heart center and gathers at focal centers (*cakra, khorlo*) throughout the spinal area. In Vajrayāna meditation, the bodhicitta experience manifests in this tangible way as bindu, exponentially enhancing the efficacy of the practice. The bindu point can be moved through the channels by means of one's awareness to clear away obscurations of emotions, concepts, and habitual patterns. Then it is possible for the vital breath to move freely and for there to develop, in Vajrayāna language, an identity of prāṇa and mind.

The mind and the breath reflect each other in quality, as every meditator knows. Even in mundane experience, emotions or moods carry with them particular breathing patterns. When we are angry, our breathing is choppy, abrupt, and harsh. When we are thinking deeply about an intellectual problem, our breathing is calm, steady, and smooth, though probably not deep. When relieved, we breathe deeply, expelling air that may have been held in.[20] In the basic calm-abiding practice, the synchronization of mind and body occurs with the mind following the exhalation of breath through the nostrils. In Tibetan subtle-body yoga, it occurs when the mind rides the movement of the subtle breaths through the subtle channels of the body and brings this awareness-energy into the central channel.

The central vertical channel (*uma, avadhūti*) is psychically situated near the spine, joining the base of the spine with the crown of the head. Its visualized color varies from tantra to tantra, but it was described by Nāropa to be "lustrous like an oil lamp, straight like a plantain, and hollow like a reed."[21] On either side of the central channel, two parallel primary channels are visualized, the *lalanā* (*kyangma*) and *rasanā* (*roma*). While the central channel is said to be the diameter of a medium straw of wheat, the two flanking channels are the diameter of the thinnest straw of wheat.[22]

Because of karmically borne habitual patterns, we fall into dualistic thought, which is reflected by the subtle breath moving only through the tiny networks of channels throughout the body, or only the left and right channels near the spine. We then become involved in distinguishing subject and object, and other such dualistic habits. This leads to the arising of all the painful emotions of attachment, aggression and bewilderment, which cause all manner of suffering and delusion binding us to saṃsāra.[23] For those who are not engaged in meditation training, this pattern does not change until death. Then there is a dramatic change in the subtle body, as the vital breath moves first into the flanking channels and then into the central channel. For ordinary beings, this produces great fear, for the cohesion of the gross-body elements gradually dissolves at death, and the subtle mind that arises feels annihilation. Yogis and yoginīs who have trained in meditation on the subtle body can utilize the dissolving of the gross-body elements for spiritual purposes at death.[24]

Yogic practice in tantra, when it is successful, prepares for this process by moving the subtle breaths, clearing the channels, and bringing the vital breath into the central channel in meditation. This frees the mind of dualistic thought, allowing the natural luminosity to be seen directly. When the vital breath enters the central channel in meditation practice, it is said that the breath begins to flow smoothly and evenly through both nostrils, gradually becomes more subtle, and then stops for a time without any accompanying sluggishness or lack of clarity.[25]

The sūtra path of Buddhism points to liberation through the practice of meditation but does not provide the detailed training to bring about this experience quickly. Instead, it relies on the conventional means of accumulating merit and wisdom, and the practice of the gradual path. The skillful means of tantra in Vajrayāna Buddhism utilizes the yoga of the subtle body to clarify the mind and accelerate the process of realization. The yogic practice of the Vajrayāna is designed to accompany the two accumulations described in the sūtras. One accumulates merit through cultivating discipline in meditation practice and in one's daily life; one accumulates wisdom through hearing, contemplating, and meditating on the teachings of one's guru. Then the yogic practices of the subtle body have the potential of clearing away habitual patterns of dualistic thinking.

When one has practiced the two accumulations and received direct authorization from a qualified guru, one can learn the subtle-body practice of bringing the vital breath from the flanking channels into the central channel and transforming the dualistic patterns of thought into wisdom-prāṇa. It is described in this way by Saraha:

> *Do not discriminate, but see things as one,*
> *making no distinction of families.*
> *Let the whole of the threefold world*
> *become one in the state of [great bliss].*[26]

A transformation takes place in the cultivation of the "inner heat" (*tummo, caṇḍāli*) yogic practices, which are discussed in the section "Feminine, Masculine, and the Subtle Body." Then it is possible to realize the nature of mind and phenomena directly and to experience nondual bliss. This practice is called "sampannakrama with signs." Once it has stabilized sufficiently, the visualized prāṇa, nāḍīs, and bindu are dissolved, and the nature of mind is seen directly. This is called "sampannakrama without signs" and represents the essential, more profound practice.[27]

The experience generated in this practice is called "great bliss" (mahāsukha, dewa chenpo), which is the wisdom of bliss and emptiness, the highest realization of meditation. This experience is not fabricated or created by conceptual mind. Instead, as Trungpa Rinpoche wrote:

> mahāsukha is an actual experience of bliss, a physical, psychological, total experience of joy that comes from being completely without discursive thoughts, being completely in the realm of nonthought. It is uniting with the non-dual awake state of being.[28]

The blissfulness of this experience is the joy that is complete freedom from fabrication and the limitations of the filters of ego. It is joy that has absolutely no barrier to direct, unmediated experience of all the details of the phenomenal world, the velvet of peony petals, the piquancy of red peppers, the flash of recognition in a lover's eyes.

Ḍākinīs and the Sacred Landscape of the Subtle Body

In the rich Tibetan tradition of sacred geography, guidebooks (*lam-yik*, or *ne-yik*) were a popular genre of tantric literature that combined a Tibetan worldview with Buddhist descriptions of the path to enlightenment.[29] While these books appeared to guide ordinary pilgrimages, the lore surrounding them is decipherable only by the advanced tantric yogin or yoginī who is journeying to realization. In this lore, the subtle body is a microcosm of the sacred landscape of these pilgrimage sites, and the yogic path is a pilgrimage of inner integration.

This is the terrain described by Khenpo Tsultrim Gyamtso Rinpoche. In an elusive, esoteric form, the ḍākinī dwells in the sacred landscape of the twenty-four sacred places. As Rinpoche sang:

By dwelling in the fields of the twenty-four
Sacred places of body, speech, and mind,
They accomplish the benefit of others.
These are called sacred-realm ḍākinīs.[30]

The twenty-four sacred places (*yülchen nyershi*) have several levels of meaning. On an outer, geographical level, they refer to twenty-four sites in India and the Himālayas that are especially sacred in Vajrayāna Buddhist practice. According to tantric lore, these twenty-four sites (eight lofty, eight earthly, and eight underground) were originally ruled by the wrathful Rudra[31] and his demon-vassals. At the beginning of the present era of strife and conflict, the Buddha Vajradhara, moved to compassion by the suffering of these realms, arose as a wrathful heruka deity and danced the nondual wisdom of all the buddhas of the three times, trampling Rudra and his retinue and liberating these sacred places into the absolute expanse of great bliss.[32]

These locations are considered especially powerful places of practice and serve as pilgrimage spots in Tibet and India. The most famous mountains among them, especially Mount Kailāsa, are associated with the body, speech, and mind of Cakrasaṃvara and Vajrayoginī and have served as retreat sites for many famous practitioners.[33] The Lachi Snow Range was particularly important to Milarepa. It contains the mountain ruled by Tseringma, his wisdom ḍākinī convert, who is an example of a sacred-realm ḍākinī of the twenty-four sacred places.[34]

These sites are considered soaked with the blessings of the great yogis and yoginīs who practiced there, and retreats performed in such places are supported by their blessings.[35] These places are protected, of course, by the sacred-realm ḍākinīs who open the gates of wisdom of the dedicated practitioner. However, it is said that these twenty-four can be found within any sacred valley, and they will shrink and disappear when conditions conducive to practice disappear.[36] The discovery of their literal locations is said to depend upon the mind of the practitioner.

In the unexcelled and inner tantras, the twenty-four sacred places also refer to the physical body maṇḍala. On this inner level, sites inside the body or on its surface represent sacred spots in which one visualizes, during creation phase, the seed syllables and figures of deities. The deities and even the specific physical locations vary according to the tantras, but they also are guarded by the sacred-realm ḍākinīs in the form of seed syllables. On both outer and secret levels, in completion-phase practice these twenty-four sites are associated with the subtle-body channels and the movement of the vital breath and mind in tantric meditation practice. Here one enacts the pilgrimage within one's own body, performing subtle-body yoga with the support and protection of the sacred-realm ḍākinīs. The details of these practices are among the most guarded treasures of creation and completion practice.

As protectors of the authenticity of the twenty-four sacred places on these various levels, the sacred-realm ḍākinīs support the yogins and yoginīs who practice on all of these levels. These ḍākinīs, who have realized the luminous mind, carry out the command of the lineage gurus and protect these teachings and realizations from those who are not properly qualified. Having prepared properly, the practitioner must open his or her heart and sincerely request the teachings, putting aside all emotional and conceptual obscurations and experiencing deep devotion and respect. When they see that the practitioner has the proper intention, the sacred-realm ḍākinīs unlock the code of these protected teachings and unbar the minds of the yogins and yoginīs so that transmission may take place.[37]

The sacred-realm ḍākinīs are profound protectors and catalysts in meditation, expressing the vitality of tantric practice. From this point of view, the utter complexity of phenomena is seen clearly and simply; the vast landscape of the twenty-four sites is seen as an outer expression of one's own body and mind. As Saraha sang concerning pilgrimage to these sites:

When the mind goes to rest,
and the bonds of the body are destroyed,
then the one flavour of the Innate pours forth,
and there is neither outcast nor brahmin.

Here is the sacred Jumna and here the River Ganges,
here are Prayaga and Benares, here are Sun [lalanā] *and Moon* [rasanā].
I have visited in my wanderings shrines and other places of pilgrimage,
but I have not seen another shrine blissful like my own body.[38]

Although receiving empowerments, engaging in pilgrimages, and performing rituals are all important aspects of Vajrayāna practice, it is realization that is essential. Through yogic practice, narrow frames of reference and ambition for attainment are transformed. The most sacred experience, the ultimate realization, is right in the present moment.

The ḍākinī is understood in Tibetan Buddhism to be the emblem and protector of the yogic tradition of the subtle body, the energetic confluence of the psychophysical human life. In hagiographic literature, ḍākinīs appear in visionary form to those who practice yoga, giving support, instruction, and even food offerings. Their appearance is particularly associated with solitary retreat, the proper place for the yogic practice of the subtle body. Solitude is necessary for yoga, as it creates the appropriate physical and psychological environment to access the experience of renunciation associated with the ḍākinī symbol of the charnel ground.[39] When one meditates in solitude, with proper motivation and careful fulfillment of the requirements of the practice, it is possible to accomplish the yoga of the subtle body. As Shabkar sang:

If you stay alone, you will tame your emotions.
If you stay alone, renunciation will dawn.
If you stay alone, you will be diligent.
If you stay alone, you will develop bodhicitta.
If you stay alone, the ḍākinīs will gather near you.
If you stay alone, the dharmapālas will surround you.
If you stay alone, meditation experiences and realization will arise.
If you stay alone, you will reach Buddhahood.
If you stay alone, a time will come when you are capable of benefiting others.
There is no way fully to describe
The benefits of solitude.[40]

In the context of solitary retreat, ḍākinīs are the preeminent symbol of the protection of the practitioner and of the mind, the sacredness of the subtle body, and the intensity of renunciation and sincere application necessary to the practice of yoga.

The practicing yogin or yoginī experiences the subtle body adorned with ḍākinīs. Alone or with their consorts the ḍākas, ḍākinīs are visualized in the various important sites in the subtle body as indicators and protectors of the sacredness of yoga. But the deities visualized are not merely token symbols; they reflect the essential power of the subtle body and its potential to clear away confusion and open the gates of wisdom. For this reason, the realm of subtle-body yoga is the realm of the ḍākinī in Tibetan Buddhism.

Feminine, Masculine, and the Subtle Body

In order to allow for the birth of [ultimate ḍākinī, the wisdom
that realizes emptiness], one must eliminate the gross forms of
consciousness
by means of the inner heat (tummo) practice that is a particular
form of bliss.
This bliss is the means of eliminating coarse consciousnesses:
therefore, the inner heat represents [a] meaning of ḍākinī."

—HIS HOLINESS THE FOURTEENTH DALAI LAMA[41]

Feminine and masculine qualities also manifest in the landscape of the subtle body as the flanking energetic channels, which are depicted somewhat differently in different tantric systems.[42] These channels flank the nondual central channel, in which their vital breaths and bodhicittas ultimately join in yogic practice.

In the tantric context, bodhicitta has a multivalent reference that reflects the several levels of meaning of all phenomena.[43] In the Mahāyāna traditions of Tibet, bodhicitta refers to the awakened mind that aspires to liberate all sentient beings. It is an attitude of cheerful altruism, based on insight into the interdependence of all beings. The persistent presence of this attitude is an indication that the practitioner has the motivation associated with the bodhisattva vow. The aspiration to attain enlightenment for the sake of all beings is the basis of all practice in Tibetan Buddhism.

In tantra, bodhicitta is described more experientially as compassionate motivation that also experiences the limitless quality of great bliss (mahāsukha), adding a quality of inexpressible joy to altruism. Simultaneously, the term *bodhicitta* refers to the essential concentrated energy of the subtle body joined with awareness, which particularly appears at the focal centers of the channels, suggesting the embodied expression of bodhicitta experience. And at the same time, the term refers in an outer way to the sexual fluids of the woman and man, menstrual blood (*dül*) and semen (*khu-wa*), which are considered by-products of the subtle-body points.[44]

The right and left flanking channels with their corresponding subtle breaths are described in some detail in the tantras and yogic commentaries; they are often spoken of as feminine and masculine, respectively. For example, in the *Cakrasaṃvara-tantra*, the right channel (rasanā, roma) is depicted as red tinged with white and is said to be governed by the fire element, the feminine dynamic, and the sun. The breaths (prāṇa, lung) that move through the rasanā are warm and fiery. In contrast, the left channel (*lalanā, kyangma*) is depicted as white tinged with red and governed by the masculine energy, the moon, and the water element; its vital breath is cool. These two aspects are complementary, and their union is essential in yogic practice.

A more important depiction of the masculine and feminine aspects is connected with the focal centers at the crown of the head and below the navel. The energy that resides at the crown is described as white, but it is more like brilliant crystal or diamond and is often referred to as icy cool, the moon, and the father. Below the navel is the mother energy, which is called the sun. It is hot and fiery, red in color. Yogic practice joins the dualities of masculine and feminine, bringing the masculine energy of the crown of the head together with the fiery feminine energy of the lower channels. When they meet, the fiery mother melts the icy father. Tiny energy drops of bodhicitta, the size of sesame seeds, melt and fan the flames below the navel, causing them to burn more intensely. Thus the process continues. When this practice is performed yogically, the breaths from the flanking channels join in the central channel, and wisdom and skillful means are joined in yogic realization. The practitioner experiences a lessening of emotional obscurations and the dawning of coemergent wisdom.

When the deities are depicted in union with their consorts in the iconography of Tibetan tantra, meaning arises at various levels. The iconography of subtle-body meditation is a portrait of yogic practice, the joining of the feminine and masculine breaths, energies, and bodhicitta in the central channel. Together the heruka and ḍākinī represent the experience of great bliss, the experiential union of penetrating wisdom and radiating compassion that is essential to removing obstacles to awakening. When these two are joined in this way, the yogic path is vital and complete.

When the masculine and feminine are joined in the central channel, the burning sensation is called *caṇḍālī (tummo)*, the experience of blissful heat at or below the navel, which leads to the experience of great bliss.[45] Tummo is explained as having two aspects: *tum* refers to the fierce or wrathful suppression of stains and defilements that obscure the true nature of mind, and *mo* is a feminine gender ending, since the realization thus engendered is the mother of all awakenings or buddhas.[46] The inner heat is essential to the realization of great bliss, the taming and purification of the subtle body, creating the conditions for the direct experience of the nature of the mind. As Saraha said:

> *Where vital breath and mind no longer roam about,*
> *Where Sun* (rasanā, roma) *and Moon* (lalanā, kyangma) *do not appear,*
> *There, O man, put thy thought to rest,*
> *This is the precept taught by Saraha.*[47]

When the mind rides the vital breath and enters the central channel, it comes to rest in its own nature.

The yogic tradition says that when the inner heat is ignited, this is the blessing of the ḍākinī. In fact, the blazing heat and the bliss it generates are sometimes called the ḍākinī, as His Holiness the Dalai Lama said in defining *ḍākinī* on page 176. From this perspective, the ḍākinī represents the subtle-body network of channels, the yogic practices of inner heat and bliss that open the way, and the dawning of wisdom that realizes emptiness or vast space.

The inner heat practice embodies the qualities of the realization of the inner and secret ḍākinīs, who ignite the experience of the yogin or yoginī with their heat on various levels. The outer ḍākinī burns in the body as the experience of inner heat with the movement of bodhicitta fueling the flames of wisdom within the channels and junctures of the subtle body; the inner ḍākinī blazes in the visionary experience as the fierce meditational deity dancing in the burning charnel ground; and the secret ḍākinī's power burns in the mind as the arising of wisdom from confusion, illuminating the nature of mind.

The Ḍākinī as the Symbol of Subtle-Body Yoga

In Tibetan Buddhism the ḍākinī is, above all, a symbol of embodiment in esoteric yogic practice. There is something natural about a feminine symbol representing the centrality of embodiment in yogic practice. Women have been associated with the body and embodiment in many cultures. In traditional domestic settings, women's lives revolve around bodily expression and nurture, birth-giving, suckling, menstruating, and caring for the young or infirm.[48] In religious settings, they tend to somatize their mystical experience with physical enactment.[49] As women came to epitomize embodiment, they rose or fell in status, depending upon prevailing views of physicality and sexuality.

Reflecting her yogic roots, however, the ḍākinī symbolizes embodiment in a slightly different way from domestically bound women in most cultures. Her body is beautiful and voluptuous as theirs may be, but it is naked and adorned with shards of bone, skull-cups of blood, and rotting heads, showing her unique relationship with embodiment. She is associated with the body—both alive and dead—but has transcended the fear of death and boldly displays the attitude of "single taste." She represents the bodily destiny of women but nurtures the practitioner and the teachings rather than ordinary babies or relatives bound by saṃsāra. As female, she dwells in the mysterious territory between birth and death, but the ambiguous and dangerous nature of the ḍākinī derives from her association not with nature but with phenomena's emptiness, the ultimate ambiguity.[50]

In her symbolic form, she at once confirms and reverses traditional Tibetan views of gender. While she embraces the conventional roles of women in the realms of nurture, embodiment, and relationship, the context of those realms is somewhat different. These areas apparently influence female and male practitioners in different ways, as we will examine in more detail in chapter 7. For the male, she joins the qualities of sensuality with reminders of death from the charnel ground, arousing lust and revulsion at the same moment. Her radiant body is beautiful and luminously empty. The bliss she bestows is not ordinary sexual bliss; it is yogic bliss that arises from the realization of impermanence, emptiness, and radiant appearance all at once. For the female, the ḍākinī represents embodiment that is not a defilement, nurture that is not a fate, and relationship that is not subordination. Even while she affirms qualities that have been associated with womanhood in every culture, she questions the entanglements of home, family, subjugation, and vanity that have bound those qualities.

In these ways, the ḍākinī serves as a powerful feminine symbol that reinforces, reverses, and challenges cultural notions of gender in Tibetan society, even while she points to multiple meanings that have nothing to do with gender. The gender of the ḍākinī is not incidental to her representation; at the same time, the meanings that her feminine form carries point to the lack of inherent existence of all phenomena and the infinite expanse of the nature of mind.

Specifically in the context of this discussion, the ḍākinī represents the subtle yogic body, an intricate network of energetic channels joining many sensitive centers throughout the body, each of which is considered endowed with her special blessings. Joining the network of the ḍākinīs engenders bliss for both female and male tāntrikas, and mastery of the yogas of the subtle body is mastery of the ḍākinīs who reside there. These are the inner meanings of the ḍākinī in tantric iconography.

Conclusion

In the yogas of the subtle body, the ḍākinī manifests in several important ways. First, she is the ruler of the twenty-four sacred places, the auspicious realms found in the outer landscape of the physical world as well as the inner landscape of the human yogic body. In the outer world, she guards the teachings, bestows empowerment, and nurtures the pilgrim's meditative experience. In the inner realms, she guards the sacredness of the yogic body through protecting seed syllables and bestows meditative success on the yogin or yoginī who practices properly with beneficial intention.

Second, the ḍākinī is the feminine component of the subtle body as the red flanking channel that carries winds and secretions of a fiery, hot nature, complementing the white channel that expresses the cool, watery nature. She is also the blazing heat at the navel center, complementing the icy coolness at the crown of the head. Tibetan lamas emphasize that the feminine and masculine principles are always present in complementary fashion in the bodies of all men and women and that the spiritual goal of practice is to unite these two aspects in meditation.

Third, the actual process of bringing the subtle breaths into the central channel through the practice of inner heat is itself considered an aspect of the ḍākinī. Her seed syllable A is the source of the heat generated by the practice, and this blazing fire melts the coolness at the crown. When they are joined at the heart center, the practitioner experiences great bliss, a direct experience of nonthought.[51] The experience of inner heat is considered the ḍākinī's blessing, and she is supplicated to bestow this blessing on the yogin or yoginī.

Finally, the subtle-body yoga practice itself is considered to be the ḍākinī, the arising of the experience of bliss-emptiness that allows the fundamental nature of mind to manifest to itself. This is the fullest meaning of sky-dancer, the actual accomplishment that opens the gates of wisdom.

SIX

The Outer-Outer Dakini

THE DAKINI IN HUMAN FORM

Woman is essentially wisdom,
Source of spontaneous prajñā and subtle-body.
Never consider her inferior;
Strive especially to see her as Vajravārāhī[1]

—MILAREPA

IT WAS JUST BEFORE dawn on the morning of August 19, 1967, in the tiny Himālayan kingdom of Sikkim on the northern edge of India. On the lush mountainside above the mist-filled valley lay the old monastery built by the ninth Karmapa, called Rumtek, "the monastery wreathed in a thousand rays of rainbow light."[2] His Holiness the sixteenth Karmapa, patriarch of the Karma Kagyü lineage, stood out on the veranda overlooking the valley, enjoying the many-colored birds who awakened with cheerful song. Just at 5:10 A.M., when the sun punctured the sky with rays of light, His Holiness suddenly sent his attendant for a small bowl of white rice. Taking the bowl in his hands, he murmured prayers of praise to the dawn, tossing rice at the close of each stanza. He turned to his attendant and jubilantly announced, "Khandro Ugyen Tsolmo has been reborn!"[3]

Just at that moment of dawn, in a village sixty kilometers away, a baby girl was born to Sönam Paldrön, wife of His Holiness Mindröling Rinpoche, one of the most eminent tülkus of the Nyingma lineage of Tibet.[4] The line of Mindröling has been filled with celebrated yoginīs, and it was fitting that the baby girl be born to this lineage. The infant was the emanation of Khandro Ugyen Tsolmo, a deeply realized nun and renowned abbess of the nunnery at Tsurphu in Tibet. As a young woman, Ugyen Tsolmo had been the prophesied consort of the fifteenth Karmapa, Khakhyab Dorje (1871–1922).[5] As an elderly nun, she had escaped from Tibet with the sixteenth Karmapa and had settled into the nunnery at Rumtek with her many devotees.

Mindröling Rinpoche was a close friend of the Karmapa and thought nothing of the special visit he paid to his newborn daughter, conferring on her the name Karma Ugyen Tsolmo. But after consulting with Dilgo Khyentse Rinpoche, the Karmapa confirmed with her father that the child was an enlightened emanation of the yoginī. When the girl was ten months old, an official announcement of the yoginī's rebirth was quietly made public, and several monks from Rumtek came to pay their respects. The Karmapa himself came yearly to give her empowerments and teachings.[6]

Eventually, as the baby grew into girlhood, the nuns who were Karma Ugyen Tsolmo's former students went to His Holiness to ask about her. We have heard she has been found, they asserted. Yes, she had. Had she been recognized? Yes, and her recognition had been confirmed by other great and realized teachers. So, insisted the nuns, enthrone her!

This was an unusual request. A number of lineages of realized women in Tibet had emanated again and again in successive lifetimes of practice and teaching. But they were usually not officially recognized and empowered as tülkus, as male emanations were; instead, they were considered incarnate ḍākinīs.[7] These women were called *jetsünma,* an honorific title signifying great realization and exemplary teaching.[8] They were raised in a "brocaded life" of honor, dedicated meditation, and training in Buddhist traditions, but they were not given a monastic education or expected to carry out official duties as their male counterparts were.[9] The nuns' insistence that she be enthroned and empowered as a rinpoche was unexpected. But eventually His Holiness could not refuse them.

The young girl was first enthroned[10] as Khandro Rinpoche in 1976 in Kalimpong when she was nine years old. Her lineage of mostly female emanations has been traced back to the great yoginī Mingyur Paldrön (1699–1769)[11] and finally to the great savior Tārā. This is a line of incarnate ḍākinīs of the Nyingma lineage to whom are attributed deep realization

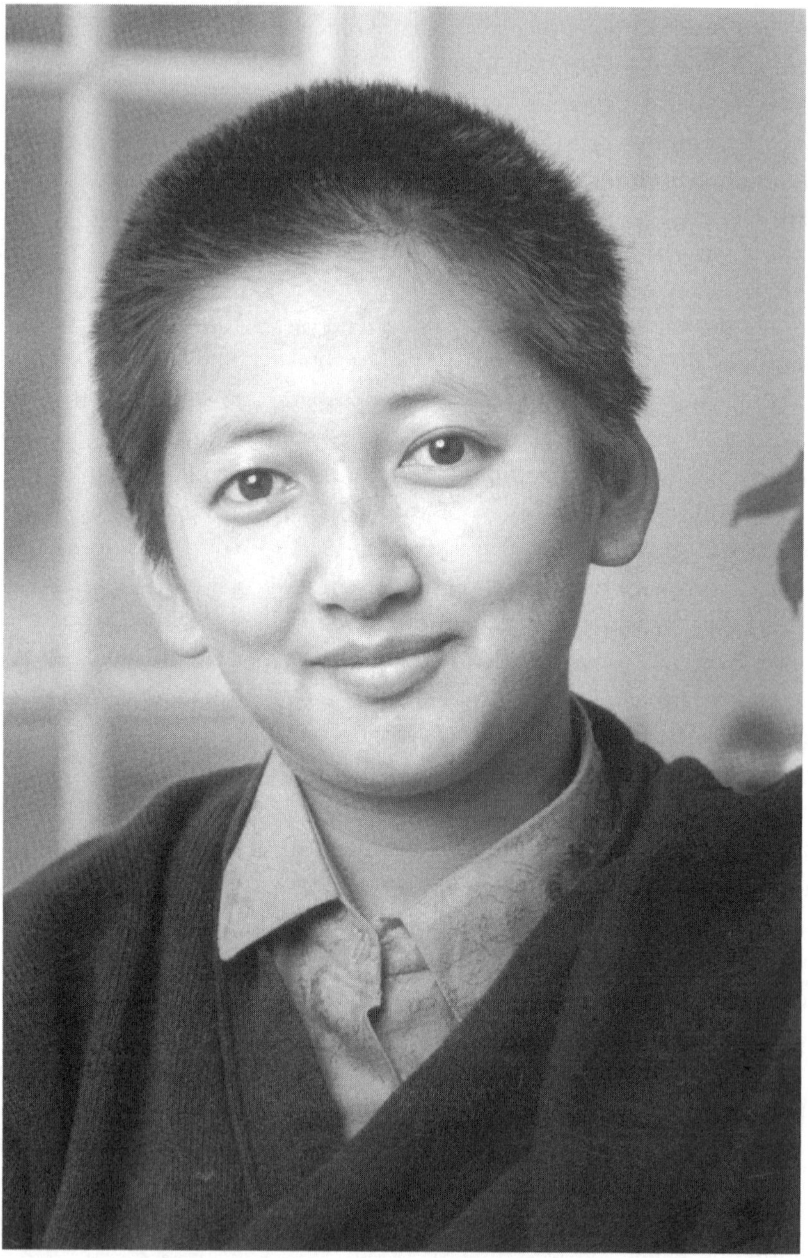

Ven. Khandro Rinpoche, an emanation of Tārā.

and powerful, direct teaching. Khandro Rinpoche was trained in both Kagyü and Nyingma traditions, often the only girl among many monks and tülkus. She was raised in Dehra Dun by her father and received a Nyingma monastic education there at Mindröling Monastery.[12] Her briefer Kagyü training was in the monastic college at Rumtek, under the direction of the Karmapa. She was also educated at a convent school in Dehra Dun, at the request of the Karmapa, Dilgo Khyentse Rinpoche, and her mother. Since the early 1990s, Khandro Rinpoche has been traveling and teaching in Europe, Asia, and North America, and has established a nunnery and retreat center in India called Samten Tse especially for Asian and Western women monastics.

Rinpoche is highly respected among her tülku counterparts in Asia, though her status as a recognized incarnate lama causes perhaps some uncertainty and discomfort. Certainly she is called an incarnate ḍākinī, but it is not common for ḍākinīs to receive a monastic education or to inherit the roles and responsibilities of a tülku. However, as she continues her teaching, duties, and responsibilities her reputation spreads throughout the Tibetan Buddhist world, and she represents the future promise of the development of a female tülku tradition.

This promise contrasts sharply with the life of another line of female incarnations, the Samding Dorje Phagmo.[13] This lineage has been associated with the ḍākinī Vajravārāhī, the Vajra Sow, and with the Samding (Soaring Meditation) Monastery. Samding is located in southern Tibet on a mountain above Yamdrok Lake near Gyangtse, an area considered potentially dangerous for all of Tibet because of the fiery waters of Dremo Lake that threaten to overflow and flood the entire country. The ḍākinī incarnation took her seat in this strategic spot in order to prevent the destruction of the dharma in Tibet. The first incarnation is said to have taken her seat in 1717, and she terrified the Dzungur Tartars who threatened the monastery by transforming herself and her eighty monks into hogs, an exhibit of the genuineness of her Vajravārāhī manifestation. The invading Tartars are said to have immediately filled the monastery with booty looted from other monasteries in the region as tribute.

The Samding ḍākinī served as abbess to a monks' monastery that historically contained relics of her previous incarnations. She was traditionally trained in meditation and textual studies, following a strict schedule of semiretreat and pausing only to give blessings to visiting devotees. Unlike her monastic charges, she dressed in yoginī clothing, wearing her hair long and combed back without any ornamentation. Her name became famous beyond the boundaries of Tibet in Mongolia and Central Asia and she was accorded privileges shared only by the Panchen and Dalai Lamas.[14]

The Samding Dorje Phagmo and her successors were beloved for four incarnations. Jetsün Chönyi Dechen Tsomo, the fourth incarnation, created a lasting spiritual impression with her profound learning, her commitment to retreat, and her powerful teaching. The depth of her realization produced rumors that she had grown sow bristles on her back, signifying her physical connection to Vajravārāhī, the Vajra Sow. The Lhasa government bestowed on her the title of Huthukthu, a Mongolian honorific meaning "saint."

With the fifth and sixth incarnations, however, political problems brewed, endangering the authenticity of the lineage and greatly reducing the faith of her devotees. The fifth was said to be dark and pockmarked, with no spiritual disposition, while a ḍākinīlike contemporary was believed to be the undiscovered true incarnation. Under suspicious political circumstances, the sixth was enthroned in 1937 before the death of the fifth, leading to a lengthy and expensive lawsuit carried out on her behalf by her powerful father, Thonpa Chazo. This caused the sixth to be reviled by the Tibetan people, making her vulnerable in the 1950s to exploitation by the invading Chinese, who flattered and courted her and made her a titular government official. As part of her retraining she eventually renounced her status as an incarnation, calling it mere superstition, married, and took up private life in Lhasa. It is said that Samding Monastery has probably been completely destroyed.

Symbol and Actuality: Human Ḍākinīs

Probably the most confusing aspect of the Tibetan ḍākinī tradition is the phenomenon of human ḍākinīs. It is commonly understood that human women are sometimes called ḍākinīs, but how does this appellation refer to the complex conventions examined here? That is, if ultimately ḍākinīs are beyond gender, what does it mean to say that human women are ḍākinīs? This area is all the more challenging because of the range of interpretations that have appeared in Western scholarly studies. At one extreme, the ḍākinī is taken to be a goddess figure, inherently female, who acts on women's behalf.[15] At the other extreme, the ḍākinī is said not to be female at all but is referred to as "she."[16] The way to resolve these extremes is to understand under what circumstances human women are ḍākinīs.

This topic is all the more provocative because of the traditional ambiguity of the ḍākinī's identity. As we saw in the previous chapters, there are a variety of female manifestations in the rich pantheon of Tibetan deities, spirits, and demons. Some are malevolent, some are peaceful, and some are realized. Within ḍākinī realms, worldly ḍākinīs who have no allegiance to dharma are considered powerful and dangerous, capable of cannibalizing victims at whim. These ḍākinīs bear close resemblance to protector ḍākinīs who may not be realized but have sworn allegiance to protect dharma practitioners and serve as allies in meditation practice. Especially important are the completely enlightened wisdom ḍākinīs who guide and instruct the yogin or yoginī. Human ḍākinīs may also be potential spiritual consorts who have the unique ability to accelerate the removal of obstacles for themselves and their partners through sexual yoga.

Human women have power simply because they have female bodies, which are seen in Vajrayāna sacred outlook to be emanations of the wisdom principle. Therefore the tantric practitioner is bound to see all women as ḍākinīs. But appreciating the special gifts of human women and understanding which women are important for one's spiritual development is a central part of ḍākinī lore. Because of this, the identification of types of human ḍākinīs is important in the practice traditions of Tibet.

Types of Human Ḍākinīs

The conventions regarding human ḍākinīs developed in an oral tradition of ḍākinī lore that has never been systematized or formalized. There is no definitive list of human characteristics that identify a ḍākinī. However, from observation we can distinguish five general ways in which humans may be considered ḍākinīs.[17] The first, most determinative way concerns auspicious birth. A ḍākinī may be born with characteristic physical marks, or she may be the recognized rebirth of a previous incarnation, as in the case of Ven. Khandro Rinpoche. Contrary to certain Mahāyāna teachings that considered a male body necessary for enlightenment,[18] Vajrayāna developed female versions of the thirty-two auspicious body marks by which an incarnate ḍākinī could be recognized. Though it occurred rarely, it is said that tülkus would sometimes choose the female body for rebirth and continue their compassionate activity as women.[19]

Second, great women tantric gurus in the Tibetan Buddhist tradition are also called ḍākinīs by virtue of their excellent realization and manifestation. This title has been applied to remarkable yoginīs such as Yeshe Tsogyal, Machik Lapdrön, Niguma, and Sukhasiddhi, all of whom initiated new cycles of teachings and were venerated because of their great realization. Their ḍākinī qualities are generally described as parallel with the three bodies of buddhahood.[20]

Third, human women are called ḍākinīs when they are the mothers, sisters, or consorts of incarnate lamas. Considering mothers to be ḍākinīs parallels Buddhism's veneration of the mother of the Buddha, Mahāmāya, whose special characteristics are praised in the Lalitavistara accounts.[21] Such special mothers are also considered emanations of the Great Mother Prajñāpāramitā. Sisters are often considered female counterparts of their realized brothers and may be given equivalent training and recognition. Consorts are considered ḍākinīs out of respect for their intimacy with the lama, but also because it is possible that together they practice the spiritual yoga of sexual union (karmamudrā). More will be said about this practice in the sections to follow.

The fourth category of human ḍākinī is that associated with the practices of the great ḍākinī yidams such as Vajrayoginī or Vajravārāhī, or the great sādhanas of the heruka and ḍākinī in union (yuga-naddha, yab-yum). A woman is a ḍākinī if she participates in tantric rituals such as the performance of the sādhana or the tantric feast (*gaṇacakra, tsok-khor*) that honors these yidams. For that matter, any tantric practitioner, whether male or female, who carries the Vajrayāna commitments especially of the practice of the feminine yidam is also considered an embodied ḍākinī, foiling the notion that only women can be considered human ḍākinīs.

Finally, subsuming all categories, every woman is understood to be a ḍākinī manifestation by virtue of having a female body, which is said to be an emanation of emptiness and wisdom. Tantric precepts are tied to this understanding of women, and it is considered a violation to disparage women in any way, especially to denigrate their spiritual qualities or the purity of their bodies. While these precepts may reverse patriarchal cultural attitudes toward women prevalent in India and Tibet, their intent is to propagate sacred outlook with regard to the female gender.[22]

In the sections that follow, we shall develop these basic classifications further, exploring the physical manifestation of ḍākinī in the bodies and lives of human women and men.

Physical Signs of the Ḍākinī

In the hagiographies of the great yoginī Yeshe Tsogyal, it is said that she was born with the characteristic marks of an incarnate ḍākinī. Her complexion was a healthy rosy white, signifying the mixing of the two bodhicittas, and she had a complete set of teeth the color of conch shells. Her bluish-black hair fell to her waist, and she was able to sit in half-lotus posture with knees firmly planted on the floor. Upon receiving a butter offering from her mother, the baby astonished her parents by singing:

I, your child, a yoginī [emanation],
Am nourished by the food of pure essences
And unclean foods I now have long forgotten.
But, mother, I will eat—that you may gain in merit.

Essential teachings will be what I eat.
And all saṃsāra will be what I swallow.
Awareness, pristine wisdom, will be now my fill.
Ah Ye![23]

Literature on the physical signs of embodiment associated with an enlightened being first appeared in the Indian Mahāyāna tradition, in which buddhas were said to manifest characteristic marks associated with "superior beings" (*mahāpuruṣa*) of Indian society. These marks were initially gender-specific; among the thirty-two major marks, an enlightened being was said to manifest "a penis covered with a sheath." Of course, there ensued many issues concerning gender and enlightenment in the Mahāyāna tradition, based on these stipulations.[24]

Vajrayāna developed a parallel tradition in which incarnate wisdom ḍākinīs also had recognizable physical signs at birth indicating the remarkable qualities of their realization. These signs are indicated in esoteric sources but never became standardized, and many of these records remain obscure. However, some texts indicated thirty-two major marks and eighty minor ones, parallel to those of "superior (male) beings." Other texts gave five major signs associated with the feminine form, such as strategically placed moles, a third eye, slightly webbed fingers, pink fingernails like mother-of-pearl (*nyachi*), and a multicolored halo of light similar to a rainbow in which appear the syllables OṂ AH HŪṂ.[25] Most indications are

The Indian princess Maṇḍāravā.

that ḍākinīs are visions of loveliness within some conventional range, with graceful lines, elegant garb, and radiant complexions. However, it is also clear from the hagiographies that ḍākinīs are generally perceived as lovely even when they are broadly built, hairy, coarse-complexioned, or very dark.[26] There are genres of messenger ḍākinīs and protector ḍākinīs who appear as withered crones or fanged flesh-eating demonesses; they may be feared even while the magnificence of their appearance is appreciated as beautiful by their subjects.

When the princess Maṇḍāravā was born to the royal family of Zahor, the aged Brahmin doctor who inspected her burst into tears of joy, proclaiming her to exhibit the classic thirty-two and eighty auspicious marks of a buddha. He continued:

> she is not of human lineage; she is a wisdom-ḍākinī who has appeared in the human realm. Whoever will be her husband will be an emperor (*cakravartin*), and if she decides to abandon the world and practice the dharma, she will spiritually guide the land of Zahor. No one has ever had such auspicious marks.[27]

It is interesting to note that her husband would manifest the destiny of wheel-turning emperor associated with such marks, but that her spiritual accomplishments are associated with her alone. Later, she became a main consort of Guru Rinpoche, who had prophesied her birth.

A recurring motif concerning incarnate ḍākinīs, but not male buddhas, is secrecy. When an infant girl was recognized as a ḍākinī, she was to be raised with special care and affection, but in secret. Yeshe Tsogyal's parents hid her away for ten years, realizing that her remarkable appearance and rapid development could cause gossip.[28] Similarly, Machik Lapdrön's father cautioned her mother, "Don't take her outdoors, don't take her into town. Keep this girl's existence a secret!"[29] Maṇḍāravā was an exception, for when she was recognized as an incarnate ḍākinī, all the subjects of the kingdom and all gods and spirits celebrated her birth for three months. However, throughout her spiritual journey her parents endeavored to keep her out of the public eye, practicing meditation and austerities within the confines of the palace.[30]

The characteristic marks of the incarnate ḍākinī are of many types. One trait marking the births of wisdom ḍākinīs is their association with resounding utterances of seed syllables, reminding the practitioner of the relationship between the ḍākinī's outer form and her inner and secret dimensions.[31] The conception of Yeshe Tsogyal arose from the red seed syllable E encircled by white vowels, and the white syllable VAṂ encircled by red consonants, which shot like a shooting star to the home of her parents. The sonorous utterance of a ḍākinī-version Vajra Guru mantra set the stage for her birth.[32] An important seed syllable that expresses the nature of the embodied ḍākinī is HRĪḤ, the yidam Vajrayoginī's essence mantra. Machik's mother, Bumcham, heard the A syllable of Prajñāpāramitā and the Vajrayoginī mantra being recited in her womb during her pregnancy. At her birth, HRĪḤ appeared on the baby's tongue, ablaze with light:

> At the crown of her head shone a white light the size of a fingertip, marked with the white syllable A. . . . [Her father examined her and said,] "In the middle of the girl's central eye there is a white syllable A, as fine as a hair, and she also has all the other signs of a ḍākinī."[33]

A second distinctive trait marking the body of a ḍākinī emanation is the vertical eye placed at the middle of the forehead, signifying extraordinary wisdom. At birth, the baby Machik displayed a vertical third eye in her forehead, gazing into space without blinking, clicking her tongue. As she grew and matured, she quickly learned many mantras and sūtras, showing special affinity for the Prajñāpāramitā-sūtras.

A third distinctive trait is the ḍākinī's association with fire imagery, especially in descriptions of her wisdom or her activity. When Machik was eight years old, her tutor exclaimed to her mother, "Chomo, this daughter of yours is no ordinary individual, but seems to be a kind of ḍākinī. I am unable to contain her intelligence. Her wisdom is like a wild running forest fire, consuming everything."[34] Maṇḍāravā often blazed fire in her wrathful emanations, and when her outraged father the king attempted to execute her with her consort Guru Rinpoche, they were placed in the center of a fiery pyre. After twenty-one days of burning, the king found the couple dancing at the center of a lotus flower surrounded by a cool lake, unscathed by the flames.[35]

Sometimes a ḍākinī emanation will take on an appearance that is the antithesis of the enlightened physical characteristics, as a parody of their significance. This is seen especially in the visionary wrathful, terrible forms of the ḍākinī, as in the famous encounter between Nāropa and the wisdom ḍākinī Vajrayoginī during his years of scholastic study at Nālandā. When she confronted him concerning the true depth of his understanding of the texts he studied, she displayed thirty-seven ugly features:[36]

> Her eyes were red and deep-hollowed; her hair was fox-coloured and dishevelled; her forehead large and protruding; her face had many wrinkles and was shrivelled up; her ears were long and lumpy; her nose was twisted and inflamed; she had a yellow beard streaked with white; her mouth was distorted and gaping; her teeth were turned in and decayed; her tongue made chewing movements and moistened her lips; she made sucking noises and licked her lips; she whistled when she yawned; she was weeping and tears ran down her cheeks; she was shivering and panting for breath; her complexion was darkish blue; her skin rough and thick; her body bent and askew; her neck curved; she was hump-backed; and being lame, she supported herself on a stick.[37]

Nāropa was terrified by this apparition, and after reflecting on it he took each of the thirty-seven features as an object of contemplation. Through this he realized that conditioned existence is miserable because it carries thirty-seven kinds of dissatisfaction; the physical body, with thirty-seven impure substances, is impermanent and mortal; and coemergent wisdom arises because of the thirty-seven transmutations of emotional and conceptual obscurations possible in yogic practice.[38] He experienced great renunciation and devotion and followed the ḍākinī's advice to seek a guru.

It is not unusual for ḍākinīs to disguise themselves as miserable old women, especially those who appear in prophetic roles to radically redirect the priorities of the arrogant or intellectual practitioner.[39] In this case, the ḍākinī's manifested form was an unusual teaching device for the intellectual Nāropa, shocking his mind into direct perception and sacred outlook. Her physical form as the hag awakened Nāropa effectively, and so we can see that the thirty-seven horrific features were an appropriate and compassionate manifestation of the ḍākinī.[40]

In any case, wisdom ḍākinīs are said in the Tibetan tradition to take human form and to exhibit their remarkable qualities in physical as well as spiritual ways. Their motivation for taking human birth is parallel to that of buddhas, particularly to tame beings and support them in their spiritual development, as well as to protect the integrity of the Vajrayāna teachings in particular. These wisdom ḍākinīs manifest as great gurus of the Vajrayāna, such as Machik; as "sisters" of their prominent gurus, such as Niguma;[41] or as consorts of famous gurus, such as Yeshe Tsogyal, whose consort was Padmasambhava, Guru Rinpoche of Tibet.

Female Tantric Gurus

The second category of embodied human ḍākinīs is the tantric guru who achieves fame for the depth of her realizations and the skill of her teaching. The namthar literature of Tibetan Vajrayāna is dotted with biographies of such human emanations, usually considered manifestations of particular ḍākinīs. Some of these ḍākinīs became teachers with many disciples, such as Yeshe Tsogyal, Maṇḍāravā, and Machik Lapdrön, and their stories are popularly repeated in the major tantric lineages.

More commonly, these female tantric gurus were enjoined to pass their teachings to only a few disciples, strictly maintaining the secrecy of the transmissions they received. Because of this, they are not always well known in their lineages and are sometimes considered "accomplished yoginīs" rather than tantric gurus in their own right. The reasons for this injunction by the ḍākinīs who give them transmission can only be guessed. Certainly, in patriarchal societies, realized women carry certain risks in credibility when they assume the role of the guru. This can be seen in the life stories of female gurus such as the treasure-discoverer Chomo Menmo (1248–1283), one of the human emanations of Yeshe Tsogyal.[42]

According to hagiographic accounts, Chomo Menmo's father was a comfortable landowner and her mother herself a human ḍākinī, and many miracles accompanied her birth. She was nursed tenderly in infancy, but when she was five her mother died, and when her father remarried she began to endure hardships. She was forced to graze cattle and do menial chores. In the spring of her thirteenth year, she fell asleep while grazing her cattle in the mountains near one of Guru Rinpoche's meditation caves.[43] A beautiful voice awakened her, beckoning her into the cave. She saw there a group of ḍākinīs celebrating in a grotesque charnel ground, and their leader Vajravārāhī warmly invited her to join their circle, drawing a text from behind a rock. Placing the text on the crown of Chomo Menmo's head, Vajravārāhī then immediately empowered her and presented the text to her, entrusting it to her care. "This contains the instructions of the

Gathering of All the Secrets of the Ḍākinīs. If you experientially cultivate it in utmost secrecy, you will obtain the supreme accomplishment."[44]

Chomo Menmo quickly became a fully matured yoginī and spontaneously expounded teachings. Some people became devoted to her, but most discounted her realization and gave her the derogatory nickname Chomo Menmo, saying, "Having fallen asleep on the mountainside, she has been possessed by a *menmo* spirit."[45] Chomo Menmo became disheartened by the lack of faith in her realization and left her home to wander aimlessly. When she met the great tertön Chökyi Wangchuk, they recognized the auspiciousness of their connection and became spiritual consorts,[46] which led to their mutual maturation. It was auspicious for him to have met her, because he was struggling with the realization of a potent treasure text (terma) that promised destruction for its discoverer. With her help and blessing, he was able to receive the key to the treasure from the ḍākinīs, the first of eighteen he eventually discovered. He could not have done this without Chomo Menmo's help.[47]

After they had exchanged their extensive teachings and empowerments, Chökyi Wangchuk advised Chomo Menmo that it was premature for her to propagate the profound terma volume she had received from the ḍākinīs. Instead, she should practice it in secrecy and wander through central Tibet benefiting beings inconspicuously, bringing them to an experience of great bliss. Then she would attain in this life the level of a fully matured human ḍākinī. Accompanied by two yoginī attendants, Chomo Menmo followed his advice for years, benefiting many. In the summer of her thirty-sixth year, she performed a feast offering at the summit of Trak Lhari in central Tibet, and she and her two attendants flew like *garuḍas* in their human bodies off to the land of the ḍākinīs, the Copper-Colored Mountain in Uḍḍiyāṇa. They were witnessed by local cowherds, who were deeply moved by the sight. Her terma text was thus returned to the ḍākinīs and kept there until its eventual discovery by the great and prolific tertön Jamyang Khyentse Wangpo (1820–1892), with whom Chomo Menmo had a karmic connection.

Chomo Menmo joined the ranks of other important female treasure-discoverers who received new texts directly from the hands of the protector ḍākinīs but were forbidden to pass on the teachings to more than one human disciple.[48] Sometimes this injunction came from the mouths of the ḍākinīs; at other times, as in the case of Chomo, it came from her spiritual consort after she had faced public ridicule. This could be seen as an example of patriarchal suppression, for while women have been recognized as full of spiritual potential in the Indian and Tibetan traditions, they have been barred from positions of leadership in institutional life, as has been clearly indicated by many scholars.[49] Generally it may be observed that Tibet has many highly accomplished yoginīs in its history, some of whom have had a few students. But few of them have achieved the rank of tantric gurus of renown.

This accounts for the dearth of yoginī lineage stories in the Tibetan tradition, for it is the students of great teachers who compile their gurus' biographies. But when great yoginīs have been discouraged from taking students or giving empowerments, their stories become mere rumors. Scholars such as Hanna Havnevik have noted it is difficult to begin collecting the stories of great yoginīs because very few are remembered by Tibetan monastic or lay people, and few Western scholars have given this task priority. Nevertheless, she and other scholars have begun to collect what remnants are available regarding great yoginīs, both historic and contemporary.[50]

When yoginīs were able to step into the limelight as tantric gurus, they did so after undergoing the hardships and surrender traditionally required of male teachers. But they also had additional difficulties because they did not conform to the narrow roles required of women. Yeshe Tsogyal endured all the traditional austerities and hardships in her training, but at one point in her journey she protested to Guru Rinpoche about the special obstacles for a woman tāntrikā:

> I am a timid woman and of scant ability; of lowly condition, the butt of everyone. If I go for alms, I am set upon by dogs; if food and riches come my way, I am the prey of thieves; since I am beautiful, I am the quarry of every lecherous knave; if I am busy with much to do, the country folk accuse me; if I don't do what they think I should, the people criticize; if I put a foot wrong, everyone detests me. I have to worry about everything I do. That is what it is like to be a woman! How can a woman possibly gain accomplishment in Dharma? Just managing to survive is already hard enough![51]

Throughout her journey Yeshe Tsogyal worked with these obstacles in skillful ways, ignoring the gossip when she joined Guru Rinpoche in tantric partnership, converting her rapists, finding an additional consort when that was required by her practice, defeating Bön shamans who belittled her, and attaining full buddhahood as a woman.[52]

Machik Lapdrön was an example of a yoginī who became realized without a famous guru as a tantric partner and who also endured hardships in her quest for realization. As a child her gifts in memorization and recitation were amazing, and she specialized in Prajñāpāramitā texts. Having developed great renown as an *ācārya,* or learned master, she was confronted one day by Kyotön Sönam Lama, a wandering yogin of great learning and realization. He asked her, "Young Ācārya, you seem very learned indeed in the Prajñāpāramitā texts, but do you really know their meaning?"[53] When she declared that she did, he asked her to explain it to him. When she described the bodhisattva paths and stages, he commented that she did indeed seem to know how to explain the meaning but that she had not yet personally realized it and integrated it into her mindstream. He asked her to practice the essence of the Prajñāpāramitā, letting go of all mental grasping and opening to the nonconceptual state. "This understanding of nonduality is a great fire which destroys the darkness of ignorant clinging to a self. The essence of all teachings is to thoroughly examine the nature of your mind. So you should do it!"

As she applied herself to the lama's instructions, a completely fresh experience beyond conceptualization dawned, and the belief in the existence of a self permanently disappeared. As an expression of her realization, Machik spontaneously changed her demeanor and habits, signifying her surrender of all attachments and preferences customary to her station: She gave up lavish clothing and jewelry and dressed only in beggars' rags and cast-offs; she gave up the company of friends, teachers, disciples, and monks and associated only with lepers and beggars; she abandoned her hermitage and the monastery and slept wherever she was, even by the side of the road; she gave up the solitude and simplicity of retreat and wandered aimlessly everywhere; she gave up healthy and pure food and ate anything (except meat), no matter how rotted or filthy; she gave up craving for praise and compliments and remained serene in the face of slander, blame, or abuse. All experiences, whether pleasurable or painful, she experienced as having a single taste in the vast expanse of things as they are.[54]

This experience of abandoning the accoutrements of life as a conventional woman was pivotal in Machik's journey. Traditional accounts are full of commentary about the circumscribed life of a Tibetan woman,

Machik Lapdrön, founder of the Chö tradition.

bound by family and intimate relationships, household demands, constraints on travel, the desire for wealth and lovely clothing, and the threat of slander or gossip. These spontaneously disappeared when Machik directly realized the essence of the Prajñāpāramitā. This transformation prepared her for the events to follow, including receiving a succession of transmissions of the Chö and other teachings from herukas and ḍākinīs. Still, when she joined with her prophesied tantric partner Thöpa Bhadra, she encountered suspicion and embarrassment on the part of her hostess and consulted her guru about the suitability of such a union. Only when her teacher suggested that it was auspicious and that she should marry did Machik settle into the relationship.[55]

The Ḍākinī as Mother, Sister, or Maid

In the tantras, the ḍākinī is often referred to as mother, sister, and maid, with ambiguous meanings attributed to each. The *Hevajra-tantra* speaks of the mother as the birth-giver for the world, an allusion to the Prajñāpāramitā, who always wishes the tāntrika prosperity and supports tantric practice. The sister shows the division between relative and absolute truth and is constant in her affection.[56] In the hagiographic literature, mothers, sisters, and other such female relatives play important roles in the lives of great gurus.

Mothers of great yogins or yoginīs are considered especially important human ḍākinīs, for how could a remarkable being like an incarnate lama or realized practitioner be born from a lesser being? The tradition of remarkable mothers can be traced back to the example of the mother of the Buddha, Mahāmāyā, who was said to be endowed with thirty-two auspicious qualities.[57] Sometimes the mother of an incarnate ḍākinī is considered a ḍākinī, as in the cases of Yeshe Tsogyal, Maṇḍāravā and Machik Lapdrön, whose mothers had many visions of ḍākinī visitations during conception and pregnancy. The great ḍākinī Dagmema, who was the wife and consort of Marpa, uniquely displayed her teaching powers at the tragic death of her son Tarma-dode when she remained calm and imparted to him the necessary instructions on ejection and transference of consciousness.[58] These mothers derived their designation as ḍākinīs from their association with remarkable yogins or yoginīs, but sometimes the mothers of these great meditation virtuosos were tantric masters in their own right. When the young prince Kambalapāda was crowned king, he proved to be a skilled and successful leader, much to his mother's chagrin. She urged him first to renounce his kingdom and become a monk, and then to renounce monastic life to pursue meditation at the foot of a tree. Eventually she encouraged him to become a wandering yogin without even a begging bowl to his name. Then she appeared to him in full glory as a wisdom ḍākinī; she gave him Cakrasaṃvara initiation and continued to guide him throughout his life.[59]

The terms for *sister* (*che, bhaginī*) in Tibetan and Sanskrit are ambiguous, for they could refer to any close female relative, even a wife. The great yoginī Niguma is called in some sources Nāropa's wife and in others his sister, though accounts of their arranged marriage appear in one of his biographies.[60] She was a Brahmin girl who converted to Buddhism after their wedding, becoming a devoted disciple of her new husband. After eight years of unhappy marriage, they agreed to a divorce, with Niguma offering to take the blame for the failure of their union. She exclaimed:

> You cannot just discard me by reproaching me with not being a Buddhist. Considering that it is uncertain when death will come, there is no safety anywhere. I shall not hinder you practising the dharma but will do whatever possible to help. So renounce the world saying that I have faults.[61]

Nāropa agreed, and in their divorce proclaimed women to be full of guile and his wife full of faults. Nevertheless, afterward they became dharma companions (*che drok*) on the path of meditation and were called brother and sister. She is said to have worked closely with Nāropa's chief student, Marpa, as translator. The later independent accounts of Niguma depict her powerfully as a wrathful, dark ḍākinī, a tantric master in her own right fervently sought for her teachings. Niguma's Six Yogas closely parallel Nāropa's famous teachings; they both received them from Buddha Vajradhara. Niguma gave these teachings to her spiritual son Khyungpo Naljor, requesting that he keep them secret by allowing them to be passed only to one disciple at a time for seven generations before being propagated more widely.[62]

The term *maid* refers to the wife or consort of a great yogin. This is one of the most important roles for human women, for tantric partnership is viewed as a particularly rich opportunity for both partners to develop realization. The intimacy of the relationship provides the setting for the sharing of wisdom, as the hagiographies attest. The sexual yoga practice, which will be discussed in more detail later in this chapter, joins meditation with physical embodiment in a very direct fashion. Reflecting this, the wives or consorts of lamas elicit instant respect in Tibetan culture.[63]

But even the domestic details of daily life between lama and mate provide a setting for direct dharma teaching. Saraha asked his wife to prepare him radish curry and then entered deep samādhi for a period of twelve years. When he emerged from his meditation, he immediately demanded, "Where are my radishes?" She replied, in the voice of the ḍākinī:

> A solitary body does not mean solitude. The best solitude is the mind far away from names and conceptions. You have been meditating for twelve years, yet you have not cut off the idea of radishes. What good will it do to go to the mountains?[64]

Hearing this, Saraha devoted himself to the inner practice of cutting through concepts and directly seeing the nature of reality.

The centrality of the mate for the tantric guru is still recognized in contemporary Tibetan Buddhism. It is customary for the gurus and peers of great meditation masters to insist they take a consort in order to vitalize their practice and lengthen their lives. This was the case for the fifteenth Karmapa, whose consort was the previous incarnation of Ven. Khandro Rinpoche, described at the beginning of the chapter. In an example of a male consort, Guru Rinpoche selected several different partners for Yeshe Tsogyal to extend her practice.[65] In a contemporary example, the great Dzogchen master Dilgo Khyentse Rinpoche became quite ill after an extended austere retreat, and so he married Khandro Lhamo, a simple young woman from an ordinary farming family. As a result of this union, his health improved and he had many deep visions. She was recognized as a ḍākinī.[66]

In the Nyingma and Kagyü lineages, when an incarnate lama who had chosen the noncelibate yogin path decided to marry, traditionally the prospective wife needed to fulfill the criteria for human ḍākinīs. Careful divinations and prophesies were consulted for suitable candidates, who were privately tested in ways similar to tülkus. Once the appropriate candidate was located, the marriage ceremony consisted of a mutual enthronement as heruka and ḍākinī, for wedding rituals are not usually religious occasions in Tibet. This is not always contemporary Nyingma practice, however.[67]

Embodied Ḍākinī as the Practice and the Realization

The fourth way in which humans are recognized as ḍākinīs comes from their participation in and accomplishment of the sādhana rituals of ḍākinī yidams. In this case, the gender of the practitioner does not really matter. When devoted practitioners, male and female, keep their Vajrayāna vows and commitments, they promise to always see themselves in the form of the ḍākinī yidam. This means that in creation-phase practice they visualize themselves as the ḍākinī, and throughout their daily lives—waking and sleeping, cooking and washing up, feeling content or furious—they are also to see themselves as the deity.[68] They commit to seeing others as the deity as well, appreciating the continual presence of the ḍākinī in the details of everyday life. When tantric practitioners have made this commitment, they are to be understood as human ḍākinīs, whether they are male or female. For that matter, the dawning of realization—meditation experience itself—is the ḍākinī.

Tantric practitioners also understand themselves to be the ḍākinī in relationship with the guru, especially in the practice of certain forms of devotional guru yoga practice. When the guru's blessing is supplicated with devotional yearning (*mögü*), the guru is visualized as the meditation object in a purified form, a heruka, while the practitioner visualizes herself or himself as the wisdom ḍākinī Vajrayoginī with all the traditional ornaments, blazing with fire. This practice expresses the qualities of the ḍākinī as spiritual subject with relation to the root guru and the lineage of enlightened teachers.[69] That is, when he or she is devoted to the guru, the male or female practitioner is a ḍākinī.

Female participants in the tantric sādhanas and feast offering practices (gaṇacakra, tsok-khor) of yidams are especially considered ḍākinīs because they fully identify with the yidam during the practice. In the ritual literature of the tantras, the role of the human and visionary ḍākinīs is pivotal. Certain aspects of the ritual such as initiations traditionally must be performed by wisdom ḍākinīs, and the presence of ḍākinī, whether human or visionary, is required for an authentic feast offering practice. At certain points in the practice, the worldly ḍākinīs, either affiliated with a dharma teacher or unaffiliated, are summoned to the feast and pacified with offerings of food and liquor. For this reason, the feast offering ritual literally refers to "a circle or assembly" of ḍākinīs, whose practice opens the gates of wisdom for all the tantric practitioners.[70]

Some scholars have traced the changes in the ritual role of women as tantra developed in India and was assimilated into Tibetan monastic practice.[71] According to these studies, women played prominent roles in tantric lineages and rituals in India, but this role was subsumed under male prerogative in monastic Tibet, where women did not hold the full monastic ordination that men enjoyed. In these contexts, it is argued that ḍākinīs were no longer human women but merely visionary forms who appeared as self- or front-visualizations in creation-phase practice. It has been argued that the ḍākinī is no longer embodied in human form but in an external, objectified form controlled and utilized by male practitioners only.[72]

On the other hand, the ḍākinī phenomena have continued not only within lay yogin(ī) communities. Certain Tibetan nuns were recognized as emanations of ḍākinīs by virtue of their remarkable practice. Hanna Havnevik found numerous references to ḍākinī nuns, who were to be treated with special respect because of their mastery of inner-heat yoga (tummo), clairvoyance, walking through walls, attainment of the rainbow body (ja-lü), and other remarkable accomplishments.[73] This is possible only for nuns who are able to receive proper instruction in tantric practice, which is often denied them. However, nuns have proven to be particularly skilled in yogic practice because of excellent motivation. Khenpo Tsultrim Gyamtso Rinpoche commented that he has found it especially inspiring to work with nuns, who lack the worldly motivations for pursuing the monastic path with which monks must often contend. He said with a dazzling smile, "I have had great success with my nuns!"[74]

As Vajrayāna Buddhism flourishes in the West, there is opportunity for the gaṇacakra ritual to return to its original form. In Western communities of sādhana practitioners, gaṇacakra feast offerings have been performed by male and female practitioners together who all understand themselves to be embodiments of the ḍākinī (or of the heruka and ḍākinī in union).[75] Officiant functions are shared by women and men, and an all-male feast offering, although rare, might be viewed by all as less fully expressing the tantric commitments of the yidam. Gaṇacakras are opportunities for the full ritual expression of the transcendent passion associated with the ḍākinī and heruka, and this may arise more predictably in practice when both genders are represented.

The category of embodied ḍākinī also applies in tantric literature to the phenomenon of women practitioners who attain enlightenment. Yeshe Tsogyal was approached shortly before her death by one of her main female disciples. Choked with grief, Dorje Tsomo of Shelkar asked Yeshe Tsogyal to take her to the abode of Guru Rinpoche (*Pema Ö*), or at the very least to leave her with special instructions and precepts. In response, Yeshe Tsogyal gave her complete instructions on the path to enlightenment (defined here as "lotus light," or pema ö) through various levels. First, to become a ḍākinī, or one who dances in space, she was to transform her subtle body through yogic practice.[76] Then, to become a siddhā she was to master her mind through yoga, taming the emotional obscurations (*kleśa, nyönmong*). To attain buddhahood, she was to realize inseparable emptiness-awareness through Mahāmudrā. And finally, to attain the rainbow body, she was to dissolve the physical body through the realization of Dzogchen. Then she would have developed the spontaneity associated with the absolute nature of phenomena (*chönyi sesa*) and would truly, fully become a ḍākinī, one who dances in the sky. This, for Yeshe Tsogyal, was the "palace of lotus light" of Guru Rinpoche, enlightenment itself.[77] Shelkar Dorje Tsomo went on to become a famous yoginī and consort with Namkhai Nyingpo, one of the most renowned disciples of Guru Rinpoche.[78]

These categories of human ḍākinīs gradually widen from an exclusive group of ḍākinīs who inherited their state from previous lives to a broader context of meditative realization open to any dedicated tantric practitioner. In the broadest understanding of the term, the ḍākinī is every woman in every station of life, whether or not she is a tantric practitioner.

Every Woman Is Part of the Ḍākinī

Women, by virtue of being female, have inherent in their bodies and minds certain qualities of the ḍākinī, whether they know it or not.[79] The embodied woman is to be revered in Vajrayāna as the representative of the Mother Prajñāpāramitā. In a reference in the *Caṇḍamahāroṣaṇa-tantra,* the Lady Prajñāpāramitā said to her devotee Caṇḍamahāroṣaṇa:

> *Wherever in the Three Worlds a womanly form is seen,*
> *that is said to be my form, whether she belongs to a low family or not low. . . .*

Each in her own form is resolute in benefiting all living beings. . . .
When those women are honored, they give [success] instantly
To those who desire the welfare of all beings.
Therefore one should honor women.[80]

Or, as Maṇḍāravā declared at her birth, disclaiming her uniqueness, "There are millions of female bodhisattvas just like me who come into this world like rain pouring down."[81]

How is it that women are part of the ḍākinī? Contemporary lamas answer that women are born women because of their karma, which involves both physical and mental factors. But by the very nature of their female bodies, women manifest the dynamic of the ḍākinī and have a unique ability to radiate the ḍākinī's qualities to the tantric practitioner who is engaged in sacred outlook.

Respect for women is therefore foundational in Vajrayāna practice and vow. A landmark thirteenth-century text by Sakya Paṇḍita outlined the parameters of these Vajrayāna commitments (samaya, tamtsik). They parallel the vinaya rules of the Buddhist monastic tradition and the "skillful actions" of a bodhisattva in the Mahāyāna tradition,[82] suggesting what it is to break a vow and to jeopardize one's sacred commitments. As in the vinaya, a Vajrayāna root downfall (*tungwa*) is a deed that violates the heart of one's commitment and can endanger the vow itself. The text explains, "The sin of not keeping these is that the vows are spoiled. If one spoils them thinking it does not matter, one will be caught by Māra and will therefore suffer."[83]

Among the root downfalls are expected ones such as disparaging one's teacher, the community of Vajrayāna practitioners, the Buddhist teachings themselves, or bodhicitta, the awakened mind. Two are of special import for this study. One, the eighth root downfall, is "physically abusing oneself out of disrespect for the five aggregates, which are in actuality the five buddhas."[84] Since the body is the support for offerings and the seat of bliss in empowerments and yogic practice, and the ground for the realization of primordial bliss, it is to be cared for and regarded as sacred. This vow indicates the importance of the sacredness of the body in tantric practice.

In addition, the fourteenth root downfall is associated with respect for all women, as embodiments of the most sacred aspects of tantric practice—female, feminine, and wisdom:

> If one disparages women who are of the nature of wisdom, that is the fourteenth root downfall. That is to say, women are the symbol of wisdom and *śūnyatā,* showing both. It is therefore a root downfall to dispraise women in every possible way, saying that women are without spiritual merit . . . and made of unclean things, not considering their good qualities.[85]

As women are expressions of the outer ḍākinī principle, they are the symbol of wisdom and śūnyatā by virtue of their female bodies. If one "tries to trick or blatantly disrespects"[86] a woman, especially a wisdom consort, and then feels satisfaction about it, this is a violation of samaya.

How is it that women's bodies are a symbol of wisdom and śūnyatā? This requires an understanding of sacred outlook. On a secret, absolute level, there is no essential difference between sexes or genders. But, as the aspects of the absolute arise and take form, there are specific expressions that differentiate into female and male. These expressions are different from the conventional primary and secondary sexual characteristics discussed in early classification texts.[87] From the point of view of tantra, such descriptions are mundane and have little to do with the sacred view of reality.

Women's bodies express the vastness of space because of their wombs and vaginas, which are understood as powerful symbols of emptiness in their own right. From a tantric point of view, manifestation arises as a dynamic dance of qualities that express themselves in the phenomenal world. And because of the physical space within women's genitalia and reproductive systems, their bodies, psychologies, and mind experiences uniquely express the dynamic qualities of emptiness. Likewise, men's physical bodies express the unique qualities of skillful means and compassionate action, engaging with their surroundings on a psychological and mind level as well. It is actually impossible to separate these physical traits from their meanings in tantric understanding.

Nevertheless, it is common in Tibetan Buddhist literature assimilated from Indian Buddhism to see the female body referred to as inferior. As mentioned, one of the Tibetan words for woman is *kyemen,* meaning "inferior birth." This has been explained clearly by Rita Gross as a realistic assessment of the lives of women in Tibetan society.[88] Although Tibetan women have had opportunities and freedoms that set them apart from their Indian sisters, they have nonetheless lived in a patriarchal society in which their avenues for formal spiritual practice are comparatively limited. When the wisdom ḍākinī Yeshe Tsogyal described to Guru Rinpoche the special plight of women,[89] he acknowledged that the low birth of women is not connected with any inherent qualities in their bodies or minds:

> *Yoginī seasoned in the Secret Mantra!*
> *The ground of Liberation*
> *Is this human frame, this common human form—*
> *And here distinctions, male and female,*
> *Have no consequence.*
> *And yet if bodhicitta graces it,*
> *A woman's form indeed will be supreme.*[90]

Yeshe Tsogyal acknowledges the obstacles that women face on the spiritual path in a patriarchal society that subjects women to special scrutiny. But, as Guru Rinpoche says, if a woman has strong aspiration, she has higher potential.

How can it be that a woman may have higher potential? There are two answers. The first answer relates to the power of Vajrayāna practice to turn the greatest obstacles into the most potent spiritual benefits. Of course a woman's spiritual capacities, based on her body and mind, are equally suited to dharma practice. But if her aspiration is strong, her potential may be greater because of the patriarchal and other obstacles she faces. Working with obstacles in a focused, nonrejecting way transforms their intensity into fuel for the journey. For a highly motivated woman in a patriarchal society, the adversity inherent in her life as described by Yeshe Tsogyal and others is powerful teaching concerning egolessness, suffering, and impermanence.

A second answer relates to the ways in which women's bodies, psychologies, and minds are linked with the dynamic of wisdom. Women, through their physical form, have a capacity to penetrate to the nature of situations and to understand and know them. With the right supporting conditions, they have tremendous ability to realize the nature of the mind. With the wrong conditions, women can become confused by their own wakefulness and wander in frustration on the spiritual path. The next section explores the ways in which women may have the propensity to develop wisdom, given these proper circumstances.

Prajñā, Upāya, Women, and Men

Women are crazy and men are stupid.

—VEN. CHÖGYAM TRUNGPA RINPOCHE

On an ultimate level, there is no real difference between women and men. Our natures are empty of inherent existence, vast and expansive, free of conceptual elaboration. Yet there are sacred masculine and feminine energies that are an essential part of the mind-body complex. These energies are not determined by biology. In the Vajrayāna view, it is more that biology has emanated from these fundamental energies of mind and phenomena; they constitute each of us. Each lama I interviewed was definite that masculine and feminine energies flow in our minds, emotions, subtle bodies, and bodies, whatever our sex or gender.[91]

Ultimately our minds have no gender, but penetrating insight and skillful means intertwine in all our experience. On a subtle-body level, all humans have feminine and masculine channels and winds, which intermingle and may in meditation meet in the nondual central channel. Our physical bodies have both feminine and masculine qualities, but depending upon our karma and the physical bodies we have inherited, we have differentiated abilities to radiate feminine or masculine energies. Always, the physical body expresses the qualities present in the subtle body and the mind.[92] These three are interdependent.

On the level of appearance and manifestation, women and men are distinct and complementary in their physical forms and psychological experiences. From the view of Vajrayāna Buddhism, both feminine and masculine qualities are inherently positive, awakened, and beneficial, but because of ignorance and habitual patterns they can manifest in painful ways. Motivated by powerful self-centeredness, relationships between women and men can arouse dramatic streams of emotionality, conceptuality, and fantasy leading to pain and alienation. But whether manifested in awakened or painful ways, the qualities of feminine and masculine energy remain consistent. Feminine manifestation is associated with energetic heat and intensity, masculine manifestation with steady power and groundedness.

Penetrating insight (prajñā, sherap) as manifested in the lives of human women is a subtle, pervasive, and very intelligent energy, a kind of sharpness or sensitivity. In its basic nature it is awareness, but in daily life it manifests as sensitivity that can be quite intense and hot, related with emotionality. This sensitivity has more allegiance to dynamics than to content. There is a Tibetan saying, "Women's intelligence is at a very sharp angle, and empty."[93] This means that women have a heightened ability to identify problems and to penetrate them without clinging to results.

The heat and intensity of women's energy can trip emotional triggers that can create enormous chaos. This can be beneficial when intractable situations present themselves. For example, when bureaucracy becomes overbearing or when stubborn logics and habitual styles are employed, intense emotionality can liberate the ponderous environment. The sensitivity of women's intuition can see injustice, emotional subtlety, interpersonal dynamics, and hidden meanings; when there are imbalances and flaws in specific environments, women's sharp, penetrating qualities can identify and adjust them. This emotionality can also be very warm, generating compassion and care for others.[94]

However, when intense emotionality is indulged, feminine intelligence can become self-serving. When this happens, feminine wisdom can become wild and even dangerous, subverting its own intelligence.[95] Women have a capacity for responsiveness that can be fickle and provocative. Its fascination with sharpness may become habitual, so that when problems are identified, feminine energy may not have a particular allegiance to solutions. A metaphor to describe feminine wisdom is the sharpness of a knife, which is very penetrating but can be too sensitive, unstable and even dangerous if not used properly. In this case it is important to have a counter-energy, strong and skilled, to control that sharp blade and protect things that are not to be cut.[96]

On the other hand, when skillful means (upāya, thap) manifests in the styles of human men, there is strength, solidity, and resiliency. In contrast to feminine energy, the masculine is obvious and oriented toward the material world of manifestation and action.[97] It is also more grounded, more sleepy, and when out of balance could be considered a "stubborn, resentful presence."[98] Generally, however, it is praised because it is strong and faithful.

In its positive manifestation, masculine means is tolerant, patient, and accommodating. The fundamental masculine qualities are immovability and bluntness.[99] Men have the wisdom to know what is happening, just or unjust, good or bad, negative or positive, and to simply let things be as they are.[100] Masculine energy is known for loyalty, reliability, and the ability to join in groups to achieve common goals.

On the other hand, masculine energy can be too accommodating, even lazy, and tends to be dull and oblivious. Without the stimulation of the feminine wisdom, the masculine can go to sleep or be lulled into merely habitual routines or bureaucratic solutions. Or, when confronted by the wild and self-serving feminine, the masculine can become stubborn, cold, and stolid. When threatened, the masculine can become blunt and heavy-handed, retaliating without accuracy. The masculine needs a relationship with sharpness because although it is very strong it is not precise or cutting.[101]

Alone, either of these energies can become an obstacle to spiritual development, according to the Vajrayāna. One without the other is very difficult and creates an imbalance in the practitioner. The sharpness of our mind-body complex yearns for more grounding, and our dullness craves excitement and clarity. Unifying these two qualities, bringing them into balance, is one of the goals of Vajrayāna practice.

As the tāntrika becomes more attuned to these polar energies in her or his experience, they are found to reside everywhere. For example, it is possible to see the interplay between the feminine and masculine energies in solitary meditation. They are experienced as two common extreme states of mind, obstacles that disturb mindfulness practice. Much of our meditation vacillates between wildness on the one hand and drowsiness or dullness on the other.[102] One moment we are bothered by excess discursiveness mixed with vivid emotionality that makes settled state of mind impossible. Ten minutes later we find ourselves nodding off to sleep, spaced out and blank. The practice is to work with these two obstacles in meditation, understanding that they come from a common root.

When penetrating insight and skillful means acknowledge their interrelationship, however, it is possible to synchronize these energies and revitalize our human experience. We could not even directly experience the world without the cooperation and interplay of the two energies. When we experience, for example, visual perception, seeing the color red involves the masculine aspect, but distinguishing the vivid tone of red, its vibrating intensity, in contrast to other colors or other reds, requires the feminine quality. If we have too much masculine, we see the color but do not discriminate it. If we have too much feminine quality, our sense perceptions jump from thing to thing without really seeing anything fully.[103]

Desire and Sexuality in Buddhist Tantra

When the Buddha sat under the tree of awakening, one of his primary discoveries was the role of desire and passion in human life. He recognized that human life is filled with anxiety and sorrow and suggested that they arise from desire (*tṛṣṇā, sepa*), a kind of craving that unwittingly drives humans into continuous experiences of pain. The common quality we share is that all of us wish to be happy and not to suffer.[104] We pursue pleasure and devise elaborate schemes to elude pain.

In order to give perspective to this human quality, Tibetan teachings point out that this is not true of other beings in the same way. Humans have a unique propensity for desire: we dream, fantasize, wish, and yearn throughout our lives. Passionate attachment pervades our experience in a variety of forms. The consumerism that saturates contemporary life is driven by this desire.

Beings in other realms or spheres of existence, however, are dominated by different emotional styles. When we witness the lives of animals in the wild, we see that they are compelled by a need to survive, and fantasy and yearning are not a part of their makeup. In the spring, they give birth to their young and devote themselves to methodically feeding and raising them in the warm summer months. As winter nears, animals hurry around to gather their winter stores, ensnared in their instinctual focus on the basic needs of life. In the Tibetan scheme, the realm of the gods is characterized by blissful ignorance, the jealous gods (*asura*s) by jealousy, the animal realm by plodding ignorance oriented toward survival, the hungry ghosts (*preta*s) by arrogance, and the various hell realms by aggression. The unremitting suffering of these realms is driven by these emotional styles.

The irony of human life is that our very desire for pleasure results in suffering. Whatever we have, we wish for more or for something different. When we have what we want, we eventually lose it, and when we get what we want, we decide it is not what we really wanted. Unexamined, this impulse toward pleasure creates an endless series of frustrating situations. Until we recognize the drivenness of human life toward unfulfilled desire, we cannot experience a respite from our suffering. Buddha Śākyamuni's teaching of the Four Noble Truths accurately pinpointed this.[105]

Desire, when liberated from self-centered preoccupations, has the intelligence to resonate to the emotional experience of others. This means

Cakrasaṃvara and Vajrayoginī in passionate embrace.

that we have momentary psychological experiences that resemble the unrelieved ordeals of each of the other five realms of existence: We experience moments of intense jealousy, echoing the experience of the jealous gods. We experience raging anger or cold disdain similar to the beings of the hot and cold hells. Like animals and god-realm beings, we fall into the numbing ignorance of daily routine or the blissful ignorance of idealism. Like hungry ghosts, we are haunted by the yearning for satiation. Because of these temporary experiences, we can understand the intensely painful experiences of other realms, and we are sensitized to the endless patterns of suffering and hopelessness in the world. We can feel empathy and compassion for other suffering beings and, if we reflect, the desire to liberate them from their misery.

When desire turns away from habitual self-centeredness and turns toward others, spiritual transformation is possible. This is described in Buddhism as the practice of the bodhisattva, one who is committed to clarity of understanding and to the welfare of others. The fuel for this practice is desire that has been transformed into the awakened heart, a spontaneous openness and warmth that transforms habitual self-centeredness into liberation. The practice of the bodhisattva would have no fuel if it were not for the power of our desire, and with strong commitment and clarity of mind transformed desire becomes a kind of contagious fever of compassion.

How do we liberate desire and turn its intelligence and intensity toward awakening for ourselves and others? In tantra, this fundamental quality of human existence is liberated with very skillful methods. The intensity of desire can be liberated only by desire itself. As the *Hevajratantra* states, "that by which the world is bound, by that same its bonds are released, but the world is deluded and knows not this truth, and he who is deprived of this truth will not gain perfection."[106] The passionate quality of human experience can only be liberated through desire itself, and then it is described as a "mingling of passion and absence of passion."[107]

One of the distinctive features of Tibetan Vajrayāna, especially in the practices of the Anuttara-yoga-tantra, is the inclusiveness with regard to desire and especially sexuality in a spiritual context. This is a way to work directly with desire, but it requires a strong foundation of training. According to Anuttara-yoga, training in the three vehicles is essential to spiritual development, especially in working with our most primitive emotions.

In order to work with our self-centered desire, we train in the foundational vehicle, the Hīnayāna, in which we learn self-restraint, renunciation, and simplicity. Desirelessness is one of the treasured spiritual qualities of the practitioner who has mastered the Hīnayāna. However, after cultivating discipline in this way, we retain a residue of aggression; we have rejected too much of the intelligence of desire and have cut ourselves off from the suffering of others.

In the broad vehicle, the Mahāyāna, aggression is the greatest obstacle to the practice of compassion; we cannot benefit beings if we are angry toward them or toward their suffering. With Mahāyāna training, aggression is transformed into patience and care, and we are able to begin to relieve the suffering we encounter. While the Mahāyāna acknowledges the close relationship between desire and compassion, there is still the danger that desire can lead to so-called idiot compassion, which is tainted by our own personal agenda.

Having completed the training of the first two vehicles, we discover a residue of blindness or obliviousness that inhibits our further development. We have in some way diluted the intensity of the world in our altruistic dreams, motivated by the futility of avoiding painful emotions, difficult life passages, and underlying habitual patterns. When we continue our training in the diamond vehicle, the Vajrayāna, we directly address this oblivious quality.

Vajrayāna training and practice give us immediate proximity to all aspects of our experience, removing the blinders that remained from the previous practice. But the residue that remains this time is passion. However, it is said that at this point passion need not be an obstacle to spiritual growth. By now it has ideally been refined through spiritual training and represents the warm heart combined with the intensity of Vajrayāna experience and practice. If it becomes the object of contemplation, it holds great power for bringing the mind to the essential point.

In the Anuttara-yoga tradition, there is really no distinction made between passion in this sense and compassion. When purified of self-centeredness, passion is expressed as devotion to others, caring skillfully and utterly about their welfare; it is also expressed as joy in living and appreciation of the unique beauty of each moment. Experiences of realization naturally carry with them the burning heat of joy and compassion—otherwise they are not genuine realization experiences. However, this is also a dangerous path, for if passion seeks to serve the ego, the explosive result creates havoc. Hence, the dynamic of sexuality in Anuttara-yoga tantra is always pyrotechnic and potent.

The ordinary chemistry between men and women is a powerful expression of the fundamental dynamic of phenomena. For this reason, the realm of gender relationships is of utmost interest for the tāntrika, for the dynamic experienced there exposes the heart of the world. The sharp edginess of women reaches for the blunt pragmatism of men; at the same time, men yearn for the emotional intensity of women. Sexual yearning is, at its heart, no different from spiritual yearning. Appreciating contrast and complementarity is central to the tāntrika's life, as is tracing the dance between men and women in ordinary discourse. And sexual passion is a central expression of this dynamic, which goes to the heart of the tāntrika's body and mind.

The play of these two energies is complex in interpersonal relationships. When feminine and masculine are at war, their neurotic aspects are heightened. The feminine becomes more emotional, wild, and destructive and the masculine more obstinate, harsh, and insensitive. Even when there is attraction between the feminine and masculine, if self-centered interests predominate these weapons are used and great suffering and alienation can result. The Vajrayāna practitioner must learn to appreciate difference and acknowledge the gifts of both genders in order to maintain sacred outlook in relationships.

In the dynamics of sexual attraction, both explicit and implicit, powerful forces are at work. Desire in human life is, at its root, an expression of the yearning for wholeness and is fundamentally healthy. Yet working with this desire in harmony with practice is a great challenge for the Vajrayāna practitioner. It is difficult to honor passion without being overwhelmed by a self-centered desire for gratification.

What are the benefits of contemplating the nature of passion? Tantric practices have often been misunderstood by the uninitiated, for they are seen as ways to practice spirituality through self-gratification. But self-gratification is contrary to the tantric path of meditation. Why would one arouse passion without self-gratification as motive and method? Generally, these practices are valued because they transform ordinary passion into the basis for the experience of great bliss, or mahāsukha.

The Vajrayāna tradition provides powerful and skillful methods that accelerate inner development in direct, tangible ways. Ordinary methods of meditation may only slowly or intermittently grant the benefits of nonthought in the practitioner's experience. Cultivating great bliss is a powerful tool to hasten the removal of emotional and conceptual obscurations in one's practice. When these are cleared away, wisdom and compassion arise spontaneously.

This progress is important, for it frees the practitioner to be more available to the needs, both spiritual and material, of the many suffering people of the world. When one is able to turn all one's inner resources to the process of waking up, compassion is liberated and the spiritual benefits for all are more quickly evident. Since desire and passion are so basic to our human life, it is important to work with them properly, employing them as fuel for generating wakefulness and compassion.

Sexual Yoga and the Ḍākinī

> In order to develop inner heat *(tummo)*, under certain circumstances and conditions, one should rely on a female consort as one's assistant, and this is [a] meaning of ḍākinī.
>
> —HIS HOLINESS THE FOURTEENTH DALAI LAMA[108]

Each of us is on one level a complete universe, with masculine and feminine elements counterbalancing each other in subtle body and mind. But on the level of tangible manifestation we are not all that complete according to tantra, and sexual desire can be the indication of yearning for completeness. By virtue of having a female body, a woman radiates the feminine qualities more strongly, and it is natural for her to yearn for the masculine qualities. Similarly, it is natural for men to yearn for the feminine qualities. Ordinarily, sexual desire creates enormous confusion regarding our embodiment, which can become a great obstacle to our awakening. One way to wholeness in Vajrayāna is to discover, through physicality, the interrelatedness of the masculine and feminine qualities on all levels of experience. Various practices bring into union the dualistic tendencies that perpetuate our suffering. For this reason, contemplating the nature (*neluk*) of passion is an important part of the spiritual path.

There are traditionally three ways to realize the nature of passion in the yogic traditions of tantra.[109] First, in creation-phase practice one can visualize the yidam deities as yab-yum in sexual union, as discussed in the inner ḍākinī description of Vajrayoginī and Cakrasaṃvara. Second, one can practice tummo (caṇḍalī), or the generation of internal heat, through the subtle-body practices of the vital breath moving into the central channel. Third, one can practice so-called sexual yoga (*karmamudrā, lekyi chaggya*) with a consort. Realizing the true nature of passion in all of these forms transforms ordinary passion into the basis for the experience of great bliss (mahāsukha), which greatly accelerates the removal of emotional and conceptual obscurations in one's practice. The purpose of exploring the nature of passion is to bring about realization where it has not already occurred; from this point of view, the experience of bliss is a great expedient in the practice of tantra.

In creation-phase practice, the tāntrika visualizes herself or himself as the yidam either alone or with a consort. When the yidam deities are carefully visualized in yab-yum, there is tremendous passion, communication, and connection between them, such that one cannot distinguish one deity from the other. They are considered two-in-one. The tāntrika is simultaneously male and female passionately joined, and if one asks which is which, the practice is already lost. Yet it is important that this practice not be pursued from the view of conventional passion. As Jamgön Kongtrül Lodrö Thaye advised:

> When you identify your awareness with the masculine and visualize the form of the feminine too intimately, there is still the danger that the toxic effect of desire will resurface, resulting initially in the loss of vital energy and ultimately in coming under the power of desire. In general, it is inappropriate to pursue mundane thoughts and afflictive emotions while meditating on a deity.[110]

This practice arouses the experience of bliss as the tāntrika embodies in psychophysical form the joining of masculine and feminine elements as heruka and ḍākinī. Bliss melts the conceptual mind, heightens sensory awareness, and opens the practitioner to the naked experience of the nature of mind.

The subtle-body yoga focuses on the energetic mind-made body that links the vast and inexpressible qualities of the mind with tangible embodiment. In meditation practice, the tāntrika rides the vital breath with awareness through the energetic channels, eventually bringing them together in the central channel. The internal heat produced in the practice generates an experience of bliss. This practice powerfully overcomes confused perception by establishing the foundation for the arising of mahāsukha, the experience of nonthought in which vividness is unmediated and one can powerfully realize the natural state.

The practice of karmamudrā, or sexual yoga, has little similarity with the self-gratifying passion depicted in coffee-table books on tantra. Instead the partners meditate on bliss aroused through sexual union and its attendant fiery emotionality, sensuality, and imagination. This practice is closely linked with subtle-body yoga: with the arising of sexual bliss, the vital breath leaves the flanking channels and enters the central channel, and the bodhicitta essence-drops ignite intense, radiating heat and joy. This experience too creates the conditions for the arising of mahāsukha.

There is a great difference between contemplating the nature of passion in these practices and actually pursuing passion. It is important that sexual passion be understood as dangerous if it is not processed, seen, and understood. Conventional sexual passion is usually ego-driven, manipulative, insecure, and self-gratifying. If this kind of passion is followed unquestioningly, dramatic scenarios of great personal suffering will arise for oneself and for others. Guru Rinpoche warned Yeshe Tsogyal of the traps of ordinary sexual passion, saying that in such situations women are the most lethal demons for men, and men for women. This kind of obsession is likened to misplaced devotion. Here he dramatizes lust in a caricature, showing its inevitable outcome.

> Your daily practice is to cultivate lust. Your essence-mantra is to engage in smutty talk. Your gesture of homage is to make flirtatious signs. Your circumambulations are to roam to the place of your fancy. Your fortitude is given to the activity of passion. You try to destroy your delusion with your lower torso. You give your confidence to your secret lover. Your gratitude is for whomever makes love with the most exertion. . . . Rather than being a helper for going higher, you are the hook that pulls the practitioner down. You aren't the enhancement of bliss, but the harbinger of prejudice and misery. To take a consort while expecting to be liberated through passion becomes a cause for increasing jealousy and disturbing emotions.[111]

In a less dramatic depiction, Khenpo Tsultrim Gyamtso Rinpoche explained that the pursuit of conventional sexual passion has three stages:

joy, giving way to nonconceptual bewilderment, leading to joylessness (*chagdral*), an experience in which passion disappears and becomes a form of hatred.[112] But he suggested that the tantric yoginī or yogin must not reject passion; instead, the powerful realm of sexual passion must be mined and clarified through practice so that its profound spiritual power can be tapped for inner transformation.

The great siddha Tilopa advised his disciple, the scholarly Nāropa, to seek a consort as part of his training. When Nāropa found a suitable woman, he was at first quite happy, but when great discord arose he became miserable and wasted away, emaciated with distress. Tilopa asked him, "Nāropa, are you happy?" Nāropa answered, "I suffer by being constantly engaged with my self-dividedness in an apparent dual world." In response, Tilopa gave him instructions on sexual yoga and mahāsukha, saying:

> *Nāropa, you should strive*
> *For saṃsāra and nirvāṇa's unity.*
> *Look into the mirror of your mind, which is [mahāsukha],*
> *The mysterious home of the ḍākinī.*[113]

In working in this way with yogic discipline, Nāropa was asked to transform conventional passion into fuel for the spiritual journey.

The most important transformation has to do with motivation; self-gratification cannot have any place in karmamudrā practice or the other practices described. As the *Hevajra-tantra* says, "This practice [of sexual union with a consort] is not taught for the sake of enjoyment, but for the examination of one's own thought, whether the mind is steady or waving [*sic*]."[114] Motivation must be based upon the inspiration to attain enlightenment for the benefit of all sentient beings. Renouncing self-gratification is also reflected in the practice itself. Through karmamudrā, practitioners generate bliss mutually in each other's subtle bodies through passionate play; simultaneously, both partners contemplate the nature of bliss through meditation. This practice highlights in an intensified way the synchronization of body and mind essential to yoga. Renouncing sexual release, the partners contemplate bliss mutually filling their bodies. Then, moving the bodhicitta through all the channels of the body, they experience the pervasion of bliss. This bliss clears the pathways and channels of their subtle bodies, making it possible to experience the radiant clarity of the mind in an immediate way.

Practice with a consort is said to advance one's practice quickly and effectively. As Yeshe Tsogyal matured in her practice, her guru told her that she could not progress without a spiritual consort of her own:

> Mistress, without a valiant partner as a skillful means, there is in truth no way for you to undertake the practice of the Secret Mantra. When an earthen vessel has not been fired, it cannot hold anything; when there is no wood, no fire is possible; when there is no fall of rain, no shoots will spring. And so, in the land of Nepal, whether he has found his way from Serling in India, there lives a youth who goes by the name of Atsara Salé, Salé the Indian. He is a hero, a ḍāka, and an emanation of Hayagrīva. He is seventeen years old and has on his breast a red birthmark at the level of his heart. Search him out and make him your companion. You will instantly reach the level of Great Bliss.[115]

As she went to seek him out, Yeshe Tsogyal sang a song that reflected the importance of practice with a consort, recognizing that a time would come when she would no longer need a consort. She begged the family who held him as bondman in these words:

> *There, where the perfect Buddha dwelt,*
> *No need was there for skillful means.*
> *The Buddha now has gone, so on such means I must rely.*
> *Tomorrow, means and wisdom will unite.*
> *When the fruit is truly gained,*
> *No need for Salé will there be.*
> *But while I tread towards this goal,*
> *I need him. Therefore sell him.*
> *This is my request.*[116]

As she practiced with several different prophesied consorts, they together transmuted ordinary dualistic passion into awareness. She sang of gaining control of the channels, vital breath, and bodhicitta and realizing her own body, speech, and mind as the three bodies (kāyas) of the Buddha.[117]

This practice gives full fruition to the maṇḍala: the most subtle and vast aspects of the mind are joined with fully embodied experience; one of the most problematic and confusing aspects of human life becomes the basis for spiritual development; and the customary alienation found in Western religion between the life of the spirit and the life of the flesh is transformed into a celebration of embodied spirituality. Karmamudrā practices may have been at one time a part of the path for all tāntrikas, and it is clear that in Indian Buddhist tantra such practices were commonplace. However, as Buddhist tantra became mainstreamed and practiced in conjunction with vows of celibacy, the detailed lore of these practices was deemphasized and in many cases lost. Greater emphasis has been placed upon the visualization of yab-yum deities and tummo practices, the other two methods of generating bliss and contemplating the nature of passion. Gampopa, the great twelfth-century Kagyü master who joined the yogic and monastic lineages of Tibet, is said to have attained full enlightenment while maintaining the monastic vows of celibacy.[118] Another tradition developed in which the celibate monk waited until the moment of death to complete the ultimate realization of buddhahood. It is said that Tsongkhapa, the great advocate for literal observance of monastic vows, postponed full enlightenment until the moment of death, when he united with a consort in a visionary realm, thus completing his yogic discipline and attaining the rainbow body.[119]

There have remained debates, however, about whether karmamudrā is essential to the attainment of full enlightenment. The tantras begin with descriptions of the Buddha in union with a ḍākinī consort.[120] The *Guhyasamāja-tantra* asserts that to achieve his final realization, the Buddha entered into the samādhi known as "diamond glory enjoying all desires"[121] and experienced bliss with the ḍākinīs of the four directions and the center simultaneously. Tantric lore says that Śākyamuni joined with Sujata the milkmaid as his consort at the foot of the bodhi tree and thus attained enlightenment.

There have always been strong yogic traditions in Tibet, outside of the monastic commitments, in which karmamudrā has been regularly practiced. These have been particularly carried in the Nyingma lineage, as well as in the Kagyü lineages that have been especially close to the Nyingma. In Tibet, the practice of karmamudrā was probably confined to hereditary lamas, treasure-discoverers, or other noncelibate yogic practitioners (*ngakpas*); in exile communities, while the monastic lineages have continued to be important, there are still living teachers who continue the karmamudrā practice in *ngak-phang* lineages.[122] These traditions have preserved and propagated all three methods for contemplating the nature of passion.

The lifestyles of lay yogis who practiced karmamudrā sometimes had the effect of scandalizing the monastic establishment, especially among the Gelukpa order, which emphasized strict monastic discipline. This was especially true with occasional Dalai Lamas who practiced as yogins instead of following the monastic path. Most renowned in this regard was the beloved sixth Dalai Lama, Rigdzin Tsangyang Gyatso (1683–1706, maybe 1746) who was famous for his beautiful voice and passionate poetry. The young sixth Dalai Lama was born into the family lineage of Pema Lingpa (1450–1521), the great Nyingma treasure-discoverer. Tsangyang Gyatso was raised in great secrecy in order to perpetuate the deceit that the Great Fifth was still alive, and this greatly shaped his view and experience as a practitioner. In seclusion, he was trained primarily by masters of the Nyingma tradition, including the regent of the Great Fifth and Terdaklingpa of Mindröling and the abbot Pema Thrinley of Dorjedrak.[123] Great teachers of the Nyingma lineage speak of the young Dalai Lama's training in certain yogic practices during his sequestered youth and use his life example to demonstrate the essence of such practices.

When Tsangyang Gyatso was enthroned at age fourteen, he declared that he had no interest in monastic vows, and he lived as the Dalai Lama in the Potala dressed as a layman with long hair, jewelry, and flowing blue silk clothing. He enjoyed celebrations with friends, the archery range, and long passionate nights with various young women of Lhasa. While his lifestyle was shocking to the monastic establishment, he was extremely popular among ordinary Tibetans, who proudly painted his lovers' houses yellow. As Lhasa gradually became a yellow city, his popularity only grew.

The passionate poetry of the beloved sixth Dalai Lama has lived on in Tibet's folk traditions, differing little from purely secular expression, but there are several poems that suggest his connection with karmamudrā sexual yoga:

Not one night without a lover have I slept.
Nor one drop of the precious [bodhicitta] have I spent.[124]

The bodhicitta (changchup sem) referred to here is the tantric code for seminal emission, as we have discussed. One feature in many karmamudrā practices is the male's withholding ejaculation, suggesting that the young

Dalai Lama had motivations other than self-gratification for his liaisons. The most tantric of his songs speaks of union with a wisdom ḍākinī:

Pure glacial waters from Crystal Peak
And dewdrops from a vajra-plant,
Fermented with the yeast of ambrosia,
Brewed by the ḍākinī of wisdom.
If drunk with pure commitment
The misery of lower states
Need never be experienced.[125]

The glacial waters and medicinal dewdrops refer to the white male bodhicitta, and the yeast of ambrosia (*dütsi men-gyi phap*) refers to the red female bodhicitta. When they are fermented together by the wisdom ḍākinī and tasted with sacred commitment (*tamtsik*), ordinary suffering can be avoided. In other words, the karmamudrā practitioner can experience bliss that completely removes him or her from conventional habitual experience.

Types of Consorts

In the tradition of karmamudrā, choosing a consort is a delicate business. First, one's motivation must be appropriately spiritual, free from ordinary lust and attachment. Then, the choice must be discreet, since the conventional world does not understand the mysteries of tantra.[126] Finally, the candidate must be qualified, according to classical guidelines.

The lore on the choice of consorts is heavily weighted in the Tibetan tradition toward female consorts, probably because of the patriarchal nature of monastic establishments, textual recording, and yogic lineages. While there is evidence of lore concerning the choice of male consorts, it is difficult to identify texts or teachings on the subject, though lamas say that the qualifications for female consorts can be extrapolated to apply to male consorts as well. Qualified female consorts are routinely considered ḍākinīs. As Guru Rinpoche instructed King Trisong Detsen, this is how one chooses a female consort:

I myself am unsullied by desire or lust;
and such faults as attachment do not exist in me.

But a woman is a necessary accoutrement to the secret teachings.
She must be of good family,[127] *committed to the dharma,*
and a keeper of the vows;
lovely of form and complexion,
she must excel in skillful means, discrimination and learning;
she must be filled with the power of compassion,
and marked with the signs of a wisdom-dakini.
Without such a one,
the maturation and liberation practices are obstructed;
the result, the achievement of the secret teachings
does not occur.[128]

Various sources provide different descriptions of the qualified ḍākinī consort. Ngari Panchen described a qualified consort as one who has received the necessary empowerments, who upholds samaya, and whose mindstream is properly matured. For example, it is important that her emotions be liberated from confusion.[129] In later advice from Guru Rinpoche to Yeshe Tsogyal, he added to these criteria that she must be intelligent and good-natured, have great faith and mastery of the six perfections of a bodhisattva, not be promiscuous, and live neatly and cleanly.[130] An additional requirement has to do with the way in which the respective male and female consorts express the qualities of the five buddha families. For example, the *Hevajra-tantra* recommends consorts from the vajra family or from the family of one's yidam; this practice with others should be done only when absolutely necessary. The *Hevajra-tantra* also describes the proper physical characteristics for both men and women and their corresponding deities and consorts.[131] Other sources give different advice.

Generally, the classifications of three kinds of embodied ḍākinīs (sacred-realm-born, coemergent, and mantra-born) are applied specifically to types of consorts, based on their levels of realization.[132] According to this schema, the spiritual level of the consort directly affects the level of realization that the yogin achieves, and so discriminating choice is important. The three are described in descending order of realization:[133] the sacred-realm-born ḍākinī who abides in the places of pilgrimage is the highest of the three in realization, having attained the subjective clear light (ösel); the coemergent ḍākinī, a particularly fearless woman who is without embarrassment, has realized the stage of completion (sampannakrama, dzog-rim); and the mantra-born ḍākinī has practiced intently and has realized the stage of creation (utpattikrama, kyerim). In parallel form, the yogin could hope to attain the same level of realization as his consort, and her assistance in the practice of karmamudrā was essential in this result. There is no available information on corresponding spiritual levels for male consorts.

The ḍākinīs of each of these levels of realization were further categorized according to their sexual style and attributes in a spiritual manner parallel with the erotic traditions of India. The tantras give the following four families of female consorts at any spiritual level of realization: the lotus (*padminī, padma*), the conch (*śaṅkhinī, tungchenma*), the picture (*citriṇī, rimochen*), and the elephant (*hastinī, ridak chen* or *langpo*).[134] In the *Saṁvarodaya-tantra,* these four are associated respectively with the four retinue ḍākinīs by family: the lotus is blue, of the *vajra* family; the conch is red, of the *padma* family; picture is yellow, of the *ratna* family; and elephant is green, of the *karma* family.[135] It is important to note that there are parallel categories of sexual style for males as well, and we may assume that these functioned in the yoginī's choice of consort. The categories for men are the rabbit (*śaśa, ribong*), the buck (*ridakpo*), the bull (*vṛṣa, lang*), and the stallion (*aśva, ta-chok*).

The Tibetan classifications of the sexual styles of men and women were probably assimilated by Buddhist tantra from the *Kāma-sūtra* tradition of fourth-century India.[136] In Vātsyāyana's text, the sexual categories were based specifically on physical body types, especially on the size of a man's penis or the depth of a woman's vagina.[137] In a late Tibetan text, these descriptions are expanded to include personality traits and social and psychological styles. Also, the Tibetan descriptions added a fourth male style, the buck, to the original three.[138]

Each of the four kinds of female consorts had particular benefits, though there appears to be variation among different sources on their details. The lotus-type consorts are known for happy and joyful personalities, their love of singing beautiful melodies, and expansiveness. In sexual union with a padminī, the experience of expansive bliss is contagious and crescendos in gradual stages.[139] Following the Indian tradition, the *Saṃvarodaya-tantra* from the group of Cakrasaṃvara tantras described the lotus-type consort in this way:

> Her face is of round shape; the nose has the form of a sesamum-flower. The nails are of the colour of copper; the back is like (that

> of) a turtle; and her feet are flat. Both breasts are of the shape of *tāla*-fruits; and her hairs are curled. There are three wrinkles of good fortune (over her navel); her breast is very beautiful. She walks like a rutting elephant; she has the scent of a lotus and the voice of a goose.[140]

The lotus-type consort was praised in biographies of living wisdom ḍākinīs, such as Machik and Bandhepa. Tāranātha details similar esoteric signs of the padminī, in writing of Machik.[141]

> In particular on her navel there was an image of a red lotus with three roots; between her breasts—an image of rosaries of precious stones, reaching down to the navel, and on each of her shoulders—images of the *svāstika.* At the back of her ears she had coils similar to those of a conch or lotus. Under her tongue there was an image of a sword of the color of the [lotus] flower marked with the [syllable] TĀṂ (symbolizing the first syllable of the name Tārā). Between her eyebrows she had the image of a banner with the sun and moon represented on it, and the image of a wheel with spikes.[142]

In an early twentieth-century Tibetan text, Gedün Chöpel described the padminī in a somewhat different way, including psychological traits as well:

> She is beautiful, with smiling face; her body is slender and supple. She has no freckles, and her color is ruddy and white. She has shiny very long black hair, and her eyes move about like a frightened deer. Her nostrils are small; her eyebrows are thick. She likes clean clothes and simple food. She wears only few adornments, like flowers and so forth. She is altruistic and a doer of virtue. She has abandoned desire for other than her own husband. Her breasts are soft, round, and big. Her vagina is about six finger breadths deep. Her menstruation emits a fragrance like a lotus; therefore she is of the lotus type.[143]

Generally speaking, the padminī is particularly valued because among the four she is the most passionate in tendency, and she gradually arouses bliss in her partner.

In contrast, the conch-type consort is also very joyful but more volatile; her vagina is deep and narrow; and sexual union with her produces a very sudden arising of bliss and restrains the emission of bodhicitta for both partners. The *Saṃvarodaya-tantra* describes these characteristics of the śaṅkhinī:

> She has long hair and a long nose; she is neither too thin nor too fat; her breasts are of the shape of orange-fruits; she enjoys eating curds and milk. . . . A *śaṅkhinī* smells like a donkey and is rough to the touch like the tongue of a cow. She has the voice of a crow.[144]

Gedün Chöpel again integrates psychological dimensions into his description of the śaṅkhinī:

> The large conch type is thin and tall. Her neck is crooked; the tip of her nose goes upward. The shape of her face is long and of beautiful color. She eats various foods again and again. She is clever at protecting her household, her servants, and those around her. She talks well; her mind is clear, and she is only a little secretive. It is easy for her to become acquainted quickly with all whom she meets. She has little respect for her elders, but it is said she mixes compatibly with her own family. Her jealousy and passion are great. Her genitals are warm and ten finger breadths deep. Her pubic hair is thick, and her secretion comes out easily. A sour odor is emitted from her body and vagina. . . . The three qualities of being talkative, having a facile tongue, and having a crook in the neck are taken as being unmistakable signs of this type.[145]

Kālasiddhi, the ḍākinī-girl raised in the charnel ground, was a classic conch-type consort of Guru Rinpoche who became enlightened meditating on the emptiness of the elements of the human body.[146]

The picture-type consort has enormous emotional range, and sexual union with her is sustained, maintaining the bliss without impulsive bodhicitta emissions. The *Saṃvarodaya-tantra* describes the citriṇī in this way:

> Her body is very short; but her breast is beautiful; her breasts are of the shape of [a sacred fruit]. She has abandoned shame and is

> very wrathful; she always takes pleasure in quarreling. Her shanks are crippled; and she lies on her back. She has a hanging underlip and the voice of a turtle dove. A *citriṇī,* who smells of meat and has her arms spread out, is said to be sporting an amorous enjoyment.[147]

Gedün Chöpel says this of the citriṇī, again adding attributes of personality:

> The picture type is of medium height. She is not very fat and not very thin. She has roving long eyes which are like the petals of a lotus. Her nose is like the sesame flower. She wears clothes of various colors and a garland of yellow flowers. She likes all kinds of pictures. She is enthusiastic to hear interesting stories. She keeps various small birds, parrots, and so forth. Always a group of children stands around her. Her body is as beautiful as a painted picture; therefore she is said to be of the picture type. Her reproductive organ is roundish and eight finger breadths deep. Her pubic area has little hair, and her menstruation is clear.[148]

The elephant-type consort has special capacity for realizing the ultimate truth and engendering this experience also in her partner because her torso, arms, and legs are large and very steady, and she can remain still for long periods of time. The hastinī is described this way in the *Saṃvarodaya-tantra:*

> She smells of liquor; her shanks are stout; she has a round nose and a line of hair (above the navel). She is mad with passion; her body is stout; she moves to and fro; (the yogin) should make her sport amorously by the "chest-opening-embrace" (*uraḥsphoṭabandha*); she is like a pill to the touch. A *hastinī* has the voice of a crane and is pleased with songs and instrumental music.[149]

Gendün Chöpel's description is similar, but includes her personal preferences and emotional style:

> The elephant type is short; her limbs are broad. Her mouth and nose are thick. Her hips are larger than anything else. Her eyes are

reddish; her hair, coarse; her shoulders, rounded. Her breasts are very large and hard like stone. She eats a great deal, and her voice is strong and anxious. She covers her whole body from head to foot with adornments. She likes adultery and low gossip. Most of this type separate from their husbands. She acquaints with large men of great strength and with all others she finds. As she has strong passion burning hard, she wants to sleep with even son and father. She needs to copulate many times each day. Though a hundred men do it, she is not satisfied. Her genitalia is very hairy and burns with heat like fire. It is always dripping wet and has an odor like that of an elephant. An adulteress like her is not suitable as a wife, but as she is vigorous in the act, she is renowned as the superior of maid servants.[150]

As for male consorts, fewer sources are available, but Gedün Chöpel described samples of each of these types. His descriptions differ from the *Kāma-sūtra* and other Sanskrit sources, which base male types primarily on the attributes of sexual organs:

The rabbit type has medium-sized body; his thoughts are good and his face smiling. He is a doer of virtue and mixes with good friends. He has abandoned cohabiting with others' wives. He respects those above him and helps those below. He eats and wears what can be attained easily. He does not worry about the past and the future; always lazy, he stays playfully happy. His masculine member when erect is about six finger breadths. The shape of his jewel [head of the penis] is bulbous and soft. He copulates quickly and his seminal fluid is ejected quickly. His seat and seminal fluid smell pleasantly. . . .

The buck type has prominent eyes and large shoulders. He respects his teachers and does not like the work of cleaning. His intelligence is sharp, and when he moves, he runs and jumps. He is always singing; he wears good adornments and clothes. He speaks truthfully, and his appetite is big. He always gives food and parties to his friends. He has little hair in the pubic region and the arm pits. His penis is about eight finger breadths long. . . .

The bull type has a big body and handsome countenance. His nature is unstable, and he has little embarrassment. It is easy for

> him to make friends, and it is easy for him to split from them. He eats a great deal and is skillful at singing and dancing. His behavior is wayward, and his passion great. He does it with all the women he can find. His phallus is about ten finger breadths long. His sweat and seminal fluid have a bad smell. . . .
>
> The stallion type is fat, and his body rough and big. His color is blackish; his feet are long, and he moves quickly. He is excitable; he likes deceit and falsehood. He keeps company with all women, young and old. This type is extremely passionate. If they would agree, he would do it with even his mother and sister. He goes with all the unsuitable—close relatives, daughters of clergy, and so forth. However much he copulates, his strength is not lost. It is difficult for him to stay even one day without a woman. His phallus is hard and very thick; when erect, it is about twelve finger breadths. His seminal fluid is considerable and has a bad smell. . . .[151]

What are we to make of these long and detailed descriptions of physical types, differing from source to source? Several observations are in order. First, these classical texts indicate a direct relationship between the body and the temperament of each type of consort, demonstrating a holistic understanding of the person. This lore indicates again the importance of embodied existence in tantra and an appreciation of the rich possibilities associated with embodiment. It is clear from these descriptions that the body is not viewed as an inert object; instead, holistic vitality and style emanate from the dynamic interaction of all aspects of embodied existence. Second, one can immediately observe that the physical appearances and temperaments of ḍākinīs (and of ḍākas, for that matter) range across a wide spectrum, each having its own charms, powers, and attractions. Rather than stereotypes that assign beauty or sexiness only to the petite, slim, pale blonde woman or to the tall, muscular, athletic man, it is clear that every body type or personality has its attractions.

While I was interviewing Khenpo Tsultrim Gyamtso Rinpoche in an attempt to distinguish the classifications of the different types of consorts, he began to laugh. When I asked why, he gave a characteristically Tibetan answer:

> All these categories, they are just Indian. They have to do with India, and these categories apply to their cultural situation. That's

not going to help people in the West. The thing to do here is to look at what's actually important. It is important that the consort you practice with has faith [*tepa*], exertion [*tsöndrü*] and wisdom [*sherap*]. That's all. And it has to be someone that you like and someone who likes you. Mutual getting along. You like that person, they like you. Somebody who is a companion and is going to help you on the path, and that you could practice with—it's not about infatuation.[152]

Milarepa and Karmamudrā

Milarepa, the twelfth-century Tibetan yogin, was dedicated to solitary retreat and spoke often of the entrapments of family, home, and domestic responsibility. He was not seduced by sexual desire in any conventional sense, as can be seen by the attempts of various worldly female demonesses and spirits. At the same time, he was known for nurturing dedicated and realized female disciples. When Milarepa tamed the worldly ḍākinī Tseringma, the Lady of Long-Life, and her retinue, she eventually became a wisdom ḍākinī who was an eligible candidate for karmamudrā practice. Milarepa recommended this practice for her as an important way to understand the process of bodily emanation in the intermediate state (*pardo*), adding that arousing Prajñāpāramitā through the practices of inner heat and karmamudrā would help her understand the third abhiṣeka and to vanquish instinctive jealousy.[153]

One day Tseringma and her retinue of four ḍākinīs arrived at Milarepa's cave, beautifully attired and carrying the classic offering substances: incense, food and drink, musical instruments, soft clothing, and flowers. After making these offerings, serving him, and singing and dancing, Tseringma and her retinue offered themselves as the "supreme bliss-emptiness offerings of the wisdom of the four joys." This refers to the tradition that of all offerings one could make to the guru, the best is the offering of karmamudrā.[154]

As they approached, they assured him that they represented the four classic physical types of qualified consorts: the lotus, conch, picture, and elephant. Milarepa responded with the benefits of each, succintly summarizing the intricate lore: the lotus-type consort promotes bliss, the conch-type speeds ecstasy, the picture-type prevents obstacles to holding the bliss, and the elephant-type aids the realization of the nature of reality.[155]

Milarepa then accepted their offering, acknowledging them as the four perfected consorts and thereby accepting them as appropriate practitioners of the four stages of karmamudrā practice, consistent with the tradition of Tilopa's instructions to Nāropa:[156] (1) Falling (bap tang) refers to how the bindu descends, but it also means the naturally empty quality of phenomena. It is likened to a "smith hammering a metal mirror, making the four types of joy descend slowly like a tortoise from the head to the [secret center]. . . ." These four types of joy are ascending experiences of bliss associated with the cultivation of mahāsukha, leading to the nonconceptual state.[157] (2) Holding (*jiltang*) or pooling describes how to practice when the bodhicitta descends; it is held and retained within the body. This is described as similar to holding "a lamp in a storm, constant in one's inner vision the reality of coemergent joy." (3) With turning back (*dokpa*), the next yogic step, the bodhicitta is sent upward through the channels passing through the heart center and the throat center to the crown of the head. This practice is likened to "an elephant drinking water, to make the four joys ascend (to the head region) and to keep them stable." Each level of ascent through the centers evokes a new level of awareness, likened to the stages of enlightenment (bhūmis). (4) The last one, spreading out (*dren*), extends the bodhicitta through all the intricate channels. This is when the experience of bliss pervades the body. The analogy is that of "a farmer watering his crops carefully to saturate every pore and experience the joy as consummation." This pervasion of coemergent joy purifies all obscurations and obstacles, states of mind, and the subtle body itself, yielding buddhahood. Milarepa practiced these four stages with each of the consorts, inspiring each of them to realization.[158]

In Milarepa's teaching, he interpreted the meaning of karmamudrā in a commentary on the Tibetan term, *lekyi chag-gya.* Karmamudrā expresses the nonduality of the various polarities of the spiritual path, such as bliss and emptiness, this and that, and nirvāṇa and saṃsāra. It is the "speed-path of union," which is full of retained bliss and the realization of the three levels of outer, inner, and secret.

This is the path of bliss—of emptiness, of no thoughts,
and of two-in-one,
a path of quick assistance by a goddess.
Following this inspiring way
you, fair ladies, will reach liberation,

and, in the realm of no-arising will remain.
Oh gifted fairies, you are indeed well qualified.[159]

The practice of karmamudrā confers what is called the third empowerment (abhiṣeka, *wang*) in tantric ritual, leading directly to the fourth empowerment of nonconceptual wisdom. The third empowerment is associated with removing obscurations of the mind so that the mind blessings of the deity and the lineage can enter the mindstream of the practitioner. The third empowerment is also called the prajñā-jñāna abhiṣeka, referring to the realization of nondual awareness through union with the consort. Thus the ritual union with the ḍākinī, the symbol of one's innermost wisdom, leads to nondual awareness of the nature of mind in the fourth abhiṣeka.

SEVEN

Living Encounters with the Dakini

My Lady, you are the ruler of naked space
The holder of the key to the secret treasury
You are inseparable with Padmasambhava
Please invoke and consecrate from the magical halo.

My Lady, you are the ruler of the ḍākinīs
The protector of the continuity of warm-breath
Your command whispers in echoing space eternally
Awaken me in the space with the sprinkle of vajra saliva.

Ḍākinīs' pure magic
Arising in the colorful halo
Kindness painfully pricks through
Awaken me with your beautiful whisper
Sane victory over dilemma
Young warrior's heart is longing
Your blessing of nourishment and love
Ripen the siddhis of immovable devotion.

—VEN. DZOGCHEN PÖNLOP RINPOCHE[1]

WE HAVE EXAMINED THE structure of the ḍākinī symbol on various levels, interweaving meditation and manifestation as understood in the

Tibetan Vajrayāna tradition. These sources are most essential, tied to the experience of the ḍākinī both as a personification of the practitioner's wisdom and as the principle of the nature of meditative realization. Now let us bring this understanding to an examination of the appearance of the ḍākinī in tantric lore, drawing on both classical and contemporary sources. From this lore, we shall derive a paradigm of activity, showing when, how, and in what forms the ḍākinī appears, what she imparts to the tantric practitioner, and the qualities of the experience. We will then reflect on the meaning of these appearances and how they may lead us to a more intimate understanding of the symbol of the ḍākinī.

The hagiographies (namthars) and histories (*chöjung*) of the great yogins and yoginīs are dotted with ḍākinī encounters, but there is a wealth of new material from contemporary sources as well. The classical stories were recorded and transmitted primarily by the students of the great yogins and yoginīs; the contemporary stories, for the most part, have yet to be recorded in literary form. Yet on a rare occasion a lama may tell close students of a ḍākinī encounter, the lama's own or his or her teacher's. It seems there is hesitance to tell one's own stories, for it may be construed as boasting or inappropriately sharing secret teachings. Yet the ḍākinī lore is among the most treasured aspects of contemporary Vajrayāna Buddhism.

Ḍākinī as Messenger and Intermediary

One of the most celebrated genres of literature concerning the ḍākinī is the hagiography, in which she appears in vivid form to the practitioner as either a visionary figure or a human woman. Many of these stories are collected in the canon of tantric literature as parts of the namthars of important teachers or as vignettes in longer sacred histories of the major lineages. Such stories are also a popular way for realized teachers to transmit the essential lore of the ḍākinī to their students. Sometimes these stories include personal accounts of such encounters. When the structure of the ḍākinī symbol is understood, they convey powerful messages about Vajrayāna practice and realization.

How does the wisdom ḍākinī manifest in this lore? When the ḍākinī appears in visions or dreams in her action mode, she is said to carry out the activities of wisdom and is often called a karma ḍākinī.[2] This action form is not really different from the wisdom aspect of the ḍākinī but appears in whatever way would be effective and beneficial. The wisdom ḍākinī is a manifestation of the mind aspect of the guru and practitioner, while the karma ḍākinī is the guise that wisdom takes when executing its realization. The karma ḍākinī takes forms that are more fluid and emulate the human or other realms in which she acts and communicates. In this area, the karma ḍākinī is often the one who actually appears to the tantric practitioner, mirroring one's delusions, energizing one's meditation practice, and activating one's realization.

Because the karma ḍākinī is the action principle of profound realization, she is shockingly direct, immediate in her spontaneity, and ruthless in her compassion. And the benefit for tantric practitioners is that she is a more accessible dimension of the ḍākinī principle.[3] The karma ḍākinī has a variety of styles of manifestation, depending upon the circumstances and the practitioner's state of mind. In Vajrayāna Buddhism, there are traditionally four kinds of skillful and appropriate actions (leshi) that arise from wisdom: pacifying (shi), enriching (gye), magnetizing (wang), and destroying (trak).[4] These four karmas are strategies spontaneously enacted by the awakened mind when working with intractable situations, either in practice or daily life.

Karma ḍākinīs appear in all of these forms as a way of dispelling obstacles, supporting wakefulness, and protecting the authenticity of tantric transmissions. When appearing in the gentle pacifying form, the ḍākinī invites obstacles into the expanse, inspiring openness and warmth in the practitioner, and overcoming neediness, depression, and hopelessness. Enriching nurtures the practitioner's dignity and basic presence and inspires confidence that can support further development of the qualities of wakefulness. If obstacles still remain, the ḍākinī takes on magnetizing qualities, drawing the practitioner into allegiance to wakefulness and the surrender of obscurations that obstruct his or her progress. In the magnetizing mode, the ḍākinī becomes slightly more intimidating and powerful, but still benevolent.

When these three strategies are unsuccessful in accomplishing the activities of compassionate wisdom, the karma ḍākinī takes on a wrathful appearance, destroying what needs to be destroyed. "It is said in the tantric tradition that, if you do not destroy when necessary, you are breaking the vow of compassion which actually commits you to destroying frivolousness."[5] The wrathful, terrifying form of the ḍākinī is able to directly and effectively remove obstacles for the tantric practitioner and for the tantric teachings. Often in wrathful form, the ḍākinī takes on all the qualities of worldly meat-eating ḍākinīs indigenous to the charnel grounds of India, with gnashing teeth and voracious appetites thirsting for human blood.

It is difficult to specifically isolate the karmas that the karma ḍākinī manifests, since the first three actions are gentler forms of compassion. In the classical hagiographies, she often appears in her inner wisdom ḍākinī aspect, which manifests all four karmas simultaneously, depending on the mind of the practitioner. She appears in visions as a naked dancing woman adorned with charnel ground ornaments, carrying a hooked knife (*kartari, triguk*) and a skull-cup of blood, the deathless nectar of wisdom. She is described as beautiful in a conventional sense, in the full bloom of youth, radiant in appearance, with a body made of light. Her characteristic marks are evident, especially the third eye blazing vertically in her forehead.

When the karma ḍākinī appears in these gentler aspects, it may be as a beautiful young human woman in regal garb, adorned with robes and jewelry, drawing the longing and supplication of the practicing yogin or yoginī. Such a ḍākinī appeared to Longchenpa, wearing silken robes and turquoise and gold ornaments, her face concealed by a golden veil. The great yogin clasped the hem of her dress and cried, "Please, bless me, sublime one!" She removed her gem-encrusted crown and placed it on his head, blessing him and promising to always bestow success in his practice.[6]

The ḍākinī gives direct advice in these encounters—what teacher to seek, where to practice retreat or travel on pilgrimage, what empowerments or teachings to request, and where and when to give the tantric teachings to fortunate students. The ḍākinī also gives meditation instructions that can aid the disheartened practitioner. The tailor Kantali was instructed to "sew together appearance and emptiness with the needle and thread of mindfulness and knowledge. When you have sewn these clothes with the the needle of compassion, meditate [that you are] clothing all beings of the world."[7]

The advice given by a realized ḍākinī is considered prophecy that carries with it the promise of the supporting auspicious circumstances to ensure eventual success. A beautiful ḍākinī clothed in leaves appeared to Marpa, instructing him to return to Tibet and prophesying his success in propagating the teachings.[8] Dagmema advised Milarepa in his arduous ordeals in his quest for teachings from Marpa, and though many obstacles arose she eventually guided him to success.[9]

The ḍākinī not only guides students to their teachers but also prophesies important disciples to tantric gurus themselves. In a dream, the ḍākinī appeared to Milarepa, proclaiming that he would have one disciple like the sun, another like the moon, and twenty-five other accomplished ones who would be like stars.[10] Gampopa was the sun and Rechungpa the moon; the names of the additional twenty-five ornament the biographies and songs of the "laughing vajra" guru.

It is just this combination of directness and fluidity in the karma ḍākinī that inspires such respect and trepidation in the tantric practitioner. In her wisdom aspect, she accurately sees the practitioner's specific circumstances and understands exactly what he or she may need. In her activity aspect, the ḍākinī takes on a form that directly mirrors the present situation, arouses the most profoundly personal responses, and mercifully intercedes even when the intervention appears ruthless. The karma ḍākinī evokes the personal subjectivity of the tantric practitioner and brings it into resonance with what is sought in spiritual practice.

Not all ḍākinīs appear in young and beautiful form; in horrific form they have the power to open the practitioner's mind in a direct way. This is how the karma ḍākinī appears in "destroying" mode, removing particularly intractable obstacles to practice. The great master Tilopa was constantly under the tutelage of an ugly old ḍākinī-woman, Vajrayoginī in disguise, who saw his spiritual potential and guided his development.[11] Of particular significance is the "laughing and crying" ḍākinī who appears in horrifying form. Nāropa saw the ugly hag who pointed out his intellectual blindness to the true meaning (*ngedön*) of the teachings he studied.[12] This is the karma ḍākinī in her destroying mode, removing obstacles for the obstinate tantric practitioner for whom a gentler approach would not be effective. Her horrific appearance has the effect of stopping conceptuality in its tracks and terrifying arrogance into submission.

When the minister of Bengal, Kuśalanātha, was converted by the great master Kāṇhapa, he developed great skill in meditation, which manifested as an uncanny ability to understand obscure foreign languages. One midnight, a huge, ugly old woman infested with leprosy appeared to him, struggling to her feet with the help of a stick after being murdered. When she declared to him that she was hungry, he recognized her as the powerful wisdom ḍākinī Vajravārāhī and immediately offered her food, drink, grains, nourishment, and pleasing objects. He then begged to be her disciple, and she blessed him, placing her hands on the crown of his head, and asked him to visualize her dissolving into his crown. When he did so, she disappeared. Kuśalanātha then realized the empowerments he had been given and became a realized siddha. After ruling in an ordinary manner for some time, he finally left his governmental duties and lived as a yogin, benefiting beings.[13]

The ḍākinī may appear as a humble woman in a low-caste profession such as wood-gatherer, prostitute, barber, arrowsmith, or barmaid. These ḍākinīs are particularly adept at pointing out arrogance and conceptuality, especially regarding class or gender superiority. The "black yogin" Ngakpa Chöpa was instructed by a weaver woman, who pointed out his yogic pride;[14] Lūipa was served by a prostitute who identified a remnant of high-caste arrogance in his unwillingness to eat putrid food.[15] These ḍākinīs derive particularly from Indian heritage in which they are considered impure and inferior because of both their caste and their gender. But in Tibet they continued to play a role, challenging the conceptuality of yogins of noble birth or high monastic rank.[16]

The typical appearance of a ḍākinī is in visionary form, but upon occasion she enters the body of a human, especially a yoginī, in order to give her transmission. An example of this is found in the 1339 chronicle of Longchenpa's initial transmission of the *Heart Essence of the Ḍākinī* treasure teachings to eight of his yogin and yoginī disciples. In a series of appearances, five different ḍākinīs descended (bap) into yoginī disciples of the master, performing (thrap) in her body and voice.[17] Each played different roles, correcting ritual details, confirming his identity as the treasure-discoverer, authorizing his writing of commentaries, and prophesying the future of the *Heart Essence* teachings.

In her visionary appearances, the ḍākinī may also assume a nonhuman form such as a yak, dog, or tigress. When Gyalwa Tötsangpa (1189–1258) wandered in the Kailāsa region, a ḍākinī appeared in the form of a female wild yak and led him to a remote cave. She then melted into the rock walls, leaving only the imprint of her horn. He meditated there for several years and attained realization.[18] The Indian princess Maṇḍāravā was able to take myriad forms at will, and her most famous animal form was that of the pregnant tigress who foraged in the charnel ground. In this form, she served also as the mount of the wrathful form of Guru Rinpoche, Dorje Tröllo, who embodies uncompromising crazy wisdom (*yeshe chölwa*).[19]

When the discouraged Indian yogin Asaṅga emerged from twelve years of fruitless retreat, he encountered a ḍākinī in the form of a bitch lying beside the road, the lower part of her body infested with maggots.[20] When he was moved to compassion, she transformed into Buddha Maitreya, who said he had been with Asaṅga all through his retreat, in various forms, including that of a swallow living in a nest in the wall of the cave. Kukkuripa the renunciant was moved by the suffering of a starving bitch, whom he cared for while he practiced in his cave near Lumbinī. Throughout twelve years of retreat, attainment, and subsequent travel and teaching, Kukkuripa never forgot his loyal companion and returned to her. One day when he patted her, she immediately became a ḍākinī and granted him the supreme realization of Mahāmudrā.[21] In Marpa's accounts, after realization Kukkuripa lived on an island in a poison lake with the bitch as his consort along with hordes of other dogs.[22] In the cases of both Asaṅga and Kukkuripa, it was the ḍākinī in the form of the dog who had the ability to touch the siddha's heart and to arouse in him the aspiration to practice wholeheartedly for the benefit of others. This is why the ḍākinī appeared in this form; when she transformed into a ḍākinī-woman, it is because of the change in Kukkuripa's attitude and perspective rather than a change in the ḍākinī herself.[23]

While usually the ḍākinī appears in visual form, she may also manifest only through her voice, singing a melodious song or whispering messages in the practitioner's ear. In his twenty-third year, the Nyingma visionary Melong Dorje heard a ḍākinī's voice declare that he had cut off the stream of rebirth.[24] Rikdzin Terdak Lingpa was enticed to take birth by the "ḍākinī's song that is the pure melody of awareness."[25] Jālandhara was practicing meditation in a charnel ground; entering a blissful state, he heard the voice of a ḍākinī say, "O noble son, you should know that your mind is the nature of reality itself."[26] The yoginī Chomo Menmo was awakened and enticed into a cave by the melodious voice of Vajravārāhī.[27] Sometimes the voice cannot be clearly heard or understood. When the ḍākinī whispered in Jigme Lingpa's ear, he caught only fragments of her words and they appeared nonsensical. When he asked her to speak more clearly, her voice grew softer until it trailed off. Nevertheless, bliss pervaded his body.[28] The ḍākinī's voice is haunting because it is said to be empty.[29]

Determining the Ḍākinī's Identity

For both male and female practitioners, a recurring theme in the appearance of the ḍākinī is the ambiguity of her identity. Stories abound about the greatest enlightened yogins or yoginīs who often do not recognize her when she appears; and when they do notice her ḍākinī characteristics they are unsure whether she is a worldly ḍākinī or a wisdom ḍākinī. If a mistake is made, the consequences could be disastrous. Taking a worldly ḍākinī to be enlightened could endanger one's spiritual development or even one's life; her powerful message could be that of a demoness or obstructing spirit. Not recognizing a worldly ḍākinī could incur her wrath, creating many obstacles and difficulties.[30] Not recognizing a wisdom ḍākinī at all represents a missed opportunity that could mire one in personal obstacles. Because of this, efforts to determine her appearance and identity are a central part of her lore.

Manuals and classifications of the various marks of the ḍākinī appear throughout the tantric tradition. There is, of course, no agreement about standard characteristics, but the consistent themes have been discussed. Once the signs have been identified, the yogin or yoginī must then determine whether there also exists a karmic connection between the ḍākinī and the practitioner. This is probably much more difficult, as many factors interact to establish the auspicious coincidence of personal connections between practitioner and guru, ḍākinī, or protector.

In a dream, Namkhai Nyingpo was instructed by a golden ḍākinī to seek a specific human ḍākinī girl as a consort. In a nearby town he found the girl Dorje Tso in a guild of weavers, busily engaging in her craft. Determining that she possessed the prescribed thirty-six marks of a wisdom ḍākinī, he then checked whether auspicious connections existed between them. The yogin threw his guru's single-strand crystal rosary into the sky, and it melted into the top of Dorje Tso's head like snow in hot sand. This ensured the presence of the appropriate circumstances to carry out the golden ḍākinī's prophecy.[31]

In a contemporary story, His Holiness Dilgo Khyentse Rinpoche, had a dream that he recounted to his students. One night he was circumambulating the Great Stūpa of Boudhnāth near his monastery and saw an old beggar woman crouched just outside the stūpa walls. As Rinpoche circled the stūpa, he became concerned about the woman's safety because she sat there long after curfew, a time when robbers or vagrants might molest her. As he rounded the stūpa gate, he saw her again and stepped forward to caution her, asking if she needed help. At that moment, the old woman raised her head with a dazzling smile and remarked, "You have been supplicating me all of these years in your practice, and you don't recognize me?" Instantly, he saw her as his yidam deity.

Why is the ḍākinī not recognized by these great masters? She is the symbol of their innermost spirituality, their inspiration, and particularly their direct realization of emptiness and luminosity. She cannot be recognized in a moment of conventional mind. Seeing her requires that habitual patterns, arrogance, and conceptuality fall away and the doors of perception open to naked awareness. This must be an unexpected, even shocking experience. She is the very subjectivity of the tantric practitioner.

Once the ḍākinī's identity is determined, the tantric practitioner pays special attention to following her advice. Her prophecies carry with them clarity of vision, comprehension of auspicious coincidence, and care for the welfare of the practitioner; they can circumvent potential disastrous consequences. It is for this reason that many of the ḍākinī tales have been recorded and repeated. Not following her advice could precipitate calamity. The Indian master Ārthasiddhi was continually asked by ḍākinīs to propagate teachings in Tibet; when he repeatedly delayed, a dark blue ḍākinī wearing bone ornaments raised her hooked knife in a threatening manner and asked him to dissolve his consciousness into her heart as she killed him. When he obeyed her, she transported his consciousness to Tibet, where it entered the womb of Bumcham, the mother of Machik Lapdrön. For this reason, ḍākinī prophecies are taken very seriously and followed carefully.

The prophecy of the ḍākinī also serves as confirmation and legitimation of meditative experience, imbued with authority. This legitimation may be necessary for the propagation of new, controversial terma teachings or for teachers who have not been recognized as tülkus. Self-legitimation, however, carries with it certain perils.[32] Citing the authority of the ḍākinīs can be dangerous, for exploiting their blessing for ambition, fame, or wealth brings obstacles. When Rechungpa returned from India with Tilopa's teachings of the "formless ḍākinīs," he displayed stubborn arrogance to his guru, Milarepa, bragging that he had "witnessed the fulfillment of the ḍākinīs' prophecy." Milarepa warned him of impending danger, remarking, "goddesses cherish the formless ḍākinī teachings, [but] he who strives to become too big is liable to be slain by villains." And many obstacles arose for Rechungpa subsequent to his master's prediction.[33]

Timing and Quality of Encounters

The wisdom ḍākinī is likely to appear to tantric practitioners at important junctures in their lives when a change of some kind is inevitable. Perhaps there are new conditions in the practitioner's life, or perhaps there has been a ripening of circumstances that make a personal change possible. If a crisis has not already arisen, the appearance of the ḍākinī will certainly precipitate one. Dharmapa had taught the dharma for many years but had not practiced. After a ḍākinī appeared to him in a dream, he sought a teacher, practiced intensively, and became a siddha.[34]

The appearances most predictably take place at the boundaries of conventional experience. In the hagiographies there are typically three auspicious circumstances: in visions, in dreams, or in solitary retreats. These visions or dreams are most likely to occur in transitional moments, signified in the accounts as at the first light of dawn. The yoginī Darbum Chödrön told her teacher Milarepa of a dream she had "this morning at first light in a vision while asleep"[35] in which Buddha Akṣobhya appeared, attended by many ḍākinīs. On pilgrimage, the yogin Praṇidhāna Siddhi (Mönlam Drup) slept one night in a charnel ground. At dawn, two successive visions of ḍākinīs appeared to him in a dream, each asking him to persevere quickly in his practice so that he could begin teaching in Tibet.[36] A bluish-black wrathful ḍākinī appeared in a dream to the yoginī Machik, asking her to take a consort in sexual yoga for the benefit of her family and the propagation of her teachings. When the ḍākinī vanished, Machik awoke to the dawning sky.[37]

The dawn (*thorang*) is a favorite Tibetan allegory for the first arising of insight in meditation practice. It is a time when light suffuses the sky, seemingly coming from no particular place, radiating everywhere without duality. The dawn is an image of liminality, the "between" quality, between life and death, between dark and light, between poles of duality. At these transitional times, according to Tibetan Buddhism, the mind has tremendous potential to awaken to its own wisdom. This is expressed in great detail in the pardo teachings associated with the *Tibetan Book of the Dead* (*Pardo Thödröl*). This is the moment of the ḍākinī's skillful means, when visionary appearance has the greatest potential for benefit.

The dream state is another such liminal, transitional experience in which the mind has great potential for openness, and this is why wisdom ḍākinīs often teach in dreams.[38] The yogin Khyungpo Naljor was advised by his ḍākinī-guru Niguma to watch his dreams carefully. That night he had a vivid dream in which a huge demon swallowed him; immediately his teacher appeared to him and warned him not to awaken but to hold the dream clearly in his mind. As he did this, Niguma initiated him into her Six Dharmas[39] practice, commenting later that he was the only yogin in all of India ever to receive the Six Dharmas in one session of sleep.

Milarepa cautioned a female disciple, however, to not take everything in her dreams as prophetic. Generally, dreams are merely projections of our habitual patterns, and if we take them literally, we continue to experience confusion. The practice of dream yoga involves the recognition of appearance and emptiness in the dream state as well as the waking state. When the practitioner realizes this quality, messages in dreams can be taken for what they are, nonarising appearances that radiate wisdom. Milarepa cautioned his disciple in this way:

Do not view the dream visions as real, yoginīs.
Eliminate attachment to inherently painful saṃsāra, yoginīs.
See the deluded affairs of the immature to be illusion, yoginīs.
Bear in mind the precepts given by this lama, yoginīs.
Focus yourselves on the explicit goal of mahāmudrā, yoginīs.[40]

Great care must be taken in noting dreams, for it is only in special, very clear dreams that the ḍākinī's prophecy is evident.

Ḍākinīs also frequently appear to the solitary meditator in remote settings such as retreat, another example of the liminal state in between life and death, sanity and insanity, confusion and wakefulness. Because the mind is open to its own wisdom on retreat, the retreatant is especially loved by ḍākinīs.[41] Milarepa spent the majority of his years in solitary retreat and was frequently visited by ḍākinīs who offered him provisions, support, and protection. In response to questions about his retreats, Milarepa sang, "abiding in this cave, alone, is the noblest service to the ḍākinīs!"[42] When the young Longchenpa began his practice, he became saddened and disillusioned with monastic corruption and sought solitary retreat. After he had spent five months in a dark retreat in the Gyame Chikla Cave, a beautiful ḍākinī appeared in a vision, foretelling his destiny as the transmitter of important cycles of Dzogchen teachings. But even a short time in the forest can yield these transformative experiences. When the young king Dzalendara went for a walk to ponder a problem in his court, he encountered a ḍākinī who took him away to Uḍḍiyāṇa, the land of the ḍākinīs, for a brief interlude of the practice of a yogin.[43]

Whether painful or pleasurable, lucid or opaque, ḍākinī encounters have an intensely intimate quality. Sometimes this is symbolically expressed by a gift put directly in the practitioner's hand, such as a treasure box, conch, or skull. At other times the intimacy is evoked by a touch, a whisper, or a gaze. The ḍākinī may appear naked and evoke nakedness in the practitioner, and her body gifts express the intimacy of connection, as we shall see in the next section. In any case, because she represents the inner subjectivity of the tantric teachings and the practitioner, she is able to touch the heart of the matter with a simple stroke or a single illuminating demonstration.

The tantric practitioner experiences a profound response to these striking encounters with ḍākinī. After initial encounters, tāntrikas are often shaken to their depths at the new perspective that they have been shown. Jigme Lingpa was left with a thrilled, electrified feeling (*sibur*).[44] Longchenpa described his experience in this way:

> The continuity of his ordinary memory and thought had become broken in the preceding moment, and he spaced out as if fainting in a state of intense red vision with a blue tinge. Then his awareness projected out into the coarser manifestations of spontaneity, and he spaced out within the upper original purity. . . .[45]

Merely upon hearing the name of his guru, the ḍākinī Niguma, Khyungpo Naljor burst into tears, and every hair on his body trembled with excitement.[46] Upon receiving the heart mantra of Ekajaṭī, Chogyur Lingpa reported experiencing a "vast magnificence, reminiscent of an earthquake" and promptly saw her in a clear vision.[47]

Eventually, however, adepts experience extended blissful states as a result of these visionary encounters. Longchenpa "remained immersed for a long while in a blissful, radiant, non-discursive contemplation."[48] Jigme Lingpa reported that he had "expanded into the great openness and bliss of recollecting awareness (*trenrik detong chenpo*).[49] Machik's son, the yogin Thönyön Samdrup, received a cup of nectar from a ḍākinī while on retreat and after drinking it experienced bliss spreading throughout his body, so that all craving for ordinary food vanished.[50] The tertön Pemalingpa reached the penultimate stage of Dzogchen, recognizing whatever appears as the play of reality itself. Because of this realization, he was able to soar through space like a bird and pass unimpeded through mountain cliffs.[51] Other such miraculous powers are often reported following the ḍākinī's blessing, prophecy, or transmission.

The result of such an encounter may be a radical life change, especially to seek a teacher or a set of teachings prophesied by the ḍākinī, or to travel to a sacred site she recommended. After his encounter with the ḍākinī, Nāropa immediately abandoned his teaching post at Nālandā, giving up all his possessions and books. Even when the "five hundred scholars, together with their patron the king and his ministers, unanimously begged him to stay," Nāropa remained firm in his resolve to find Tilopa and receive teachings from him.[52]

There is always a sense of urgency in the encounter with the ḍākinī. If the yogin or yoginī ignores her advice on these matters, great obstacles and calamities can arise. When Jamgön Kongtrül Lodrö Thaye was only fifteen years old, he had visions of Guru Rinpoche and received many important blessings and teachings. When he remained indifferent to these transmissions, auspicious coincidence was lost. This manifested on a subtle level with the agitation of the ḍākinīs and on an outer level with the young lama's extreme illness:

> At that time [his consciousness] transferred out of his body, whether in reality or in a dream he could not tell. He met Guru Rinpoche and his consort and conversed with them a great deal. Finally, they advised him to retake his incarnate frame. Encouraged by that dream omen, and by the venerable Jamyang Khyentse Wangpo, he established [a practice that repaired his tantric commitments], whereupon a most radiant spherical canopy of rainbows arose in the cloudless sky, and his physical constitution, too, became [free from ailment].[53]

There are numerous other examples of the dangers of ignoring the ḍākinīs' advice regarding the timing of teachings, seeking teachers, and engaging in pilgrimages. When the advice is followed, there are great protections in place; when it is not, the perils can be extreme.

Transmission as the Blessing of the Ḍākinī's Body

In service to the tantric lineages, sometimes the ḍākinī gives the practitioner direct empowerment, blessing, or authorization. This may be done in the customary way, through speech, conferring the teachings of the whispered lineage, and through direct mind transmission. But often her transmissions are quite unusual, tracing the pattern of characteristic feminine imagery of the sort found in other religious traditions. In this pattern she draws on the experiences of women in conventional roles, inverting them and utilizing them to dramatize the emptiness of all phenomena.[54]

Women in Tibetan society, as we discussed in chapter 1, were closely circumscribed by biology, which tied them to childbearing, nurture, and the hearth—in short, their bodies tied them to their destinies. Ḍākinīs represent freedom from all those strictures, and they display naked bodies that glow with attractiveness and youth. Yet these bodies are not as they appear. The ḍākinī is decorated with charnel ground ornaments and dances in a field of decaying corpses. Nevertheless, her body is vividly colored and appears insubstantial, composed of light with a quality of transparency, displaying its radiant but empty nature. The interior of her body is vast and limitless space, though it may also display deities and visions. The bodies of ḍākinīs personify the wisdom that realizes the impermanence of mortality as well as phenomena's emptiness of inherent existence. She portrays the nakedness of awareness itself, stripped of concept and emotionality, burning with the intensity of unmediated realization.

From this point of view, it is no surprise that the ḍākinī guides and blesses the disciple with her radiant body. The body that usually entraps the conventional woman is the empowered medium of the ḍākinī. When the ḍākinī blesses her disciples with her body, she introduces them to her most basic nature as the Great Mother Prajñāpāramitā, direct and experiential emptiness.

The tantric teachings themselves are given body analogies when likened to the ḍākinīs. Dharma is called the "life heart of the ḍākinīs" (*khandro-me sog-nying*), or the "heart blood of the ḍākinīs" (*khandro-me nying-trak*). It is also called the "breath of the ḍākinīs" (*khandro shallang*), emphasizing the freshness and secrecy surrounding the tantric teachings.[55] In the early lore of the worldly ḍākinī, those who would subdue her demanded that she give her living heart (*sog-nying*), offering her in return a treasure that would replace it.[56] The wisdom ḍākinī offers a glimpse of her living heart, a maṇḍala of deities swirling in the vast expanse of the interior of her body. This is seen in the story of the servant girl Kumarī, who sliced open her breast in the encounter with Guru Rinpoche.

Bodily offerings appear to be the province of all ḍākinīs, whether worldly or wise. As discussed in chapter 2, worldly ḍākinīs dwelt in charnel grounds, feasting on the bodies of the dead. But once conquered by the dharma, ḍākinīs render parts of their own bodies as offerings. In a visionary journey to the land of the ḍākinīs (*orgyen khandro ling*), Yeshe Tsogyal witnessed many ḍākinīs in human form making offerings to the queen of the ḍākinīs, Vajrayoginī:

> Some of them were slicing off pieces of their own flesh with knives, laying it out and offering it as a [sacramental] feast. For the same purpose, some were bleeding themselves, some were giving their eyes, some their noses, some their tongues, some their ears, some their hearts, some their inner organs, some their muscles, some their intestines, some their bone marrow, some their spinal fluid, some their life force, some their breath, some their heads, and some their limbs, cutting them off and arranging them as a [sacramental] feast. They offered everything to the principal ḍākinī in union with her consort, dedicating it as a devoted [sacrament].[57]

Alarmed by this vision, Yeshe Tsogyal asked, "Why are you pursuing pain like this?" and the ḍākinīs answered in a litany, If you do not instantly offer whatever you have to the qualified guru, the precious spiritual opportunity is lost and many obstacles will accumulate. What must be offered is that most dear to you—your possessions, yourself, and your awareness. For ḍākinīs, their bodies, ornaments, and implements are their awareness. And awareness cannot be possessed or held—it must be immediately offered. This is how wisdom ḍākinīs teach.

The theme of the ḍākinī cutting open her heart center to display the inner reality of her body recurs in Tibetan hagiography.[58] Maṇḍāravā gave this gift to her parents when she returned to visit them after her awakening, bestowing on them the maṇḍala of long-life deities.[59] Nāropa gave Marpa the teachings on Vajrayoginī and sent him to the Sosadvīpa charnel ground in India to receive her blessing personally. Marpa arrived there on the winter solstice, the tenth day of the waning moon, and met a young woman whom he realized to be the manifestation of the Coemergent Consort. She gave him the blessing of kyerim and dzog-rim, drawing her crystal hooked knife across her heart center and revealing a splendid garland of the seed syllables of her mantra circle inside her body cavity, with her essence syllable HRĪḤ at the center, blazing with brilliant red light. She then sent him to Bodhgayā to see the tooth relic of the Buddha and then to Tibet to become a teacher in his own right.[60]

Another common way in which the ḍākinī gives a blessing of her own body is through sexual union. Yet sexual union also is not as it appears. In conventional Tibet, a woman's sexuality was perilous, attracting unwanted suitors who would imprison the woman as domestic property. Or, if the woman pursued a relationship based on her own desires, she was condemned as an ordinary prostitute. The body of the ḍākinī, whether visionary or human, is a subtle body of vital breath, channels, and essences. She has transmuted ordinary sexual passion into spiritual fire; the passion of the ḍākinī is fundamentally the passion for realization, and her blessing arouses a similar passion in her subjects. This passion paves the way for the dawning of nonconceptual realization. When the ḍākinī joins with the yogin, she blesses him with her empty and radiant body, a direct transmission of her nature. When Tilopa was blessed by the Queen of the Ḍākinīs, she offered herself to him passionately, proclaiming him to be her consort Cakrasaṃvara. Milarepa's student Tseringma, the Lady of Long Life, offered herself to her teacher in the practice of karmamudrā.

There are many other examples, but perhaps the most famous is that of Saraha, one of the earliest adepts, who is said to have lived three hundred and thirty-six years after the death of the Buddha. Saraha was a Brahmin, the youngest of five brothers. The great heruka-protector Hayagrīva, in order to fulfill his spiritual potential, appeared to Saraha in the market in the form of a low-caste woman meticulously crafting arrows. She became his consort, and Saraha went to live with her in the charnel ground, exclaiming, "Till yesterday I was not a real Brahmin, from today I am." There is obvious irony in this statement, for consorting with a low-caste woman not his wife in a place of filthy corpses violated the essence of the Brahmin's caste code. But his exclamation suggests that by receiving the blessing of her body, he had finally been introduced to true spirituality, after years of previous spiritual training. As they lived together, they practiced, feasted, and sang songs of realization that scandalized the king and queen of the region. When they and their subjects begged Saraha to give up the sacrilege of this lifestyle that violated every tenet of his caste, he responded with a series of *doha*s that made him legendary. In the "People Dohas," he celebrated his realization with this verse:

[The yoginī] consumes the householder and the [coemergent]
shines forth.
There is neither passion nor absence of passion.
Seated beside her own, her mind destroyed,
Thus I have seen the yoginī.

One eats and drinks and thinks what occurs to the thought.
It is beyond the mind and inconceivable, this wonder of the yoginī.

Here Sun [rasanā, roma] and Moon [lalanā, kyangma] lose their
distinction,
In her the triple world is formed.
I know this yoginī, perfecter of thought and unity of the
[coemergent].[61]

Saraha is speaking here on several levels. The ḍākinī consort, who is called the bestower of great bliss, has intoxicated for him all dualism of desire and concepts, such that the distinction of self and other, mind and world, has been completely drowned. This is the cessation of the subjective mind, the devoured householder. Yet the objects of desire still remain. From this desire one can extinguish the extreme of passion, which binds one to saṃsāra, and the extreme of passionlessness, which binds one to nirvāṇa. Then the yoginī, at first the object of desire, is understood to be not only the consort but the nature of mind itself. "She" then is the cessation of the subjective mind; "she" and her magic are beyond compare. This is how the path of great bliss accelerates the realization of the yogin.[62]

The body blessing may arise in the form of the vital essence of the ḍākinī's subtle body, her red bindu or thigle. When Marpa sought a famous forest yogin, he was instructed to approach his attendant, a woman of low caste. As a ḍākinī, she represented the mind essence of her teacher. She offered Marpa a large jug of water, instructing him to use one-third for bathing and one-third for drinking. Following her instructions, he washed, and the wash water miraculously returned to the jug as his own white bindu vital essence. When the woman again appeared and performed yogic exercises over the jug, a stream of her own red vital essence flowed into the jug. She instructed Marpa to bathe again in the mixed essences, and when he did so, all his thoughts dissolved.[63] Then he drank the water and, looking into the jug, saw the maṇḍala of the Guhyasamāja deities. Finally, the forest yogin appeared and completed the empowerments.[64]

The ḍākinī also gives blessing by cutting off her own head, a tradition particularly connected with the wrathful wisdom ḍākinī Vajravārāhī. Two sisters fled from abusive marriages and sought out the guru Kāṇhapa, known for his yogic skill. After initiating them, he sent them into retreat for twelve years. They returned without offerings, and the master, testing them, suggested they offer their own heads. Immediately, they drew from their mouths swords of wisdom, slashed off their heads, and placed their heads in the master's hand, singing, "We destroy the distinction between self and others. As tokens of the indeterminate, we offer these gifts."[65] Astounded with their offering, the guru replaced their heads on their shoulders, leaving no scars, and challenged them to practice for the benefit of others.

Another way in which the ḍākinī gives transmission and blessing from her body is with her own hair. When Yeshe Tsogyal calligraphed the terma teachings for Guru Rinpoche, she did so using a brush fashioned of her own hair. In another example, the first Karmapa, Tüsum Khyenpa (1110–1193), attained enlightenment through the practice of dream yoga in his fiftieth year, after being visited by fifteen wisdom ḍākinīs. With this realization, he experienced the sameness of day and night, dreams and the waking state, and meditation and everyday life. At the moment of his enlightenment, an ornate black crown (*vajra mukut, shanak*) appeared above the Karmapa's head, woven from the hair of one hundred thousand ḍākinīs, symbolizing his knowing of the past, present, and future.[66] This constantly present crown came to symbolize the spiritual power of the Karmapas, but for centuries it could be seen only by those of elevated spiritual realization. Later, the emperor of China, Yung Lo (Ch'eng Tsu, 1403–1425), who was a devoted student of the fifth Karmapa, Deshin Shekpa (1384–1415), created a replica of the crown studded with gold and jewels and presented it to his root guru. Deshin Shekpa then displayed the crown in a ceremony, which exists to this day, in which he manifested the compassion of Avalokiteśvara. The crown and its ceremonial display have the reputation for effecting the immediate liberation by seeing (*thong-dröl*) of all beings who witness it.[67]

The hair is an intimate, personal aspect of the ḍākinī's body, signifying the close experiential contact between disciple and teacher. In the earlier tradition, the surrender of one's hair signified renunciation. Monastic vows necessitate the surrender of the hair, and it is customary in Tibetan Buddhist refuge vow ceremonies for a lock of hair at the crown of the refugee's head to be cut. But the ḍākinīs' gift of hair is the reverse of these traditions. Rather than surrendering his or her hair, the initiant receives the ḍākinī's hair, a representation of feminine wisdom or awareness. This is more akin to the custom of relics in the Tibetan tradition, in which disciples keep locks of their guru's hair as a blessing. In the case of the Karmapa, the crown woven of ḍākinī hair signifies the body blessing of one hundred thousand ḍākinīs upon the realization of the Karmapa line.

Another body blessing of the ḍākinī is that of the ḍākinī's breath, which is said to be the essence of the teachings of the "whispered lineage." The ḍākinī's breath is the dynamic, intimate communication between guru and disciple, especially in the transmission of oral instructions on tantric view and meditation. The breath is said to be warm, enveloping, and personal and to sustain the practitioner in the most difficult moments of practice. When Milarepa was leaving Marpa to go practice in solitude, Dagmema, an incarnate wisdom ḍākinī and the wife of his guru, presented him with gifts of food, clothing, and boots. Then, proclaiming that these were only material gifts, she cried many tears and presented him with a skull-cup of blessed liquor, saying:

Without forgetting your compassionate father and mother,
Remember their kindness and persevere in your practice.
Wear the cloak of the ḍākinīs' deep breath,
Let it warm you on your journey.
May we meet again in the Pure Land of the Buddha
As friends reunited.[68]

In an auspicious dream, Shabkar encountered an old, sick, starving woman lying along the road, and she begged him for food and transport. When he gave her tea and roasted barley flour and placed her on his horse, she immediately transformed into Vajravārāhī, adorned and dancing, and joyfully empowered him. Shabkar rhapsodized, "From her heart emanated rays of light that penetrated me and brought me into an increasingly clear and vivid expanse of bliss and voidness."[69] Then she granted him siddhi in the form of a miraculous bag filled with silver coins. She asked him to bestow these coins on beings with suitable karma and disappeared into the sky. As Shabkar and his retinue held the coins in their hands, they could fly anywhere they wished. Reflecting later on the meaning of the dream, Shabkar concluded:

> by giving to my spiritual sons the profound instructions, which are like the warm breath of the mother ḍākinīs, they would attain either the state of celestial and human beings, liberation, or ultimate omniscience, in numbers corresponding to those of the different silver pieces.[70]

The ḍākinī's breath is the simile used specifically for the oral instructions from one's guru, but it also more generally refers to the body blessing of the ḍākinī. The breath in this case is personal and very near, and yet its quality is ungraspable. The breath is intimately warmed space, the essence of the ultimate nature of the wisdom ḍākinī, and when she wraps her students in it, they are infused with her intangibility and her blessing at once. The breath is intimately tied to meditation practice in Tibetan tantra, whether it be the mindfulness-of-breath practices of śamatha and vipaśyanā or the subtle-body practices in which mind rides breath, or prāṇa, through the channels. The ḍākinī's breath whispers the reminder that these practices are the path to liberation, along with the vast wisdom imparted by her teachings.

In these cases, the ḍākinī's transmission was to the human progenitor of a lineage of profound meditation practices, the Dzogchen and Mahāmudrā traditions. While the customary speech and mind empowerments she gave are crucial aspects of transmission, the intimacy of the body empowerment gives the yogin a direct experience of the heart of teaching.

The wisdom ḍākinī's body, whose nature is emptiness, bestows bliss on her initiant, whether her consort, her disciple, or her devotee. This bliss, or mahāsukha, is not just conventional pleasure. It is an experience of complete joy that comes from a genuine experience of nonconceptuality, uniting with a nondual, awake state. This experience manifests as confidence, which "comes only from complete identification with the wisdom-mind of the yidam. According to the scriptures, mahāsukha and wisdom are indivisible."[71] The experience of great bliss and wisdom inseparable is the experience of Mahāmudrā, in which complete clarity dawns concerning the nature of the mind and phenomena, along with unconditioned great joy. The body blessing of the ḍākinī ensures the development of this experience.

Ḍākinī Activities: Devouring and Feeding

A second area of characteristic feminine imagery has to do with food and acts of eating, serving, and feeding. In conventional settings, women in

Tibet (as well as India) were expected to prepare food and serve others. In ḍākinī imagery, the subservient role of women with regard to food was sometimes inverted so that especially the worldly ḍākinī ate instead of serving; worldly ḍākinīs feasted on the bodies of others for their own enjoyment, becoming unspeakably vile and dangerous. Sometimes ḍākinīs, especially wisdom ḍākinīs, carried out the traditional role of food preparation and serving, especially in relationship with the authentic practitioner who needed support in retreat. In any case, many ḍākinī stories have strong themes of devouring and feeding.

Wisdom ḍākinīs sometimes literally take on the devouring activities of their worldly ancestry, giving the blessings of their body through a kind of spiritual cannibalism. When Guru Rinpoche entered the palace of the Queen Ḍākinī, Sangwa Yeshe (Guhyajñāna),[72] she was seated on a throne of sun and moon discs, dressed in charnel ground ornaments and holding a skull-cup and wooden drum. Guru Rinpoche approached her with the appropriate offerings, prostrations, and circumambulations, requesting the outer, inner, and secret empowerments. She responded by transforming him into the seed syllable hūṃ and conferring on him these three empowerments with her body: first, she took the hūṃ on her lips; then she swallowed him and he received abhiṣeka in her stomach; next she empowered him in her secret place.[73] Finally, she passed him through her secret lotus, her vagina, and with these blessings his body, speech, and mind were purified of defilements. These constituted the outer, inner, and secret empowerments he sought, purifying the three obscurations. Through this blessing and others, he came to be known as Thötreng Tsal, or "strength of the rosary of skulls."[74]

Sometimes wisdom ḍākinīs have a wrathful demeanor in their devouring activities. While meditating in retreat, Do Khyentse Rinpoche (1800–1866) concentrated with single-minded devotion on Guru Rinpoche. That night, three terrifying ḍākinīs appeared to him and said, "In the 'self' of the delusory appearances, ignorance of grasping and grasped have manifested. There is no other way but to separate you from your evil body."[75] They cut his body to pieces and, dividing it among themselves, gobbled everything, including his consciousness. He fell unconscious, and when he awoke he saw the Vajrasattva consorts standing before him, emanating light. As the light touched him, he felt his own body to be of light, and he received many blessings and prophecies from gurus and ḍākinīs.

Being consumed in this way is a great blessing of the wisdom ḍākinī, for it represents a direct joining of the emptiness-space nature of the ḍākinī with the mind of the practitioner, which are understood in the transmission to be undifferentiable. This very literal transmission points out the ultimate nature of mind in the most direct way imaginable.

When confronted with the devouring activities of worldly ḍākinīs, wisdom ḍākinīs are especially skillful in transforming them and bringing them to the dharma. Maṇḍāravā offered herself to a cannibalistic ḍākinī who resided in a palace in Camara:

> There she found Queen Bhumahing, who was red in color with orange hair standing straight up. Her fangs were so large that they touched her breasts, and she wore a flayed human skin. Her brow was a mass of wrinkles. From her mouth resounded a shrill whistle, and she devoured the ḍākinī [Maṇḍāravā] in a single instant. The ḍākinī shouted "Phat!" and transferred her consciousness so that the queen's body collapsed and fell apart. The cannibal's abdomen split open, and the princess emerged.[76]

Rather than literally swallowing the worldly ḍākinī, Maṇḍāravā allowed herself to be consumed and then overcame the demon queen with her awareness. In so doing, Maṇḍāravā subdued the cannibalistic hordes. Then she married the cannibal king and dissolved into his body, taking control of him and turning him and his subjects to the dharma.

At the same time, the ḍākinī may demand that the practitioner devour her offering. In one of Jigme Lingpa's most vivid visionary experiences, the ḍākinī who entrusted him with yellow terma scrolls (*shok-ser*) demanded that he immediately eat them, proclaiming that they carried the power of liberating through experience. When he swallowed them without chewing, the words and meanings were directly imprinted upon his mind.[77] Kalu Rinpoche told a story of a ḍākinī who bestowed her blessing on her dull-witted husband by secretly offering him a piece of half-chewed fruit that she removed from her mouth. When he devotedly ate it, he was no longer dull-witted and became a great scholar-practitioner, renowned throughout India.[78] Khenpo Karthar Rinpoche told a story of a blacksmith's wife ḍākinī who was repeatedly supplicated by a monk; finally she broke a filthy turnip in half, rubbed it against her nipples, and threw it to him. When he was confused, he was assured, "You must accept it; eat the turnip right away!"[79]

The theme of feeding appears throughout the life story of the human ḍākinī Sukhasiddhi. As the young wife and mother of a destitute family, she offered the household's last remaining rice to a begging yogin, incurring the wrath of her husband and children, who threw her out. She then traveled to Uḍḍiyāṇa, and through her diligence and care she became a successful businesswoman, brewing rice wine and opening a restaurant. Eventually she heard of a famous yogi, Virūpa, who lived partway up the mountain, and she daily sent him offerings of her best rice beer with one of his woman disciples. Enjoying the beer, Virūpa took an interest in his generous benefactor and invited her to visit. Delighted, she went to him, bringing large offerings of beer and meat. As he conferred on her an initiation, she immediately manifested as a wisdom ḍākinī in mind and body and took the name of Sukhasiddhi, "she who has accomplished bliss."[80]

Ḍākinīs are closely associated with sacramental feasts and the offering and receiving of food and drink. Offerings to ḍākinīs, both worldly and wise, bring great blessings to tantric practice, and so these offerings are an intrinsic part of the twice-monthly cycle. The feast offering (gaṇacakra, tsok-khor)[81] is an elaborate practice session in which the practitioners, through the ritual recitation, fully evoke the maṇḍala of the yidam and renew the transmissions conferred by the guru, the lineage of enlightened teachers, and the deity whom they have previously bestowed in empowerment. In order to fully confirm this blessing, the practitioners present an excellent food offering in the form of a feast, to which the ḍākinīs and their consorts are invited. The invitation appears risky, for ḍākinīs can be dangerous and carry a menacing reputation like their forebears; but without their presence, the realization of the practice is beyond reach. The food itself is a sacrament that reminds the practitioners of the unsurpassable sacredness of all realms of perception (tag-nang). Performing the feast offering and partaking wholeheartedly invokes the ḍākinī's blessings. As Kṛṣṇācārya joined a feast offering in Uḍḍiyāṇa, he was instructed by the chief ḍākinī in a long song that ended with these words:

These words have never been put into written form—
They are gathered here with me in the clear heart of the ḍākinīs.
In this way, to cause your direct understanding of all this to broaden,
You must perform the songs and dances of the ḍākinī gathering.[82]

The tantric feast is one of the most powerful practices of extending sacred outlook into all realms of ordinary experience, purifying habitual, defiled ways of interpreting them.

The brewer ḍākinī, Sukhasiddhi.

When the practitioner invites the ḍākinīs to the feast in an outer way, she or he is inviting inner experiences as well. These include the experience of bliss, bestowed by the ḍākinī in full awareness of the dynamics of the subtle body; the experience of fully embodying the visualized yidam; and the experience of the nature of mind, the secret ḍākinī. While inviting the ḍākinīs and their retinues to the feast, the practitioner is given the following instruction:

Imagine your pores filled with knowledge-holders, ḍākinīs, and so on,
like a bursting bag of sesame seeds;
in a state of deliberate mindfulness, partake without attachment.
It doesn't matter if you see it as ordinary food and drink,
whatever you eat will become a sacred feast.[83]

It is often stated in feast liturgies that the practitioner is to visualize the pores of the body filled with hosts of ḍākinīs, which manifests the full blessings that the ḍākinīs bear to the tantric practitioner. When one experiences this completely, the blessings of the wisdom ḍākinīs have descended.

Legends of tantric feasts of ḍākinīs date back to pre-Buddhist worldly ḍākinīs in the Indian tradition, in which ḍākinīs would gather in charnel grounds for their own feasts. These gatherings were events of great foreboding for ordinary householders, who avoided charnel grounds especially on those occasions, but practitioners like Khyungpo Naljor who sought wisdom ḍākinī teachers braved the dangers to seek out their gurus.[84] Early in Indian Buddhist tantra, sacramental feasts were central in the ritual celebrations associated with ḍākinīs, and they were often convened by female tantric practitioners.[85] In the namthar tradition, ḍākinīs sometimes gather near a retreat site of a solitary yogin or yoginī, nurturing him or her with their feast offerings. The starving Milarepa often received "nourishment" from ḍākinīs, but it is clear this was no ordinary food. On long retreat, Milarepa dreamed he cultivated a field and lush crops sprang up, providing grain to support his practice. In remembering the dream, he sang:

I fill the granary with the fruit of excellent instructions,
Without the support of mental concepts.
This excellent grain, roasted and ground by ḍākinīs,
Is the hermit's food for inner growth.[86]

The ḍākinīs' blessing allows the oral instructions to be understood and applied, and so the grain that nourished him was a different kind of food. Later, when Milarepa was stranded by snow on retreat, he was asked how he was able to get food. He responded, "Most of the time, I was in the state of samādhi and hence required no food. On feast days, many ḍākinīs offered me food in their [tantric feasts]."[87] The food of tantric feasts may nourish on a literal level, but the real nourishment comes from the blessings of the tantric lineages and the ḍākinīs. In another place, when Mila and disciples were living in retreat, many ḍākinīs came and offered them a sacramental feast. They addressed Mila, "It is good for you during devotions to accept food and clothing from human beings, and also to receive a little heavenly nourishment from the ḍākinīs. We will always bring provisions for you." Mila responded, "The possessions, facilities, and food of the common people can never match the merits of enlightenment and the power of realization. Therefore, worldly needs are dispensable."[88] He then sang them a long song about what really nourished him.

Gender Differences: Yoginī Encounters with the Ḍākinī

Most of the hagiographies are records of encounters between male yogins and female ḍākinīs. Western studies of the ḍākinī have made much of this, drawing Jungian or feminist conclusions suggesting that the ḍākinī is an archetypal or patriarchal projection of all that men lack. There is much to support these interpretations. Yogins' accounts of ḍākinī encounters emphasize the practitioner's perspective, his response to her appearance, including his emotional state and spiritual experience, and his interpretation of the events. The ḍākinī emerges without personal history or identity, often without a name, and she disappears as quickly as she appears. By her actions, she is clearly not an ordinary being even if she is a human woman. Therefore it is most easy to objectify and abstract her.

A number of yoginī hagiographies have now been translated.[89] Even though these accounts have been passed through predominantly male lineages of students, they bear the stamp of the characteristically female experience of the spiritual path.[90] Most accounts of yoginīs appear to follow the pattern of yogin hagiographies, with descriptions of personal obstacles, searches for a teacher, trials and ordeals, practice, and realization. But the different kinds of obstacles encountered are characteristic of women in patriarchal systems. Most of these accounts devote the majority of their preenlightenment stories to the trials of marriage obligations, relationships with in-laws, and social ostracism.[91] Especially difficult are the injunctions for the girl to marry, often against her will, though she prefers a life devoted to practice. If she marries, she often suffers at the hands of a domineering husband or in-laws;[92] if she does not, she is confined by her parents to a solitary and protected life.[93] Upon rare occasions her spiritual gifts are recognized and she is allowed to seek a teacher.[94] But even when she receives teachings and transmissions, she is often bound to silence or is ridiculed or suppressed in her attempts to communicate her experience.[95] Often these yoginīs perform their practices and retreats in the company of other yoginīs in a relationship of mutual support.[96]

As for visionary encounters, ḍākinīs appear frequently to these yoginīs in forms closely resembling those that appear to men. Sometimes they appear naked with the customary charnel ground ornaments; at other times they are beautiful and clothed in silks and jewels. The timing of their appearances, the ways they teach, and the methods of support and guidance also accord with those of yogin accounts.

Specific themes that are characteristic of yoginī encounters appear in the story of the conception of the yoginī Machik Lapdrön. When ḍākinīs visited her mother Bumcham in a remarkable dream, a series of brilliant ḍākinī retinues successively bathed her with milky-white fluid and made offerings to her, requesting, "Mother, please be a mother to us."[97] Then a wrathful night-blue ḍākinī appeared before her, standing one cubit above the ground. She drew her hooked knife and sliced open Bumcham's heart, crying, "This heart of yours, obscured by ignorance, I'll pull it out and I'll eat it." She tore out Bumcham's heart and quickly caught the spurting blood in a skull-cup; she thirstily drank it, sharing with her ḍākinī retinue. The night-blue ḍākinī then drew from her silken girdle a pure white, clockwise-turning conch shell, adorned at its center with the seed syllable A. She blew it in a clear blast that echoed through the universe, and offered it to Bumcham as a replacement for her mortal heart. She and her retinue then blessed Bumcham with radiating light and dissolved into space. Bumcham's experience of the dream had no fear or pain; rather, as her heart was being torn out and replaced with the conch, she felt contentment, lucidity, and joy pervading her body.[98]

In this account, the ḍākinīs approached Bumcham as one of themselves who did not necessarily know that she was. In their supplication to her as Mother, they reminded her of her own nature as Yum Chenmo, the Great Mother, and asked her to be mother to them, the ḍākinīs. When the night-blue ḍākinī cut open Bumcham's chest, she demonstrated that she and Bumcham were mirror images—Bumcham's chest and the ḍākinī's chest were the same. But since Bumcham had not yet realized this, the ḍākinī took out her conventional heart or identity, obscured by ignorance, and gobbled it down. The empty and radiant body of the ḍākinī consumed Bumcham's ego-clinging on the spot. At that point their natures were one.

In its place she gave the tantric symbol of the feminine, a right-turning conch shell adorned with the A syllable, the seed syllable of Prajñāpāramitā. The right-turning conch (*tung-gye kyil*) is much rarer than the left-turning one and is considered extremely valuable especially because it is a natural object, not made by human hands.[99] This gift was signaled with the single blast blown by the ḍākinī to the farthest reaches of the universe, a nonconceptual tone of the essence of the ḍākinīs.

Yoginī encounters with the visionary ḍākinī contain several themes that point out the continuity of her own nature with the yoginī's. The ḍākinī consistently appears as an ally and support, even when wrathful. She mirrors the yoginī in embodiment, explicitly accentuating her feminine qualities, and eventually the yoginī herself manifests as the ḍākinī with special powers and characteristics. In contrast to her interactions with yogins, the ḍākinī confirms the yoginī's practice and realization instead of serving as an oppositional force, and the ḍākinī gives her body gifts in the areas of sexual yoga and of health and longevity.

First, the ḍākinī appears not as an oppositional figure but as an ally, mirror, or companion of the yoginī focused primarily on empowering and encouraging her. We have seen in the yogin accounts that the ḍākinī may appear in horrific guise, especially when confronting intellectual or class arrogance or intractability. She is especially likely in these contexts to appear as an ugly old hag or a wretched woman of low caste or disgusting profession. No such accounts occur in the available yoginī records. Rather, the ḍākinī appears in supportive or confirming roles, accepting the yoginī as a sister or ally. The thirteen-year-old cowherd Chomo Menmo is ushered into a terrifying charnel ground by Vajravārāhī and her retinue with the words "Welcome! girl of our enlightened family." She is then immediately empowered and entrusted with an important ḍākinī text and invited to feast with the hosts of ḍākinīs.[100] When Machik is overcome with the vision of Tārā in the form of a ḍākinī, she wonders whether an ordinary person like herself could benefit beings in any way. Tārā responds by revealing to her that her basic nature is the Great Queen Prajñāpāramitā herself, and encourages Machik to persevere in her practice.[101] This does not mean that ḍākinīs do not take on wrathful appearance with yoginīs, for the dark blue ḍākinī who cut out Bumcham's heart was most certainly wrathful; however, there is no hint that Bumcham was in any way frightened or reversed by the experience.[102]

There are occasional contrasexual examples of apparitions that manifest the qualities of ugliness and deformity. When the young yoginī Dorje Tso congratulated herself for becoming the consort of the gorgeous, virile Guru Rinpoche, the guru took on the ugly form of a decrepit old beggar to disabuse her of her obsession. He became

> an old man with hair whiter than a conch and eyes paler than blue, his head at the same level as his shoulders, drool and snot reaching his chest, and eye-bags hanging down to his cheeks. This frightful, nauseating magical appearance was there when the girl woke from her slumber.[103]

Seeing her attachment, the girl went into retreat and practiced the dharma. This vision of ugliness is all the more horrible in a figure to whom the practitioner is expected to be sexually attracted.

In addition, the yoginī does experience a challenge to her views parallel to those received by yogins, but these challenges come from gurus or male yogins encountered along the way. We have already described how Machik Lapdrön was confronted by Kyotön Sönam Lama, who queried her about her personal realization of the Prajñāpāramitā.[104] His treatment of her was, however, relatively gentle, and she experienced profound deepening in her practice as a result of his guidance.

Second, the ḍākinī bestows her body gifts on the yoginī in characteristic ways different from the way she gives them to yogins. She acts as a mirror for the yoginī, transforming her own view of her body as a ḍākinī's body, which is by nature radiant, empty, and beautiful. Bumcham's encounter with the wrathful ḍākinī left her feeling blissful, and even though she was forty-eight she daily took on successively younger appearance.[105] In a rare gender-reversal, Maṇḍāravā's mother experienced during pregnancy many ḍākas anointing her body with a special perfume. She became far more beautiful than before, "more youthful and radiant as each month went by."[106] When Gelongmo Palmo (Bhikṣunī Lakṣmī) the Kaśmiri princess prayed to the bodhisattva Avalokiteśvara (Chenresik), her advanced leprosy was completely healed and she was invited to dance in clouds of ḍākinīs.[107] When Yeshe Tsogyal was on retreat in the desolate mountains of Tibet, she practiced the austerities of tummo while completely naked, fasting for a period of one year. Suffering greatly and near death, she prayed fervently to the Three Roots, the guru, yidam, and ḍākinī, for guidance and support. At that moment, a brilliant red ḍākinī appeared to her, completely naked, without even bone ornaments, and thrust her vagina (*bhaga*) against Yeshe Tsogyal's mouth. Drinking deeply of the copious flow of blood, the yoginī experienced nonconceptual bliss. Her health was restored and she felt as strong as a lion.[108]

In the body gift of sexual yoga, the ḍākinīs counsel yoginīs to couple with particularly appropriate consorts, or they serve as matchmakers, delivering messages from prospective siddha consorts. Machik Lapdrön received visits from a succession of ḍākinīs counseling her to unite with Thöpa Bhadra. The last was Śaṅkapāli, the "conch protrectress," who was sent by the siddha on his behalf to persuade her of the auspiciousness of their connection.[109] Yeshe Tsogyal, while hosting a tantric feast for hundreds of worshipping ḍākinīs, bestowed on the human participants the symbolic initiations of the secret ḍākinīs. Then under her guidance her human and ḍākinī guests joined in union and reached the enlightenment stage of irreversibility.[110]

Feminist commentators have lamented the rarity of male ḍākinī (ḍāka) appearances to yoginīs, speculating that women are deprived of the spiritual guidance of a male symbolic partner, especially in sexual yoga or in the generation of great bliss.[111] Maṇḍāravā's mother experienced such a visitation from ḍākas, and the hagiographies abound with visionary male guru appearances to yoginīs, fulfilling these deficiencies. These gurus may appear in human form, or they may take the symbolic form of the heruka, the enlightened masculine principle.[112] In the hagiographies, yoginīs sometimes engage in sexual yoga with their gurus or with consorts of their guru's or ḍākinīs' choosing, to their mutual benefit. Yeshe Tsogyal and Maṇḍāravā practiced with Guru Rinpoche, and Yeshe Tsogyal's guru recommended several other spiritual consorts to her.[113]

In the case of visionary empowerments through sexual yoga, there are accounts in yoginī hagiographies in which the yoginī dreams of union with an attractive visionary enlightened-but-generic male. Sometimes it is unclear that the union entails sexual yoga. For example, when the nun Sudharmā practiced in retreat, she dreamed that an immaculate white man placed a crystal vase on her head three times, which illuminated the three world realms. Later, she gave birth to an extraordinary son, who was the yogin Garap Dorje, the founder of the Dzogchen lineages.[114] In three similar accounts, the placing of the vase caused bliss to pervade the yoginī's body, simulating the effects of sexual yoga.[115] In some stories of the conception of human ḍākinīs, symbolic visitation comes simultaneously to the mother and father as beams of light or visions of precious objects, either during lovemaking as in the case of Maṇḍāravā or in simultaneous dreams as in the case of Yeshe Tsogyal.[116] These visitations also produced experiences of pervading bliss.

A third difference in the yoginī encounters with the ḍākinī concerns the yoginī herself taking on the form of the ḍākinī. This is a common theme. As the yoginī develops spiritually, she takes on splendid physical forms typical of the ḍākinī, as in the case of Maṇḍāravā, who appears as the wrathful Siṃhamukhā "lion-headed ḍākinī,"[117] or Yeshe Tsogyal, who appears in twenty-five emanations, all aspects of the Great Queen Prajñāpāramitā.[118] Sukhasiddhi became a wisdom ḍākinī, and though she was already sixty-one years old, she took the form of a sixteen-year-old girl.[119] The yoginī does not necessarily admit her transformation. When curiosity-seekers approached the yoginī Drenchen Rema to ask if she were a ḍākinī, she replied angrily, "I have no powers!" and pelted them with stones. But the stones did not hurt them and instead cured all of their diseases, confirming that she was indeed a ḍākinī. This was verified for her in a series of dreams in which she herself was a central ḍākinī with ḍākinī retinues.[120]

This suggests that the ḍākinī can be seen in much the same ways by both female and male tantric practitioners, with certain exceptions. For both women and men, the ḍākinī is the symbol of naked awareness, the egoless wisdom-mind that serves as the ground of tantric practice. She is also the semiwrathful yidam manifestation of the wisdom-mind that consumes in fiery display the structure and habits of conceptual mind. She is the symbol of the channels and winds of the subtle body, and the bliss generated by the practice of yoga. And by virtue of her female body she is the human woman wherever she is encountered. The unique way in which the ḍākinī is experienced by the female practitioner is in relation to her own body and manifestation as woman. She serves as the seal and blessing of women's physical embodiment and as an ally and support in their practice. She endeavors to inspire women to practice authentically, and when women become enlightened they themselves manifest as the ḍākinī.

EIGHT

Protectors of the Tantric Teachings

The assembly of ḍākinīs who dispel obstacles and
adverse circumstances
Is contained within one's own innate nature;
In that state there is no need to offer tormas.
Leaving the six sense-consciousnesses in their
natural condition,
The yogin is content.[1]

WHEN PRINCESS MAṆḌĀRAVĀ EXPERIENCED the attacks of a mighty demon obstructor and his retinue against a wisdom maṇḍala, she took the wrathful form of the mighty Queen Prajñāpāramitā to confront them. With her hundred heads and thousand arms, she brandished terrible weapons and stomped heavily with a hundred legs. She wore charnel ground ornaments and blazed with primordial wisdom fire. She leaned forward and sang this threatening song:

> Hum! Hum! Bhyoh! Bhyoh! I am the blazing ḍākinī of the three realms of existence. With my blazing vajra sword I shall slice you wicked malefactors to pieces. My power in this world is boundless and vast as the heavens. My every gesture propels the ocean's waves. My power holds sway over all that is peaceful in the world and beyond; whatever remains I shall press between the palms of

> my hands. Now, you eagle-like demons and malefactors, prepare for the moment of your annihilation! Rulu! Rulu! Hum! Bhyoh! Bhyoh! Bhyoh! Bhyoh!"[2]

The demons were overwhelmed with fear and humbly offered the ḍākinī the very essence of their lives, vowing to protect the dharma. The key to the wisdom ḍākinī's power was her embodiment of the wisdom of Prajñāpāramitā: insight into the fundamental emptiness that is the heart of Vajrayāna view and practice. Maṇḍāravā exemplifies the ḍākinī as the protector of the Buddhist teachings, especially the secret teachings of the Vajrayāna. This chapter explores the ways in which the wisdom ḍākinī protects Vajrayāna, the guru-disciple relationship, oral transmission, tantric lineages, and the inner meaning of the essential teachings themselves.

In many cases, ḍākinī protectors are former worldly ḍākinīs who have been bound by oath to a Vajrayāna guru and who carry out the wishes of the guru and the lineage of teachers. For her the tantric teachings are her heart blood, or the very essence of her life. She has dedicated all of her power to the support and protection of the teachings, and she does not take kindly to misuse of her essence. The greatest violation for the ḍākinī protector is to propagate the tantric teachings without permission. This can be seen in the colophon of the *Mila Gurbum,* in which the author writes:

> *Three times did I seek my guru's permission*
> *To write this book.*
> *He smiled at me, [but] did not grant it*
> *Until the third time.*
> *I dare not violate the rules*
> *Because the ḍākinīs are most severe and strict.*
> *My guru says this story should be told*
> *Only to great yogis in the future*
> *As a reference for their devotions;*
> *But from others it must be secret kept.*
> *Lest I violate the ḍākinīs' rules and wishes*
> *I now sincerely pray to them*
> *To conceal this story from those*
> *[who cannot profit by it],*
> *And never let it widely spread.*[3]

The ḍākinī knows that tantric realization flourishes in an environment of intimacy, inexpressibility, and direct experience. Too much talk or dissemination can kill yogic realization. For this reason, ḍākinīs especially favor those who practice silently in solitary retreat.

When wisdom ḍākinīs serve also as protectors, they take on the guises of the worldly ḍākinīs at their most wrathful, complete with long, sharp fangs, rolling bloodshot eyes, clenched teeth, and terrifying weaponry. We have seen examples of how wisdom ḍākinīs take on a wrathful appearance to awaken the individual practitioner from arrogance, intellectual opinionatedness, or laziness. These same methods are employed in the conversion of demons and protection of the transmission of the dharma.

Auspicious Coincidence and Uḍḍiyāṇa

There are two primary types of transmissions that preserve guru-disciple communications in Tibetan Vajrayāna, and the ḍākinīs play important but different roles in each. First is the lineage of oral instruction called the "long transmission of pronouncements," or *kama,* handed down through a historic lineage of human gurus. Examples can be found in the tantric teachings received by human gurus like Tilopa and Nāropa, or Guru Rinpoche and his immediate disciples.

The second is the "close lineage of discovered treasures," or terma, which appears from the continuous direct communication of Guru Rinpoche. These treasures of constantly fresh teachings are discovered by enlightened treasure-discoverers, or tertöns. In this transmission, actual scriptures were concealed and subsequently discovered at appropriate times by realized gurus through their visionary power. The strongest terma tradition is that traced back to Guru Rinpoche. He is said to have understood that the Vajrayāna teachings that he transmitted would benefit from broader expression in future, turbulent times.[4]

While these two lines of transmission are distinct in the Nyingma tradition, ḍākinīs play a similar role in each. They guard and protect the teachings entrusted to their care, and they ensure the ongoing integrity of those teachings' discovery and dissemination. In each of these two lines, the authentic transmission of the tantric teachings is likened to the "warm breath of the mother ḍākinīs." The "whispered lineage," or kama, often uses that well-known analogy. Termas were said to embody the "unfading, moist breath of the ḍākinīs," a constantly intimate and fresh form of blessings.

It is said in the kama teachings that the ḍākinīs guard the integrity of oral transmission in five respects, called the five certainties. The powerful, personal teachings of the "hearing, or ear-whispered lineage"[5] can be transmitted only if (1) the teachings are presented in a properly arranged place, with auspicious indications; (2) the teacher is a qualified guru; (3) the students have sufficient devotion and dedication; (4) the time is ripe and appropriately auspicious; and (5) the teachings are appropriate in content and presentation.[6] Ensuring these five criteria is the ḍākinīs' responsibility.

Hagiographies indicate that these five prevail in both the kama and terma transmissions.[7] Ḍākinīs appear at key moments in the transmission of new lineages, warning of obstacles, limiting the audience, testing the confidence of the students and the guru, and even correcting the details of the rituals and pronunciation. The proper configuration of all of these components is spoken of as *tendel,* auspicious coincidence, which in a Tibetan context refers to the constellation of appropriate conditions for a successful transmission. *Tendel* is the abbreviation of the Tibetan term for interdependent origination (*pratītyasamutpāda*), suggesting that each of these five factors equally influences the other four, none of them being primary. The devotion of the students mutually draws out the guru's ability to transmit the teachings; the ripeness of the time mutually influences the appropriateness of the setting of the teachings. In each aspect, the ḍākinīs' and other protectors' blessings ensure the chemistry of the transmission.

Similar concern about tendel dominates the discovery of terma texts.[8] Potential tertöns carefully regard the auspicious coincidence of factors, including their readiness to discover, translate, and transmit these teachings to worthy disciples. They do preparatory practices, usually in retreat, waiting for auspicious signs such as visions, dreams, and prophecies. Ḍākinīs are prominent in such signs, for it is they who hold the teachings secret until tendel prevails. At the point where Longchenpa successfully received the *Heart Essence of the Ḍākinīs* terma, he sang this verse in appreciation:

When ḍākinīs deliver prophecies tonight
On the tenth day of the waning half of the lunar month
[A day when the ḍākinī's influence is believed very strong],

This is a sign of the internal conjunction of auspicious factors,
A sign of pure commitments among the faithful,
A sign of the nonbiased emergence of welfare for the living,
And a sign of traversing the ocean of cyclic existence![9]

In the terma tradition, it is essential that treasure-discoverers maintain close ties with the ḍākinīs, who are the source of the visionary experience necessary for a successful discovery.

When there is no suitable recipient of the tantric texts, they are said to be kept sealed in the invisible expanse and guarded and preserved by ḍākinīs. The invisible expanse is considered the special province of the ḍākinīs and is given the legendary name of Uḍḍiyāṇa, or, in its Tibetan version, Orgyen.[10] This place is said in legends to be a western paradise outwardly associated with three possible geographical locations: the Hindu Kush, the region of the Swat valley (to the northwest of contemporary India, near the Afghani border in Pakistan), or South India in the region of Kañcī.[11] The original Sanskrit name can be understood to mean "vehicle of flying," or "going above and far." In Vajrayāna legend, Uḍḍiyāṇa was said to be a beautiful and prosperous place ruled by King Indrabhūti. When King Indrabhūti asked the Buddha for teachings that would not require him to give up his throne, kingdom, wealth, or family, Buddha secretly gave him empowerments of inner tantras. All the inhabitants of this land, even the insects, practiced these teachings and became accomplished, vanishing in rainbow bodies. Desolate and uninhabited, Uḍḍiyāṇa was then transformed by compassionate water spirits (nāgas) into a lake. The water spirits also began to practice the tantric teachings, and their sons and daughters became ḍākas and ḍākinīs. At that point Uḍḍiyāṇa became renowned as the "land of the ḍākinīs."[12]

Uḍḍiyāṇa is particularly associated with Guru Rinpoche, Padmasambhava, the "lord of the ḍākinīs." It was in the middle of Dhanakośa Lake in Uḍḍiyāṇa that the king discovered him as a wondrous child, sitting on a lotus flower. The land is occupied by all sorts of ḍākinīs, both worldly and wise, who gather in four famous cities housing one hundred thousand myriads of ḍākinīs. These cities are built around dazzling temples whose stores preserve many volumes of tantric texts.[13] One such city is Dhūmasthira, the "place of smoke." The great contemporary master Dudjom Rinpoche wrote that the village of Dhūmasthira appears today to be an ordinary town, but because the women who live there belong to an ancient race of ḍākinīs they still have worldly power. Its central palace, Dharmagañji, cannot be seen conventionally, but it still "contains some tantras of the way of secret mantra which have not yet appeared in India; for the ḍākinīs have kept them secured in the invisible sphere, so that they are not ordinary objects of perception."[14]

While these realms are elaborated in tantric legends, their meaning can be found in the practices. Even while lamas speak rhapsodically of Uḍḍiyāṇa and its environs, they remind their students that Uḍḍiyāṇa can only be found esoterically. For the practitioner of subtle-body yoga, Uḍḍiyāṇa refers to the network of channels and vital breath in which the blissful heat of the ḍākinīs is generated. For the practitioner of the tantric sādhana, Uḍḍiyāṇa is the pure maṇḍala in which the yidam deity dwells. For the practitioner of the formless completion-stage practice, Uḍḍiyāṇa is the natural, self-arisen primordial wisdom-mind, complete and perfect just as it is.[15] These levels accord with the levels with which we have described the ḍākinī herself. And these are the levels at which the hidden teachings of tantra are sealed and guarded by the ḍākinīs.

Symbols Hidden and Revealed

The ḍākinīs also protect by holding the teachings in indecipherable language. In the transmission of the tantric teachings, only a small portion is contained in recorded texts. Texts cannot carry the entire teaching; no text carries the inner meaning, details of practice, or realization experience. The text is merely the outer instrument that holds the ground for the tacit meaning carried in the oral tradition. It is well known in the Tibetan tradition that tantric texts must be introduced through the oral instructions of a qualified guru. For this reason, the literal language of tantric texts is often incomprehensible to the uninitiated. Tantric language is called "twilight language" (*sandhā-bhāṣā, gongpe-ke*), signaling the same transitional, liminal quality that we described in terms of ḍākinī encounters. It must be experienced to be understood.[16]

The oral tradition of transmission as well as the personal inner realization of the meaning are protected by the ḍākinīs on behalf of the tantric lineages. If the lineage of oral instructions is lost, Tibetans believe, the essence of the teachings returns to the celestial realm, Uḍḍiyāṇa, protected by ḍākinīs. If the texts themselves are lost, they also return to the ḍākinīs' care to be rediscovered later.[17] When Milarepa burned the ḍākinī texts brought back from India by his conceited disciple Rechungpa, he first asked the ḍākinīs to reclaim them and keep them under their care. Acknowledging his arrogance, Rechungpa finally exclaimed, "What is the use of books without a guru?" Hearing this, the ḍākinīs returned the texts to him intact.[18]

In the terma tradition also, we can see how the protection of the ḍākinīs is important. It is especially in the kind of terma called "entrustment to ḍākinīs" (*khandro te-gya*) that sky-dancers are central.[19] In this form of terma, Guru Rinpoche's consort Yeshe Tsogyal received myriad teachings from her guru, remembering them all with perfect recall, one of her most beloved traits.[20] She collected all of these oral instructions and calligraphed them in secret script on yellow scrolls of paper (shok-ser), using her own hair as a brush. She then sealed the scrolls and concealed them in various locations, such as "indestructible rocks, wealth-filled lakes, and immutable chests."[21] As Dudjom Rinpoche wrote:

> Since [such treasures] were translated from the secret symbols of the ḍākinīs, the texts are profound and their blessing great. The unworthy, no matter how keen their intelligence, are like blind men examining an elephant and cannot appraise even a portion of them. The revealers of treasure are genuinely beyond the perceptual range of ordinary beings.[22]

When these scrolls are discovered, they are said to reawaken in the tertön a direct understanding of the treasure that is concealed in his or her awakened mind nature.

The script used by Yeshe Tsogyal is said to be "ḍākinī symbolic script" (*khandro dayik*), which is illegible except to the highly realized or auspicious tāntrika who can call on the ḍākinīs for help in deciphering it.[23] There appear to be several different kinds of these scripts, including ḍākinī scripts and other secret types. They may be in Indic or Tibetan languages but incomprehensible in meaning; or they may be in magical script (*trülyik*), which is symbolic in content but rapidly mutates while being read; or there may be secret or known fragmentary scripts that can be understood only with the whispered transmission.[24]

In an outer manner, then, it is understood that the ḍākinīs are the chief class of terma protectors, responsible for concealing them until the time is ripe and delivering them into the hands of the tertöns. The ḍākinīs also protect the practitioners of the terma texts, preserving the integrity of the terma teachings in their application. As the renowned tertön Nyoshul Khen Rinpoche remarked, "The terma teachings of the short and direct lineage are like the warm, fresh breaths, from which the moisture of blessings has not yet evaporated." On an inner level, it is ḍākinīs who wield the power to conceal or reveal the meaning of symbolic scripts specifically, and symbols in general, in tantric Buddhism. As is said in the tantras, concerning the ḍākinī code:

> *Ḍākinīs make use of symbols.*
> *They are skilled in symbols and symbolic replies.*
> *They link the ultimate essence to symbolism.*
> *Ḍākinīs are the life-force of symbols.*[25]

This means that the ḍākinīs have dominion over the secret treasury of termas, and only they or their peers have the power to directly understand their meanings. They skillfully use symbols to express this subtle meaning, and they link the ultimate meaning of the teachings with the symbols when they transmit them to worthy disciples. For this reason, the ḍākinīs are the vital essence, the life force, that brings these teachings alive. Without the aid and support of the protector ḍākinīs, the terma teachings would be incomprehensible.

At times the ḍākinīs appear to tertöns in visions, prophetically guiding their discoveries; at other times they lead the search with rains of flowers, canopies of rainbow light, or wisdom melodies of song. They may also serve as human consorts of the tertöns. Tertöns themselves are most often not celibate monastics; rather, they are more commonly yogins or householders, with consorts playing a dominant role in the discovery of the treasures. In fact, most tertöns consider tantric practice with a consort to be part of the necessary auspicious circumstances for the discovery of terma.[26] Tertöns are also women, as in the case of the contemporary tertön Khandro Khachi Wangmo, who was considered an incarnate ḍākinī. When she discovered the terma ritual objects on Bonri mountain in Nyingchi, she revealed the objects to those assembled as a ḍākinī herself, stripped to the waist and in a visionary state.[27]

Actual sexual union is not necessary for the human ḍākinī to guide the tertön. In a contemporary example, Yage Kunsang Drolma fled an unwanted arranged marriage and sought refuge in the nunnery of Rindzin Nuden Dorje, with whom she had a previous karmic connection.

> When they met, she requested that he ordain her as a nun and that he cut her hair. This haircutting was symbolic of their union. After the ordination Rindzin went to the place known as Khandro Bumdzong and found all the hidden texts.[28]

Later, when Lama Rindzin experienced obstacles in his discoveries, he sent his monks to the nun Yage Kunsang, requesting her to aid him. She came in procession with the monks and performed a ritual with her lama, described as another symbolic expression of their sexual union. Then the lama was able to rediscover the last chapter. The nun Yage Kunsang was called a perfect practitioner of the monastic code. Though she kept her hair long like a yoginī, she developed "the smell characterizing very good Vinaya practitioners. Lama Rindzin Nuden Dorje was a pure monk and Yage Kunsang was a pure nun. They both followed the Vinaya rules and they didn't commit any fault."[29]

The reason that ḍākinīs play such an important role in terma protection and discovery is that they represent the inner wisdom-mind of the tāntrika. While the search for terma may appear an outward one, it must be accompanied by an inward deepening. The true hiding place for terma is in the mind, and the essence of all terma is mind terma.[30] Although Tibetan Buddhists in exile are always concerned with the preservation of endangered Tibetan texts, of greater concern is the preservation of mind transmissions. This is why Tibetans have endeavored so assiduously to save the tülku lineages of transmission. Inquiry into the nature of the ḍākinī is, at its heart, an inquiry into the true nature of our own minds. The outer presence of the ḍākinī in the tertön's life is meant to be a reminder of the essential discovery of the secret ḍākinī.

Ḍākinīs are famous as purveyors of symbols. When Saraha met the arrowsmith woman in the market, he watched her carefully and realized that she was giving spiritual instruction. Seeing him there, she turned and said, "My dear young man, the Buddha's meaning can be known through symbols and actions, not through words and books."[31] He responded, "You are not an ordinary arrowsmith woman; you are a teacher of symbols."[32] To the uninitiated, the symbol is opaque and the teachings are hidden; to the worthy and ripened student, the symbol is offered and revealed. This means that, simultaneous with the protection they give to the tantras, ḍākinīs offer teachings. They communicate symbolically and give symbolic gifts; when confronted with symbolic gestures or sounds, they respond unerringly with symbolic replies.[33]

In the kama lineage, ḍākinī symbolic language also obscures the meaning of the teachings for the uninitiated practitioner. When Marpa prepared to return to Tibet, he offered a sacramental feast in honor of his guru Nāropa. As a parting gift, the great guru sang an indecipherable song to his young Tibetan disciple, using the śūnyatā language of the Prajñāpāramitā:

A flower blooming in the sky,
The son of a barren woman rides a horse
Wielding a whip of tortoise hair.
With the dagger of a hare's horn
He kills his enemy in the space of dharmatā.
The mute speaks, the blind man sees.
The deaf man hears, the cripple runs.
The sun and moon dance, blowing trumpets.
The little child turns the wheel.[34]

Then Nāropa told Marpa that he would come to understand this song only if he returned once again for teachings.

Many years later in Tibet, Marpa had a visionary dream in a "state where sleep and luminosity mix." In it three beautiful ḍākinīs appeared to him, clothed in silks and wearing ornaments of bone, melodiously singing the meaning of Nāropa's previous teaching:

The ḍākinī is the flower blooming in the sky.
The son of a barren woman riding a horse is the [whispered] lineage.
The whip of tortoise hair is the inexpressible.
The dagger of a hare's horn is the unborn.
This kills Tilopa in the space of dharmatā.

Tilopa is the mute, beyond word, thought, and expression.
Nāropa is the deaf man, the dharmakāya mountain of dharmatā.
Lodrö is the cripple, who runs on the mountain with the gait of
luminosity, free from coming and going.
The moon and sun are Hevajra and consort.
They are two dancers, but one taste.

The [conch shells] proclaiming fame in the ten directions
Sound for worthy vessels.
The wheel is Cakrasaṃvara.
Its turning is the [whispered] lineage wheel itself.
O child, turn it without attachment.[35]

Here the ḍākinīs pointed out the nondual essence of Mahāmudrā, the inexpressible nature of the mind and experience, the essence of the ḍākinī's whispered lineage. They use all the famous allegories of ḍākinī language, pointing to the lack of inherent existence of all phenomena, its fundamental vast and luminous quality. They also bless the masters of Mahāmudrā, the lineage beginning with Tilopa.

Immediately upon waking, Marpa was overwhelmed with devotion and hastily departed for India to see his teacher one last time. He was too late—Nāropa had already died.[36] Nevertheless, the aging Marpa sought his teacher for many months in which he received a series of visions, each of which was filled with more indecipherable ḍākinī poetry. Finally at Phullahari in Nepal he received the Cakrasaṃvara teachings from Nāropa himself, and, impressed with the profundity of the teachings, Marpa exclaimed, "Knowing one thing liberates all!"[37]

The ḍākinī's protection is reflected in the integrity of the symbols, but once the communication takes place the ḍākinīs know that the symbols have served their purpose. After the ḍākinī gave Jigme Lingpa an amulet box, the treasure of Samantabhadra's heart-mind, she vanished with the words "Symbol's dissolved!"—a typical ending of a treasure-discovery vision.[38] This is a reminder that the symbols themselves have no inherent existence and that their appearance points to various meanings but the ultimate meaning is always the vast and luminous expanse.

On the most subtle level, the ḍākinīs are embodiments of the essence of the tantric teachings, the personal and direct realization of things as they are coupled with the skillful means needed to apply this realization in everyday life. The ḍākinī herself and her symbolic language elicit this realization; just seeing these scripts or hearing the language is considered a blessing from the lineage, for they can arouse liberation by seeing (thongdröl), a method of awakening that is occasioned by direct, unmediated sense perception.[39] The ḍākinī acts on behalf of the lineage of teachings, uncovering the naked awareness itself. Reverence for her is reverence for the capacity of living, panoramic awareness to dawn. Disrespect for her dishonors this capacity and allows it to die.

Why is it that ḍākinīs play such an important role as protectors of both the kama and terma Vajrayāna teachings? Tulku Thondup, citing Dodrup Chen III, says that this is because it is the natural quality of the female to care for and preserve.[40] But a further clue can be found in understanding the motherly qualities according to Vajrayāna Buddhism, in which the space from which everything arises, known as Mother Prajñāpāramitā, can also be protective, sharp, and cutting.[41] One true form of the Mother is the wrathful, wild protector, as Maṇḍāravā showed in her manifestation of the Queen with one hundred heads and one thousand arms, blazing with scorching fire. When she stomped her hundred legs, the entire earth shook. In this act, she demonstrated the inherent power in the direct experience of Prajñāpāramitā, the realization of emptiness in the Vajrayāna sense.

The Wisdom Ḍākinī Protector Ekajaṭī

The most important protector of the Vajrayāna teachings, especially the inner tantras and termas, is Ekajaṭī.[42] She is known as the protector of mantra, for she supports the practitioner in deciphering symbolic ḍākinī codes and properly determines appropriate times and circumstances for revealing tantric teachings. Because she completely realizes the texts and mantras under her care, she reminds the practitioner of their preciousness and secrecy.

Ekajaṭī is considered the Queen of Mantra and the first ḍākinī principle, the mantra protector (*ngak sungma*). Her name means "one topknot" (*Ralchigma*), and her hair is arranged in a single bun with a turquoise forehead curl. This and her other features signify her blazing allegiance to nonduality. Ekajaṭī's single eye gazes into unceasing space, a single fang pierces through obstacles, a single breast "nurtures supreme practitioners as [her] children."[43] She is naked, like awareness itself, except for a garment of white clouds and tiger skin around her waist. The tiger skin is the realized siddha's garb, which signifies fearless enlightenment. She is ornamented with snakes and a garland of human heads. In some representations, she stands on a single leg. Her body is dark in color, brown or deep blue.

Ekajaṭī stands on a flaming maṇḍala of triangular shape. She is sur-

Protector Ekajaṭī, Queen of Mantra.

rounded by a fearsome retinue of mamo demonesses who do her bidding in support of the secret teachings, and she emanates a retinue of one hundred ferocious iron she-wolves from her left hand.[44] For discouraged or lazy practitioners, she is committed to being "an arrow of awareness" to reawaken and refresh them. For defiant or disrespectful practitioners, she is wrathful and threatening, committed to killing their egos and leading them to dharmadhātu, or the ultimate realization itself. She holds in her right hand the eviscerated, dripping red heart of those who have betrayed their Vajrayāna vows. She is supplicated every evening at sunset by Vajrayāna practitioners and requested to support and protect the integrity of the teachings and the practice.

When Ekajaṭī appears to yogins in hagiographies, she is especially wrathful. She speaks in sharp piercing shrieks, her eye boils, and she gnashes her fang. At times she appears twice human size, brandishing weapons and served by witches drenched in blood.[45] Visions of her are considered highly auspicious, to be treasured. Lushül Khenpo Könchok Drönme carried with him throughout his life the vision of an old, ugly, and angry-looking woman upon whom he consistently meditated as a divine being. Late in his life, she transformed into a pure vision of Ekajaṭī, the protector of the tantras.[46] Ekajaṭī is known as protector of terma teachings, along with the male protectors Vajrasadhu (Dorje Lekpa) and Rahula. However, since the treasure teachings are particularly associated with ḍākinīs, Ekajaṭī is of special importance.

Ekajaṭī especially protects the Dzogchen, the most closely guarded teachings in Tibetan Buddhism. It is said that Śrīsiṃha himself entrusted the *Nyingthik* teachings to her care.[47] To the great master Longchenpa, who initiated the dissemination of certain Dzogchen teachings, Ekajaṭī offered uncharacteristically personal guidance. In his thirty-second year, Ekajaṭī appeared to Longchenpa, supervising every ritual detail of the *Heart Essence of the Ḍākinīs* (*Khandro Nyingthik*) empowerment, insisting on the use of a peacock feather and removing an unnecessary basin. When Longchenpa performed the ritual, she nodded her head in approval but corrected his pronunciation. When he recited the mantra, Ekajaṭī admonished him, saying, "Imitate me," and she sang it in a strange, harmonious melody in the ḍākinī's language.[48] Later she appeared at the gathering and joyously danced, proclaiming the approval of Guru Rinpoche and the ḍākinīs.[49]

On Behalf of the Tradition: Founders of New Lineages of Teaching

One important responsibility of the wisdom ḍākinīs is the initiation of new lineages of teachings. Since they are the protectors of tantras, they often are the source of new teachings, which they fiercely protect until the circumstances are ripe for their dissemination. Sometimes they have received the teachings from enlightened ḍākinī realms such as Uḍḍiyāṇa, or they serve as intermediaries for other celestial realms. At other times they have retained custody of discovered texts that have yet to be propagated.[50] In any case, some of Tibet's most popular practices originated with the transmission by ḍākinīs. For example, Avalokiteśvara's famous six-syllable mantra *Oṃ mani padme hūṃ* was transmitted to the second Karmapa, Karma Pakshi (1204–1283) directly from the ḍākinīs.[51]

Their role in the initiation of new cycles of teachings can be seen in the number of text colophons that prominently display ḍākinī names. Of course this can also be understood in light of our discussion of spiritual subjectivity. Just as new teachings are given by ḍākinīs, they are received by the ḍākinī as well—the inner realization of the tantric practitioner. As Khenpo Jigme Phüntsok remarked, the words of Jigme Lingpa's terma text were written *for* ḍākinīs, the innermost spirituality of those who read it. When the tantric teachings are realized, it is the inner ḍākinī in each practitioner who receives them and therefore is realized.[52]

What can we learn about the ḍākinī as initiator of new tantric lineages? Her paradigm is consistent with the roles described here. She acts on behalf of the tantric teachings as messenger and intermediary, and she is the predominant protector of the integrity of the teachings and their transmission. But in this special role, there are additional aspects to her manifestation. She must pay special attention to testing the yogin or yoginī who is to receive the teachings, examining his or her purity of Vajrayāna commitments, personal confidence, and inner conviction in inherent wakefulness. All three aspects are necessary if the new line of teachings is to prosper. Ultimately, these three are not really separate.

Ḍākinīs have many powers at their command and will often pose as worldly, demonic ḍākinīs to ensure that the practitioner is ready to receive the teachings he or she seeks. In this guise, they flaunt their flesh-eating ferocity, gnashing their teeth or brandishing their weapons. Or they may create a series of daunting obstacles that the practitioner must overcome in order to prove himself or herself worthy. The yogins or yoginīs do not always succeed without help. When Marpa asked to receive the ḍākinī whispered lineage teachings from Nāropa, cautious ḍākinīs took on flesh-eating guise and attacked him, and he fled. At first his guru did nothing to help him, but then a terrorized Marpa supplicated Tilopa to protect him. Tilopa manifested wrathful replications of himself and chased down the ḍākinīs, demanding their support.[53]

When the practitioner manifests commitment and confidence, the wrath of the ḍākinīs dissolves, and they become attentive teachers or devoted students. This pattern, established with the subjugation and conversation of the worldly ḍākinīs, is repeated with wisdom ḍākinīs who serve in protecting and confronting roles. As the stainless ḍākinīs of nirmāṇakāya manifestation said to Tilopa:

We are to you as the butterfly to the lamp;
The butterfly hopes to extinguish the lamp,
But instead dies in the light.
Just so, we hoped to harm you,
But you overpowered us.[54]

The ḍākinīs are also committed to testing the purity of the commitments of the yogin or yoginī. A particularly telling moment of this kind of testing can be found in the transmission of the *Heart Essence of the Ḍākinīs* (*Khandro Nyingthik*) teachings that have been so important in the inner tantras of the Nyingma lineage. The great dharma king Trisong Detsen had a daughter called Pemasel, or "clear lotus," who fell gravely ill and died at the age of eight. Guru Rinpoche immediately came to her, and with the hook of his contemplation caught her consciousness and revived her, giving her the transmission of the *Khandro Nyingthik.* Guru Rinpoche then announced to her father that her illness resulted from evil karma from a murder she had committed in a previous life.[55] She would experience five "impure" lives in which she would work off the effects of this evil karma, and she would then have seven "pure" lives in which she would experience the blessing given her by Guru Rinpoche. During these seven lives, she would become an important tertön.

In one of these subsequent lives as a man, Pema Lendreltsel (1291–1313) actually rediscovered the *Khandro Nyingthik* teachings but did not follow the injunctions of the ḍākinīs to keep them utterly secret.[56] When meeting with the third Karmapa, Rangjung Dorje (1284–1339), he yielded to the

Karmapa's request to see the terma texts, take them as blessings on his head, and finally receive full empowerment for them. Immediately following, a series of calamities occurred that led to his early death.[57] Twenty-six years later his successor, Longchen Rabjam (Longchenpa, 1308–1364), learned this from Vajravārāhī in a vision, who declared that if Pema Lendreltsel had practiced these teachings in secrecy, he would have benefited many. "Since in fact he didn't keep them secret, he wasn't able to live out his full life span."[58] Now that he had been born as Longchenpa, the prophecy could be continued.

Longchenpa was careful not to repeat his predecessor's mistake. When he sought permission to pass on the transmission of the *Khandro Nyingthik* teachings, he turned to five different ḍākinīs for guidance, each of whom played a role concerning the auspiciousness of the transmission. Ekajaṭī corrected the liturgical details, Vajravārāhī confirmed his identity as an authentic tertön, Dorje Gyudrön served as his "word protector" (*kasung*), Yeshe Tsogyal aided in the symbolic transmission to the audience, and the worldly protector Remati tested his confidence. Later Guru Rinpoche appeared in a vision, surrounded by hosts of ḍākinīs, to bestow the treasure texts upon Longchenpa.

Later Vajravārāhī again appeared to Longchenpa, assuring him that he held the meaning of the teachings but that he should limit the guidance he gave others on this practice. When he asked how it was that she appeared to him, she answered:

> Am I a deity who must be meditated upon, a mantra to be recited, an object of offerings? Don't you understand that I am always present for all yogīs and yoginīs with intact commitments and realization? I have been in seamless union with you in all your rebirths.[59]

Because the commitments of Longchenpa and his disciples were strong, Vajravārāhī and the other ḍākinīs authorized the transmission of the *Khandro Nyingthik* and accompanied him at the time of the transmission. They also remained as continuous protectors of the teachings in successive months. Needless to say, Longchenpa's long, devoted, and very productive life was characterized by great reverence for and resonance with the host of ḍākinīs who accompanied him.

The ḍākinī must also test the confidence of the practitioner to discover whether he or she has sufficient personal conviction in inherent wakefulness, a prerequisite for tantric realization. When the great yogin Khyungpo Naljor went to the secret places of India and Nepal, seeking an authentic, enlightened teacher, all the teachers he met directed him to the great wisdom ḍākinī Niguma, consort of the adept Nāropa.[60] She was said to have attained the highest enlightenment and dwelt in the state of Vajradhara. When he heard her name, tears poured from Khyungpo Naljor's eyes, and the hairs of his body trembled with excitement. When he asked where to find her, he was told that she could not be found conventionally. Only those of perfected sacred outlook could see her, as she had attained the rainbow body. However, she sometimes appeared at the great charnel ground Sosaling Grove at the time of the tantric feasts of the ḍākinīs.

Taking the five hundred measures of gold he had amassed as an offering, Khyungpo Naljor eagerly traveled to Sosaling charnel ground on the feast day and immediately had a vision of a dark brown ḍākinī, adorned in the customary manner, dancing high in the sky above him. Dressed in charnel ground ornaments, she transformed herself into many ḍākinīs, dancing everywhere in space. Thinking this must be Niguma, Khyungpo Naljor prostrated many times, circumambulated, and requested tantric teachings. The ḍākinī responded ferociously, testing him: "I am a flesh-eating demoness [shasa khandro]. When my retinue arrives you will be in great danger. They will surely devour you. You must quickly flee."[61] Unafraid, the yogi again respectfully requested the teachings, and the ḍākinī retorted that she could give teachings only if he offered a great deal of gold.

Khyungpo Naljor offered her his five hundred measures of gold, and to his surprise, the ḍākinī accepted the gold and immediately tossed it into the forest. Joyfully, he concluded, "This is the [wisdom] ḍākinī herself, for she discards such a quantity of gold without remorse."[62] He realized that a worldly ḍākinī would have had attachment to gold and would have kept at least some of it. And, uttering the seed syllable HRĪḤ,[63] she emanated an elaborate maṇḍala and gave him the root and branch transmissions of the Six Yogas.[64] Later, Khyungpo Naljor was to study with a succession of impressive ḍākinī gurus and to prove a worthy disciple of each.[65]

Probably the most famous test of the yogin's confidence appears in the "superior biography" of Tilopa, the human guru and founder of the Kagyü lineage of teachings, the most famous of which are the Mahāmudrā meditation teachings. In the text, an old woman appeared to the child Tilopa

Niguma, founder of the Shangpa Kagyü.

in a vision, sending him to seek the teachings of the whispered lineage from the stainless Queen of Ḍākinīs. The old ḍākinī advised him, "You are an emanation who possesses the prophecy and commitment for these. If you take them by force, you will get them."[66] It was clear from the prophecy that all depended upon Tilopa's confidence in his own inherently enlightened nature. Armed with three symbolic implements,[67] Tilopa set out to obtain the teachings. With the support of his ḍākinī mentor, his body was immovable, his speech was unwavering, and his mind could not be reduced to fear. These three vajra prides, beyond any sense of ego, are what gave him the confidence to win the teachings.[68]

As he approached the monastery of the Queen Ḍākinī, he encountered a series of wrathful worldly ḍākinīs who threatened his progress, saying, "We are devouring ḍākinīs. We eat flesh and thirst for blood." Responding, "Because I am not frightened even by many ḍākinīs, not one tip of my hair has trembled!"[69] he boldly entered the monastery. Though threatening ḍākinīs attempted to stop him, Tilopa demanded to see the Queen, the dharmakāya wisdom ḍākinī. When he approached without the customary prostration of respect, her attendant ḍākas and ḍākinīs expressed disapproval. The Queen Ḍākinī said:

He is the father of the buddhas of the three times, Cakrasaṃvara.
Even if a hail of vajras fell from the sky upon him,
He could not be conquered.[70]

When he requested the teachings of the whispered lineage, she continued to test him, saying that these teachings were locked by the commitments, prophecies, and siddhis and he would not be able to open them. When he confidently proclaimed, "I have the key of the ḍākinī's prophecy!" the ḍākinīs let out a chorus of horselaughs. The Queen challenged him with a ḍākinī riddle, which he confidently solved, declaring his meditative realization. Impressed, the Queen Ḍākinī completed the empowerment, proclaiming Tilopa as her consort, as Buddha Cakrasaṃvara, the supreme bliss, and protector of beings, and blessing him by offering herself to him passionately. She gave him the oral instructions of the whispered lineage and appointed him master of the tantras. He became the first human guru of the "whispered lineage," which was carried through his line of successors beginning with Nāropa.[71]

In each of these accounts, the ḍākinīs were testing the readiness of the yogins to receive tantric instruction. Conventionally speaking, the practitioner begins the spiritual journey idealizing and idolizing the guru and the teachings, especially when contrasted with himself or herself. But the Vajrayāna teachings require that the practitioner uncover fundamental confidence in her or his own enlightened nature. Without this conviction, all the empowerments and blessings of all the buddhas of the three times will have no effect. Practice will merely confirm the miserable state of the practitioner. But with fundamental confidence, the practitioner can actually receive the empowerments, benefit from them, and put them into practice. The ḍākinī tests the practitioner to see if such confidence is present.

Conclusion

DAKINI'S WARM BREATH: QUINTESSENCE OF A TANTRIC SYMBOL

The teachings of the whispered lineage
are the ḍākinī's warm breath.

—MILAREPA[1]

WHEN GURU RINPOCHE ENCOUNTERED the maidservant Kumarī at the palace gate, he did not recognize her to be a wisdom ḍākinī until she revealed herself to him in all her glory. Why would such a great teacher, superior in realization and accomplished in the ways of the world, not see Kumarī as she really was? If the great Guru Rinpoche himself could not recognize the ḍākinī, how can the ordinary Vajrayāna practitioner see her face?[2]

The story of Guru Rinpoche's encounter with Kumarī reveals the powerful ambiguity of the ḍākinī, her hiddenness, and her inexpressibility. Because she is nonconceptual, she cannot be known as an object of experience; because she holds the keys to direct realization, she is an emissary of awakening. She represents the lineages of awakening traced all the way back to the Buddha, but at the same time she represents personal awakening in the present moment. Guru Rinpoche demonstrated sudden awakening, the unexpected opening of conventional mind to the dawning of nondual wisdom. When such an experience happens for Guru Rinpoche, we know that it is possible for every practitioner of tantric Buddhism to encounter the ḍākinī with all her depth of meaning.

How are we to interpret this encounter? In the final analysis, not every aspect of the ḍākinī carries equal consideration. Considering this adds certain tools to the interpretation of ḍākinī lore. Let us review Paul Ricoeur's "hermeneutics of suspicion," which identifies the most essential qualities of the symbol as distinguished from those aspects of the ḍākinī that are subject to cultural bias and interpretation.[3] From this perspective, what is most essential to an understanding of the ḍākinī? When is her reality least mediated or culturally bound? According to Ricoeur's method, the meditative dimensions of the ḍākinī are the practitioner's most direct access to the essence of the symbol. Following the traditions we have described, the ḍākinī can be found especially in the ritual and formless practices (utpattikrama, kyerim; sampannakrama, dzog-rim), which include performance of the sādhana of the yidam(s), the various practices of the subtle-body yoga, and the formless Mahāmudrā practice of resting in the nature of mind. Those aspects of greatest "suspicion," most subject to cultural influence and misinterpretation, are the cultural dimensions, drawn from interpretations that render women the living embodiments of the ḍākinī and from the hagiographic stories of ḍākinī encounters. Taken as independent accounts, these ways of speaking of the ḍākinī are the most susceptible to misinterpretation. When these sources are interpreted within the context of meditation practice and ritual, the lore of the ḍākinī-woman or ḍākinī encounters has potential depth of meaning.

From this perspective, we may return to Guru Rinpoche's encounter with Kumarī. Taken at face value, as an independent encounter between the yogin and the ḍākinī, it is easy to misunderstand the message of the ḍākinī. A Jungian might find Guru Rinpoche to be meeting his unconscious, the emotional or intuitional aspects of himself previously unacknowledged. A feminist interpretation might deem Kumarī to be the gynocentric goddess who instructed Guru Rinpoche on proper respect for women, the source of all wisdom. Both of these interpretations rely too heavily on the cultural boundedness of the encounter and upon a dualistic understanding of yogin and ḍākinī.[4] Interpretations that rely on the meditative contexts of the ḍākinī symbol come much closer to an accurate reading of the story. Kumarī represented to the yogin the inner meaning of his yogic experience and the requisite preparation for the meeting with the

Queen Ḍākinī. If Guru Rinpoche were to receive the blessing empowerment from the Queen Ḍākinī Secret Wisdom, it was essential that he yogically prepare. First, his sacred outlook was tested in a classic ordeal necessary to prove his intention and remove his obstacles; next, Guru Rinpoche was introduced to the maṇḍala of peaceful and wrathful deities of Mahāyoga-tantra that would be fully revealed to him in the empowerment to come. This encounter gave him the necessary respectful attitude, confidence, and sacred outlook to enter into the inner sanctum of the maṇḍala of the deities of Mahāyoga-yāna.[5]

What is possibly most provocative about the ḍākinī lore is the idea that the ḍākinī is a feminine symbol and at the same time is utterly beyond gender. While Kumarī is a feminine figure, within her body was revealed the limitless expanse in which the maṇḍala of peaceful and wrathful deities could be seen. Viewed through Ricoeur's hermeneutics of suspicion, this suggests that the essence of the ḍākinī is genderless, yet she takes feminine form in the realm of symbol. As a feminine deity, she represents the lack of inherent existence of gender even as she redefines the meanings of gender for herself and for all human beings. If the practitioner bases interpretation upon meditative experience, he or she may find the embodied or visionary ḍākinī powerful in liquefying concepts—including those of gender—even while she takes the gendered form of a beautiful or terrifying woman. In one flash, she communicates that the world of duality is a perfect and only means of expression of that which is beyond duality. How she is seen depends upon the sacred outlook (tag-nang) of the practitioner.

There are, of course, many unresolved or unfinished areas of meaning for the ḍākinī that must be elaborated in further studies. If the ḍākinī is a feminine principle, tantric Buddhism is based upon a hidden masculine principle as well that needs further exploration. The heruka, or blood-drinker (trak-thung), epitomizes the masculine principle of energy and skillful means that empowers situations, making them more creative. This wrathful yidam drinks of the blood of self-cherishing, confusion, and doubt and liberates impediments to full manifestation. He is the wisdom ḍākinī's powerful consort, and joined together in blissful union they represent the full possibilities of awakening. His qualities arouse the ḍākinī in all her manifestations. In keeping with the essence of the ḍākinī qualities, a study such as this one cannot end without expressing intense yearning for the complete elaboration of the heruka as well.

Yet the contrasexuality of the ḍākinī and heruka creates other haunting questions. In our critiques of the Jungian and feminist models of interpreting the ḍākinī lore, a major concern was the excessive reliance on the contrasexuality of the ḍākinī with reference to the practitioner. We asked whether the ḍākinī's feminine gender and sexual mode suggest that she is relevant only to the male practitioner, and we determined that she was relevant to both male and female practitioners, though in somewhat different ways. This question returns in a somewhat different form at this point. Does the yab-yum "father-mother" pairing of the heruka and wisdom ḍākinī suggest that only heterosexual models of relationship are relevant in tantric lore? What about homosexual models of relationship? How are they to be interpreted, given the contrasexuality of heruka and ḍākinī?

While this must be explored in more detail in future studies, it is important to note that the subtle-body, visionary, and essence aspects of ḍākinī and heruka are not tied to inherently existent or biologically bound sex. Gender is understood in a Buddhist context to be a construction of various factors, much as can be found in contemporary writings. In Tibetan presentations of the physical body, the woman's is said to be more closely associated with the ḍākinī, and the man's with the heruka, but these associations are not based on tangible physical traits. Exactly what this means needs further exploration. Because the essential qualities of each of these are tied especially to the nature of mind itself, certain ambiguities persist concerning physical manifestation. What remains to be done is a serious application of the tantric principles of heruka and wisdom ḍākinī to homosexual identity and relationship, and to the study of embodiment.[6]

With these various yearnings, ambiguities, and "suspicions" in mind, let us choose a central nonpersonified image from the ḍākinī lore that may succintly express the core of her meaning. The "warm breath of the mother ḍākinīs" (*khandro trölung* or *khandro khalung*) expresses the most important, meditative qualities while embracing the feminine symbolic as well. This warm breath is an intimate image used in the oral traditions of Vajrayāna Buddhism indicating teachings and practices that are unsullied by intellectualizing, sectarian disputes or controversies, or overly stylized ritual.[7] The tantric teachings are transmitted through various lineages, but all of them rely on the personal relationship with a qualified guru. The oral transmission of teachings is often called the whispered lineage, transmitted "mouth to ear" from guru to disciple in intimate and personal communication. The term *khalung* refers to the "mouth-breath" of the guru whispering instructions to the student; *trölung* is "warm breath," showing the personal quality of the communication. The warm mouth-breath is also considered damp with saliva, like steam or vapor, indicating its fresh, alive qualities: the experience is always new, and yet there is continuity. The communication is living instruction, which carries the continuity of lineage.[8] Those teachings and practices that still contain the vitality and authenticity of the unbroken practice lineages are said to carry the "warm breath of the ḍākinīs," invoking the centrality of the guru-disciple relationship.

From this perspective, every word of Vajrayāna is the ḍākinī's breath. The undertone of those words is the A, the dharmatā, the intimate life-breath of all phenomena. The vital essence of Vajrayāna is carried in the practice of all tāntrikas, who constantly realize the living quality of the continuity of the lineage. The ḍākinī holds this fresh and living quality close and guards its integrity. Her spacelike nature (*kha*) is the essence of the breath, ungraspable as a thing. Yet when directly experienced, like the breath, it pulsates with the vitality of realization. This living ungraspability makes the breath an ideal meditation object in Buddhist practice. While it cannot be limited or suppressed, it is as immediate and tangible as one's very life. The breath pervades, sustains, and defines our existence. There is no boundary around the breath, but there is immediate, ineffable experience of it.

Breath also relates closely to the yogic traditions of the subtle body, in which the yogic breath (*prāṇa, lung*) moves energetically throughout the body through refined pathways or channels. This breath is considered the essence of life itself, animating and sustaining all living beings. The outer manifestation of this vital energy is the movement of inhalation and exhalation through the nostrils. On a subtle level, it is the energetic movement of the breath through the channels, giving us the ability to sense beauty, experience emotional suffering, and express understanding. This subtle vital breath (sog-lung) is the most basic source of synchronized mind and body. The network of channels of moving breath throughout the body-mind is spoken of as the network of ḍākinīs (ḍākinī-jāla). When one speaks of the warm breath of the ḍākinīs, the inner meaning invokes the profound meditation practices that clear away obstacles through subtle-body yoga (tsa-lung).

It is also important to acknowledge the meaning of the warmth of the ḍākinī's breath. Of course, warmth refers to the intimacy of communication and of personal practice—completely alive, fresh, and moist. But the warmth of the breath is also the quality of wisdom in Vajrayāna Buddhism. When we suddenly awaken to fresh aspects of experience, wisdom is often fiery hot, consuming the obscurations of emotionality and conceptuality. This warmth is experienced literally in subtle-body yoga as caṇḍāli (tummo), the blissful heat that opens the practitioner to nonconceptual insight. It is also the mind quality of wisdom, which destroys obstacles and awakens insight. The warm breath of the ḍākinīs is the expression of conceptual mind liquefying and wisdom dawning.

The warm breath of the ḍākinīs is said to be present when the wisdom-mind of the practitioner, steeped in devotion, meets the blessings of the lineage of realized ones in the transmission of the oral instructions for meditation. This warm breath remains in the practice of meditation, providing support and nourishment for the meditator. And it continues with the awakening of nonconceptual wisdom. But the warm breath is also a protection, guarding the motivation of the meditator as well as the authenticity of the teachings. When the protective cloak of the ḍākinīs is present, authentic practice is sustained; when it is absent, the practice may wither and languish. When we understand the image of the ḍākinī's warm breath, we discover the key to her centrality in the tantric traditions in which the ḍākinī symbolizes the spiritual subjectivity of the practitioner, the fruits of meditation experienced in a constantly fresh, immediate way as the dynamic display of wisdom.

NOTES

PREFACE

1. In the Tibetan tradition, it is believed that, through compassion, enlightened teachers are capable of reincarnating through successive generations, carrying with them seeds of previous lives, realizations, and meditative attainments. This legacy can be actualized through rigorous training and ritual empowerments, which necessitates the early discovery of such a child. This discovery is expedited through predictions made by the previous incarnation and by visions experienced by devoted students and contemporaries. Trungpa's autobiography, *Born in Tibet,* was one of the first by a Tibetan lama, published in England in 1966.
2. For a collection of essays that describe this moment in feminist liberation, see Spretnak 1982.
3. Trungpa 1973a, 23.
4. Ibid., 24.
5. *Hevajra-tantra* II.iii.53, Snellgrove 1959, 99.
6. While this has been said consistently in Vajrayāna scholarship, it is remarkable how rare it is to actually execute such a methodology. In the recent comprehensive volume on Tibetan literature, Skorupski wrote of the opacity of tantric language, "Since [twilight language] makes use of analogy, double meanings, and rich, and at times far-fetched, symbology, it is difficult to establish the exact significance and meaning of words and whole passages.

The deliberate use of intentional language is often justified on the grounds of preserving the secrecy of tantric teachings. It is possible, however, to explain its use as a peculiar mystical language whose intention is not to provide literal and concrete expositions, but to indicate or evoke particular psychic and spiritual trances that are to be attained." Inexplicably, no mention is made of the importance of oral instructions from a qualified lama. Cabezon and Jackson 1996, 106.

7. This delineation refers to configuration of the tantras from both the Nyingma and Sarma "nine yāna classifications," referring to the nine vehicles of Tibetan Buddhist teachings. Each of these vehicles is a complete cycle of teachings of the Buddha, graded from most elementary to most sophisticated. The Tibetan Buddhist practitioner is to understand something of the essence of the lower yānas before engaging in the practices of the higher ones. The last three, slightly different from school to school, are called the "higher tantras" and comprise the Anuttara-yoga-tantra (unsurpassable meditation tantra) in the Sarma school and the Mahāyoga, Anuyoga, and Ati-yoga tantras (Great Meditation, Further Meditation, and Beyond Meditation tantras) in the Nyingma school. These yānas emphasize potent meditation methods that uncover the intrinsic enlightenment in the practitioner, accelerating her or his progress to realization.
8. These are all Anuttara-yoga-tantra texts; see footnote 7. Sources for the *Cakrasaṃvara-tantra* have been Chögyam Trungpa and the Nālandā Translation Committee 1986, 1989; 1976, 1979, 1985; and Dawa-Samdup 1919, 1987. For the *Saṃvarodaya-tantra,* Tsuda 1974. For the *Abhidhānottara-tantra,* selections in Kalff 1979. For the *Hevajra-tantra,* Snellgrove 1959, vols. 1 & 2; Farrow and Menon 1992; Willemen 1983. For the *Guhyasamāja-tantra,* a father tantra important in Anuttara-yoga-yāna, see Gäng 1988; Wayman 1977.
9. Dudjom 1991, vol. 1, 275–89; vol. 2, 78, n. 1105.
10. Cf. Nālandā 1997; Situpa 1988; Thrangu 1993. Guenther 1963; Thrangu 1997; Trungpa 1994. Trungpa and Nālandā, 1980; Thrangu 1992, 1995. Chang 1977; Kunga and Cutillo 1978 and 1986; Lhalungpa 1977. Stewart 1995; Thrangu 1993; Douglas and White, 1976; Thinley 1980.
11. T. Tulku 1983; Dowman 1984; Douglas and Bays 1978; Schmidt 1993; Chönam and Khandro 1998.
12. Goodman 1983; Gyatso 1998. Harding, in press.
13. Obermiller 1964; Chimpa and Chattopadhyaya 1970; Roerich 1949; Dudjom 1991; Thondup 1996.

14. Such as the *Hevajra-tantra,* according to one of Snellgrove's theories. Snellgrove 1959, 14.
15. Monastic colleges.

INTRODUCTION

1. Her names are given in the *Pema Kethang* as Sūryacandrasiddhi (Accomplished Like the Sun and Moon), Guhyajñāna or Sangwa Yeshe (Secret Wisdom, meaning ḍākinī), and Lekyi Wangmo (Karma ḍākinī Powerful Lady). Douglas and Bays 1978, 219.
2. The forty-two peaceful deities are Samantabhadra and Samantabhadrī, the five male and female buddhas, the eight male and female bodhisattvas, the six *munis,* and the four male and female gatekeepers. The fifty-eight wrathful herukas are: the five herukas and consorts, eight yoginīs, eight *tramen* goddesses, four female gatekeepers, and twenty-eight *iśvarīs*. Dzogchen Pönlop Rinpoche, commentary on "Aspiration of Samantabhadra," July 1998, Boulder, Colorado. These are also the deities encountered in the intermediate state (*pardo*).
3. Willis 1987a, 57, 58. Willis composed an important essay that summarized interpretations of the ḍākinī. Willis 1987a, 57–75. There is no need to repeat her excellent work on the subject.
4. Snellgrove 1957, 175. This is an improvement on the early interpretations, such as that of L. Austine Waddell, who depicted the ḍākinī as a "demoniacal" figure, best understood as a "witch" or a "fury." Subsequent work on the topic of the transformation of the ḍākinī has been done by Martin Kalff, who examined the ḍākinīs of the Cakrasaṃvara tradition. Through a description of the ḍākinīs of one tantric cycle, he demonstrated in a preliminary way how the Buddhist tradition was "able to integrate the wrathful, morally ambiguous feminine aspect" of the wild pre-Buddhist forms. Kalff 1978.
5. In his early work, Guenther was likely to ignore Tibetan conventions of the abbreviated form of *khandro,* inexplicably translating it in the male form as *ḍāka,* which he called "cipher of transcendence" or "sky-walker." See particularly his translation of the life of Nāropa (1963). In a dual-gender commentary on this, he wrote, "The Tibetan explanation of the word is that 'sky', 'celestial space' is a term for 'no-thingness' and 'to go' means 'to understand'. The Ḍāka or the Ḍākinī is therefore an understanding of no-thingness." Guenther 1973, 103 n. 1. Quoted in part in Willis 1987a, 62.

6. Kalff 1978, 1979; Herrmann-Pfandt 1990; Klein 1995; Gyatso 1998.
7. Donald Lopez (1998) has cleverly suggested that the myth of Shangri-La perpetuated by Euro-American fantasies has in turn influenced Tibetans' view of their own culture.
8. An exception to this feminist critique can be found in Gross (1998b), who with an equally strong feminist understanding identifies the victimized mentality in such charges of abuse. Her perspective is, however, unique among feminist critiques.
9. For a bold and eloquent articulation of these concerns, see Dzongsar Khyentse 1997. The article concludes with a poem, of which the final stanza expresses the content. "This nature of mind is spontaneously present./That spontaneity I was told is the dakini aspect./Recognizing this should help me/ Not to be stuck with fear of being sued."
10. Ortner 1996, 1–42; 173–80. The development of these aspects of ḍākinī manifestation is the subject of the following chapters.
11. *Ḍākinī-guhya-jvāla-tantra.* See chapter 1 for details.
12. In a study of Tibetan Buddhist religion, four aspects can be identified, each requiring different methods of investigation: doctrine, practice, institutional structure, and symbol. Janice Willis emphasized the importance of considering the ḍākinī as symbol above all. 1987a, 58.
13. Because the word *female* fits more the realm of living, existing female humans rather than the realm in which nonontological appearances arise from emptiness, as in the case of the ḍākinī, the word *feminine* applies more accurately to the symbolic realm.
14. Bynum 1986, 1991 passim.

CHAPTER ONE

Gender, Subjectivity, and the Feminine Principle

1. Evans-Wentz 1937, 1927. Jung's impact on interpretation in Tibetan studies is treated in Lopez 1998, chap. 2, and in Gomez 1995.
2. Lopez 1998, 59. With a cruel twist given by Lopez, we may ask if Tibetans have accepted the Jungian interpretation of the ḍākinī exported back to them as the best representation of their own cultural understanding. In addition to Tibetan ideas that may have influenced his views of the anima, he cited the Chinese *p' o* as a direct example of the anima. 13, 57–58.
3. Jung 1904, 11 §152, 486, 850; 12 §246; 13 §278; 16 §410; 18 §263.
4. Jung 1978, §850.

5. Jung 1966, 1977, 191–92.
6. Jung 1978, 75.
7. Tucci 1961, 1969, vii, 37; Eliade 1961, 1969, 225–26. They apparently drew on Jung's essays on the maṇḍala in 12, 25–224.
8. As Govinda began the foreword of his autobiography, "Why is it that the fate of Tibet has found such a deep echo in the world? There can only be one answer: Tibet has become a symbol of all that present-day humanity is longing for, . . . within the innermost being of man, in whose depth this past is enshrined as an ever-present source of inspiration." 1971, xi.
9. Guenther 1963, ii–iii.
10. Subsequently, Katz carefully studied the applicability of the anima to the understanding of the ḍākinī, finding areas of benefit as well as areas of peril. Katz 1977, 1992; Willis 1987a; Herrmann-Pfandt 1990; Gyatso 1998.
11. From *Collected Works* 13 §58. Quoted in Hillman 1985, 5. Jung was an innovator in that he was able to separate sex and gender before this was done in common parlance. Singer 1976, 1989, 187–88.
12. The appendix of Jung 1966, 1977, 304, calls the anima the "unconscious subject-imago"; "the image of the subject in his relation to the collective unconscious"; "the anima is the face of the subject as seen by the collective unconscious." Quoted in Katz 1977, 15.
13. The elements that I observe are not necessarily the ones Katz recognizes, but they have been influenced by his fine article. He notes the areas of confluence to be contrasexual appearance, function of inspiring and leading, appearance in dreams, visions and actual women, source of power, teacher and guide, preliminary to therapy or meditation instruction, wrathful and peaceful appearances (multivalence of image generally), concreteness of image, leading to the transformation of the individual, and psychogenic origins. Katz 1977, 36. The main flaw in Katz's article is his undue reliance on sources like Guenther for the interpretation of the ḍākinī, when Guenther himself has been deeply influenced by Jung in this matter.
14. This problem can be seen in Herrmann-Pfandt's interpretations of polarity in ḍākinī lore. Particularly when she compares the relationship between ḍākinī and yogin to the ḍākinī's relationship to yoginīs this paradigm is shown to be faulty. 1990, 153–55. And many of Herrmann-Pfandt's objections to the patriarchal use of ḍākinī imagery appear to be a critique of Jung rather than a critique of Tibetan Buddhism. 1990, 470–75.
15. Hillman 1985, 7.
16. This point is made almost in passing in Katz 1977, 29. A thoroughgoing

critique of Jung's androcentrism can be found in Wehr 1987. What he described as "natural" in women (passivity, excess emotionality, ineffectuality) is actually deeply shaped by the social forces of androcentrism and patriarchy, says feminism. Jung was so absorbed in psychological investigations that he never paid attention to the social forces at work on the lives of men and women. And because of a deeply spiritual sensitivity, and the tendency to absolutize the psychological patterns of the unconscious, he legitimated the damaging effects of patriarchy on women by making the wounded feminine into an archetype. Feminists also challenge Jungians for their appropriation of relationships with real women, further objectifying and enslaving them. Analysts such as Hillman and Naomi Goldenberg have reconfigured much of Jungian theory to more accurately fit the experiences of women.

17. Jung remained perplexed about the inadequacy of this symmetric model of which he was so convinced. "So far as my experience goes, a man always understands fairly easily what is meant by the anima; indeed, as I said, he frequently has a quite definite picture of her, so that from a varied collection of women of all periods he can single out the one who comes closest to the anima type. But I have, as a rule, found it very difficult to make a woman understand what the animus is, and I have never met any woman who could tell me anything definite about his personality." Jung 1904, 10 §41.
18. Katz (1977, 29) mentioned the importance of the ḍāka for the yoginī, based on his study of the siddha namthars of India, and this theme has appeared in many studies of the ḍākinī. The ḍāka may have been important in early tantric Buddhism in India, but he never really made the journey to Tibet except in rare instances in which he is a carryover from the Indian tradition. Generally speaking, the ḍākinī appeared in Tibetan namthars and liturgies with the nameless consort. It seems the ḍāka has some of the same ambiguities as Jung's animus.
19. In her study of Jigme Lingpa, Janet Gyatso made similar observations concerning the parallel rather than oppositional modes of the ḍākinī with the yogin. While they are different, they share much in common: "they both have bodies, they both become enlightened, they both teach. What the liminality of the ḍākinī facilitates, then, is not a symmetrical, mutually confirming couple, but rather, an asymmetrical relationship in which the two parties engage in similar activities but in different ways. In the hagiographical material, she is seen teaching her partner that he can do what he is doing in another key, in a style that is less dualistic and more evocative of experiences

of bliss and emptiness but that does not entail an absolute break with—or 'otherness' from—saṃsāric patterns." 1998, 251.

20. Ibid., 252.
21. Katz notes that Jung calls the anima empty as well, but uses this word to suggest that real women who have a weak personality structure take on the projections of men, playing out the role of their anima to them. Katz rightly points out the difference in usage between the two meanings. 1977, 30–31.
22. Jung 1953, 1973, 39.
23. Katz 1977, 34–35. Katz accurately points out that Buddhists would hold no "essence" apart from appearance, which delivers them from the dangers of solipsism.
24. This topic is developed in chapter 4.
25. Examples of the former can be found in the work of Mary Daly (1973), Carol Christ (1979), and Judith Plaskow (1989). For an excellent summary of these movements, see Gross 1996, chap. 4.
26. These sweeping feminist interpretations of the ḍākinī have been challenged in a preliminary way in the work of Anne Klein, who distinguished the feminine symbol from the ordinary lives of Tibetan women (Klein 1985b, 111; 1995, 50–57). Janice Willis suggested that while the ḍākinī appears in feminine form, "she" is not "female," and cautioned modern-day women practitioners "who pride themselves on being 'already halfway there' owing solely to their sex" to remember the absolute aspect of the ḍākinī. (Willis 1987, 72).
27. Herrmann-Pfandt 1990. This is the only comprehensive treatment of the ḍākinī, a German doctoral dissertation, an impressive encyclopedic study drawn from the author's original translations of many Buddhist tantric texts, which mixes the critical methodologies of Tibetology with Jungian psychology and feminist critique.
28. Herrmann-Pfandt 1990, 474.
29. Campbell 1996, 186.
30. Campbell 1996, 128–129. Using radical feminist and psychoanalytic methods, Campbell critiqued Tibetan notions of the ḍākinī, remarking that she is "the secret, hidden and mystical quality of absolute insight required by men, and . . . her name became an epithet for a sexual partner." The lama, however, retains the power of the teachings and transmits its meaning while using the abstract feminine as a complement. The female body and subjectivity is then coopted completely by the patriarchal system. This, she maintained, is damaging for women, for they can never be autonomous teachers or even practitioners in their own right, and they are kept under the dominion of male

Tibetan hierarchies. For this reason, the ḍākinī can only be understood to be a symbol of patriarchal Buddhism that guards male privilege.

31. Shaw 1994, 32, 38. Shaw's study was focused on tantric Buddhism in India, in which she attempted to reconstruct a history of women in early tantric circles from original translations of Indian Buddhist tantras. She acknowledged the ambiguity between the humanity and divinity of the ḍākinī common to tantric literature, but this acknowledgment seriously affected her methodology, for she draws historical conclusions based on symbolic expressions of the ḍākinī in the tantric literature she studied.
32. Ibid., 12–13. In this method, Shaw cited the influence of the work of Elizabeth Schüssler Fiorenza. It is interesting to note that historical materials have played a quite different role in Christian scripture and theology than they have in Buddhism, especially tantric Buddhism.
33. Ibid., 13.
34. Aziz 1987, 1988; Klein 1985b, 1995. See also Miller 1980; Ortner and Whitehead 1981; Ortner 1996.
35. Falk 1980; Gross 1993; Schuster-Barnes 1987; Sponberg 1992; Klein 1985b. The most important, sustained analysis of this kind has come from Rita Gross (1993), who has judged androcentrism within Buddhism to be inconsistent with the gender-free liberative teachings of the Buddha and suggested a reconstruction of the institutions to reflect the original "feminism" of the Buddha.
36. As Nancy Schuster-Barnes explained, monastic saṅgha rules and traditions forced women to remain outside of Buddhist institutional life, which significantly affected women's influence on doctrinal debates, sectarian developments, and lineages of dharma transmission. 1987, 129–31.
37. Campbell 1996, 137. "Reductionism, incorporation, and assimilation of the female into the male domain renders her as 'other,' a category in which she is defined by and through her relation to the dominant force—the male. In other words she is unable to define herself, and must rely on the 'enlightened' men of the lineage to establish her position vis-à-vis their own. . . . The absence of a female-centered symbolic, articulated in the context of a female subjective, has given rise to an ambiguous presence within the institutions of Buddhism, and has created a situation of compromise for women practitioners," according to Campbell. 140–41.
38. Herrmann-Pfandt 1992, 471–76.
39. Lacanian psychoanalytic theory and Marxist sociological theory have deeply influenced this notion of subjectivity in feminism. Because of the powerful

influence of postmodernism and its critique of subjectivity, feminists such as Luce Irigaray have developed a new interpretation of subjectivity without an essentialist view of the self. This work influenced Anne Klein's (1995) work.

40. Gross 1993, 296. Gross's appendix succinctly defines the key terminology of feminism for the beginner, applying it in a preliminary way to a study of Buddhism.
41. Ortner 1996, 21–42. This article, entitled "Is Female to Male as Nature Is to Culture?," first published in 1974, set the stage for discussion of culturally constructed differences in gender. Using a structuralist approach, Ortner suggested that male dominance was universal, though culturally constructed.
42. Wilson 1996.
43. Ibid., 150–51.
44. Ibid., 13. This is a classic statement of two of the misperceptions (*viparyāsa*) of taking to be beautiful that which is by nature ugly and taking to be permanent that which is by nature impermanent.
45. Most feminisms have discarded religion as hopelessly patriarchal, responsible more than any other social institution for the enslavement of women. Only such feminists as Carol Christ and Luce Irigaray have pleaded that "because religion has such a compelling hold on the deep psyches of so many people, feminists cannot afford to leave it in the hands of the fathers." Christ 1979, 273.
46. These are the options pursued in Christian feminism, in the former case by Mary Daly and Carol Christ, and in the latter case by Elizabeth Schüssler Fiorenza 1986.
47. Ricoeur 1976, 63.
48. Ricoeur 1978b, 38.
49. Eliade 1965, 205. Eliade and Ricoeur speak of the appropriateness of a phenomenological approach to symbols. Phenomenology works with description rather than investigation of origins, reasons, or applications. In phenomenology of religion, symbols are described using recognizable language on the literal level of meaning, but the power of the symbol speaks through the words, giving richness and deeper meaning.
50. This differs in marked ways from postmodernism, in which subjectivity negatively connotes an excessive sense of individuality. *Subject* has two meanings that suggest weakness and victimization—subject to the control of another person and subject to one's own identity by conscience or self-knowledge. In either case, the subject is the counterpoint to the object, which imprisons the very notion. Foucault and others have called such subjectivity the act of

the privileged and have deemed it a myth and an expression of the logic of paranoia. Ricoeur and Eliade speak from a perspective of phenomenology, which suggests that the way to overcome this dilemma is through understanding subjectivity as arising from symbol, creating the occasion for the emptying of the isolated self into a broader, more encompassing reality.

51. Lhalungpa 1977, 50.
52. Ricoeur 1972. This contrasts with the structuralist views of anthropologists such as Clifford Geertz, who view symbols as media to an ultimate meaning that has been created by history. Such a view robs symbol of its magic and transformative power. Bynum 1986, 9.
53. In this critical dimension, Ricoeur responds to Freud, for whom suspicion was the dominant mode with regard to symbols. Ricoeur considered suspicion to be a healthy component of the hermeneutic, modifying the fundamentalism, idealism, and naïveté associated with unquestioning belief in symbols. Ricoeur 1965, 1970, 447; White 1995, 88. This notion of suspicion was also employed by Fiorenza 1986, 3–40. Perhaps the Vajrayāna equivalent of suspicion is vajra pride, discussed in chapter 4.
54. In this interpretation of Ricoeur's hermeneutic, I refrain from many of the points made in White's adaptation to feminist hermeneutics of symbols because of its reliance on the Western preoccupation with God the Father.
55. This is contrary to the work of Clifford Geertz, who suggested that symbols are close to proximate signs, and that female-referring symbols are especially attractive to women, serving as a "model by and for" women. See Bynum 1986, 9.
56. Ricoeur 1981, 94.
57. Klein 1995, 61–88. When Klein speaks of mindfulness in this section, it is more in accord with descriptions in Indian and Tibetan Buddhist texts that contrast *śamatha* and *vipaśyanā* practice (*shi-ne* and *lhak thong*), in which mindfulness is associated with the cultivation of one-pointedness and calm, and insight or awareness is associated with clarity regarding the meaning of one's experience. For this reason, I use the generic term *meditation* rather than Klein's *mindfulness.*
58. Klein 1995, 83. This is similar to what Janet Gyatso called "subjectivity without essence." Gyatso 1998, 269.
59. This perspective differs from that of French feminists such as Hélène Cixous and Luce Irigaray, who argue that women have a separate symbolic order, and with Julia Kristeva, who locates female meaning in the semiotic, a kind

of nonsymbolic marginality derived from the physical context, which is the prerogative of women.

60. Bynum 1986, 165–71. See also Ricoeur 1985 for more detail on the importance of symbols in shaping personal subjectivity.
61. Bynum 1986, 2–3.
62. Ibid., 13.
63. Tibetan Buddhism under Han Chinese rule certainly has distinct new elements, such as preoccupation with national identity, such that Tibetans often adhere "publicly to the official culture while masking their true sentiments," as Kapstein has observed. But, when faced with the alternative to a sense of conflict, many young Tibetans are reaffirming traditional Tibetan religious identities, fueling the religious revival that is currently underway in Tibet. Goldstein and Kapstein 1998, 144–145. See also Zangpo 1997.
64. This has been thoroughly demonstrated by Aziz 1987, 1988; Klein 1985b, 1995; Miller 1980; Ortner and Whitehead 1981; Ortner 1996.
65. These are the eight worldly concerns (*jikten kyi chögye, aṣṭau lokadharmāḥ*) that keep the mind ensnared in conventional thinking.
66. Harding, in press. Similar litanies of obstacles can be found in other accounts by Yeshe Tsogyal (Dowman 1984, 89) and Nangsa Obum (Allione 1984, 76–84).
67. Harding, in press.
68. Ibid., 90.
69. Gross 1993, 81–82; Aziz 1987, 81.
70. For a more extensive treatment of this, see chapter 6.
71. Dowman 1984, 86; T. Tulku 1983, 102.
72. Das 1992, 250.
73. Samuel 1993, 287, 310. For a great deal more on the historic dilemma of Tibetan nuns, see Willis 1987b, 96–117; Tsomo 1987, 118–33; Havnevik 1990; Aziz 1988.
74. Klein 1995, 51–52, and anecdotal.
75. Aziz 1988, 32.
76. These experiences are recorded in the biography of Nangsa Obum (Allione 1984, 46–59, 61–140) and in the contemporary autobiography of Dawa Drolma, mother of Chagdud Tulku Rinpoche (Drolma 1995). For more on the delok phenomenon, see the life of Shuksep Lochen Chönyi Zangmo, also called Ani Lochen, a Dzogchen teacher who late in the nineteenth century went through the delok experience. Thondup 1996, 250–55. Much more work needs to be done on the delok phenomenon in yoginīs of Tibet.

77. Klein 1995, 52. Klein observed that the hereditary tradition of hailmasters, for example, is not carried by women, but that there is no reason it cannot be.
78. Aziz 1988, 32–33. She attributed this bias to the prevalence of the influences of orientalism and colonialism on Tibetology, a tendency that is doomed to move the field into merely "an esoteric specialty with limited relevance to the rest of modern human experience." This view is shared by Havnevik, who added that it is also a Tibetan issue, for her informants could give little information, "indicating that only a few of the famous female religious specialists were recognized as important incarnations" (1990, 135).
79. Throughout his book, Samuel used the terms *clerical* and *shamanic,* which are appropriate in the context of his own definitions in anthropological research but have had more difficulties for Buddhologists and religious scholars. For this reason, *monastic* and *yogic* will be used in this work. Samuel 1993, 5–22.
80. Ibid., 10.
81. Ibid., 360 and passim.
82. Willis 1999, 148–49.
83. Trungpa 1982. She also appears in Milarepa's namthar, but in Marpa's her abilities as a yoginī and teacher are more prominent.
84. Allione 1984, 236; Samuel 1993, 351–53.
85. Dowman 1988, 143; Willis 1999, 151. More about all these women teachers appears elsewhere in Willis.
86. Samuel 1993, 606 n. 16. The namthar of Jetsün Mingyur Paldrön was translated by Marilyn Silverstone at Shechen Monastery in Boudhnath, Kathmandu.
87. Willis 1987, 73.
88. Willis spoke of the ḍākinī in this way, as a "feminine principle." Speculating why the ḍākinī takes feminine form, she wrote, "An attempted answer would require at least a book." 1987, 73. It is important to note that there is no Tibetan word for "feminine principle." Whereas the term was consistently used in English by Ven. Chögyam Trungpa Rinpoche to refer to the aspects of spiritual experience that I describe, they were generally called aspects of the ḍākinī, or *khandroma,* by the lamas whom I interviewed.
89. From a series of interviews, July 1994, Boulder, Colorado.
90. Chönam and Khandro 1998, 6. Elsewhere Gyatso expresses her ambivalence about these terms in reference to the ḍākinī. "The ḍākinī species is paradigmatically feminine. For the purposes of the following discussion, I favor the term 'female' when referring to beings with certain sexual organs or to

the biological functions of those organs, and I employ the term 'feminine' to denote attitudes and attributes conventionally associated with such females. It will be apparent, however, that this distinction cannot always be maintained in analyzing the role of the ḍākinī, nor can we necessarily assume that sex, including its organic 'givens,' is not finally a convention itself." Gyatso 1998, 248.

91. Chönam and Khandro 1998, xi.
92. This was described by Gyatso as the "voice" of all autobiography that is associated with the feminine. She went on to show that the ḍākinī is the autobiographer for Jigme Lingpa's secret autobiography. Gyatso 1998, 108. In this, she cites Jacques Derrida and Philippe Lejeune (260–64).
93. Gyatso borrows the word *semiotic* from Kristeva, who rejects notions of symbolic, claiming them to be patriarchally constructed to reflect the Oedipal tendencies of the father. An intriguing idea, but it seems a stretch into unnecessary obscurity. Gyatso 1998, 251.
94. The famous formulation is, respectively: *nye drak, sap drak, la drak, zang drak.* See Kalu 1986, 118.

CHAPTER TWO
The Ḍākinī in Tibetan Buddhism

1. Trungpa 1999, 6.
2. Chang 1977, 661.
3. Gyatso 1998, 246.
4. Snellgrove 1959, 135.
5. Willis 1987a, 57.
6. It is curious that the term appears among a series of examples in Pāṇini's famous Sanskrit grammar, the *Aṣṭādhyāyī* (iv.2.51), which was probably composed near the end of the fourth century B.C.E. The non-Brahmanical origins can be attested by the associated meanings, related to low-caste musicians and musical instruments and ghoulish attendants of Śiva. Cf. Monier-Williams 1899, 1976, 430; Guenther 1993, 32 n. 41.
7. Herrmann-Pfandt 1990, 116–117; 1996, 39–44, 47–51.
8. Danielou 1964, 1985, 288, 302. Among the main attendants of Śiva, under the category of gaṇas, the "categories" include all the minor deities that are counted in groups. Under the command of the "lord of categories" Gaṇapati, they dwell on Pleasure Mountain (Kailāsa). There are nine kinds of gaṇas, such as *āditya*s, *rudra*s, and *vasu*s. The minor figures include *preta*s,

piśācas, bhūtas, ḍākinīs, śākinīs, and *bhairavas*. Danielou also lists ḍākinīs under "minor form of the goddess." In this list are attendants of Durgā, such as yoginīs, who are "represented as ogresses or sorceresses; ḍākinīs are called female imps, eaters of raw flesh. They are attendants of Kālī. Pūtanā was a demoness who tried to poison the child of Kṛṣṇa. She is described in the Mārkeṇḍeya-purāṇa as a ḍākinī." 288. Other speculations about the origin of the ḍākinīs are various. P. C. Bagchi (1975, 51) suggested that they can be traced to the Dags of Dagistan in central Asia. Bhattacharji (1970, 1988) suggested they are related to the *ghoṣinīs*, female attendants of Rudra in the *Atharva Veda*. See also Herrmann-Pfandt 1990, 115 n. 1; 1996, 42–44.

9. See O'Flaherty 1980, part 2; Kinsley 1997, 1–8, 67–90.
10. O'Flaherty 1980, 1982, 277–79; Herrmann-Pfandt 1996, 39–70.
11. An old account of tantric witches is given by Satindra Narayan Roy (1928), from the popular cult of Orissa, contrasting the dangerous unmarried ḍākinī women to the Vaiśnavite practitioner who follows caste considerations.
12. Quoted in O'Flaherty 1980, 1982, 279.
13. The origin of these texts is uncertain, probably because they were passed through esoteric oral traditions of practice before emerging in an identifiable way in Pālā India. Hence, this date refers primarily to the discoveries of Western scholarship, which is somewhat contradicted by tantric histories themselves, which trace the tantras to Buddha Śākyamuni. Bhattacharyya 1996, 121; Snellgrove 1987, 144–60.
14. The ḍākinī emerges in the Mārkeṇḍeya-purāṇa VIII.108 (300–500 C.E.) in this form. Other Hindu cult texts that mention the ḍākinī were Ḍākinī-kalpa and the Mahānirvāṇa-tantra. The earliest cultic description of the ḍākinī appeared in Gangdhār inscriptions in Madhya Pradesh, dated 423–424 C.E., associated with the "cult of the seven mothers." See Herrmann-Pfandt 1990, 116 n. 5, 7, 9.
15. N. Bhattacharyya 1996, 94; Brooks 1990; Muller-Ortega 1989.
16. B. Bhattacharyya 1964; N. Bhattacharyya 1996. Kinsley (1997, 92–96) also described how Tārā first developed as a Buddhist deity and eventually was assimilated into Hinduism.
17. Chinnamastā, for example, a tantric deity popular in Hindu tantra, is depicted as severed-headed, with two attendants, Varṇinī and Ḍākinī. B. Bhattacharyya, who edited the Sādhanamālā, formulated the theory that some Hindu deities must have been Buddhist ones originally, including Tārā, Chinnamastā, and Mañjughoṣa. Thus, by comparing the iconography, the dates of the manuscripts, and the mantras, Bhattacharyya concluded that

Chinnamastā is originally Buddhist, and this statement has not been disputed by most scholars. The Buddhist Chinnamastā was usually known as Vajrayoginī or Vajravārāhī and was worshipped at least by the seventh century. The Sādhanamālā states the Siddha Śabarapa (variant spelling Śabarīpa) is credited with the introduction of a new cult of Vajrayoginī (*Sādhanamālā* vol. 2, cxliv ff). Cf. Benard 1994, 12–14.

18. Coburn 1984.
19. For an excellent study of the assimiliation process associated with the development of the Great Goddess traditions of India, see Pintchman 1994.
20. Śakti, from the Sanskrit root *śak*, "to be able," connotes power above all.
21. Pintchman 1994, 97–98.
22. Snellgrove 1959, 44. Snellgrove could not be more clear on this point, going on to say that the term appears only in isolated mantras, as in *Sarvatathāgatatattvasaṃgraha, Narthang Kangyur Gyü,* vii. 346b I.
23. Miranda Shaw (1994, 33), culminates her presentation of her methodology with this claim, after repeatedly merging interpretations of Śaivite, Śākta, and tantric Buddhist understandings. This could only be said in the absence of oral commentary, in which common terms are interpreted differently in these different traditions. What is missing in her work and the work of other tantric scholars is an understanding of the assimilation of common mythic themes, terminology, and practices to different understandings and ends.
24. Alicia Matsunaga's (1969) study of the Japanese notion of *honji-suijaku* traces the assimilation of deities to Buddhist interpretations dating back to the Indian tradition, through China, and especially Japan. Similar interpretations have been done, using different terminology, such as the work of Samuel (1993) on assimilation in Tibet.
25. This attitude parallels that of the Vaiśnavite attitudes toward the ḍākinī in tantric Hinduism, detailed in Roy 1928.
26. Suzuki 1932, 1973, 221. She is also unfavorably depicted in the Caturaśitisiddhapravṛtti by Abhayadattaśrī. Herrmann-Pfandt 1990, 119, n. 22. See also Herrmann-Pfandt's treatment of the Indian ḍākinī's close association with animals, 1996, 51–57.
27. Sutton 1991, 18. Suzuki had earlier commented that sections of the text must have been written later than the main body, chapters 2–7 of the Nanjio edition, for they are incongruous with the sūtra's main message. Sutton quotes Hauer as suggesting that since the meat-eating chapter appears in Guṇabhadra's translation in 443, along with an entire chapter of tantric-

style dhāraṇīs, this stratum of the text reveals the changing environment of Buddhism in India at that time.

28. Bhattacharyya 1974, 1996, 85–107. Bhattacharyya's work on the historical development of Indian tantrism places the developmental phase of Śāktism between 300 and 700 C.E.
29. *Nirvāṇa-tantra, Picchilā-tantra, Yoginī-tantra, Kāākhyā-tantra,* and *Niruttara-tantra.* Kinsley 1986, 122. See also Loseries-Leick 1996 for details on Tibetan assimilations of Kālī.
30. Snellgrove 1987, 147–60. When Snellgrove describes these non-Buddhist deities as Śaivite, he is not suggesting that they are particularly Hindu either. As he explains, the "Śaivite identification represented the continuing Indian tendency to bring all locally indigenous manifestations of religion into the Hindu fold, mainly by means of cross-identification of divinities, and thus in origin such fearful gods, being no more Hindu than Buddhist, could be interpreted in accordance with differing philosophical and religious traditions." 157.
31. Ibid., 158.
32. This area needs further study. Miranda Shaw began this work, though her emphasis is more on the history of women in early Indian tantric Buddhism. A study of the figure of the ḍākinī cannot be completely subsumed by a study of women, and precipitous conclusions can be drawn in both directions by mixing the two studies. The social and political implications are probably different from the theological ones. For classifications of Buddhist goddess figures, see Herrmann-Pfandt 1990, 124–125.
33. I agree with the comments of David Kinsley (1986, 1987), who writes of the Hindu tradition, "I have resisted the theological assumption found in much scholarship on Hindu goddesses that all female deities in the Hindu tradition are different manifestations of an underlying feminine principle or an overarching great goddess. . . . Although the centrality of a great goddess is clear in some texts and although this goddess does tend to include within her many-faceted being most important Hindu goddesses, her presence is not indicated in the majority of texts that speak of Hindu goddesses." 4–5.
34. Herrmann-Pfandt 1990, 124–126.
35. Herrmann-Pfandt indicates that her research shows that ḍākinīs especially relate to the categories of yidam, dharmapāla, and guru. Ibid., 126.
36. Kvaerne 1995, 120, 130, 131.
37. This view is influenced by the descriptions of the development of the feminine principle in the Hindu Great Goddess tradition, defined as the forces at

work in the ongoing creation of the world, presented by Pintchman 1994. In contrast, the Tibetan Buddhist feminine principle is not cosmogonic and has little to do with creation in the ultimate sense. See chapter 3.

38. Willis 1987a, 57–75.
39. Herrmann-Pfandt 1990, 115 n. 2. Monier-Williams (1899, 430) ascribes to it Sanskritic roots, citing Pāṇini and Patañjali. Giuseppe Tucci (1977, 69, n. 96) suggests that the word comes from *ḍai,* "to fly." Herbert Guenther (1993, 32 n. 41) describes it as a crude or vulgar word from regional non-Sanskritic dialects (*deśī*), not pure, refined, or reflective of the sacredness of Vedic reality. David Snellgrove (1959, 135) suggests, similar to Tucci, that the possible root is *ḍī,* "to fly." Monier-Williams has no such root as *ḍai* and instead has *ḍī,* suggesting the veracity of Snellgrove's suggestion. *Ḍā* appears to be a shortened form of *ḍākinī* and also is a kind of drum, associated with *ḍamaru,* the kind of drum carried by ḍākinīs.
40. Danielou 1985, 288. Also Monier-Williams 1976, 430, 1061.
41. See Klein 1995, 159.
42. The classic depiction of the ḍākinī is in "dancing posture" (*kartap*), as in the descriptions of Vajrayoginī in her sādhana. Trungpa and Nālandā 1980.
43. See, for example, Vajragarbha's commentary on the *Hevajra-tantra,* in which he gave this definition: "concerning the concept 'ḍākinī,' we designate this idea as belonging to one who has realized a state of being that resembles the sky which means total contemplation toward the sky" (Herrmann-Pfandt 1990, 141).
44. C. Tulku 1989. Herrmann-Pfandt 1990, 141 n. 3.
45. Das 1981, 300.
46. Herrmann-Pfandt 1990, 142–143.
47. Snellgrove 1987, 106.
48. This term is not exactly equivalent to *ḍākinī,* for it appears with special reference to the yidam Vajrayoginī. Also, it must be noted that Khachö is a special paradise for a level of realization short of full enlightenment, mentioned often in the *Milarepa Gurbum* and the siddha hagiographic literature.
49. Gyatso 1998, 305 n. 1; Chang 1977, 311 n.3.
50. In Guenther's early work, he made the mistake of translating *khandro* in a male form, which he later corrected. A discussion of gender issues in the Tibetan language appears in Neumaier-Dargyay 1992, 41–43, in which she suggests that Tibetan syntax is "naturally inclusive" and laments the forcing of gender distinctions when translating into modern languages of the Indo-Germanic families. She feels this raises issues that were not necessarily pres-

ent in the Tibetan context. Her point has many interesting implications for this study. Of course, the Sanskrit texts that served as sources for many tantras and namthars had gender-specific syntax, so gender orientation was embedded in tantric literature from India.

51. Edou 1996, 102; Schmidt 1996.
52. Kalff 1978, 149–50; Herrmann-Pfandt 1990, 118–22. In certain texts, such as the gaṇacakra liturgies, the distinction between these two has been preserved in Tibetan, while in hagiographies and in the descriptions of the retinues that surround gurus the distinction between worldly and wisdom ḍākinīs remains obscured.
53. Ngakpa Dawa Chodak, personal communication, October 1998, Boulder, Colorado. I would suggest that the ambiguity of the ḍākinī's identity is part of her manifestation, in contrast to Janet Gyatso's suggestion of a kind of "intermediate" ḍākinī between worldly and wisdom manifestations. Gyatso 1998, 247, 306 n. 16.
54. This is referred to as *tendel,* auspicious coincidence, the Tibetan understanding of interdependence. More will be said about this notion later, in Chapter 8. Gyatso 1998, 178–80.
55. Aris 1988, 28.
56. The unfortunate Pema Lendreltsel was the reincarnation of the princess Pemasel. When he discovered the *Khandro Nyingthik* teachings, he was to practice them in secret for some time and was promised the mastery of inner radiance and the ability to greatly serve others. "Because he did not maintain secrecy, he did not live out his full span." Dudjom 1991, 582. He was succeeded by Longchen Rabjam, who carefully relied on the wisdom ḍākinīs for authorization and advice, thus ensuring the future of the *Khandro Nyingthik* teachings. There is ambiguity concerning his mistake, which was not clarified in my interviews with lamas: was his error in his choice of a ḍākinī, or in sharing the text prematurely with Rangjung Dorje?
57. Dudjom 1991, 503. He is speaking here of modern-day Swat, the supposed geographical location of Uḍḍiyāṇa, the birthplace of Padmasambhava. In addition, he says there are still tantras hidden there that have not yet appeared in India, for the ḍākinīs there have kept them secret "in the invisible sphere, so they are not ordinary objects of perception."
58. Shasa khandros are closely related to the *piśāca*s, a class of fierce, malignant, goblinlike demonesses in the *preta,* or hungry ghost, realm. They are particularly known for consuming human flesh, though the carnivorous appetites of the piśācas are not that discriminating. According to Tibetan chronicles,

it is common for Tibetan demons to be depicted as meat-eating, thus assuring their Buddhist mentors of their barbaric tendencies. Gyatso 1987; 1998, 77.

59. *khandro ling-gi nyül-le.* T. Tulku 1983, 194; 22.
60. Douglas and Bays 1978, 142–43. Much more will be said in chapter 4 about the importance of the charnel ground for understanding the Vajrayāna wisdom ḍākinī.
61. Milarepa had an extended encounter with a sinmo (rākṣasī), a powerful demoness who eventually swore loyalty to the yogin and the dharma. Chang 1963, 38–57. Janet Gyatso analyzes the myth of the supine demoness, addressing her gender, symbolism, and meaning in the context of Tibetan mythology. Gyatso 1987, 33–51.
62. The very meaning of *jikten* (worldly) is mortal, subject to destruction and death. Schmidt 1996.
63. Samuel 1993, 161.
64. She came to be known as the ḍākinī of long life, but before her conversion to Buddhism she had the ability to shorten life. She is one of the twelve sister earth goddesses—Tenma (tenma chu-nyi)—who are protectors of Tibet.
65. Chang 1977, 336.
66. There are three general classes of worldly deities of Tibet, of which the mamos represent one class, the worldly deities of inciting and dispatching (*mamo bötong*). The other two classes are the deities of offering and praise (*jikten chötö*), and the deities of exorcism (*möpa trag-ngak*). All three categories were assimilated into the Mahāyoga practices called the "Eight Sādhanas" (*druppa ka-gye*).
67. Sutherland 1991, 166; Kinsley 1986, 1987, 151–60.
68. Nebesky-Wojkowitz 1975, 269–75.
69. Dowman 1985, 181–183; Robinson 1979, 117–20. Alternate spellings are Lwabapa and Lawapa.
70. Padmakara 1999, 84; Dowman 1984, 78; T. Tulku 1983, 95.
71. Dudjom 1967. T. Tulku 1978, 370–71.
72. Tāranātha 1970, 214. In this account, Tāranātha uses the terms *tramen* and *ḍākinī* interchangeably. Tramens are wrathful demonesses not usually associated with ḍākinīs; they are female vampires, resurrected corpses who eat human flesh. It is explained that he practiced the wrathful Yamāri (Yamāntaka) practice, under the blessings of his yidam Vajravārāhī, and propagated the *Rakta-yamāri-tantra* and *Raktayamāntaka-sādhana.* 245. Cf. Dowman 1985, 50–51.

73. Douglas and Bays 1978, 370.
74. Chang 1977, 304.
75. Karma Chagme, "Pacifying the Turmoil of the Mamos." Translated by the Nālandā Translation Committee.
76. Ibid.
77. Mamo is prominent in the "maṇḍala of the Eight Yidam deities" of the Mahāyoga-yāna tantras, the seventh yāna of the Nyingma classification of tantras. Mahāyoga has eighteen principal tantras with eight primary wrathful yidams, whose practice has great power to increase skillful action in the world. Each yidam relates to an aspect of the practitioner's personal obscurations, whether they be emotional, conceptual, or karmic. In the group of eight wrathful yidams, most of them herukas, the sixth is the wisdom ḍākinī Mamo.
78. This is one way in which Tibetan literature explained the distinction between worldly and wisdom ḍākinī, modeling in her the journey of the individual tantric practitioner from confusion to enlightenment. Herrmann-Pfandt 1990, 120.
79. Chang 1977, 318. The account of these encounters spans a number of chapters in the *Milarepa Gurbum.* See Chang 1977, 296–361. Another description occurs in Tenzin Chökyi Lodrö's *Guidebook to Lapchi.* Huber 1997, 131–33. This series of events recapitulates the paradigmatic account of the Buddha under the tree of enlightenment, in which he was harassed by the māras, who were assimilated into Tibetan lore.
80. Chang 1977, 319. One cannot miss the parallels with the experience of the Buddha under the tree of awakening, in which he was attacked by Māra and his hordes. It seems that sitting still, experiencing no fear of the elements or the mind, calls the local demons and major spirits to rise up in protest. Such fearless awakened mind is a violation of the worldly cult of ignorance fostered by conventional mind. In Buddhist lore, every sincere practitioner must face these forces on retreat in order to build momentum in the practice.
81. Chang 1977, 300.
82. Ibid., 319.
83. Ibid., 342. A parallel account appears in Tenzin Chökyi Lodrö's *Guidebook to Lapchi* (Huber 1997, 133–34), with emphasis on the final subjugation of Tseringma and the subsequent taming of all the denizens of Lachi, so that thereafter it became a place of practice completely supported by its resident spirits. See Chapter 5.

84. Chang 1977, 344–45.
85. Later, they also became his *karmamudrā,* carefully selected consorts in his practice of the "action seal" practice of sexual yoga, which is known for clearing away obstacles for the realization of Mahāmudrā, the ultimate awakening according to the meditation tradition of Milarepa, the Kagyü. See chapter 6.
86. The yeshe khandro is considered a sky-dancer on the level of the seventh bodhisattva bhūmi. Ven. Khandro Rinpoche, interview, October 16, 1997.
87. See chapter 5, and chapters 7 and 8 for more detail on this material.
88. T. Norbu 1981, 1985, 64.
89. Ven. Khandro Rinpoche, interview, October 16, 1997.
90. This description appears in Willis 1987, 75, in her conversations with Geshe Jampel Thardö.
91. Thondup 1992, 43.
92. Padmakara 1999, 10; cf. Dowman 1984, 12; cf. T. Tulku 1983, 17–18.
93. Tibetan Buddhism has an understanding of emanation whereby enlightened tülkus who are reborn will gradually remember their realization and training from previous lives, maturing into even further spiritual development in this life. It is explained that they must, however, go through rigorous training, practice, and testing to uncover this realization, as an example, out of compassion for all beings who also must undergo such practice, training, and testing. For, indeed, all beings inherently have the spiritual potential of buddhahood, but it must be uncovered, just as it was uncovered for Yeshe Tsogyal.
94. Dowman 1984, 189 n. 2.
95. Thondup 1983, 1992, 45.
96. Thondup 1983, 1992, 45; Dudjom 1991, vol. 1, 907; vol. 2, 113.
97. Ven. Tsoknyi Rinpoche, interview, July 1994, Boulder, Colorado; Willis 1987a, 75; Guenther 1993, 31; C. Tulku 1989. These four also correspond to the four verses of Khenpo Rinpoche's spontaneous song, as we shall see. Ven. Tsoknyi Rinpoche emphasized in his teachings that while these three levels are "like" the three kāyas, it would be best not to use the three-kāya terminology, "as the three kāyas express the male side of things, but if you want to express the female side of things, to keep the energy of the female, you need different terminology."
98. *Khenpo* is the highest monastic degree offered in the Kagyü and Nyingma schools, and this he received from His Holiness the sixteenth Karmapa. *Geshe Lharampa* is the corresponding highest monastic degree offered in the

Gelukpa school, and this he received from His Holiness the fourteenth Dalai Lama.

99. Ven. Khenpo Tsultrim Gyamtso Rinpoche, interview, October 12, 1994, Boulder, Colorado. Michele Martin, the translator, later gave a copy to Edou, who published it without commentary in Edou 1996, 104. Khenpo gave brief commentaries on that day and in July 1997. His close student, Ven. Dzogchen Pönlop Rinpoche, gave commentaries in November 1996 that greatly helped the interpretation of this teaching.

100. *ngak-kye khandro, lhen-kye khandro, shing-kye khandro.* In other sources (Hopkins 1977; Wayman 1973; Shaw 1994) this classification appears to refer only to suitable consorts. In no known source are there parallel descriptions of the level of attainment of male consorts.

101. Tsongkhapa's text was translated with the fourteenth Dalai Lama's commentary by Hopkins 1977, 27–28. Tsongkhapa's commentary on the *Cakrasaṃvara tantra,* the *Bedün Kunsel,* was quoted by Shaw 1994, 170. In Hopkins's translation, there are actually two ways of describing these three categories, which seem to be somewhat different. One interpretation is also quoted in Edou 1996, 104. Shaw draws from another translation that appears to be yet another interpretation of Tsongkhapa's.

102. Tsuda 1974, 266–72.

103. This is an example of creative applications of the teachings that seem typical of Tibetan Vajrayāna gurus in the West, applying sometimes obscure categories to a new interpretation that relates directly to the experience of their Western students.

104. In an early interview, Ven. Tsoknyi Rinpoche listened intently to my questions and then asked for paper and began furiously diagramming. He insisted that I structure my book in the way I have done, clearly outlining the categories and the labels I was to give each category. When I asked what text to consult on these categories, he said that there are texts but they have the categories mixed up, and that he was trying to give me a helpful method. Interview, July 1994, Boulder, Colorado.

105. This is all the more evident because Khenpo Rinpoche's presentation has a different order, as we will see.

106. This text comes from the Cakrasaṃvara cycle of tantras. In the text, these last two are referred to as secret and most secret, a variant on the form I am presenting here. Lamas are hesitant to speak in this way to any but their closest disciples, as the most secret is actually inexpressible. The German passage itself is difficult but can be summarized: The first ḍākinī is one who

overcomes coarse thoughts and has body colors and hand marks related to the empowerment of the vase; the second ḍākinī, of the secret empowerment, is the ḍākinī related to the winds of the breath and the channels, as well as the ascending heat; the third ḍākinī, associated with the prajñā-jñāna empowerment, goes beyond the bliss felt in the body and mind as happiness and is the coemergent bliss ḍākinī; the fourth ḍākinī of the fourth empowerment is the essence of the mind, which is the taste of emptiness, accessed through recognition. Herrmann-Pfandt 1990, 143–44 n. 15; cf. Gyatso 1998, 305 n. 7. A similar threefold presentation of the outer, inner, and secret ḍākinī came from Janice Willis's interviews with Geshe Jampel Thardö: "the *outer ḍākinī* is those varied forms in which the ḍākinī appears, whether human or deific, benign or wrathful, beneficient or malevolent; the *inner ḍākinī* manifests when the advanced meditator successfully transforms him or herself into the great ḍākinī (usually Vajrayoginī, herself); and the *secret ḍākinī* is the formless power, energy, and pure bliss of Voidness." 1987, 75. Note that what is missing is the subtle-body ḍākinī, the most esoteric of the ḍākinī teachings.

107. *mkha' 'gro dang ni mkha' 'gro mar/ kun rdzob lus snang khyad yod kyang/ od gsal phyag rgya cen po la/ngo bor dbyer ba rdul tsam med//* The translator noted with surprise that Rinpoche spoke here of ḍāka as khandro and ḍākinī as khandroma. This formulation is rarely seen in Tibetan, as we noted.
108. *rig dang skal par ldan pa rnams/ rdo rje theg par zhugs byas de/ sngags kyi dngos grub thob pa la/ sngags skyes mka' 'gro ma zhes grogs//*
109. Ven. Khenpo Rinpoche, oral commentary, October 12, 1994. Ven. Dzogchen Pönlop Rinpoche, November 1996, Boulder, Colorado. H.H. Tenzin Gyatso, the fourteenth Dalai Lama in Hopkins 1977, 27–28. Also quoted in Edou 1996, 104.
110. *rtogs ldan bla ma mnyes pa yis/ gnyug ma'i rang ngo 'phrod pa'i mthus/ gnas lugs mngon sum rtogs pa la/ lhan skyes mka' 'dro ma zhes brjod//*
111. Ven. Khenpo Rinpoche, oral commentary, October 12, 1994, Boulder, Colorado. Ven. Dzogchen Pönlop Rinpoche, November 1996, Boulder, Colorado.
112. Tsuda 1974, 271.
113. *sku dang gsung dang thugs kyi gnas/ nyi shu tsa bzhi'i zhing rnams su/ gnas ni gzhan don byed rnams la/ zhing skyes mkha' 'gro ma zhes bya//*
114. VIII.25–26. Tsuda 1974, 266–67.
115. See the presentation of this vignette in the introduction.
116. Guenther 1993, 31.

117. In chapter 7 we will examine these depictions and discuss how one might understand them from the point of view of the wisdom ḍākinī's subjectivity.

CHAPTER THREE
The Secret Ḍākinī

1. Hladiš 1999, 11.
2. Tārā was telling her that she was the queen of *vajradhātu,* or the most profoundly vast space, beyond any reference point of space, in contrast to form or nonspace. Vajradhātu is the fathomless ground of everything in Vajrayāna Buddhism.
3. This entire section is taken from Edou 1996, 150–52.
4. Ibid.
5. Thondup 1983, 1992, 56.
6. Ibid. 20.
7. Neumaier-Dargyay argued that this "mind of perfect purity" (*bodhicitta, changchup sem*), which is synonymous with the All-Creating Sovereign (*Künje Gyalpo*), is beyond gender, yet is depicted allegorically as feminine. She hinted that the Tibetan could just as well be Künje Gyalmo, interpreted as All-Creating Queen. Neumaier-Dargyay 1992, 28–30, 41–42. This is an enticing notion, but because the gender of the Tibetan is so clearly masculine (*po* ending, rather than *ba,* which is neutral, or *mo,* which is feminine), it is probably a stretch.
8. The discussion in chapter 2 explored the difference between depictions of the feminine in Tibetan Vajrayāna and other traditions of the feminine. The following discussion focuses specifically on the "mother."
9. Coburn 1982, 1986, 153–65.
10. From "Ḍākinī Wisdom," a taped seminar given in Seattle, November 16, 1989. Tapes distributed by Chagdud Gompa Foundation.
11. Quoted from the *Ratnaguṇasaṃcayagāthā* XII.1–2. This text is the versified summary root text of the *Aṣṭasāhasrikā-prajñāpāramitā* (hereafter referred to as Aṣṭasāhasrikā). Translated in Conze 1973a, 31.
12. According to Conze, the personification of Prajñāpāramitā as a deity can be traced back to the fourth century, though examples of her iconography before 800 C.E. have not survived. (Conze 1960, 22–23). After 600 C.E., in the tantric phase of the development of Prajñāpāramitā she is personalized, and sādhanas were composed to honor her. During this phase she is represented in definite iconography that became quite popular in the late Indian and

Tibetan traditions. Typically, she is represented in a peaceful form blazing in the color of gold, holding a Prajñāpāramitā text on top of a blue lotus, while seated on a lunar disk on top of a red lotus. Her hands are placed in the mudrās of teaching (*dharma-cakra-mudrā*) and of granting fearlessness (*abhāya-mudrā*), and she wears the ornaments of a celestial bodhisattva. See Snellgrove's translation of a short sādhana to Prajñāpāramitā from the Sādhanamālā, from Conze et al. 1964, 252–54. See figure on page 82.

13. *Aṣṭasāhasrikā* xii. 254; xxviii.456; *Aṣṭadaśasāhasrikā* 327. Conze 1973a, 172–173.
14. Conze 1967, 123–47, 243–68. In certain cases I have altered Conze's terminology to fit contemporary translation conventions.
15. *Aṣṭasāhasrikā* vii. 176. Conze 1973a.
16. *Aṣṭasāhasrikā* vii.171. Ibid.
17. *Pañcaviṃśatisāhasrikā* 328; *Abhisamayālaṅkāra* iv.4. in Conze 1975, 345.
18. For more on seed syllables, see the section in this chapter 3.
19. This text, which represents a discourse between the Buddha and Ānanda, opens with the usual preamble and closes with the usual conclusion. However, when it comes time for the customary teaching, the Buddha utters a single sound, the first letter of the Sanskrit alphabet, the A. The Sanskrit of the text has been lost (*Bhagavatī prajñāpāramitā sarva-tathāgatha-mātā ekākṣarā nāma*). In Tibetan it is found in Narthang (*Na-tsok* 255b–256a). Conze 1973b, 201.
20. This is a quote from the early-twentieth-century Nyingma master Dodrupchen Jigme Tenpe Nyima. Gyatso 1992, 185 n. 8. For more on the *A-Ra-Pa-Ca-Na* formulation, see 173 n. 8.
21. Machik Lapdrön received the Chö teachings from three different sources and combined them into one tradition that is called the Chö of Mahāmudrā. One of these transmissions was from the Indian sūtra tradition traceable to Buddha Śākyamuni, while the other two came from Tārā and Yum Chenmo themselves. Edou 1996, chapter 5.
22. Ibid., 30.
23. Ibid., 17, 178 n. 7.
24. Harding 1994.
25. Kunga and Cutillo, 1978, 21.
26. Nyoshul Khenpo 1995, 94. On a three-year retreat, Rinpoche spontaneously sang this song to his mother Chökyi Nodzom, but it is also obviously addressed to the Great Mother Prajñāpāramitā, for it is full of double references.
27. Urgyen 1995, 59–62. "If one wishes for a thorough understanding of this

matter one has to take the sky as a simile: the point is that Reality is unborn, and that as the main characteristic the mind is ceaseless. Like the sky so is Reality; by means of the sky as simile [Reality] is pointed out. The imperceptible Reality is taught by pointing at [something else which is] imperceptible." This classic meditation comes from the "mind section" (*sem-de*) of the Dzogchen teachings. Canonically, this practice is described in the *Künje Gyalpö'i Do,* translated by Neumaier-Dargyay 1992, 59.

28. These two aspects are introduced as the secret ḍākinī. "Knowing ying is yeshe." Ven. Tsoknyi Rinpoche, interview, July 1994, Boulder, Colorado.
29. Urgyen 1995, 61–62.
30. Harding 1994.
31. Thondup 1992.
32. This is the wisdom behind Janice Willis's use of the convention "she" in her article on "Ḍākinī: Some Comments on *Its* Nature and Meaning." [italics mine] Willis 1987a, 72–75.
33. Ibid., 62. In this article, Willis quotes Herbert Guenther's gloss of the Tibetan in Guenther 1973, 103 n.1.
34. Gyaltsen 1990, 104. A somewhat different version of this song appears in Trungpa 1982, 66 and 72, with a more lengthy commentary on the ḍākinī. This song is treated in more detail in chapter 8.
35. Klein 1995, 61.
36. Klein 1995. Klein's treatment of subjectivity pivots on a systematic investigation of the supposed "I" based upon the Gelukpa tradition of the great meditation master Tsongkhapa. She recommended weeks or months of observation of this "I" and suggested that this search will be fruitless. While the concept of the self is habitual, it is extemely fragile upon reflection and reveals only an "empty subject which is a dependent arising." (133) From this one moves to a different dimension of subjectivity, which is the natural clarity of the mind (*ösel*) as taught in "great completeness" Dzogchen meditation practice, though she does not elaborate on how her readers are to make this shift. Her presentation also directly addresses postmodern critiques of conventional subjectivity.
37. Ibid. 88; Gyatso 1998, 265–271. "Subjectless subjectivity" is slightly different from Klein's and Gyatso's presentations. Given her Gelukpa analytic and Dzogchen context, Klein's has a bias toward emptiness or space as opposed to contents. Gyatso, who wrote with reference to autobiography, spoke of "subjectivity without essence," referring to Jigme Lingpa's construction of identity. This study, which relates more to the structure of the ḍākinī symbol

and its relevance for spiritual subjectivity, deals more with the relationship between space and form, especially the feminine form of the ḍākinī—hence "subjectless subjectivity."

38. Trungpa and Nālandā 1980, 86. I must acknowledge that all of the instructions on the ritual dimensions of the secret ḍākinī came from my root teacher, Chögyam Trungpa Rinpoche, for which I am very grateful. These are not instructions one would receive casually from books, brief encounters with lamas, or other teachers, since they are the core of the ritual understanding of the ḍākinī. While much of what he taught is found in fragmentary fashion elsewhere, Trungpa Rinpoche gave it coherence, context, and commitment.
39. Quoted in Padmakara 1994, 312.
40. Ibid., 310.
41. International Translation Committee 1998. The gender of the teacher is not important, but it must be acknowledged that most Tibetan gurus are male, for reasons we have already discussed. Certainly on occasion the ḍākinī herself is the guru, as such human female gurus as Machik Lapdrön, Yeshe Tsogyal, and Maṇḍāravā. Or in the rare instances of the origination of new lineages of teachings, visionary ḍākinīs serve as gurus, such as the teachers of Tilopa, Khyungpo Naljor, and Longchenpa. This is discussed in further detail in chapter 6.
42. Guenther 1963, 80.
43. Chang 1977, 419.
44. Harding 1996, 36.
45. Ibid.
46. Trungpa 1982, 233. This is discussed in another way by Trungpa 1973a, 222–24, and in Trungpa 1991a, 163. This presentation has similarities with Snellgrove's (1987) criticism of the usual understanding of "symbolic" in Western interpretation: "But when modern apologists use the term 'symbolic' as though to suggest that the external practices were never taken in any literal sense, they mislead us. Central to tantric practice is the refusal to distinguish between the everyday world (saṃsāra) and the experience of nirvāṇa." 160.
47. *Prajñāpāramitā-hṛdāya-sūtra.* Ven. Chögyam Trungpa Rinpoche's Mahāmudrā-style commentary on this formula is summarized in this way: "Form is form, emptiness is emptiness, things are just what they are and we do not have to try to see them in the light of some sort of profundity." Trungpa 1973a, 189.
48. Trungpa 1992, 45. An example of how this manifests in classical Vajrayāna

literature can be seen in Tilopa's introduction of thirteen symbols to Nāropa, and Nāropa's immediate understanding of their meaning. Guenther 1963, 37–41.

49. Kalu 1986, 110.
50. Trungpa and Guenther 1975, 58.
51. Trungpa and Nālandā 1982, xxxix. Another word for symbol in Tibetan is *da,* discussed in chapter 8.
52. A final, hidden meaning of *mudrā* is the consort, the giver of bliss. Union with the consort expresses intimacy with all of one's experience, in which there is no separation between experience and experiencer. Mudrā expresses nonduality in gender and all seemingly polarized manifestations in the world. The term is used this way particularly in connection with the third *abhiṣeka,* in which the karmamudrā, or consort, is taken as an expression of the realization of knowledge. In the early tradition, one literally took a young consort as a part of the ritual. It has long been understood, however, that in current practice the consort is generally visualized instead.
53. The ḍākinī was Ekajaṭī, the protector of mantra, about whom much more is said in chapter 8. Dudjom 1991, vol. 1, 580; Germano and Gyatso 2000, 319.
54. Trungpa 1973c, 23.
55. In Sanskrit, consonants are pronounced as the initial sound followed by the vowel sound *ah,* so that the alphabet is pronounced *ka, kha, ga,* etc. Vowels are indicated as ornamentations of the letter A, with the implication that all vowel sounds are variations of A.
56. Kongtrül 1995, 55.
57. Trungpa 1999, 37–40.
58. Ibid., 46.
59. Ibid., 46–47.
60. It is a famous seed syllable in Anuttara-yoga-tantras such as the Cakrasaṃvara, Hevajra, and Kālacakra tantras.
61. The Hevajra specifically refers to EVAṂ as the *saṃvaram sarvabuddhānām* and *saṃvaram ḍākininān,* and the commentaries refer to the ḍākinīs in this context as enlightened beings who fly through space, irrespective of gender.
62. *Hevajra-tantra,* II.iii. 2–6. Snellgrove 1959, 1980, 94; Farrow and Menon 1992, 180.
63. *Hevajra-tantra,* I.i.1. Farrow and Menon 1992, 4, from the commentary by Kṛṣṇācārya, the Yogaratnamālā.
64. This is, of course, the esoteric meaning, for *bhaga* most often refers to wealth,

happiness, and good fortune, the bhagavan being one who possesses (*vat*) these great blessings.

65. Kongtrül 1995, 29.
66. Ibid.
67. Ibid.
68. This is a shift from *jñāna,* or *yeshe,* to *prajñā,* or *sherap,* which is a shift to the feminine in which a masculine principle is present. *Jñāna* is nondual wisdom, the self-existing feminine that is beyond gender in any conventional sense; *prajñā* is penetrating insight-wisdom, the feminine principle, which has upāya, the masculine principle, as its counterpoint. Obviously, prajñā and jñāna come from the same root, *jñā,* to know—in Tibetan, *shepa.*
69. Ven. Khenchen Thrangu Rinpoche, interviews, November 1989 and November 1990, Boulder, Colorado.
70. Guenther 1971, 203–04.
71. Ibid., 203
72. Ven. Khenchen Thrangu Rinpoche, interviews, November 1989 and November 1990, Boulder, Colorado.
73. This is a fascinating word in Tibetan, for it is the term used to refer to "sacred histories," those classic literary genres in which lamas detail their understanding of lineage history and namthars, or sacred biographies of lineage figures. Famous such accounts that have been translated include those by Tāranātha and Butön, as well as the Blue Annals. In those contexts, *chöjung* refers to the history of the dharma; in our discussion here the term refers to the source or ground of all phenomena. But, given that *chö* can be translated in a variety of ways, the most general being "all matter, all knowledge of things both worldly and spiritual and all that exists and can be known," (Das 1969, 1981) we understand that any translation is inadequate.
74. Trungpa 1999, 236.
75. The three-dimensional representation, more technically accurate in yoginītantra, is a three-sided pyramid, inverted with the apex pointing down. Sometimes the chöjung is represented two-dimensionally as merely a single triangle, with apex pointing down. The chöjung is common to many tantras, with different colors, combinations, and scales depending upon the ritual requirements.
76. Trungpa 1982; Trungpa 1975, 9.
77. Poussin 1971, 98–99. The Sarvāstivādin abhidharma of Vasubandhu described dharmas, or momentary phenomena, as having three phases: arising, dwelling, and ceasing, hence "sarva asti," everything exists in the three times.

78. Trungpa 1999, 10.
79. Ibid., 37–40.
80. Trungpa Rinpoche's teachings contain inconsistencies in the presentation of these three qualities. The second quality, nondwelling, appears in several sources, but in his introductory seminar on the feminine principle this quality was called "with a nature like sky." 1999, 18–24. In other presentations this depiction seems to appear as a subset of the three qualities as I am presenting them.
81. Harding 1994.
82. Trungpa 1999, 12.
83. Ibid., 13.
84. Harding 1994.
85. Trungpa 1999, 20.
86. Edou 1996, 152.
87. Ibid.
88. Snellgrove 1959, 24.
89. Ibid., 30.
90. Trungpa 1999, 3.
91. Guenther 1993, 186 n. 122. Guenther leaves us wondering about how women practitioners relate to the feminine. He appears to have fallen into Jung's contrasexual model, which does not consistently fit the case in Vajrayāna symbol and practice. See chapter 1.
92. Trungpa 1999, 16. Ven. Tsoknyi Rinpoche, interview, June 1994, Boulder, Colorado. This must be understood properly in the context of Vajrayāna Buddhism, which is perhaps different from Hindu tantra.
93. Herrmann-Pfandt 1990, 307–09, 470–75 and passim; Shaw 1994, 20–34; Campbell 1996, 125–46, 186. Kinsley (1989, xii–xix) critiqued the notion that there is any concrete knowledge of prepatriarchal culture in India or elsewhere that could provide a direct correlation between gender hierarchies in religion and social patterns within a culture.
94. Shaw 1994, 44.
95. Ibid., 32.
96. Ibid. The problem with Shaw's interpretation is that she substitutes a problematic patriarchal society with a gynocentric cult that she says pervades tantric circles in India. It is difficult to comment on the veracity of her claims in the Indian tantric tradition without anthropological and historical studies and without oral instructions from lineage holders of the Indian tradition. In the absence of these, Shaw's interpretation zigzags between Indian Hindu

and Nepali Bajrācārya sources drawing heavily on Tibetan sources and commentaries. When gynocentric notions are applied to Tibetan Buddhism, there is a misrepresentation.

97. Simmer-Brown 1994, 68–69. Shaw said, "I don't think there is a masculine or a feminine as an abstract principle in the Indian texts that I work with. They're not concerned with an inner masculine or feminine. . . . In Tibet, tantra was appropriated into a monastic context, and it had to become something that celibates could perform by themselves. . . . [A]ll the female symbolism became very abstract—it became not an embodied ḍākinī, but a ḍākinī principle."
98. Ven. Khenpo Tsultrim Gyamtso Rinpoche, interview, October 1994, Boulder, Colorado. The rest of the spontaneous song is treated in chapter 6.
99. Ortner 1996, 1–42; 173–80. The development of these aspects of ḍākinī manifestation is the subject of the following chapters.
100. Cf. Bynum 1986; Aziz 1987, 1988; Klein 1985b, 1995; Miller 1980; Ortner and Whitehead 1981; Ortner 1996.
101. Ortner 1996, 1–42; 173–80.
102. A complete exposition of this probably requires another book; however, it is developed in certain sections of chapters 4, 5, and 6.

CHAPTER FOUR
The Inner Ḍākinī

1. Schmidt 1993, 166.
2. Dowman 1985, 43–44; Robinson 1979, 28.
3. Here I refer to systems theory from the scientific world of cybernetics, which involved a paradigm shift in many related fields. This work began in science and was pioneered by Gregory Bateson. The term is also applied to the fields of family therapy, organizational development, and business and industry.
4. This is not to say, of course, that there is no room for change or political action. From a Vajrayāna perspective, change can only be facilitated from a perspective of commitment to the maṇḍala. Then the strategies and skillful actions are suitable to the totality of the situation, rather than being based on impulsive rejection of what is unpleasant or disliked. This kind of engaged activism requires taking the long view and a contemplative perspective.
5. *Hevajra-tantra* I.iii.16. Snellgrove 1959, 59; Farrow and Menon 1992, 44–45.
6. Bynum reflected on the role of contemplating the body in medieval Chris-

tianity, suggesting that inherent in the doctrine of incarnation is the corruptibility of the body. This closely parallels the centrality of embodiment in Vajrayāna Buddhism, in which the contemplation of the body rests on an understanding of the sacredness of embodiment. Bynum 1991, 239–98; 1995, 200–26, 318–44. See chapter 6.

7. Wilson 1996, 41–43.
8. Douglas and Bays 1978, 64–66. See also Templeman 1989, 117 n. 63.
9. Bynum makes the point that most cultures attempt to mask or deny "the horror of the period between 'first death' (the departure of breath or life) and 'second death' or mineralization (the reduction of the cadaver to the hard remains—that is, teeth and bones)." This phase, which she calls "fragmentation," became theologically important in medieval Europe as a way of avoiding the threatening topic of the corruptibility of the human body. It seems that it is just this phase upon which the Vajrayāna focuses in the symbol and iconography of the ḍākinī. Bynum 1991, 295; 1995, 51–58.
10. Thondup 1996, 366.
11. Schmidt 1993, 38–39.
12. Chönam and Khandro 1998, 150.
13. The eight charnel grounds important to Guru Rinpoche were: (1) Cool Grove, Sitavana (*silwa tsel*), in the east; (2) Perfected in Body (*ku la dzok*) to the south; (3) Lotus Mound (*pema tsek*) to the west; (4) Laṅka Mound (*lanka tsek*) to the north; (5) Spontaneously Accomplished Mound (*lhündrup tsek*) to the southeast; (6) Display of Great Secret (*sangchen rölpa*) to the southwest; (7) Pervasive Great Joy (*dechen delwa*) to the northwest; and (8) World Mound (*jikten tsek*) to the northeast. Schmidt 1996, 410.
14. This is according to the *Cakrasaṃvara-tantra,* which lists a different set of charnel grounds from those important to Guru Rinpoche listed in note 12. These charnel grounds are, in the cardinal directions, counterclockwise from the east: Chaṇḍogra, Gaḥvara, Vajrajvala, and Karaṅkin, and in the intermediate points, counterclockwise from the northeast, Aṭṭahāsa, Lakṣmīvana, Ghorandhakāra, and Kilikilārava. For a commentary concerning the eight charnel grounds, see Tucci 1969, 40–42.
15. Padmakara 1994, 41.
16. Chang 1977, 303. This act parallels the tradition in Hindu tantra in which it is essential to give the wrathful goddess what she requests in order to avert further disaster. See O'Flaherty 1980, 82, 275–79.
17. Trungpa 1991a, 70–71.
18. The eight worldly concerns (*jikten kyi chögye*) summarize the attachments of

conventional life: gain and loss, pleasure and pain, praise and blame, and fame and infamy.

19. Just as in the Christian tradition praying in the desert was an essential part of spiritual development, in India the place of retreat was the forest. See Ray 1994, 44–68. In Tibet the mountains took on this significance.
20. Lhalungpa 1986, 333.
21. Chang 1977, 4.
22. Ibid., 25.
23. Padmakara 1999, 67–68; Dowman 1984, 65–66; T. Tulku 1983, 79–80. The passage goes on to describe retinue ḍākinīs in human form offering shreds of flesh from their own bodies to the central ḍākinī, Vajrayoginī.
24. Wilson 1996, 15–110.
25. Lang 1986, 63–79.
26. Johnston 1972, 72–73. These passages are also treated in Wilson 1996 (66–67), who describes this as a post-Aśokan account in which sexuality and repulsiveness are juxtaposed in a style characteristic of the period. Other examples of such accounts can be found in the stories of the renunciation of Yasa and Cittahattha. Johnston, 75–82.
27. Wilson 1996, 41–76. Lang contrasts the literature on renunciation for monks and nuns in the *Therīgāthā* and *Theragāthā,* saying that for nuns the imagery sometimes concerned the aging and deterioration of the body, but more often contemplated the snare of a tyrannical husband and a demanding family life. Lang 1986, 63–79.
28. The four *viparyāsas* (*jik-tsok la tawa*), or misperceptions, address how it is that we myopically see only the positive traits we wish to see, ignoring the true qualities of phenomena. These meditations point out that while a flower may be beautiful today, tomorrow it will wilt and be suitable only for the garbage heap. Contemplation of each of these four led directly in the pre-Mahāyāna tradition to an understanding of the four foundations of mindfulness. Mindfulness of body leads to an understanding of repulsiveness, mindfulness of feelings leads to seeing pain in what we think is pleasurable, mindfulness of mind gives rise to a direct understanding of impermanence, and mindfulness of dharmas fosters a realization of egolessness.
29. There are obviously parallels with this in the Hindu tradition, in the iconography and qualities of Śiva and Kālī. See O'Flaherty 1973, and Kinsley 1986, 1987; 1997.
30. Templeman 1989, 72–73.

31. Maṇḍāravā was one of Guru Rinpoche's important consorts and a famous ḍākinī. See references to her in chapters 6 and 7.
32. In another account, the baby girl abandoned with her mother's corpse in the charnel ground was the daughter of the Queen of Nepal. She was discovered and raised by a monkey. Later, when it was noticed that she had the webbed fingers and toes of a wisdom ḍākinī, she was given the name Śākyadevī the Nepalese (or Śākya Dema). An important consort to Guru Rinpoche, she assisted him in the concealing of treasure teachings, driving away the four scourges who attempted to obstruct him. Douglas and Bays 1978, 300–01; 314–16; Dowman 1984, 54–56, 268–69; Evans-Wentz 1970, 165–66; 176–77.
33. Chönam and Khandro 1998, 162–64. In another charnel ground, she manifested as the Lion-Headed Ḍākinī (167); in another, she manifested eight miracles to tame wrathful mamo ḍākinīs (169–71); in another, she became the Queen Prajñāpāramitā with one hundred heads and one thousand arms (172).
34. This again refers to the viparyāsas described in note 27, which summarize the misguided efforts of sentient beings to find happiness in all the wrong places. This is reversed in the form of the ḍākinī, who has no such deceptiveness.
35. These are the six classic charnel ground ornaments made of bone: necklace (*kaṇṭhi, norbu*), bracelets (*haste rucaka, lag-drup*), earrings (*kuṇḍala, nacha*), skirt (*mekhalā, karak*), crown (*cakrī, khorlo*), and cemetery ointment made of ash (*bhasma, thalwa*). Trungpa 1982, 217–18.
36. The secret center is below the fourth cakra, in the pubic area, located slightly differently in each of the Anuttara tantras. It refers to the chöjung, the cosmic cervix described in chapter 3.
37. Trungpa 1982, 235.
38. This form is particularly popular in Newari Buddhism in Nepal.
39. For more on women associated with nature through birth-giving and child-rearing, placed in a context of pancultural androcentrism, see Ortner 1996, 73–84. However, here we are looking at the symbolic power, which is the reverse side of the androcentrism that Ortner describes. In the assimilated Buddhist form of the symbol of the ḍākinī, her wisdom transcends nature altogether.
40. Chang 1977, 449.
41. Oral commentary by Khenpo Tsultrim Gyamtso Rinpoche, given for Ngedön School, September 19, 1986.
42. *Āditta-pariyāya-sutta, Saṃyutta-nikāya XXXV.28*. Rahula 1959, 95–97.

43. For a complete study of the fire of suffering and its extinction, see Thanissaro Bhikkhu 1993.
44. Chönam and Khandro 1996.
45. Dowman 1985, 205; Robinson 1979, 132.
46. The following commentary is based on the author's experience working with the *lojong* slogan of Atīśa, "Three objects, three poisons, three virtuous seeds." For further commentary on this slogan, see Chödron 1994, 28–32.
47. Harding 1996, 34.
48. Trungpa 1982, 239.
49. Trungpa 1973c, 25.
50. The lineage of the practice described here came from Nāropa, who received the transmission from his root guru Tilopa, who received direct transmission of Vajrayoginī or her equivalent representative. This is discussed in chapter 7.
51. There is evidence that this tradition did not come from Indian sources but from the earliest period of Tibetan Buddhism, the time of Padmasambhava. Herrmann-Pfandt 1990, 146–47.
52. Quoted in Kalu 1997, 189.
53. As was discussed, the prevailing pattern in Buddhism is patriarchal institutional patterns combined with androgynous soteriology. See Schuster-Barnes 1987; Sponberg 1992.
54. Dowman 1985, 73.
55. Trungpa 1982, 238; Vajrayoginī is especially central in the *Cakrasaṃvara-tantra,* as depicted here. However, she is important in many other tantras, and other yidam wisdom ḍākinīs are always associated with her. In her more wrathful form she is known as Vajravārāhī, and in this presentation this is her secret manifestation.
56. Trungpa 1982, 228. This presentation of the iconography of Vajrayoginī comes from Trungpa Rinpoche's abridged commentary on the Vajrayoginī-sādhana, which appeared in article form, and all quotes unless otherwise cited come from this commentary. Most of Rinpoche's citations come from the "praise" section of the sādhana.
57. See the quote by Jetsünma Chimme Luding in Havnevik 1990, 177.
58. Trungpa 1982, 239. For a full description of the iconography of Vajrayoginī, see also Trungpa 1991b, 147–48.
59. Ibid., 238.
60. Ibid.
61. The abhidharma texts detail the conditioned dharmas, which include the

range of identified emotional states arising from ignorance. One often sees rosaries of carved wooden heads with such expressions sold in Buddhist countries of Asia. Sometimes they depict various emotions in great detail, a graphic teaching for counting one's prayers or mantras.

62. When he appears alone, Guru Rinpoche also carries a khaṭvāṅga that represents in secret form his consort ḍākinīs Yeshe Tsogyal and Maṇḍāravā, completing his manifestation of the masculine principle. His khaṭvāṅga is topped with a trident instead of a double dorje, and it has symbolism of its own. Cf. Dilgo Khyentse 1988, 23.
63. Trungpa 1982, 239.
64. Benard 1994, 10–15. This form has never been fully embraced by Tibetan Buddhism. See chapter 7.
65. II.iv.42. Snellgrove 1959, 105.
66. Trungpa 1975, 106–09.
67. Edou 1996. There are at least two forms of the Chö practice, one of which relies especially on Machik Lapdrön as the central deity form (Chö of Mahāmudrā). The other is from the Nyingma terma tradition and relies on the Tröma Nagmo deity. I am referring especially to the latter tradition.
68. Harding and Barron 1990.
69. Other retinues include throngs of additional ḍākinis, fierce protectors of all varieties, legions of gods and demons, and dharmapālas of the four gates. With the support of these extensive retinues, she is especially revered for her "destroying" activities, which are of several kinds. She destroys obstructing forces, "annihilating them and reducing them to dust, but liberating their consciousnesses in dharmakāya." Ibid. 37.
70. Eller 1993, 1995, 136. Eller speaks clearly about the "nexus of values gathered under the goddess' skirts."
71. Christ 1979, 273–86.
72. Eller noted that spiritual feminists who are not career scholars have invested a great deal of time, research, study, and memorization in order to familiarize themselves with goddess traditions, producing resource guides and materials to serve the movement. This has no doubt nourished the audience for scholars in the history of religions, no matter how different their motivations and conclusions may appear. Eller 1993, 1995, 134.
73. Kinsley 1989, x.
74. As examples, note Bynum's research on medieval women's understanding of the Holy Spirit and Hawley's research on worship of Kṛṣṇa through the divine gopī. Bynum et al., 1986, 1–16, 231–56, 257–88.

75. Shaw 1994, 37.
76. Ibid., 41–42. Shaw speaks of Vajrayoginī's "metaphysical link" with women, saying that she took form so that "women, seeing enlightenment in female form, will recognize their innate divinity." The quote she uses to support the special favor of women is misrepresented, selected from a context in the *Caṇḍamahāroṣaṇa-tantra* that also challenges the yogin's practice. See George 1974, 80. There are two other problems in Shaw's translations of passages from the tantras and from namthars: (1) she translates passages concerning feminine and masculine as expressed in "twilight language" to mean men and women in the literal sense (cf. 27, 32, 59, 68–69) and (2) she translates passages with gender-neutral terminology to be gender-specific, favoring women (cf. 41 n. 19, 42 n. 22, 106 n. 25). She justifies the latter as a remedy for patriarchal tendencies in previous scholarship favoring men (13–15).
77. Herrmann-Pfandt 1990, 262–68 and passim; 1997, 26–29. Herrmann-Pfandt does not treat Vajrayoginī (Vajravārāhī) in detail, except to study her iconography in yum-yab, reversed from the customary form, 325–31; Campbell 1996, 140, 144. Specifically, Campbell discussed Dorje Phagmo (Vajravārāhī) as a potential exception to the passive mother image, herself a "dynamic and autonomous goddess" who has the "possibility of disrupting the traditional significance of male/active, female/passive, and thus offer[s] for women the kind of representations of the divine which might bring about a different kind of subjectivity." She builds this point on Bharati's assumptions about active and passive in Tibetan gendered iconography.
78. Campbell 1996, 141.
79. Gross 1998a, 408; 1998b, 174. This point is also made by Herrmann-Pfandt, who explained that ḍākinīs are not almighty beings in the sense of Western religion; instead they are symbols and personifications of certain aspects of the world, psyche, and enlightened nature. Herrmann-Pfandt 1991, 127.
80. Klein 1995, 22.
81. The dynamics of this process are described in the teachings on the twelve nidānas, in which the consciousness (*vijñāna,* third) becomes name and form (*nāma-rūpa,* fourth), the psychophysical personality. Then through the six senses (*ṣad-āyatana,* fifth), one develops contact (*sparśa,* sixth) and feeling (*vedanā,* seventh), from which arises desire (*tṛṣṇā,* eighth), the afflicted emotions of attachment, anger, and bewilderment.
82. Klein argued this as well, though in relation to "subjectivity without contents," discussed in chapters 1 and 3. Klein 1995, 88, 133.

83. See discussion in chapter 3.
84. While this process is described as gradual, it is important to understand that sādhanas often begin with a sudden arising of the complete self-visualization of the deity as well, the experience of which supports the entire sādhana ritual. Both classical texts and contemporary instructions give hints for intensifying one's visualization practice, suggesting that difficulties in visualization are common to both Tibetans and Western students. See Klein's (1995) comments, 185–86. For an example of such instructions in an important classical text, see Jamgön Kongtrül Lodrö Thaye in Harding 1996, 39–41.
85. See Jamgön Kongtrül Lodrö Thaye's presentation of the importance of pride of the deity, and Harding's (1996) commentary, 39–40; 16–17.
86. Self-visualization in the body of contrasexual gender can be likened to the experience of Śāriputra in the *Vimalakīrti-nirdeśa-sūtra,* who is magically caused to exchange bodies with an enlightened goddess, a progenitor of the ḍākinī. Shocked, indeed horrified, Śāriputra experiences a change in his understanding of embodiment, agreeing that he could also find no essence to his femaleness (*strībhava*). Śāriputra declared, "I no longer appear in the form of a male! My body has changed into the body of a woman! I do not know what to transform!" Thurman 1976, 63.
87. Ibid. This was Śāriputra's conclusion after the incident described in the previous note.
88. Trungpa 1982, 238.
89. Harding 1996, 41.
90. Trungpa 1982, 240.
91. Gyatso 1998, 245, 261.
92. Ibid., 261.
93. The union of heruka and ḍākinī is a symbol of various other aspects of Vajrayāna meditation practice, including elements of the subtle-body yoga, discussed in the Chapter 5.
94. As mentioned in chapter 2, blood *(trak)* was considered horribly unclean, as the *rasa* of another human being that could pollute one's family line for generations. The "blood-drinker" would ordinarily be unimaginably defiled.
95. This refers in a summary way to the "nine moods of the heruka" in a commentary by Tsewang Künkhyap, a disciple of Situ Pema Nyinje. Summarized in Trungpa 1982, 234; Guenther 1963, 44–45, n. 7.
96. I.x.e.42. Snellgrove 1959, 136–37, and n. 1.
97. The palace contrasts with the overt charnel ground characteristic of the

ḍākinī Vajrayoginī, of which she is native. For the heruka, the charnel ground and the luxury of the palace are inseparable.

98. This is more accurately called in the Sanskrit texts *ālīḍha* posture, a warrior's posture associated with shooting arrows, with one leg bent at the knee and the other drawn back for steadiness.

99. These too are symbols of the masculine and feminine, respectively, and when they are crossed in the traditional way signify their inseparability.

100. This contradicts Bharati's somewhat precipitous assertion that the assignations of passive and active were switched in Buddhist tantra, suggesting that this was true also in Tibet. "Vajrayāna Buddhists created or absorbed two types of deities, chiefly female, i.e., genuine 'Śaktis' in the Indian sense, female 'energies' which retain their purely dynamic function in Tibetan Vajrayāna (e.g. Vajravārāhī, 'the Vajra Sow'); and also, goddesses who embody the theologically genuine Vajrayāna concept of the static *yum* (cosmic mother) who is also *prajñā,* total wisdom, viz. the quiescent apotheosized Prajñāpāramitā." See Bharati 1965, 200–02. He may not have been aware that Vajravārāhī, for example, plays both roles in different practices, and that when this form is practiced, no such polarity is evident.

101. Dowman 1985, 11.

102. Herrmann-Pfandt 1990, 155; 322–24; 1997, 17–20. Herrmann-Pfandt cites five aspects of the prominence of the male consort in yab-yum depictions, summarized thus: (1) the larger size and greater number of arms and legs of the yab; (2) the yab, facing forward and making eye contact, is more overtly understood as the counterpart of the practitioner; (3) the body posture of the yab determines the position and thus the depiction of the yum; (4) when the ritual requires visualizing oneself as the deity, it often states "with consort," suggesting that one visualize oneself as the "central" deity, which is male; and (5) the practice identifies the name of the "central" deity, often calling it "heruka yab-yum," which suggests that the female consort is a nameless addition to the practice of the male deity.

103. Herrmann-Pfandt reiterated this criticism throughout her long monograph, and this is also argued in Campbell 1996, chapter 8 and passim.

104. Cf. Herrmann-Pfandt 1990, 325–28. A grand example of the reversed yum-yab can be found in the ritual of Sarasvatī (Yangchen) with Mañjuśrī in her lap, practiced by Jetsünma Chimme Luding, the Sakya woman lama who is sister to H. H. Sakya Trizin.

105. For example, in a practice of Mahākāla and Mahākālī in embrace, the self-visualization is performed with an emphasis on the male, because skillful

means is considered most important. But when the front visualization of the same practice is done, Mahākālī faces forward because the wisdom aspects are deemed more important. Example taken from Kagyü three-year retreat practice, under the direction of Khenchen Thrangu Rinpoche, Gampo Abbey, Nova Scotia.

106. Herrmann-Pfandt mentioned two that came from Indian sources: (1) *Abhidhānottara-tantra* chap. 36, folios 201.7–204.2; Peking folio 180a.1–b.8, and its related work from Tibet transmitted by Tāranātha, *Dorje Naljorma lha cudün gyi drup-thap* of Jamyang Loter-wangpo; (2) *Śri-vajravārāhī-sādhana* of Prajñābhadra, Pek. 2286, translated into Tibetan by Sumatikīrti and Marpa Chökyi Wangchuk. Line drawings of the iconography from these two Indian sources are provided in her monograph. Herrmann-Pfandt 1990, 325–26, n. 19–23; illustrations 10 and 11, 327, 329. Also 1997, 21–25.

107. In a commentary Jamyang Loter-wangpo describes the consort as blue with one face and two hands, holding a vajra and bell as in the conventional description of the *yum*.

108. Herrmann-Pfandt 1990, 330.

109. Padmakara 1999, 68–69; Dowman 1984, 66–67; T. Tulku 1983, 80–81. The text speaks of Vajrayoginī and consort, and the fact that she could witness and accept the gifts and snap her fingers in this way was taken by Herrmann-Pfandt as evidence that she faced her retinues. The translations of this text use the term *yab-yum* rather than the reversed form. Herrmann-Pfandt 1990, 331.

110. Willson 1986, 200–01. Herrmann-Pfandt doubted whether Nāropa is actually the holder of the lineage of reversed Śamvara, called Dechok Yab-yum Golok. She noted that Tāranātha was probably familiar with this practice, but Nāropa does not appear in the lineage lists of this practice. She remarked with some irony that even reversed the practice is named after the male deity. 1990, 330.

111. Herrmann-Pfandt speculated about the visualization practice, assuming that the identification with the deity emphasizes the heruka, but it appears that these speculations are based on conjecture. Specifically, she suggested that "most tantric practice is seen from and judged from a male perspective." 1990, 130. In a later article, she quoted a commentary from the Kālacakra cycle in which male or female tāntrikas visualize themselves in the same gender as their physical bodies, or only with the central deity of the yab-yum couple. This is contrary to every instruction I have ever seen or received.

Most of her conclusions concerning yab-yum arise from this misunderstanding. 1997, 20–21.

112. Ven. Tsoknyi Rinpoche, interview, July 1994, Boulder, Colorado.
113. Havnevik 1990, 177.

CHAPTER FIVE

The Outer Ḍākinī

1. Padmakara 1999, 74–75.
2. Caroline Walker Bynum has traced the intimate albeit ambivalent link between soul and body in the medieval theology of incarnation and has suggested how it affects contemporary identity formation. Bynum 1995, 13–17; 1991, 181–238. For more on this, see Gallagher and Laqueur 1987.
3. Geoffrey Samuel (1990) has been deeply influenced by Tibetan views of embodiment and has articulated an understanding of mind and body as inextricably tied in shamanic understanding. "I do not believe that there are in fact any natural, pre-given, ultimately real distinctions between mind and body, subjective and objective, self and other, consciousness and matter. The distinctions we make doubtless depend to some degree on aspects of human biology, such as the available human sensory modalities, but we learn them individually on the basis of the culture within which we grow up. Short of committing ourselves to a particular set of religious or scientific dogmas, we can have no guarantees that they are true. . . . If we accept that we are in fact talking about techniques for restructuring the self and the emotions, of realigning the relationship between one human being and others, then what the Indian and Tibetan Tantric practitioners are doing becomes something which may have direct consequences for individual and society." Samuel 1989.
4. Exceptions, of course, exist in Buddhist traditions in which the corpse of the rare deceased teacher is miraculously immune to decay, indicating his enlightened qualities.
5. Contemporary yogins and yoginīs such as Khenpo Tsultrim Gyamtso Rinpoche teach privately about their charnel ground experiences. In chapters 1 and 4 we discussed the Indian tradition of charnel ground meditations as presented in Wilson 1996, 41–43.
6. Chang 1977, 1256. Such contemplations usually arise in the study of Madhyamaka philosophy, in which lamas will characteristically ask what the hand is.

Is it the fingers, the palm, the wrist, the nails? The skin, the bones, the cartilage, the muscles? Or are all these things together the hand?

7. For development of this idea, see Sogyal Rinpoche 1992, 15–27; for a more classical interpretation, see Padmakara 1994, 39–59.
8. Chang 1977, 116–17.
9. Snellgrove 1959, 1980, 92.
10. Chang 1977, 124–25.
11. Gyamtso 1995, 2; Chang 1977, 308–09. For interpretation of this verse, I am endebted to Rinpoche for his commentary on how to apply this verse to bringing illness onto the path. Karme Chöling, Barnet, Vermont, 1994.
12. Khenpo Tsultrim Gyamtso's translator, Elizabeth Callahan, notes that the Tibetan term *nyer-len zug kyi pungpo,* translated as "the skandha of form that is brought about compulsively," means that the skandha of form is brought on by karma, and this brings suffering. Gyamtso 1995, 2.
13. Union refers to the integration of appearance and emptiness. This is the essence of deity yoga practice, in which the physical form has no substance but is radiant and full of qualities. Ibid.
14. The threat of encountering in graphic form the degeneration and decay of the human body became in Tibetan Buddhism the basis of the Vajrayāna practice of coemergent wisdom. Thomas 1980.
15. This term for physical body has the additional meaning of "lost, left behind, abandoned," referring to the body as an impermanent shell, a reference to conventional views of the body discussed in the previous section. When informed by tantric views of embodiment, the physical body is understood as a sacred maṇḍala (*lü-kyi-kyil*).
16. The difficulties of describing this in Western terms are noted by Samuel 1989, 202, 237. "[T]he subtle body has been one of the hardest concepts in Buddhist and Hindu thought for Westerners to appreciate, perhaps because it implies a lack of separation between 'body' and 'mind,' which Western science and medicine has had difficulty in accepting. The Tibetans at times speak as if the cakra and nāḍī are really physically present in the body in the form they are described in the tradition, and it is difficult to square such an internal anatomy more than approximately with that known to modern medicine. The system of cakra and nāḍī doubtless has some physical correlates but it is best understood as a kind of mental model of the human nervous system as seen from the inside. Such a model is not a straightforward description but a structuring; learning the map involves learning to

make sense of one's nervous system in a particular way." Samuel warns of "misplaced concreteness" with regard to these descriptions.

17. I have chosen the translation "breath" because of its resonance with *khandro khalung,* "the warm breath of the ḍākinīs." More commonly, *lung* is translated as "wind."
18. Karthar 1990–1991. Throughout this section, I have relied in general on Rinpoche's teachings on the *Zamo Nangdön* of the Third Karmapa, Rangjung Dorje, a text based on the *Hevajra-tantra,* the *Kālacakra-tantra,* and the Six Dharmas of Nāropa. Because it is a restricted text, however, I have quoted no details.
19. Trungpa and Nālandā 1980, 357; 1982, 235. For an interpretation from the Gelukpa tradition, see also Sopa 1985, 153, 155.
20. Chang 1963, 13.
21. Quoted in Guenther 1963, 161. Guenther notes the importance of not being deceived by the description of "hollow like a reed," which might suggest a physical tube. This simile is used to suggest emptiness, nonsubstantiality, and serves not as a physical description but as an aid to visualization. "[If] we try to concretize it it will break in our hands."
22. There are various traditions concerning the description of the subtle body. For the Karma Kagyü, the *Sabmo Nangdön* is an authoritative description of the 72,000 nāḍīs.
23. This pattern is described in detail in the writings of all Buddhist schools, perhaps nowhere more eloquently than by Nāgārjuna and his Sanskrit commentator Candrakīrti in the *Mūlamadhyamaka-kārikās* XVIII.34–354. While these texts describe the conundrum, there is little meditation instruction concerning the method to liberate oneself from these habitual patterns. This is the missing link that the oral instructions of Vajrayāna provide.
24. This is described thoroughly in the *Pardo Thödröl,* known as the *Tibetan Book of the Dead.* With the dissolution of the physical elements and the skandhas, there is a moment of complete dissolving in which the pardo of dharmatā dawns and the complete space of mind is available. For ordinary beings, this is experienced as a faint or blackout, but for yogis and yoginīs it is a powerful spiritual opportunity. Fremantle and Trungpa 1975; Sogyal Rinpoche 1992.
25. Chang 1963, 60–61.
26. Snellgrove 1954, 1964, 228.
27. Trungpa and Nālandā 1980, 357; Trungpa 1982, 235.
28. Trungpa 1982, 239–40.

29. Huber 1997 is an excellent description of such a guidebook. There is also a chapter on this genre in Cabezon and Jackson 1996.
30. For a focused commentary of this verse, see chapter 2, "Four Aspects of Ḍākinī."
31. Rudra is the quintessential Vajrayāna representation of the inflated ego out of control. This deity is also called in Tibetan literature Mahādeva, Maheśvara, and Bharaiva and historically seems associated with the Śaivite traditions of India. Rudra represents the heterodox, demonic forces of the world subjugated by Guru Rinpoche when he entered Tibet. Here we see a reenactment of that encounter, which the Vajrayāna Buddhist practitioner experiences regularly in the creation phase of sādhana practice, in which the ego is subjugated by the yidam deity. The twenty-four sites sometimes include eight charnel grounds at the boundary of the maṇḍala, yielding a total of thirty-two sacred sites, but that is rarer in the Cakrasaṃvara tradition. Cf. Huber 1997, 120–34.
32. Ricard 1994, 342–43, n. 10.
33. Mount Kailāsa was an important practice site, for example, for Shabkar (1781–1851), the inveterate pilgrim and siddha, who visited many of these sacred sites. The White Lion-Faced Ḍākinī abides at Mount Kailāsa in upper Tibet and is associated with the heruka and ḍākinī's body; the Striped Tiger-Faced Ḍākinī lives at Lachi in central Tibet and is associated with speech; the Black Sow-Faced Ḍākinī dwells at Tsari, in lower Tibet and is associated with the mind. Cf. Ricard 1994, 271–72.
34. An actual description of geographic Lachi can be found in Huber 1994a, 39–52. The more traditional guidebook is found in Huber 1997, 120–34.
35. One list of the twenty-four sacred places: Pullīramalaya, Jālandhara, Uḍḍiyāṇa, Arbuda, Godāvarī, Rāmeśvara, Devīkoṭa, Mālava, Kāmaru, Oḍra, Trīśankuni, Kośala, Kaliṅga, Lampāka, Kāñcī, Himālaya, Pretādhivāsinī, Gṛhadevatā, Saurāṣṭra, Sauvarṇadvīpa, Nagara, Sindhu, Marudeśa, and Kulatā. Trungpa and Nālandā 1982, 243–44.
36. Ricard 1994, 442, n. 1.
37. Ven. Dzogchen Pönlop Rinpoche, interview, November 1996, Boulder, Colorado.
38. Saraha's *Dohakośa.* Snellgrove 1954, 1964, 230.
39. See chapter 4 for more detail on this experience.
40. Ricard 1994, 417.
41. Quoted from an interview in Edou 1996, 103. The other two meanings of *ḍākinī* that His Holiness cites are discussed in chapters 3 and 6.

42. It is difficult to generalize about the placement of the nāḍīs even within a specific tantra as lineages of transmission vary. Some transmissions place the nāḍīs according to the gender of the yidam; others according to the gender of the practitioner. Also variant are the colors of the respective nāḍīs, and which is considered feminine or masculine. This description is therefore quite a general one.
43. Bodhicitta, like phenomena in general, arises with an outer, inner, and secret understanding, as described here. Samuel 1989, 204–5.
44. Guenther 1963, 162–63; Lati and Hopkins, 1979, 14–15. Ringu Tulku Rinpoche, interview, April 1997.
45. This is the depiction in the Six Dharmas of Nāropa. *Hevajra-tantra* I.1.31., Snellgrove 1959, 36–37, 50. This is sometimes said to be an experience parallel with *kuṇḍalinī* in Hindu tantra, but it is important to understand that caṇḍālī in this case refers to the experience of heat itself, not to a deity, and that the actual practices of tummo are among the most closely guarded in Tibetan Buddhism. When these practices are not accessible, scholars have been known to erroneously assume parallels with the more available literature and commentaries on Hindu kuṇḍalinī practice. (Samuel 1993) In Hinduism, Caṇḍālī, literally the "wild one," is associated with heat generated through the yogic practice, and she is a feminine deity who presides over its generation. In Tibetan tantra, caṇḍālī is not a deity but an experience.
46. This definition came from the teachings of Loppön Phurba Dorje, translated by Sarah Harding, March 1999.
47. Snellgrove 1954, 1964, 227. See also Guenther 1993, 113.
48. Ortner 1996. Ortner argued that women's association with embodiment has occurred in various societies because of the socialization of men and women in patriarchal cultural settings. Of course, as Ortner pointed out, women are not inherently closer to nature, for their social roles have reinforced identities that are purely cultural constructs. See 41–42.
49. Cf. Bynum 1991, 186–222.
50. The "ultimate ambiguity" refers to the power held by bodhisattvas to tolerate the reality of emptiness, called *anutpattika-dharma-kṣānti.* See Thurman 1976, 164–65. This contrasts with the work of Ortner (1996), who states that women mediate between culture and nature, are closer to birth and death, and thus are considered ambiguous and dangerous. Sherry Ortner has done most of her fieldwork on gender with Himālayan women, especially Ortner 1974, 73–84.
51. The ḍākinī is sometimes given the name Avadhūtī, which is also the name

for the central channel, for the heat travels up the central channel bringing the bliss of union associated with her. Snellgrove 1959, 36–37.

CHAPTER SIX
The Outer-Outer Ḍākinī

1. Vajra Sow, the queen of all wisdom ḍākinīs. This verse exhorts the Vajrayāna practitioner to see all women as embodiments of wisdom and as sources of the subtle body. Milarepa, in the third of *Six Secret Songs*, Kunga and Cutillo 1978, 17.
2. Holmes 1995, 29. After His Holiness the sixteenth Karmapa fled his ancient Tibetan monastic seat, Tsurphu, in 1959, he sought to establish a seat for the Karma Kagyü outside of Tibet. The Mahārājā of Sikkim offered him Rumtek, the site of a Karma Kagyü monastery founded by the ninth Karmapa, Wangchuk Dorje. On this site, His Holiness built a new monastery, also called Rumtek, which opened in 1967. Douglas and White 1976, 118–20.
3. This account is compiled from several interviews with Khandro Rinpoche and with Dzigar Kongtrül Rinpoche.
4. Mindröling is one of the four important Nyingma monasteries in Tibet, and its tülkus have for generations has been considered among the highest lamas of the Nyingma. Hence it is customary to refer to Mindröling Rinpoche in English as "His Holiness."
5. Khakhyab Dorje was a close disciple of Jamgön Kongtrül Lodrö Thaye, one of the greatest meditation masters and scholars in Tibetan history, and a key figure in the nonsectarian Ri-me movement in late ninteenth-century Tibet. Kongtrül Rinpoche prophesied that the fifteenth Karmapa would take a consort, which he did late in life. Thinley 1980, 155–57.
6. Khandro Rinpoche and her family speculate that His Holiness knew that he would not live to see her or many of his other young tülku charges into adulthood, and so he generously bestowed many empowerments on them while they were children. His Holiness the sixteenth Karmapa died in 1981, leaving the training of the young Karma Kagyü tülkus to others.
7. Havnevik speculated that while many yoginīs were acknowledged as incarnations, no institutional structure for maintaining such incarnations was ever developed even while the *labrang,* which ensured continued institutional support for male tülkus, was supported. She does note that female incarnations were recognized regionally or by certain monasteries. 1990, 133.
8. This honorific title is used broadly for highly regarded women. While the

term *togden* is used for yogins, there is no equivalent term for yoginīs, who are called *jetsünma.* Ibid., 36, 44.

9. In fact, Khandro Rinpoche's sister, Jetsün Dechen Paldön, is just such a female emanation. She was trained side by side with her sister, and they travel and teach together throughout the world.
10. The issue of the child's enthronement was complicated by other concerns regarding her status as a Nyingma or Karma Kagyü tülku. The Mindröling tülkus felt she should be regarded as a Nyingma lineage holder, given her elevated status in the Minling line. The Karma Kagyü, however, regarded her as a Kagyü tülku and wished to bring her to their main monastery, Rumtek. The resulting controversy went on for years and culminated in three separate enthronements, serving all the parties involved. For this reason, Khandro Rinpoche was not empowered until the age of nine.
11. The text of the hagiography (namthar) of Mingyur Paldrön has been preserved in the Mindröling tradition and is recited annually in the monastery celebrations on Tibetan New Year (*Losar*).
12. Khandro Rinpoche was trained by Dagpo Tulku Rinpoche and Gyaltse Tulku Rinpoche and Khenpo Chöcho, and later by Tulku Ugyen Rinpoche. She received many empowerments from her father and from His Holiness Dilgo Khyentse Rinpoche.
13. Dhondup and Tsering 1979, 11–17. This monastery was visited by Waddell and Tucci, who wrote accounts of meeting the respective sitting incarnations.
14. Willis 1987b, 105; Havnevik 1990, 79–80, 133.
15. Shaw 1994, 27, 32, 59, 68.
16. Willis 1987a, 72–74.
17. Herrmann-Pfandt classifies these somewhat differently in five different categories. I have reshaped her categories for the purpose of this study. See Herrmann-Pfandt 1990, 131–35.
18. Falk 1980; Schuster 1981; Schuster-Barnes 1987, 113–14.
19. Havnevik 1990, 134–35. Her informants explained that tülkus may choose any form for incarnation, but since the male form was more highly regarded than the female, they could benefit more beings in a male body.
20. See chapter 1 for more detail on this point.
21. Herrmann-Pfandt 1990, 171–73.
22. Herrmann-Pfandt speculates that this precept relieves none of women's subjugation in Tibetan Buddhism because it perpetuates the objectification of women, albeit on a more subtle level. Ibid., 135, 473–74. It is probable that a similar injunction would be made to see men's bodies as sacred, but in a

patriarchal setting it is appropriate to single out women, who otherwise are objectified or denigrated.

23. Padmakara 1999, 11; cf. T. Tulku 1983, 18; Dowman 1984, 12.
24. In many Mahāyāna traditions, a male body was needed to attain buddhahood, and women were considered inferior of body. This led to a genre of sūtras in which young women manifested miraculous sex changes just before enlightenment, ensuring the Mahāyāna promise of women's spiritual potential. Schuster 1981 extensively treats this issue in Mahāyāna sūtras; the most famous of these sūtras is the *Vimalakīrti-nirdeśa-sūtra.* Thurman 1976.
25. Edou 1996, 199 n. 11. In the case of ḍākas or vīras, the male counterparts of ḍākinīs, the characteristic marks that identify them are similar to those of the ḍākinī, though not identical with the male marks of a *mahāpuruṣa.* Atsara Salé, the consort of Yeshe Tsogyal selected by Guru Rinpoche and author of her biography, was identified by an unusual red mole on his chest, teeth like clockwise-turning conches, slightly bloodshot eyes, a sharp straight nose, azure-blue eyebrows, and handsome and attractive appearance. The mahāpuruṣa marks included webbed fingers and the clockwise coils of his hair. Padmakara 1999, 49–50; Dowman 1984, 48; T. Tulku 1983, 59.
26. The preference for fair, light-skinned beauty reflects an especially Indian bias toward Āryan traits of the high caste. Yet tantric traditions of India may have originated among indigenous Dravidian peoples in which dark complexions are preferred. Given all the cultural influences on tantra in India, it is clear that standards of beauty are not consistent, and as we will see later in this chapter, something attractive is found in all physical types.
27. Quoted in Herrmann-Pfandt 1990, 172–73; Douglas and Bays 1978, 237. The actual thirty-two marks are not enumerated here or in her namthar, though they are mentioned in both places. A different version of her characteristics appears in the account of her previous life as Özer Nangyen (Chönam and Khandro 1998, 42–43). It is unclear here how the mark of "penis covered with a sheath" manifested in this girl child.
28. Padmakara 1999, 11; T. Tulku 1983, 18; Dowman 1984, 14.
29. Edou 1996, 126; Allione 1984, 157.
30. Chönam and Khandro 1998, 90–130.
31. Cf. chapters 3 and 4.
32. This famous mantra is *Hrī Guru Padma Vajra Aḥ,* Padmakara 1999, 7; Dowman 1984, 9, 11. The seed syllable EVAṂ as representing the joining of masculine and feminine is treated in chapter 3.
33. Edou 1996, 125–26.
34. Ibid., 127.

35. Douglas and Bays 1978, 296–97. Oddly, the namthar of Maṇḍāravā describes these events as the immolation of Guru Rinpoche while she languished in a prison. This is the version also told by Jamgön Kongtrül in *The Precious Garland of Lapis Lazuli* (352), Schmidt 1994, 264–65.
36. According to the account by Dorje Dze Öd, the Drikung Kagyü teacher, there were thirty-two ugly aspects of the old woman, and his account correlates this with thirty-two negative qualities of saṃsāra, in their outer, inner, and secret aspects. Gyaltsen 1990, 59–60. Another similar story of a learned paṇḍit's more polite encounter with the ugly old ḍākinī are recorded in the *Ordinary Biography of Tilopa* (Nālandā 1997, 145–46).
37. Guenther, 1963, 24.
38. Ibid., 25.
39. Ibid. There is a further discussion of the topic of the aged ḍākinī in chapter 8.
40. Chapter 1 cites Guenther's Jungian-style commentary on the appearance of the ḍākinī and the meaning of her horrible attributes. We may assume that the interpretation is his own. Guenther 1963, ii–iii.
41. There are some traditions of tantric biography that speak of Niguma as Nāropa's consort and wisdom ḍākinī, but these are contradicted by the actual Niguma sources. According to Guenther (1963), Nāropa wed Niguma in an arranged marriage that dissolved because of his yearning for the spiritual life, and "according to the widely practised habit of calling a female with whom one has had any relation 'sister' she became known as 'the sister of Nāropa' " 1963, 283.
42. Allione 1984, 205–12; Dudjom 1991, 771–74. She is one of the "two characteristic ḍākinī who were the real presence of Yeshe Tsogyal," the other being the fourteenth-century human ḍākinī Künga Bumpa, Dudjom 1991, 72, n. 1020.
43. Secret Cave of Supreme Bliss, at Khyungchen Dingwei Trak in Zarmolung. Dudjom 1991, 771.
44. The text was *Khandro Sangwa Kundü*. Ibid., 772.
45. Ibid., 773. In so doing, they associated her with minor aboriginal Tibetan deities who are consorts of the sky gods, who reside in lakes and sometimes mountains and are connected with medicine and healing. They were subdued by Guru Rinpoche but were never converted to the dharma. These deities are associated with Bön. Nebesky-Wojkowitz 1975, 198–202.
46. See the discussion of karmamudrā later in this chapter.
47. The story is told that when the treasure was unlocked, its essence was a vulture as large as a garuḍa. Riding on its back he came into the presence of Vajrasattva, who bestowed the empowerment of the terma. In an outer sense,

this is spoken of as Chökyi Wangchuk's challenges in translating the difficult text. Dudjom 1991, 763; Herrmann-Pfandt 1990, 298, n. 8.

48. She appears as one of two women on the list of 108 tertöns. Other examples include Pemasel, the first tertön of the *Khandro Nyingthik,* and her two female successors, Rikma Sangye Kyi and Chomo Pema Drol. Eventually these teachings were propagated by Longchenpa, but not without precipitous obstacles on the way. Harding In press, 3–6; Dudjom 1991, 554–55; Thondup 1996, 98–99. The special role women have played in terma lineages is discussed in chapter 8.

49. Gross 1993; Sponberg 1992; Schuster-Barnes 1987; Klein 1985b; Aziz 1987; Havnevik 1990.

50. Havnevik 1990, 135. Of course this task was begun in 1984 with Allione's collection of yoginī biographies, now in its second edition, 2000. For additions to Allione's work, see Willis 1999, Havnevik 1990, and Madrong 1997. I would like to add to their lists Khandro Ugyen Tsolmo, whose life story began this chapter; Mingyur Paldrön of Mindröling; and Shanzen Jetsün.

51. Dowman 1984, 89; T. Tulku 1983, 105–06.

52. These events are sprinkled throughout the accounts of her life. See, for example, Dowman 1984, 24, 118–19, 44, 89, 113, 77–82, respectively. Cf. Padmakara 1999; T. Tulku 1983. According to Havnevik's research, the concern about gossip still pervades the yoginī's life in contemporary Tibetan communities. 1990, 147–49.

53. Edou 1996, 132; Allione 1984, 161.

54. Allione 1984, 162; Edou 1996, 133.

55. Edou 1996, 144; Allione 1984, 171. Machik skillfully pacified the embarrassment and concern of her benefactor by singing a verse acknowledging it.

56. I.i.v; v. 16–18. Snellgrove 1959, 60 n. 7; 62 n. 2. Mother and sister refer in brief to the eight kinds of female relatives: mother, sister, daughter, niece, maternal uncle's wife, maternal aunt, mother-in-law, and paternal aunt. (II.v.59) These eight refer to the eight blissful consorts who are attendants to the maṇḍala of Hevajra. For detailed commentary, see Farrow and Menon 1992, 257.

57. This tradition is traced in the *Lalitavistara.* Feminist critique considers this question indicative of the patriarchal concerns in assigning ḍākinī classifications to some women like mothers, sisters, or consorts, since it is evidence of status derived from the male rather than from the woman's own accomplishments. And even if she is considered a ḍākinī, she is usually viewed as subordinate to her realized offspring. Herrmann-Pfandt 1990 175–76.

58. Trungpa and Nālandā 1982, 166–69.
59. Robinson 1979, 117–19; Dowman 1985, 123–29; Dudjom 1991, 485–87.
60. Guenther 1963.
61. Ibid., 18.
62. See instructions on the practice of the Six Yogas of Niguma in Mullin 1985, 99–151; and Kalu 1986, 98–103.
63. Havnevik 1990, 184–86. Her informants commented that nuns and yoginīs command respect only after long lives of practice and accomplishment, but the wives and consorts of the lama are accorded immediate respect.
64. Dowman 1985, 68; cf. Robinson 1979, 43.
65. Padmakara 1999, 44–45, 94–95.
66. Ricard 1996, 41. Khandro Lhamo remembered working in the fields and being approached by lamas who told her they would take her to Khyentse Rinpoche's retreat, since it had been predicted that she was an auspicious consort. Although Rinpoche seemed not the least interested in taking a wife, he was very ill and near death and agreed because of a prophecy from his teacher. She described their life together in retreat with great charm and detail. This phenomenon, which is closely associated with tertöns, is discussed briefly in Gyatso 1998, 86, 140.
67. Ven. Dzigar Kongtrül Rinpoche, private communication, 1992, Boulder, Colorado. This phenomenon is also described by Havnevik 1990, 184–85.
68. This practice is described in personal essays by two Vajrayoginī practitioners. Gross 1998a, 199–210; and Pay 1997.
69. This observation accords with Gyatso's discussions with Khenpo Jigme Phüntsok, who suggested that the readers of the secret biography of Jigme Lingpa were ḍākinīs, though she did not make the connection between the ḍākinī status of the students and their devotional connections with their guru. 1998, 263.
70. Herrmann-Pfandt 1990, 369–94.
71. Shaw 1994, 4–8, 74f; Kalff 1979, 53f; Herrmann-Pfandt 1990, 307–09, 369.
72. Herrmann-Pfandt 1990, 369; Campbell 1996, 124–46.
73. Havnevik 1990, 64–84.
74. Informal comments, 1985, Boulder, Colorado. For more detail on nuns' vocation, see Ibid., 46.
75. This is in some contrast to Herrmann-Pfandt's statements that ritual feast offerings of this kind are currently practiced rarely if at all (*selten, falls überhaupt, in der ursprunglich konzipierten Form praktiziert worden sind*), which is certainly not true, especially with the advent of large communities of male

and female tantric practitioners in the West who practice these rituals together. Even if no women are present in traditional monastic gaṇacakras, men who practice the female yidams are themselves ḍākinīs when performing the ritual.

76. This is an example of the definition of ḍākinī as the accomplishment of the inner heat (tummo) yoga of the subtle body, as described in chapter 2. It is important to note that Yeshe Tsogyal prefaced her teachings by calling Shelkar Dorje Tsomo a "wisdom-ḍākinī."
77. T. Tulku 1983, 190–91; Dowman 1984, 162–63.
78. Shelkar Dorje Tsomo is listed as one of the female accomplished masters who were disciples of Guru Rinpoche, along with Maṇḍāravā and Yeshe Tsogyal. Shelkar Dorje Tsomo was known for the siddhi of crossing rivers as if they were plains. Dudjom 1991, 536.
79. Ven. Tsoknyi Rinpoche, interview, July 1994, Boulder, Colorado. "Ordinary human beings, women, are part of the ḍākinī, belong to the class [*rimpa*] of ḍākinī. Ordinary men are part of ḍāka." Do ordinary women know they are part of ḍākinī? "Some know, some don't know. But they have no need to know. The nature of women is part of the ḍākinī."
80. George 1974, 81–82.
81. Chönam and Khandro 1998, 87.
82. Dudjom 1996; International Translation Committee 1998.
83. Willis 1972, 103–4.
84. This comes from the commentary by Ngari Panchen, Pema Wangyi Gyalpo. Dudjom 1996, 120.
85. Willis 1972, 103.
86. Dudjom 1996, 122.
87. *Abhidharmakosá* II. 1–13, Poussin 1988.
88. Gross 1993, 81–98.
89. See note 51.
90. Padmakara 1999, 91; cf. Dowman, 1984, 86. This is commonly repeated in popular parlance among Tibetans. Havnevik 1990, 185; Beyer 1978, 47.
91. This notion directly contradicts the findings of Miranda Shaw (1994), who speaks of women in the Indian tantric tradition as completely and exclusively female. She states that there is no "abstract feminine or masculine principle." 35–37. Also asserted in Simmer-Brown 1994.
92. Ven. Tsoknyi Rinpoche, interview, July 1994.
93. Dzigar Kongtrül Rinpoche, interview, March 15, 1991.
94. Ven. Khandro Rinpoche, interview, August 1994.

95. Ibid. Very similar observations came in Havnevik's interviews with nuns, tülkus, and laypeople. 1990, 148–50, 184–85.
96. Ven. Dzogchen Pönlop Rinpoche, interview, November 1996.
97. Ven. Ringu Tulku Rinpoche, interview, January 1997. Again, similar observations were made by Havnevik's informants, both male and female. 1990, 184–85.
98. Trungpa 1975.
99. Ven. Dzogchen Pönlop Rinpoche, interview, November 1996.
100. Ven. Khandro Rinpoche, interview, August 1994.
101. Ven. Dzogchen Pönlop Rinpoche, interview, November 1996.
102. These two extremes are treated classically as two sides of the same condition whose antidote is presence of mind, a kind of light-handed warning system that rouses one to renewed mindfulness. Lhalungpa 1986, 23–26; Berzin 1978, 48–51.
103. Ven. Dzogchen Pönlop Rinpoche, interview, November 1996.
104. This is the most prevalent of the teachings of Tibetan lamas, as can be seen, for example, in the teachings of His Holiness the fourteenth Dalai Lama. Cf. Piburn 1990, 15–27, 52–57.
105. Thurman 1976, chapt. 10. In fact, the sūtra recounts how the great Tathāgata Sugandhakūṭa taught in his realm called "all scents beautiful scents." There he taught through sound and language; every tree emitted a beautiful scent, and upon smelling it the bodhisattva was instantly elevated to the highest bhūmis. He and his students marveled at the skillful means of Śākyamuni, who taught humans who were so dense and ensnared by desire that they needed teachings as crude and obvious as those of the Four Noble Truths. 81–83.
106. I.ix.19. Snellgrove 1959, 1980, 80.
107. I.x.9. Ibid., 81.
108. Quoted from a personal interview by Edou 1996, 103. The other two meanings of *ḍākinī* cited by His Holiness are quoted in chapters 5 and 6.
109. For this description, I am indebted to Khenpo Tsultrim Gyamtso's teachings in an interview at Rocky Mountain Shambhala Center, July 1997.
110. Harding 1996, 35.
111. Schmidt 1994, 56.
112. Personal interview, Rocky Mountain Shambhala Center, July 1997.
113. Guenther 1963, 77.
114. II.ii.c. Snellgrove 1959, 1980, 91.
115. Padmakara 1999, 45; cf. Dowman 1984, 44.

116. Padmakara 1999, 52; cf. Dowman 1984, 51.
117. Padmakara 1999, 93–99; Dowman 1984, 95.
118. Kagyü lamas claim that, albeit unusual, Gampopa attained full enlightenment by the time of his death without a yogic sexual consort. Yet there is also speculation that Gampopa's wealthy patroness was beautiful and considered a "female emanation," a euphemism for incarnate ḍākinī, so it is possible that he practiced karmamudrā, but in great secrecy. Stewart 1995, 155.
119. Shaw 1994, 146.
120. Snellgrove 1959, 1980, 47; Gäng 1988, 113.
121. Gäng 1988, 265–67; Wayman 1977, 1980, 300–02.
122. One example of a Western lineage holder of the *ngak-phang* line is Ngakpa Chögyam, a Welsh successor to the Aro Ter lineage of the Nyingma school.
123. Aris 1988, 146, 152–56.
124. Fields and Cutillo 1994, 118. Cf. Houston 1982; Barks 1992.
125. Fields and Cutillo 1994, 117.
126. The issue of secrecy in Tibetan tantra is a controversial one, subject to feminist critique discussed in Campbell 1996, 97–123; 126–30. But it is important to understand why, traditionally speaking in Tibet, it was a part of karmamudrā practice.
127. This refers to her coming from one of the classic ḍākinī families. Other issues regarding her birth parentage and so on are subject to some debate, depending upon the sources. Indian Buddhist tantric sources emphasize women of low-caste or tribal status; Tibetan sources stress consorts of high social standing.
128. T. Tulku 1983, 30–31; cf. Dowman 1984, 24.
129. Dudjom 1996, 123; Herrmann-Pfandt 1990, 300.
130. Schmidt 1994, 56–57.
131. II.xi. Snellgrove 1959, 1980, 118–19; Herrmann-Pfandt 1990, 299–300.
132. For a different description of these three kinds of ḍākinīs, see chapter 2.
133. The actual quote from His Holiness the Dalai Lama presents two conflicting interpretations of these stages. Hopkins 1977, 27–28. This presentation is supported to some degree in Longdröl Lama's *Collected Works* presentation on ḍākinīs in the Anuttara-yoga-tantra, quoted in Wayman 1973, 184. Also see *Saṃvarodaya-tantra* IX.12, Tsuda 1974, 267.
134. Guenther notes the variations of names of these types, drawing from the traditions of Tilopa, Padma Karpo, and Rechungpa, who names only three types instead of four. Guenther 1963, 77 n. 1.
135. The *Saṃvarodaya-tantra* specifically correlates the four types of consorts to

the four traditional retinue ḍākinīs of the *Cakrasaṃvara-tantra:* Ḍākinī (blue, vajra family); Lāmā (green, karma family); Khaṇḍarohā (red, padma family); and Rūpiṇī (yellow, ratna family). Tsuda 1974, 324; Trungpa and Nālandā 1986, 1989.

136. Cf. Wayman 1973, 184; Kalff 1978, 155; Herrmann-Pfandt 1990, 303–04.

137. Danielou 1994, 90–93.

138. Hopkins 1992, 153–57, 171–77. Particularly parallel to the retinue families are the places in which to entertain the four types of women, the lotus, conch, picture, and elephant corresponding respectively to the vajra, padma, ratna, and karma families.

139. Khenpo Tsultrim Gyamtso Rinpoche, interview, Rocky Mountain Shaṁbhala Center, July 1997.

140. Tsuda 1974, 324.

141. Tāranātha introduced this by speaking of Machik as a padminī, one of the four types of consorts. Compare Tāranātha to the padminī description in the *Kāma-sūtra:* "The lotus woman (padminī) has tender limbs like lotus stems; her sexual secretions smell of lotus. She has the eyes of a startled doe; the edges of her eyes are red. She hesitates, out of modesty, to expose her beautiful breasts. Her nose resembles a sesame flower. She is virtuous and respectful by nature. Her face is white like a jasmine flower. Her sanctuary of Eros seems like a full-blown lotus. Her body is thin and light and she walks delicately like a goose. Her words are mixed with sighs, like a goose, her figure is slight, her belly divided into three parts. She eats little, is modest and wise, but proud. She loves beautiful clothes and flowers." Danielou 1994, 92.

142. Roerich 1949, 220–21.

143. Hopkins 1992, 173. Gedün Chöpel was born in 1905 in Amdo and was recognized as a Nyingma tülku. He was trained in scholastic debate in the Gelukpa tradition and became a renowned debater with outrageous disguises and debate methods. In India he learned Sanskrit and studied the *Kāma-sūtra* and many other Indian texts, and he befriended scholars, missionaries, and travelers. He is known for brilliant composition of texts, the most noted of which was his *Treatise on Passion,* quoted here. His presentation of types of women and men may have an idiosyncratic flavor, but it follows the contours of more traditional presentations.

144. Tsuda 1974, 325. The śaṅkhinī is associated in the *Saṃvarodaya-tantra* with the primary retinue ḍākinī of Cakrasaṃvara called Khaṇḍarohā, "lady arisen from a piece." See chapter 4 for a fuller description of her role.

145. Hopkins 1992, 174.

146. Dowman 1984, 119, 269, 120–121.
147. Tsuda 1974, 325. The citrinī is associated in the *Saṃvarodaya-tantra* with the primary retinue ḍākinī of Cakrasaṃvara called Rūpiṇī, "beautiful form." See chapter 4 for a fuller description of her role.
148. Hopkins 1992, 174.
149. Tsuda 1974, 324–25.
150. Hopkins 1992, 174–75.
151. Ibid., 171.
152. Khenpo Tsultrim Gyamtso Rinpoche, interview, Rocky Mountain Shambhala Center, July 1997.
153. The third abhiṣeka is the wisdom empowerment, which points out the inseparability of bliss and emptiness through revealing the secret of sexual union. Upon receiving the pardo teachings, Tseringma prostrated to Milarepa, proclaiming, "Oh Jetsun! From now on I will follow you and practice karmamudrā with you until I have consummated my experience and realization of the quintessential *bardo* instruction. Please always remember and look after me." Chang 1977, 352–53.
154. Ibid., 358.
155. Ibid., 358–59. It is unclear from the text how Tseringma filled these types, for it is her four retinue ḍākinīs who fit each in a specific way. Perhaps she fulfilled all of them perfectly. After all, it is understood that the retinue are merely symbolic representations of the fullness of her realization.
156. Commentary on these four stages is taken from the namthar of Nāropa, Guenther 1963, 78. Also, Khenpo Tsultrim Gyamtso, Rinpoche, interview. Rocky Mountain Shambhala Center, July 1997.
157. These are the four joys called joy (*ānanda, gawa*), perfect joy (*paramānanda, chogga*), supreme joy (*vilakṣana, gadrel*) and coemergent joy (*sahajānanda, lhen-chig kyepe gawa*). Guenther 1963, 78.
158. Yeshe Tsogyal described each of these stages in her blissful union with her guru and consort, Guru Rinpoche. Padmakara 1999, 40–44.
159. Chang 1977, 360.

CHAPTER SEVEN
Living Encounters with the Ḍākinī

1. Supplication to Yeshe Tsogyal, entitled "Hail My Lady!" Privately published poem composed at Gampo Abbey, Cape Breton, Nova Scotia, September 1997.

2. The description here follows the more general profile of the karma ḍākinī, and does not treat her especially in her form as a human woman who qualifies as an ideal consort in the practice of karmamudrā, discussed in chapter 6. Much of this material is only reluctantly shared by Tibetan lamas, and this presentation seems to be of general interest and value.
3. Ven. Dzogchen Pönlop Rinpoche, interview, October 1997, Boulder, Colorado. Ven. Chagdud Tulku Rinpoche, interview, July 1995, Boulder, Colorado.
4. Trungpa 1976, 73–82; 1991b, 25–41. See descriptions of these in *Hevajra-tantra* I. xi, which describe the gazes, breathing, and appropriate locations for each practice.
5. Trungpa 1976, 77.
6. Dudjom 1991, 579.
7. Robinson 1979, 217; Dowman 1985, 325–26.
8. She is described as a kṣetrapāla ḍākinī (*shing-kyong kyi khandroma*). Trungpa 1982, 122.
9. Lhalungpa 1977, 48–75.
10. Chang 1977, 463, 236–38.
11. She appeared to him in a variety of scenarios in his ordinary, extraordinary, and secret biographies and represented him as a messenger to a great feast in Uḍḍiyāṇa, speaking of him as her brother. Nālandā 1997, 148.
12. Guenther 1963, 24–25. Another example is that of Saroruha, who was sent by the ugly wood-gatherer to the guru Anaṅgavajra. Herrmann-Pfandt 1990, 361.
13. Templeman 1989, 71–72.
14. Das 1992, 167.
15. Robinson 1979, 22–24; Dowman 1985, 33–35.
16. Herrmann-Pfandt points out that these examples cannot be found for yoginīs; she speculates that this is probably because women were already sensitive to lower social standing as a result of their gender, having to honor husbands even when they were ruthless and morally detestable. For this reason, she speculates, yoginīs did not particularly have this style of class-oriented arrogance that needed to be removed by practice with low-caste partners. Herrmann-Pfandt 1990, 311.
17. Germano and Gyatso 2000.
18. Ricard 1994, 346 n. 60.
19. Maṇḍāravā took on many other forms such as the Lion-Headed Ḍākinī, the Nine-Headed Ḍākinī, and so forth. Chönam and Khandro 1998.

20. Tāranātha's account is the one that speaks of the dog as a bitch, giving a clue to her real identity as a ḍākinī. Butön and other contemporary accounts say the dog became Maitreya the teacher. Chimpa and Chattopadhyaya 1970, 157.
21. Dowman 1985, 199–200; Robinson 1979, 128–30.
22. Trungpa and Nālandā 1982, 16–25.
23. Herrmann-Pfandt 1990, 290.
24. Dudjom 1991, 567.
25. Ibid., 825.
26. Robinson 1979, 161–62; Dowman 1985, 245.
27. Dudjom 1991, 771–72.
28. Gyatso 1998, 50.
29. Allione 1984, 94. This was said of the voice of the human ḍākinī Nangsa Obum.
30. Germano and Gyatso 2000, 335–36. When Longchenpa failed to recognize Namdru Remati, she was bitterly jealous and threatening. While he asked about her identity, he was not intimidated, having already received many ḍākinī visitations and treasures.
31. Harding In press. 105.
32. Gyatso explores this phenomenon in the secret autobiographies of Jigme Lingpa, suggesting both the necessity for legitimation and its perils. Legitimation is drawn from visionary experience, proof in the discovery of terma texts, and confirmation by legendary Tibetan and especially Indian sources of authority. This may suggest that the prestige of the ḍākinī in Tibet may derive in part from her Indian origins. For a complete treatment of this phenomenon, see Gyatso 1998, 148–53.
33. Chang 1977, 424.
34. Abhayadattaśrī, *Caturaśitisiddha-pravṛtti* 87–88, cited in Herrmann-Pfandt 1990, 361
35. Kunga and Cutillo 1986, 166.
36. Mönlam Drup was the previous incarnation of Machik Lapdrön, and these two ḍākinīs, Nairātmyā and Mahāmāyā, were each giving prophecy. Edou 1996, 121; Allione 1984, 151–52.
37. Edou 1996, 141–42; Allione 1984, 169.
38. Young described the important role of dreams in Tibetan religion even before the introduction of Buddhism. In Buddhist Tibet, dreams foretell auspicious births, reveal pith teachings, and guide the meditation practices of yogins and yoginīs. Her interpretation of the ḍākinī dreams followed the feminist critiques that suggest that the ḍākinī functions only in the male

imagination and that even women's dreams are coopted by men. 1999, 147–66.

39. Roerich 1949, 730–31; Mullin 1985, 97–98. Niguma's Six Dharmas closely parallel her former husband Nāropa's, received also from the primordial buddha Vajradhara. These teachings were carried through a separate lineage traced back to her primary student Khyungpo Naljor. Niguma requested that they be kept secret, passed only one-to-one, guru to disciple, for seven generations before being propagated more widely. See instructions on these practices in Mullin 1985, 99–151; see also Kalu 1986, 98–103.
40. Kunga and Cutillo 1986, 169, 200.
41. For an explanation of why this is so, see chapter 5.
42. Chang 1977, 4; also 25, 233, 235–36.
43. Holmes 1981, 8.
44. Goodman 1983, 22; Gyatso 1998, 57.
45. Germano and Gyatso 2000.
46. Mullin 1985, 96.
47. Dudjom 1991, 843.
48. Ibid., 579.
49. Goodman 1983, 25.
50. Edou 1996, 157; Allione 1984, 181.
51. Harding 1998, 23.
52. Guenther 1963, 27.
53. Dudjom 1991, 863.
54. Caroline Walker Bynum demonstrated how medieval mystical women "manipulated the dominant tradition to free themselves from the burdens of fertility yet made fertility a powerful symbol" through an inversion of meanings of the body and of food in religious language and imagery. Bynum 1991, 1987, 1995. We shall discuss the relevance of these images for ḍākinī hagiographies here.
55. See the introduction for an exposition of the meaning of this key image.
56. Douglas and Bays 1978, 370 ff; Herrmann-Pfandt 1990, 341–42; Trungpa and Nālandā 1980, 168.
57. Padmakara 1999, 68; Dowman 1984, 66; T. Tulku 1983, 80.
58. An important event of this sort was treated in some detail in the introduction. Ḍākinīs often are said to have all the deities of the tantric maṇḍala arranged within the space of their bodies, as is said of Yeshe Tsogyal in her ritual. Thondup 1983, 1992, 46.
59. Chönam and Khandro 1998, 178.

60. Nālandā 1982, 101 n. This theme appears in other ḍākinī stories as well: cf. Chönam and Khandro 1998, 178.
61. People Doha, *ślokas* 106–08. Snellgrove 1954, 1964, 235–36. Cf. also Guenther 1969, 48, 50. In his most recent book, Guenther again attempts to translate these ślokas, taking the commentaries into account, but the result is most awkward and obscure. See Guenther 1993, 113–14, 188 n. 126–27.
62. This interpretation is drawn in greatly simplified form from the summaries of Guenther of the commentary by Karma Thrinley, which drew on interpretations by Lingrepa, Rechungpa, Parphupa, and Rangjung Dorje. Guenther 1969, 48–53.
63. One can understand this in the context of subtle-body yoga practices, which accelerate the cessation of dualistic mind and the direct perception of sacred world (tag-nang). This is proper preparation for the succeeding empowerments that he was to receive.
64. Gyaltsen 1990, 105–06.
65. Dowman 1985, 318; Robinson 1979, 212–13. The guru is also called Kṛṣṇācārya, who was associated with the severed-headed Vajravārāhī practice, which he taught on his deathbed. In another account by Tāranātha, the sisters danced off into the sky, higher and higher, disappearing into rainbow light. Tāranātha's account is followed by the comment that when many worldly rākṣasas and ḍākinīs began to sever their own heads in this manner, as an antidote Vajravārāhī herself appeared in a severed-headed form, and the siddhi became common among siddhas devoted to her. Templeman 1989, 63. This tradition has much more prominence in Hindu and Newari tantra than it does in Tibet. See Benard 1994 for details. It is surprising that there is no chapter on the Chinnamastā in the recent study of the treatment of women's heads in the history of religions. See Eilberg-Schwartz and Doniger 1995. While there are interesting parallels here with other traditions, in tantric Buddhism it is the ḍākinī herself who cuts up her body and offers it. Generally, these accounts are downplayed and discouraged in the contemporary Tibetan tradition.
66. Holmes 1995, 137. According to the oral tradition, the vajra crown is traced back to a prince from before the time of Buddha Dīpaṅkara, who meditated on a mountainside for one hundred million years. In honor of his vast and profound samādhi, thirteen million ḍākinīs came, each offering a strand of her own hair, from which they wove a vajra crown, ornamented with jewels. The crown offered by the Chinese emperor was until 1959 always kept at Tsurphu Monastery. At the time of the tenth Karmapa, the Emperor of Jang

(Yunnan) had an exact replica of the Ch'eng Tsu crown made, and presented it to the patriarch. This crown was taken on the Karmapa's travels and used for the Black Crown ceremonies. It is unknown which the sixteenth Karmapa took with him into exile in 1959.

67. Thinley 1980, 41–45, 74–75; Douglas and White 1976, 34–35, 61–65. This ceremony was photographed on many occasions during the life of the sixteenth Karmapa, but the most accessible record can been seen in the film *The Lion's Roar,* Centre Productions, 1982.
68. Lhalungpa 1977, 98–100. Dagmema, whose Tibetan name is identical to Nairātmya in Sanskrit, means "no self," a reminder that her basic nature is emptiness and vast space, a confirmation that she is an embodied wisdom ḍākinī. Her relationship with Milarepa was close and very personal as he underwent the trials of receiving teachings from Marpa, and her grief at his leaving was real and heartfelt.
69. Ricard 1994, 262.
70. Ibid., 262–63.
71. Trungpa 1982, 240.
72. The Queen Ḍākinī was also known as the ḍākinī Lekyi Wangmo, Karmeśvarī, the ḍākinī who transmitted the Eight Sādhana teachings to the eight vidyādharas in the Mahāyoga-yāna tradition.
73. The three empowerments were, respectively, the Buddha Amitābha blessing, the Avalokiteśvara empowerment, and the Hayagrīva empowerment. Cf. Evans-Wentz 1970, 132–33; Schmidt 1993, 42–43. See also Douglas and Bays 1978, 219–21.
74. Dudjom 1991, 469; Douglas and Bays 1978, 223.
75. Thondup 1996, 185. Do Khyentse Rinpoche had numerous encounters with ḍākinīs throughout his life. This is merely one of many such tales.
76. Chönam and Khandro 1998, 166–67.
77. Gyatso 1998, 58, 94. In the text this is spoken of as liberation through experience (*nyong-dröl*), which is contrasted with a slightly less powerful realization, liberation through seeing (*thong-dröl*). In other words, the act of consuming overcomes dualistic habits of any kind.
78. Kalu 1994, 128–29.
79. Karthar 1990, 97.
80. Kalu 1997, 175–76. It is significant that Kalu Rinpoche told this story, for he held the lineages of two of the most famous ḍākinīs in the Kagyü lineage, Sukhasiddhi and Niguma, whose student Khyungpo Naljor passed them on

to the Shangpa Kagyü, one of the lesser Kagyü schools. This school has now all but vanished, its lineage holders extremely rare.

81. Buddha Śākyamuni is known for turning the wheel of dharma three times, thereby establishing the dharma through verbal teaching to specific groups of disciples. In Vajrayāna language, the gaṇacakra is the "wheel of gathering" turned by the second Buddha, Guru Rinpoche, establishing the Vajrayāna dharma through the joining of wisdom and skillful means in a ritual setting. The requisites for such a feast are the sacred substances of torma (sacramental cakes), meat, and liquor. Kongtrül 1995, 44–45.
82. Templeman 1984, 27.
83. Harding 1996, 56.
84. Mullin 1985, 96. Other famous yogins who attended ḍākinī feasts for teachings included Kāṇhapa, Atīśa, and Lūipa. Shaw 1994, 82.
85. This has been fully treated in Shaw 1994, chapt. 4; Herrmann-Pfandt 1991, chapt. 10. Herrmann-Pfandt traced how the women's gatherings in early Indian Buddhist tantra were appropriated by men in the development of tantra in Tibet, and this became central to her argument that the patriarchy of Tibetan Buddhism has usurped female power.
86. Lhalungpa 1977, 113.
87. Chang 1977, 25.
88. Ibid., 233.
89. For summaries of these sources, see Willis 1999, 145–58, 1987b, 96–117; Madrong 1997; Havnevik 1990. Additional information can be drawn from Allione 1984; Chönam and Khandro 1998; Dowman 1984, 1985; Drolma 1995; Dudjom 1991; Edou 1996; Gross 1987, 1989; Harding In press; Herrmann-Pfandt 1990; Padmakara 1999; Shaw 1994; T. Tulku 1983; Thondup 1996.
90. See a description of this in Bynum 1986, 13, also quoted in chapter 1. The following observations have been shaped by her suggestions concerning the characteristic qualities of women's experience of gendered symbols.
91. These obstacles are discussed in chapter 6. Similar themes can be seen in the hagiographies of the yoginīs Chomo Menmo, Drenchen Rema, Nangsa Obum, Machik Lapdrön, Maṇḍāravā, Ayu Khandro, Yeshe Tsogyal, Niguma, and Pemasel and her successors, Trompa Gyen, and Dorje Tso of the Dzogchen tradition.
92. Padmakara 1999, 12–22; Dowman 1984, 15–24; Allione 1984, 69–90;
93. Chönam and Khandro 1998, 95–112.
94. Edou 1996, 126–30; Allione 1984, 158–65, 216, 225–26, 241–42.
95. Allione 1984, 210; Dudjom 1991, 773; Harding In press, 3–4.

96. Dudjom 1991, 773–74; Allione 1984, 239–55.
97. Edou 1996, 123.
98. Ibid. The great yogin Tampa Sanggye threatened Milarepa, saying that the worldly ḍākinīs were furious because of his indiscriminate singing of songs about the most secret of teachings. In revenge they had removed his heart, breath, and life essence and dined on them in a sacramental feast. Milarepa responded by immediately singing more joyful songs. Chang 1977, 607–08. In an interesting contrasexual example, Namkhai Nyingpo of Nub received "heart within the chest" teachings that he called the "magic of the ḍākinīs," and he displayed his understanding to King Trisong Detsen by cutting open his chest with a knife of white silver and showing the deities of the *Viśuddha-sādhana.* When the king prostrated with respect, jealous ministers expelled him from the kingdom. Schmidt 1993, 86.
99. The conch is another prevalent symbol of the ḍākinī, especially of a ḍākinī consort. It is also one of the eight auspicious symbols (*tashi tag-gye*) common in Tibetan iconography. In Indian culture, it is a prevalent symbol of the feminine; in Tibet, its outer meaning is associated with its use as a musical instrument, announcing the fame of the Buddha's teachings. As such, in tantra it is associated with the power of the teachings of the whispered lineage, the oral instructions from one's guru. Dagyab 1995, 24, 54–55. See chapter 6.
100. Dudjom 1991, 772.
101. Edou 1996, 150–52.
102. Ibid., 123; Allione 1984, 153–54.
103. Harding In press, 117.
104. See chapter 6 for commentary on this.
105. Edou 1996, 123; Allione 1984, 153–54.
106. Chönam and Khandro 1998, 85.
107. Avalokiteśvara often appears in the form of a woman, and Gelongma Palmo supplicates him/her with this verse, "Moonlike mother of Buddhas, whose form is that of a beautiful goddess. . . . Empty by nature, you [emerge] from emptiness in the form of a woman and tame living beings thereby." Shaw 1994, 129; Ortner 1989, 181–82; Kalu 1984, 96–97; Willis 1999, 148–49. Gelongmo Palmo was known especially for introducing the Chenresik practice conjoined with fasting that subsequently became so popular in Tibet.
108. Just before this crisis, Yeshe Tsogyal prayed to her guru for support, and Guru Rinpoche appeared to her in his form as a heruka and nourished her with a skull-cup of chang, the white bodhicitta essence of the masculine

principle, which empowered her to continue her practice. With these two empowerments, she received both masculine and feminine blessings, though in somewhat different forms. Padmakara 1999, 73–74; Dowman 1984, 70; T. Tulku 1983, 85–87.

109. Edou 1996, 142–45; Allione 1984, 168–71.
110. Padmakara 1999, 183; Dowman 1984, 167; T. Tulku 1983, 195–96.
111. Allione 1984, 17; Gross 1993, 108–09; Herrmann-Pfandt 1990, 154; 296. Note previous discussions about the nonexistence of the ḍāka figure in Tibetan Buddhism—instead there is mention of pawos, heroes, who play a minor role. Specifically, Herrmann-Pfandt notes that there is not one Sanskrit or Tibetan source that spoke of ḍākas in service of the enlightenment of a female yoginī, though apparently she was unaware of the Maṇḍāravā account. Herrmann-Pfandt also notes that in relationship to the guru the hagiographic accounts speak only of her service to him, not his to her. 1990, 154–55. This topic is not treated in detail here, but there are certainly counterexamples of the latter in the hagiographies of the yoginīs from minor to major.
112. See chapter 4.
113. Padmakara 1999, 49–60; Dowman 1984, 44–54; Chönam and Khandro 1998.
114. Dudjom 1991, 490–91. The resulting birth was a deep embarrassment for the nun Sudharmā, who disposed of her son in an ash pit in shame. When the infant remained unscathed, she realized that he was a special child, an emanation, and she raised him with loving care. The image of giving birth is a powerful spiritual one, which can also be seen in the yogin's being inspired by the ḍākinī, which "gives birth" to the powerful tantric text as in the cases of termas.
115. Herrmann-Pfandt 1990, 293–94.
116. Chönam and Khandro 1998, 27; Padmakara 1999, 8–11; Dowman 1984, 11–12.
117. Chönam and Khandro 1998, 167.
118. Padmakara 1999, 191–92; Dowman 1984, 172–76; T. Tulku 1983, 201–05.
119. Kalu 1997, 176.
120. Allione 1984, 226–27.

CHAPTER EIGHT
Protectors of the Tantric Teachings

1. This song was sung by the yogin Shabkar, a song of Milarepa's from the *Mila Gurbum.* Ricard 1994, 83.

2. Chönam and Khandro 1998, 172–73.
3. Chang 1977, 353.
4. In the "dark age" in which obstacles proliferate, dharma teachings would need new expression and more accessible forms of profundity. The terma tradition of Tibet counterbalanced the custom of seeing a long, historic transmission of the teachings dating back to the Buddha in the sixth century B.C.E. Terma is immediate in the sense that such teachings have contemporary language, unconventional and direct themes, and powerful, personal blessings. This format has been particularly appropriate for the Vajrayāna teachings, in which the living guru is more important than the historical Buddha, and in which the chaos and degeneration of the dark age provide greater opportunity for practice and awakening. As Jigme Lingpa said, "When the canonical teachings are adulterated like milk at a fair, and are on the point of disappearing, [then the terma teachings] will spread. For the termas are unadulterated and are the swift path of practice." (Thondup 1986, 63) It is curious to me that most Western scholarship on the subject has occupied itself with the question of fraud, rather than an examination of the phenomenon itself. (Aris 1998; Gyatso 1993, 1998; Hanna 1994; Samuel 1993) This is in contrast to the work of Tulku Thondup, whose translation of the Dodrup Chen text is so informative and comprehensive.
5. *kangsak nyengyü*, "whispered lineage of the ordinary beings," in which the teachings must be presented in words by a human teacher to disciples, in contrast with the "symbol lineage of the vidyādharas" (*rigdzin dayi gyü*), in which teachings are conveyed symbolically, and the "mind lineage of the conquerors" (*gyalwa gonggyü*), in which teachings are transmitted from mind to mind. This term is usually translated as "hearing lineage" (*nyengyü*), but in order to capture the intimate connection involved, I have used the less common "whispered lineage." Padmakara 1994, 332–347; Dudjom 1991, 447, 452, 456–7.
6. Dudjom 1991, vol. 2, 141. According to Patrül Rinpoche, the perfect place is the citadel of absolute expanse; the perfect teacher is the dharmakāya buddha, Samantabhadra; the perfect students are bodhisattvas and deities; the perfect time is limitless time; and the perfect teachings are the Mahāyāna. Padmakara 1994, 9.
7. Gyatso suggests that in concern for the legitimation of the terma transmissions, indicative signs for these follow in many cases the example of the kama transmissions. See Gyatso 1998, 219.
8. Ibid., 179–80.

9. Germano and Gyatso 2000.
10. The variations of spelling and terminology are many: Udrayāna, Oḍḍiyāna, Odiyan, Urgyan, Ugyen, Udyāna. This is one of the most famous of liminal realms favorite to Tibetans, not quite mythical, not quite real, in the same domain as the legendary Śambhala.
11. This last suggestion has come from Lokesh Chandra (1980), who traced the possible connections linguistically, textually, and historically.
12. Dudjom 1991, 441–42. In the "old translation school" it is said that these teachings were given to Indrabhūti by Vajrapāṇi; in the "new translation school" version, the teachings were given by the Buddha himself.
13. Douglas and Bays 1978, 80; Dudjom 1991, 441–42. Some sources distinguish two Uḍḍiyāṇas parallel with each other, one a transcendental realm of wisdom ḍākinīs, the other a worldly ḍākinī realm. Herrmann-Pfandt 1990, 158–59.
14. Dudjom 1991, 503.
15. Thondup 1995, 166–90. In this commentary on the *Vajra Seven-Line Prayer of Guru Rinpoche,* Thondup Rinpoche gave detailed descriptions of the levels of meaning of Uḍḍiyāṇa.
16. See the discussion of twilight language in the introduction.
17. Herrmann-Pfandt 1990, 351–54. Butön Rinpoche wrote that the lost texts of the most important Indian tantras are in Śambhala or Uḍḍiyāṇa preserved by ḍākinīs. Only 6,000 of the 16,000 songs of Milarepa have survived; the remaining 10,000 were brought by ḍākinīs to the Akaniṣṭha heaven. Other texts lost at the end of the first spreading of Buddhism in Tibet were protected by ḍākinīs and have been rediscovered by worthy disciples.
18. Chang 1977, 442–51.
19. There are three kinds of terma teachings: prophetic authorization empowerment, aspirational empowerment, and entrustment to ḍākinīs. The prophetic authorization empowerment (*kabap lungten*) accords with the predictions of Guru Rinpoche, who prophesied the times, places, and tertöns based on his visionary understanding of the coming turbulent age. The aspirational empowerment (*mönlam wangkur*) is terma concealed in the essential nature of the minds of realized teachers, and this terma is discovered directly by the tertön through visionary experience.
20. Ven. Tulku Ugyen Rinpoche, the great Dzogchen master, spoke of this quality as remembrance that never forgets, which is the same as nondistraction, a quality of practitioners of high realization. Yeshe Tsogyal is called the "mis-

tress of secrets" and "queen of the expanse" because of her infallible memory. Schmidt 1994, 19.

21. Dudjom 1991, 745.
22. Ibid., 746.
23. Jigme Lingpa, for example, was aided by the "supreme ḍākinī of the five families." Goodman 1983, 28; Gyatso 1998, 59.
24. Thondup 1986, 69, 107–14, 125–33. I cannot sufficiently document the variety of scripts, as there appear to be myriad versions.
25. *Lamrim Yeshe Nyingpo,* by Guru Rinpoche. Kongtrül 1995, 36.
26. Thondup 1986, 82–83; Samuel 1993, 296; Herrmann-Pfandt 1990, 358.
27. Hanna 1994, 1–13. Havnevik also reported a contemporary woman tertön in the Bönpo and Nyingma traditions named Kachö Wangmo (d. 1987), who publicly rediscovered treasures in forty-three different places, often in the presence of thousands of people. She was imprisoned during the Cultural Revolution and ended her life on Bönpo pilgrimage. Havnevik 1990, 82.
28. Ibid., 74.
29. Ibid., 75.
30. Thondup 1986, 101–14; Herrmann-Pfandt 1990, 360.
31. This account is taken from the biography by the fifteenth-century Kagyü lama Karma Thrinley. For the full traditional interpretation of the arrowsmith woman's craft, see Guenther 1969, 5.
32. This is a common form of teaching in tantra, the employment of a pun. The word *arrow* is *mda',* which is identical in pronunciation to the word for *symbol, brda'.*
33. Kongtrül 1995, 226 n. 86.
34. Another version of this famous song was examined in chapter 3. See Trungpa 1982, 66.
35. Ibid., 72; cf. Guenther 1963, 100–01. See the previous discussion of the first section of these verses, at the end of chapter 3.
36. The term here is *chöpa la shekpa,* translated as "entered the action," which refers to an advanced stage of Vajrayāna practice in which Nāropa left behind conventional reference points such as the body and wandered freely in the world in a visionary fashion. Conventionally this may be regarded as death, but in the tantric perspective Nāropa became more available to Marpa than before, provided Marpa could perceive him. Trungpa 1982, xlvi, 223.
37. Ibid., 77–91. This transmission originated with Tilopa, who received it from Vajrayoginī and the ḍākinīs in Uḍḍiyāṇa. Nāropa received it from Tilopa

and passed it on to Marpa in this account. The Tilopa account is described in chapter 8.

38. (*da-thim*) Gyatso 1998, 57, 94; Goodman 1983, 22.
39. Thondup 1986, 112
40. Ibid., 236–37.
41. Ven. Dzogchen Pönlop Rinpoche, interview, November 1996, Boulder, Colorado.
42. Gyatso (1998) comments that Ekajaṭī appears variously in Indic Buddhism, associated at times with Tārā. In Tibet, she is called "queen of the mātṛkās." 306 n. 17. In the *Guhyasamāja-tantra,* she is called the wrathful goddess Ekajaṭā (Ein-Haarflechte). Gäng 1988, 217. She is called "queen of dralas" (*dralhe gyalma*). Nebesky-Wojkowitz 1975, 34. Another name given her is "mistress of the desire realm" (*dökham wangmo*). Thondup 1986, 114.
43. Nālandā Translation Committee 1975–1986; cf. Nebesky-Wojkowitz 1975, 33–34.
44. Nebesky-Wojkowitz describes these as four kinds of emanations of body (100,000 Nepalese women); speech (ḍākinīs); mind (black women of the Mön country); and action and virtue (numberless, undetermined). 1975, 34.
45. Dudjom 1991, 562, 570
46. Thondup 1996, 231. For a contemporary, popular story of the leprous old beggar woman transforming into Vajrayoginī, see Das 1992, 7.
47. Thondup 1996, 63.
48. Germano and Gyatso 2000, 319–20; cf. Dudjom 1991, vol. 1, 580; vol. 2, 49–50, n. 664.
49. Dudjom 1991, 587.
50. Herrmann-Pfandt 1990, 332–34.
51. Thinley 1980, 48.
52. Gyatso interviews for her Jigme Lingpa study. See Gyatso 1998, 263.
53. Trungpa 1982, 88–89.
54. From Dorje Dze Öd's account of the Kagyü forefathers. Gyaltsen 1990, 37.
55. As the senior queen of King Bhimakutra of Makuta, she had murdered the son of a junior queen. Aris 1988, 26. See also accounts in Dudjom 1991, vol. 1, 554–55; Germano and Gyatso 2000.
56. In Germano and Gyatso, Guru Rinpoche annointed the young princess with this name, signifying that she was "the One with the Dynamism of a Karmic Connection to Padma." Her successor was actually Tsultrim Dorje, who took her dying name to signify his connection with Guru Rinpoche.

57. Dudjom 1991, vol. 1, 582–83; Aris 1988, 27–28. See the description of these calamities in chapter 2.
58. Germano and Gyatso 2000; cf. Dudjom 1991, vol. 1, 582.
59. Germano and Gyatso 2000; cf. Dudjom 1991, 585.
60. Guenther 1963, i–ii; Roerich 1949, 730–31. See the brief biography of Niguma and her disciple Khyungpo Naljor in Kalu 1986, 98–100.
61. Mullin 1985, 96.
62. Ibid., 97.
63. The seed syllable of the yidam Vajrayoginī.
64. See chapter 6. For greater detail on the Six Yogas of Sister Niguma, see the translation by Glen Mullin (1985, 99–151). Kalu Rinpoche remarked, "There is really no essential difference between the Six Yogas of Nāropa and the Six Doctrines of Niguma. The notable difference is in the transmission lineage. The Six Doctrines of Nāropa came from Nāropa to Marpa and his successors, while the Six Doctrines of Niguma came through the great Mahāsiddha Khyungpo Naljor. Thereafter, the two doctrines were transmitted by the successive lineage holders so that there is to the present day an unbroken line in the Kagyü tradition of both doctrines, Nāropa's and Niguma's." Kalu 1986, 103.
65. His other ḍākinī gurus included Kanaśrī of Devīkoṭa, Sumati, Sukhasiddhi, Gaṅgādharā, and Samantabhadrī. Herrmann-Pfandt 1990, 335, n. 20 and 21. The story of Khyungpo Naljor's meeting with Sukhasiddhi is closely parallel with this account of meeting Niguma. See Kalu 1986, 106–07. For a slightly different account, see Namdak 1997.
66. Nālandā 1997, 153.
67. The three implements are a crystal ladder, a bridge fashioned of precious stones, and a key made of a blade of *kuśa* grass. The crystal ladder was actually a diamond sliver, the width of a hair, so sharp that it could cut down the iron walls of the monastery with a single slice. The key was made of kuśa grass, the kind of grass on which the Buddha sat under the tree of enlightenment, and the symbol of enlightened mind. These three demonstrated the power of Tilopa's realization and resolve. When he reached the palace, Tilopa set his ladder against the iron walls, placed his bridge over the poisonous moats, and opened the door with the kuśa grass key.
68. Ven. Chögyam Trungpa Rinpoche, oral commentary, 1973.
69. Nālandā 1997, 153. In the commentary by T'ai Situ Rinpoche, these ḍākinīs are called worldly ḍākinīs who were devoted to protecting the dharma, which

is why their worldly powers had no effect on Tilopa. In trying to tame him, they themselves were subdued. Situpa 1988, 30.

70. Nālandā 1997, 154.
71. Trungpa 1982, 72, 77–91; Situpa 1988.

CONCLUSION

1. Quoted in Norbu 1981, 1995, 49.
2. See introduction.
3. For more on this, see chapter 1.
4. For more on this, see chapter 1.
5. Douglas and Bays 1978, 219; Dudjom 1991, 469.
6. While this has been done in a preliminary way by Hopkins (1998), the actual result probably needs to be more complete than the reworking of a sex manual into a homosexual context. For more on this topic, see Leyland 1998.
7. One might say that the Tibetan tradition itself shares Ricoeur's hermeneutic, for it is this meditative, yogic understanding of the ḍākinī that is considered its most precious, closely guarded tradition. The teachings given this appellation are those that have been least sullied by cultural overlay.
8. Dzogchen Pönlop Rinpoche, personal communication, October 1997, Boulder, Colorado. Rinpoche indicated that this image can be traced back to the time of Tilopa and Nāropa.

SELECT BIBLIOGRAPHY

Allione, Tsultrim, tr. 1984. *Women of Wisdom.* London: Routledge and Kegan Paul, 2000, Revised edition. Ithaca, N.Y.: Snow Lion Publications.

Aris, Michael, tr. 1988. *Hidden Treasures and Secret Lives: A Study of Pemalingpa (1450–1521) and the Sixth Dalai Lama (1683–1706).* Delhi: Indian Institute of Advanced Study and Motilal Banarsidass.

Aziz, Barbara N. 1987. "Moving towards a Sociology of Tibet." In *Feminine Ground: Essays on Women and Tibet,* edited by Janice D. Willis, 76–95. Ithaca, N.Y.: Snow Lion Publications.

———. 1988. "Women in Tibetan Society and Tibetology." In *Tibetan Studies. Proceedings of the Fourth Seminar of the International Association for Tibetan Studies. Schloss Hohenkammer, Munich 1985,* edited by Helga Uebach and Jampa L. Panglung, 25–34. Kommission für Zentralasiatische Studien, Bayerische Akademie der Wissenschaften.

Bagchi, P. C. 1975. *Studies in the Tantras.* Calcutta: University of Calcutta.

Banerji, S. C. 1978. *Tantra in Bengal: A Study in Its Origin, Development and Influence.* Calcutta: Naya Prokash.

Barks, Coleman, tr. 1992. *Stallion on a Frozen Lake: Love Songs of the Sixth Dalai Lama.* Athens, Ga.: Maypop Books.

Benard, Elizabeth. 1990. "Ma gCig Labs sGron, A Tibetan Saint." *Chö Yang* (Dharamsala) 3: 43–51.

———. 1994. *Chinnamastā: The Aweful Buddhist and Hindu Tantric Goddess.* Delhi: Motilal Banarsidass.

Berzin, Alexander, tr. 1978. *The Mahāmudrā: Eliminating the Darkness of Ignorance* by the Ninth Karmapa Wang-Ch'ug Dor-je. Dharamsala: Library of Tibetan Works and Archives.

Beyer, Stephan. 1978. *The Cult of Tārā: Magic and Ritual in Tibet.* Berkeley: University of California Press.

Bharati, Agehananda. 1965, 1975. *The Tantric Tradition.* Rev. ed. New York: Samuel Weiser.

———. 1976. "Making Sense out of Tantrism and Tantrics." *Loka 2: A Journal from Naropa.* 52–55.

Bhattacharji, Sukumari. 1970, 1988. *The Indian Theogony.* Cambridge: Anima Publications.

Bhattacharya, Bholanath. 1977. "Some Aspects of the Esoteric Cults of Consort Worship in Bengal: A Field Survey Report." *Folklore: International Monthly* 18, 10 (October): 310–24; 11 (November): 359–65; 12 (December): 385–97.

Bhattacharya, Brajamadhava. 1988. *The World of Tantra.* Delhi: Munshiram Manoharlal.

Bhattacharyya, Benoytosh. 1964. *An Introduction to Buddhist Esoterism.* Banaras: Chowkhamba Sanskrit Series Office.

Bhattacharyya, Narendra Nath. 1970. *The Indian Mother Goddess.* 2nd ed. New Delhi: Munshiram Manoharlal Publishers.

———. 1974, 1996. *History of the Śākta Religion.* New Delhi: Munshiram Manoharlal Publishers.

Broido, Michael M. 1982. "Does Tibetan Hermeneutics Throw Any Light on Sandhābhāṣa?" *Journal of the Tibetan Society* 2:5–40.

———. 1984. "Padma Dkar-po on Tantra as Ground, Path and Goal." *Journal of the Tibetan Society* 4: 5–46.

Brooks, Douglas Renfrew. 1990. *The Secret of the Three Cities: An Introduction to Hindu Śākta Tantrism.* Chicago: University of Chicago Press.

Bynum, Caroline Walker. 1986. "Introduction: On the Complexity of Symbols." In *Gender and Religion: On the Complexity of Symbols,* edited by Caroline Walker Bynum, Stevan Harrell, and Paula Richman, 1–20. Boston: Beacon Press.

———. 1987. *Holy Feast and Holy Fast: The Religious Significance of Food to Medieval Women.* Berkeley: University of California Press.

———. 1991. *Fragmentation and Redemption: Essays on Gender and the Human Body in Medieval Religion.* New York: Zone Books.

———. 1995. *The Resurrection of the Body in Western Christianity, 200–1336.* New York: Columbia University Press.

Bynum, Caroline Walker, Stevan Harrell, and Paula Richman. 1986. *Gender and Religion: On the Complexity of Symbols.* Boston: Beacon Press.

Cabezon, José Ignacio, ed. 1992. *Buddhism, Sexuality and Gender.* Albany: State University of New York Press.

Cabezon, José Ignacio, and Roger R. Jackson. 1996. *Tibetan Literature: Studies in Genre.* Ithaca, N.Y.: Snow Lion Publications.

Campbell, June. 1996. *Traveller in Space: In Search of Female Identity in Tibetan Buddhism.* New York: George Braziller.

Chandra, Lokesh. 1980. "Oḍḍiyāna: A New Interpretation." In *Tibetan Studies in Honour of Hugh Richardson,* edited by Michael Aris and Aung San Suu Kyi, 73–78. New Delhi: Vikas Publishing House.

Chang, Garma C. C., tr. 1963. *Six Yogas of Nāropa and Teachings on Mahāmudrā.* Ithaca, N.Y.: Snow Lion Publications.

———. 1977. *The Hundred Thousand Songs of Milarepa,* vols. 1 & 2. Boulder: Shambhala Publications.

———. 1983. *A Treasury of Mahāyāna Sūtras: Selections from the Mahāratnakūta Sūtra.* University Park: Pennsylvania State University Press.

Chimpa, Lama, and Alaka Chattopadhyaya, tr. 1970. *Tāranātha's History of Buddhism in India,* edited by Debiprasad Chattopadhyaya. Simla: Indian Institute of Advanced Study.

Chödron, Pema. 1994. *Start Where You Are: A Guide to Compassionate Living.* Boston: Shambhala Publications.

Chönam, Lama, and Sangye Khandro, tr. 1998. *The Lives and Liberation of Princess Maṇḍāravā: The Indian Consort of Padmasambhava.* Boston: Wisdom Publications.

Chotso, Tsering. 1997. "A Drop in the Ocean: The Status of Women in Tibetan Society." *The Tibet Journal* 22, 2 (Summer): 59–67.

Christ, Carol. 1979. "Why Woman Need the Goddess." In *Womanspirit Rising,* edited by Judith Plaskow and Carol Christ. San Francisco: Harper and Row.

Coburn, Thomas B. 1982, 1986. "Consort of None, Śakti of All: The Vision of Devī-Māhātmya." In *Divine Consort: Rādhā and the Goddesses of India,* edited by John Stratton Hawley and Donna Marie Wulff, 153–65. Boston: Beacon Press.

———. 1984. *Devī-Māhātmya: The Crystallization of the Goddess Tradition.* Delhi: Motilal Banarsidass.

Conze, Edward. 1960. *The Prajñāpāramitā Literature.* The Hague: Mouton and Company.

———. 1967, 1975. *Thirty Years of Buddhist Studies and Further Buddhist Studies.* Oxford: Bruno Cassirer.

———, tr. 1973a. *The Perfection of Wisdom in Eight Thousand Lines and Its Verse Summary.* Bolinas, Calif.: Four Seasons Foundation.

———, tr. 1973b. *The Short Prajñāpāramitā Texts.* London: Luzac & Company.

Conze, Edward, I. B. Horner, David Snellgrove, and Arthur Waley, eds. 1954, 1964. *Buddhist Texts Through the Ages.* New York: Harper and Row.

Cooey, Paula M. 1990. "Emptiness, Otherness, and Identity: A Feminist Perspective." *Journal of Feminist Studies in Religion* 6:2, 7–23.

Dagyab Rinpoche. 1995. *Buddhist Symbols of Tibetan Culture: An Investigation of the Nine Best-Known Groups of Symbols.* Translated from the German by Maurice Walshe. Boston: Wisdom Publications.

Daly, Mary. 1973. *Beyond God the Father.* Boston: Beacon Press.

Danielou, Alain. 1964, 1985. *The Gods of India: Hindu Polytheism.* Princeton: Princeton University Press.

———. 1994. *The Complete Kāma-sūtra.* Rochester, Vt.: Park Street Press.

Das, Sarat Chandra. 1969, 1981. *Tibetan-English Dictionary.* Kyoto: Rinsen Book Company.

Das, Surya. 1992. *The Snow Lion's Turquoise Mane: Wisdom Tales from Tibet.* San Francisco: HarperCollins.

Datta, Bhupendranath, tr. 1944, 1957. *Mystic Tales of Lāmā Tāranātha: A Religio-Sociological History of Mahāyāna Buddhism.* Calcutta: Ramakrishna Vedanta Math.

Dawa-Samdup, Kazi, ed. 1919, 1987. *Shrīchakrasambhāra Tantra: A Buddhist Tantra,* Tantrik Texts, vol. 7. New Delhi: Aditya Prakashan.

Dhargyey, Geshe Ngawang. 1985. *A Commentary on the Kālacakra Tantra.* Translated by Gelong Jhampa Kelsang (Allan Wallace). Dharamsala: Library of Tibetan Works and Archives.

Dhondup, K., and Tashi Tsering. 1979. "Samdhing Dorjee Phagmo—Tibet's Only Female Incarnation." *Tibetan Review* (August): 11–17.

Douglas, Kenneth, and Gwendolyn Bays, tr. 1978 *The Life and Liberation of Padmasambhava. Padma bKa'i Thang,* as recorded by Yeshe Tsogyal. *Le Dict de Padma,* translated into French by Gustave-Charles Toussaint. Berkeley: Dharma Publishing.

Douglas, Nik, and Meryl White, ed. 1976. *Karmapa: The Black Hat Lama of Tibet.* London: Luzac and Company.

Dowman, Keith, tr. 1984. *Sky Dancer: The Secret Life and Song of the Lady Yeshe Tsogyel.* London: Routledge & Kegan Paul.

———. 1985. *Masters of Mahāmudrā: The Songs and Histories of the Eighty-Four Buddhist Siddhas.* Albany: State University of New York Press.

Drolma, Delog Dawa. 1995. *Delog: Journey to Realms Beyond Death.* Junction City, Calif.: Padma Publishing.

Dudjom, Jigdral Yeshe Dorje. 1991. *The Nyingma School of Tibetan Buddhism: Its Fundamentals and History.* Translated and edited by Gyurme Dorje with the collaboration of Matthew Kapstein. Boston: Wisdom Publications.

———. 1996. *Perfect Conduct: Ascertaining the Three Vows.* Translated by Khenpo Gyerme Samdrup and Sangye Khandro. Boston: Wisdom Publications.

Edou, Jerome. 1996. *Machig Labdrön and the Foundations of Chöd.* Ithaca, N.Y.: Snow Lion Publications.

Eilberg-Schwartz, Howard, and Wendy Doniger, eds. 1995. *Off with Her Head! The Denial of Women's Identity in Myth, Religion, and Culture.* Berkeley: University of California Press.

Elder, George R. 1976. "Problems of Language in Buddhist Tantra." *History of Religions* 15, 3:231–50.

Eliade, Mircea. 1959. "Methodological Remarks on the Study of Religious Symbolism." In *The History of Religions: Essays in Methodology.* Chicago: University of Chicago Press.

———. 1961, 1969. *Yoga, Immortality, and Freedom.* Princeton: Princeton University Press.

———. 1963. "The Structure of Symbols." In *Patterns in Comparative Religions.* Cleveland: Meridian Books.

———. 1965. *Mephistopheles and the Androgyne.* New York: Sheed and Ward.

Eller, Cynthia. 1993, 1995. *Living in the Lap of the Goddess: The Feminist Spirituality Movement in America.* Boston: Beacon Press.

Evans-Wentz, W. Y., ed. 1927, 1949, 1957, 1960. *The Tibetan Book of the Dead.* London: Oxford University Press.

———. 1937, 1954, 1968, 1970. *The Tibetan Book of the Great Liberation, Or the Method of Realizing Nirvāṇa through Knowing the Mind.* London: Oxford University Press.

Facchini, M. 1983. "The Spiritual Heritage of Ma gCig Lab sGron." *Journal of the Tibet Society* 3, 21–26.

Falk, Nancy Auer. 1974. "An Image of Women in Old Buddhist Literature." In *Women and Religion,* edited by Judith Plaskow and Joan Arnold Romero. Rev. ed. Missoula, Mont.: Scholars Press.

———. 1980. "The Case of the Vanishing Nuns: The Fruits of Ambivalence in Ancient India Buddhism." In *Unspoken Worlds: Women's Religious Lives in Non-Western Cultures,* edited by Nancy Auer Falk and Rita M. Gross. San Francisco: Harper & Row.

Farrow, G. W., and Menon, I., tr. 1992. *The Concealed Essence of the Hevajra Tantra, With the Commentary Yogaratnamālā.* Delhi: Motilal Banarsidass.

Fields, Rick, and Brian Cutillo, tr. 1994. *The Turquoise Bee: The Lovesongs of the Sixth Dalai Lama.* San Francisco: HarperSan Francisco.

Fiorenza, Elizabeth Schüssler. 1986. *In Memory of Her: A Feminist Theological Reconstruction of Christian Origins.* New York: Crossroad.

Fremantle, Francesca and Chögyam Trungpa. 1975. *The Tibetan Book of the Dead: The Great Liberation through Hearing in the Bardo.* Berkeley: Shambhala Publications.

Fremantle, Francesca, tr. 1990. "Chapter Seven of the Guhyasamāja Tantra." In

Indo-Tibetan Studies. Papers in Honour and Appreciation of Professor David L. Snellgrove's Contribution to Indo-Tibetan Studies, edited by Tadeusz Skorupski, 101–14. Tring, U.K.: Institute of Buddhist Studies.

Gallagher, Catherine, and Thomas Laqueur, eds. 1987. *The Making of the Modern Body: Sexuality and Society in the Nineteenth Century.* Berkeley: University of California Press.

Galland, China. 1990. *Longing for Darkness: Tara and the Black Madonna, A Ten-Year Journey.* New York: Penguin Books.

Gäng, Peter, tr. 1988. *Das Tantra der verborgenen Vereigigung, Guhyasamāja-Tantra.* Munich: Eugen Diederichs.

George, Christopher S., tr. 1974. *The Caṇḍamahāroṣaṇa Tantra, Chapters 1–8: A Critical Edition and English Translation.* American Oriental Series, no. 56. New Haven: American Oriental Society.

Germano, David, and Janet Gyatso. 2000. "Longchenpa and the Possession of the Ḍākinīs." In *Tantra in Practice,* edited by David Gordon White. Princeton: Princeton University Press.

Goldstein, Melvyn C., and Matthew T. Kapstein. 1998. *Buddhism in Contemporary Tibet: Religious Revival and Cultural Identity.* Berkeley: University of California Press.

Gomez, Luis O. 1995. "Oriental Wisdom and the Cure of Souls: Jung and the Indian East." In *Curators of the Buddha: The Study of Buddhism under Colonialism,* edited by Donald S. Lopez, Jr., 197–250. Chicago: University of Chicago Press.

Goodman, Steven D. 1981. "Mi-Pham rgya-mtsho: An Account of His Life, and the Printing of His Works, and the Structure of His Treatise Entitled mKhas-pa'i tshul la 'jug-pa'i sgo. *Wind Horse (Proceedings of the North American Tibetological Society)* 1:58–78.

———. 1983. "The kLong-chen snying-thig: An Eighteenth Century Tibetan Revelation." Ph.D. dissertation, University of Saskatchewan.

Govinda, Lama Angarika. 1971. *The Way of the White Clouds: A Buddhist Pilgrim in Tibet.* Berkeley: Shambhala Publications.

Gross, Rita M. 1987, 1989. "Yeshe Tsogyel: Enlightened Consort, Great Teacher, Female Role Model." In *Feminine Ground: Essays on Women and Tibet,* edited by Janice D. Willis. Ithaca, N.Y.: Snow Lion Publications.

———. 1993. *Buddhism After Patriarchy: A Feminist History, Analysis, and Reconstruction of Buddhism.* Albany: State University of New York Press.

———. 1996. *Feminism and Religion: An Introduction.* Boston: Beacon Press.

———. 1998a. *Soaring and Settling: Buddhist Perspectives on Contemporary Social and Religious Issues.* New York: Continuum Publishing.

———. 1998b. "Helping the Iron Bird Fly: Western Buddhist Women and Issues of Authority in the Late 1990s." In *The Faces of American Buddhism,* edited by Charles S. Prebish and Kenneth K. Tanaka. Berkeley: University of California Press.

Guenther, Herbert, tr. 1963. *The Life and Teachings of Nāropa.* London: Oxford University Press.

———, tr. 1969. *The Royal Song of Saraha: A Study in the History of Buddhist Thought.* Berkeley: Shambhala Publications.

———, tr. 1971. *The Jewel Ornament of Liberation, by Gampopa.* Berkeley: Shambhala Publications.

———. 1983. "The Dynamics of Being: rdzogs-chen Process Thinking." In *Canadian Tibetan Studies I,* edited by Eva K. Dargyay. Calgary, Alberta: Society for Tibetan Studies.

———. 1993. *Ecstatic Spontaneity: Saraha's Three Cycles of Dohā.* Berkeley: Asian Humanities Press.

Gupta, Sanjukta. 1991. "Women in the Śaiva/Śākta Ethos." In *Roles and Rituals for Hindu Women,* edited by Julia Leslie. 193–209. Rutherford, N.J.: Farleigh Dickinson University Press.

Gupta, Sanjukta, Dirk Jan Hoens, and Teun Goudriaan. 1979. *Hindu Tantrism.* Leiden: E. J. Brill.

Gyaltsen, Khenpo Könchog, tr. 1990. *The Great Kagyu Masters: The Golden Lineage Treasury.* Ithaca, N.Y.: Snow Lion Publications.

Gyamtso, Khenpo Tsultrim. 1995. *The Songs of Jetsun Milarepa: A Selection,* translated by Karma Tsultrim Palmo. Privately published.

Gyatso, Janet. 1986. "Sign, Memory and History: A Tantric Buddhist Theory of Scriptural Transmission." *Journal of the Association of Buddhist Studies* 9, 2: 7–35.

———. 1987. "Down with the Demoness: Reflections on a Feminine Ground in Tibet." In *Feminine Ground: Essays on Women and Tibet,* edited by Janice Willis. Ithaca, N.Y.: Snow Lion Publications.

———. 1992. "Letter Magic: Peircean Meditations on the Semiotics of Rdo Grubchen's Dhāraṇī Memory." In *Mirror of Memory,* edited by Janet Gyatso. Albany: State University of New York Press.

———. 1993. "The Logic of Legitimation in the Tibetan Treasure Tradition." *History of Religions* 33, 1: 97–134.

———. 1998. *Apparitions of the Self: The Secret Autobiographies of a Tibetan Visionary.* Princeton: Princeton University Press.

Hanna, Span. 1994. "Vast As the Sky: The Terma Tradition in Modern Tibet." In *Tantra and Popular Religion in Tibet,* edited by Geoffrey Samuel, Hamish Gregor, and Elisabeth Stutchbury. New Delhi: International Academy of Indian Culture and Aditya Prakashan.

Harding, Sarah, tr. 1994. "Excerpt from *The Precious Garland Ornament of Liberation; a History of Pacification and Severence.*" Unpublished manuscript.

———. 1996. *Creation and Completion: Essential Points of Tantric Meditation,* by Jamgön Kongtrül. Boston: Wisdom Publications.

———. In press. *Jewel Ocean: The Life and Revelations of Pemalingpa.* Boston: Wisdom Publications.

Harding, Sarah, and Richard Barron, tr. 1990. *T'hröma Nagmo: A Practice Cycle for Realization of the Wrathful Black Dakini, A Treasure of Dudjom Lingpa.* Translated under the Direction of Chagdud Tulku. Junction City, Calif.: Padma Publishing.

Havnevik, Hanna. 1990. *Tibetan Buddhist Nuns: History, Cultural Norms and Social Reality.* Oslo: Norwegian University Press.

Hawley, John Stratton. 1986. "Images of Gender in the Poetry for Krishna." In *Gender and Religion: On the Complexity of Symbols,* edited by Caroline Walker Bynum, Stevan Harrell, and Paula Richman. Boston: Beacon Press.

Hawley, John Stratton, and Donna Marie Wulff. 1982. *The Divine Consort: Rādhā and the Goddesses of India.* Berkeley: Graduate Theological Union.

Hermanns, Matthias. 1953. "The Status of Woman in Tibet." *Anthropological Quarterly* 26, 3: 67–78.

Herrmann-Pfandt, Adelheid. 1990. *Ḍākinīs: Zur Stellung und Symbolik des Weiblichen im tantrischen Buddhismus.* Bonn: Indica et Tibetica Verlag.

———. 1996. "The Good Woman's Shadow: Some Aspects of the Dark Nature of Ḍākinīs and Śākinīs in Hinduism." In *Wild Goddesses in India and Nepal,* 39–70, edited by Axel Michaels, Cornelia Vogelsanger, and Annette Wilke. Bern: Peter Lang.

———. 1997. "Yab Yum Iconography and the Role of Women in Tibetan Tantric Buddhism." *The Tibet Journal* 22, 1 (Spring): 12–34.

Hillman, James. 1985. *Anima: An Anatomy of a Personified Notion.* Dallas: Spring Publications.

Hladiš, Jirka, tr. 1999. "Praise to Dharmadhātu of Noble Nāgāruna." Master's thesis, Nāropa University, Boulder, Colorado.

Holmberg, David. 1983. "Shamanic Soundings: Femaleness in the Tamang Ritual Structure." *Signs: Journal of Women in Culture and Society* 9, 1: 40–58.

Holmes, Katia. 1981. *Dzalendara and Sakarchupa: Stories from Long, Long Ago of the Former Lives of the Gyalwa Karmapa.* Fores, Scotland: Kagyu Samye Ling.

Holmes, Ken. 1995. *Karmapa: Urgyen Trinley Dorje.* Fores, Scotland: Altea Publishing House.

Hopkins, Jeffrey, tr. 1977. *Tantra in Tibet: The Great Exposition of Secret Mantra, by Tsongkapa.* London: George Allen and Unwin.

———, tr. 1992. *The Tibetan Arts of Love, by Gedün Chöpel.* Ithaca, N.Y.: Snow Lion Publications.

———. 1998. *Sex, Orgasm, and the Gay Arts of Love: The Sixty-four Arts of Gay Male Love.* Berkeley: North Atlantic Books.

Houston, G. W., tr. 1982. *Wings of the White Crane: Poems of Tshangs dbyangs rgya mtsho (1683–1706).* Delhi: Motilal Banarsidass.

Huber, Toni. 1994a. "When What You See Is Not What You Get: Remarks on the Traditional Tibetan Presentation of Sacred Geography." In *Tantra and Popular Religion in Tibet,* edited by Geoffrey Samuel et. al. Delhi: Aditya Prakashan.

———. 1994b. "Why Can't Women Climb Pure Crystal Mountain? Remarks on Gender, Ritual and Space at Tsa-Ri." In *Tibetan Studies 1992,* vol. 1, edited by Per Kvaerne. Oslo: Norwegian University Press.

———. 1997. "Guidebook to Lapchi." In *Religions of Tibet in Practice,* edited by Donald Lopez, 120–34. Princeton: Princeton University Press.

Hummel, Siegbert. 1960. "Die Frauenreiche in Tibet." *Zeitschrift für Ethnologie* 85, 1: 44–46.

International Translation Committee. 1998. *Buddhist Ethics by Jamgön Kongtrül Lodrö Tayé.* Ithaca, N.Y.: Snow Lion Publications.

Johnston, E. S., tr. 1972. *The Buddhacārita, or The Acts of the Buddha.* Delhi: Motilal Banarsidass.

Jung, C. G. 1904. *Collected Works,* edited by Sir Herbert Read, Michael Fordham, and Gerhard Adler; translated by R. F. C. Hull. Bollingen Series 20. Princeton: Princeton University Press.

———. 1953, 1973. *Psychological Reflections: A New Anthology of His Writings, 1905–1961.* Edited by Jolande Jacobi and R. F. C. Hull. Bollingen Series 31. Princeton: Princeton University Press.

———. 1966, 1977. *Two Essays on Analytic Psychology.* Translated by R. F. C. Hull. Bollingen Series 20. Princeton: Princeton University Press.

———. 1978. *Psychology and the East.* Translated by R. F. C. Hull. Bollingen Series 20. Princeton: Princeton University Press.

Kajiyama, Yuichi. 1985. "Stūpas, the Mother of Buddhas, and Dharma Body." In *New Paths in Buddhist Research,* edited by A. K. Warder. Durham, N.C.: Acorn Press.

Kalff, Martin M. 1978. "Ḍākinīs in the Cakrasaṃvara Tradition." In *Tibetan Studies Presented at the Seminar of Young Tibetologists, Zürich, June 26–July 1, 1977,* edited by Martin Brauen and Per Kvaerne, 149–62. Zurich: Völkerkundemuseum der Universität Zürich.

———. 1979. "Selected Chapters from the Abhidhānottara-tantra: The Union of Female and Male Deities." Ph.D. dissertation, Columbia University.

Kalu, Kyabje Dorje Chang. 1986. *The Dharma: That Illuminates All Beings Impartially Like the Light of the Sun and the Moon.* Albany: State University of New York Press.

———. 1994. *Gently Whispered: Oral Teachings by the Very Venerable Kalu Rinpoche.* Barrytown, N.Y.: Station Hill Press.

———. 1997. *Luminous Mind: The Way of the Buddha.* Boston: Wisdom Publications.

Kapstein, Matthew. 1980. "The Shangs-pa bKa'-brgyud: An Unknown Tradition of Tibetan Buddhism." In *Tibetan Studies in Honour of Hugh Richardson,* edited by Michael Aris and Aung San Suu Kyi, 138–44. New Delhi: Vikas Publishing House.

Karmay, Samten. G. 1985. "The Rdzogs-chen in Its Earliest Text: A Manuscript from Tun-huang." In *Soundings in Tibetan Civilization,* edited by Barbara Aziz and Matthew Kapstein, 272–82. Proceedings of the Third Seminar of International Association of Tibetan Studies. New Delhi: Manohar.

Karthar, Khenpo. 1990–1991. *The Profound Inner Meaning,* vols. 1 & 2. Woodstock, N.Y.: Karma Triyana Dharmachakra.

Katz, Nathan. 1977. "Anima and mKha'-'gro-ma: A Critical Comparative Study of Jung and Tibetan Buddhism." *The Tibet Journal* 2, 3 (Autumn): 13–43. Revised and published as "Ḍākinī and Anima: On Tantric Deities and Jungian Archetypes." In *Self and Liberation: The Jung-Buddhist Dialogue,* edited by Daniel J. Meckel and Robert L. Moore, 302–29. Chicago: Paulist Press, 1992.

Khyentse, Dilgo. 1988. *Wish-Fulfilling Gem: The Practice of Guru Yoga According to the Longchen Nyinthig Tradition.* Boston: Shambhala Publications.

Khyentse, Dzongsar. 1997. "Distortion." *Shambhala Sun* (Summer): 24–29.

Kinsley, David. 1986, 1987. *Hindu Goddesses: Visions of the Divine Feminine in the Hindu Religious Tradition.* Delhi: Motilal Banarsidass.

———. 1989. *The Goddesses' Mirror: Visions of the Divine from East and West.* Albany, N.Y.: State University of New York Press.

———. 1997. *Tantric Visions of the Divine Feminine: The Ten Mahāvidyās.* Berkeley: University of California Press.

Klein, Anne. 1985a. "Nondualism and the Great Bliss Queen: A Study in Tibetan Buddhist Ontology and Symbolism." *Journal of Feminist Studies in Religion* 1, 1: 73–98.

———. 1985b. "Primordial Purity and Everyday Life: Exalted Female Symbols and the Women of Tibet." In *Immaculate and Powerful—The Female in Sacred Image and Social Reality,* edited by Clarissa W. Atkinson, Constance H. Buchanan, and Margaret Miles, 111–38. Boston: Beacon Press.

———. 1986. "Gain or Drain? Buddhist and Feminist Views of Compassion." *Spring Wind* 6: 1–3, 105–16.

———. 1987a. "Finding a Self: Buddhist and Feminist Perspectives." In *Shaping New Vision: Gender and Values in American Culture,* edited by Clarissa W. Atkinson, Constance H. Buchanan, and Margaret R. Miles. Ann Arbor, Mich.: UMI Research Press.

———. 1987b. "The Birthless Birthgiver: Reflections of the Liturgy of Yeshe Tsogyel, the Great Bliss Queen." *The Tibet Journal* 12, 4: 19–37.

———. 1995. *Meeting the Great Bliss Queen: Buddhists, Feminists, and the Art of Self.* Boston: Beacon Press.

Kongtrül, Jamgön. 1995 (vol. 1), 1998 (vol. 2). *The Light of Wisdom: The Root Text, Lamrim Yeshe Nyingpo, by Padmasambhava.* Translated by Eric Pema Kunsang Schmidt. Boston: Shambhala Publications.

Kunga, Lama, and Brian Cutillo. 1978. *Drinking the Mountain Stream: New Stories and Songs by Milarepa.* Novato, Calif.: Lotsawa.

———. 1986. *Miraculous Journey: Further Stories and Songs of Milarepa, Yogin, Poet, and Teacher of Tibet.* Novato, Calif.: Lotsawa.

Kvaerne, Per. 1974–75. "On the Concept of Sahāja in Indian Buddhist Tantric Literature." *Temenos* 11: 88–135.

———. 1977. *An Anthology of Buddhist Tantric Songs—A Study of the Caryāgīti* Oslo-Bergen-Tromso: det Norske Videnskaps-Akademie. Hist.-Filos. Klasse Skrifter. Ny Serie No. 14. Universitetesforlaget.

———. 1995, 1996. *The Bön Religion of Tibet: The Iconography of a Living Tradition.* Boston: Shambhala Publications.

Lamotte, Etienne. 1949. *Le Traite de la Grande Vertu de Sagesse.* Louvain. Vol. IV Belgium: Uitgeveri, Peters.

Lang, Karen Christina. 1986. "Lord Death's Snare: Gender-related Imagery in the Theragāthā and the Therīgāthā." In *Journal of Feminist Studies in Religion* 2, 2: 63–79.

Lati Rinbochay and Jeffrey Hopkins, 1979. *Death, Intermediate State and Rebirth in Tibetan Buddhism.* Valois, N.Y.: Snow Lion Publications.

Leyland, Winston, ed. 1998. *Queer Dharma: Voices of Gay Buddhism.* San Francisco: Gay Sunshine Press.

Lhalungpa, Lobsang P., tr. 1977. *The Life of Milarepa.* New York: E. P. Dutton.

———. 1986. *Mahāmudrā: The Quintessence of Mind and Meditation by Tagpo Tashi Namgyal.* Boston: Shambhala Publications.

Lo Bue, Erberto. 1994. "A Case of Mistaken Identity: Ma-gcig Labs-sgron and Ma-gcig Zha-ma." In *Tibetan Studies, 1992,* vol. 1, edited by Per Kvaerne. Oslo: Norwegian University Press.

Lopez, Donald. 1994. "dGe 'dun chos 'phel's Klu sgrub dgongs rgyan: A Preliminary Study." In *Tibetan Studies, 1992,* Vol. 1, edited by Per Kvaerne. Oslo: Norwegian University Press.

———. 1998. *Prisoners of Shangri-La: Tibetan Buddhism and the West.* Chicago: University of Chicago Press.

Loseries-Leick, Andrea. 1994. "Symbolism in the Bon Mother Tantra." In *Tibetan Studies, 1992,* vol. 1, edited by Per Kvaerne. Oslo: Norwegian University Press.

———. 1996. "Kālī in Tibetan Buddhism." In *Wild Goddesses in India and Nepal,* edited by Axel Michaels, Cornelia Vogelsanger, and Annette Wilke. Bern: Peter Lang, 417–435.

Lynch, Owen M. 1990. *The Social Construction of Emotion in India.* Berkeley and Los Angeles: University of California Press.

Mackenzie, Vicki. 1998. *Cave in the Snow: Tenzin Palmo's Quest for Enlightenment.* New York: St. Martin's Press.

Macy, Joanna Rogers. 1977. "Perfection of Wisdom: Mother of All Buddhas." In *Beyond Androcentrism: New Essays on Women and Religion,* edited by Rita M. Gross, 315–33. Missoula, Mont.: Scholars Press.

Madrong, Migyur Dorje. 1997. "A Discussion on Some Great Women in Tibetan History," translated by Sonam Tsering. *The Tibet Journal* 22, 2 (Summer): 69–90.

Makley, Charlene. 1997. "The Meaning of Liberation: Representations of Tibetan Women." *The Tibet Journal* 22, 1 (Summer): 4–29.

Makransky, John. 1997. *Buddhahood Embodied: Sources of Controversy in India and Tibet.* Albany: State University of New York Press.

Marglin, Frédérique Apfell. 1982. "Types of Sexual Union and Their Implicit Meanings." In *The Divine Consort: Rādhā and the Goddesses of India,* edited by John Stratton Hawley and Donna Marie Wulff, 298–315. Berkeley: Berkeley Religious Studies Series.

Martin, Can. 1987. "Illusion Web: Locating the *Guhyagarbha Tantra* in Buddhist Intellectual History." In *Silver on Lapis: Tibetan Literary Culture and History,* edited by Christopher I. Beckwith, 175–220. Bloomington, Ind.: The Tibet Society.

Matsanaga, Alicia. 1969. *The Buddhist Philosophy of Assimilation: The Historical Development of the Honji-Suijaku Theory.* Tokyo: Charles E. Tuttle Company.

Matsunaga, Yukei, ed. 1978. *The Guhyasamāja-tantra: A New Critical Edition.* Osaka: Toho Shuppan.

McDaniel, June. 1989. *The Madness of the Saints: Ecstatic Religion in Bengal.* Chicago: University of Chicago Press.

McGilvray, Dennis B. 1998. *Symbolic Heat: Gender, Health and Worship among the Tamils of South India and Sri Lanka.* Middletown, N.J.: Grantha.

Miller, Beatrice D. 1980. "Views of Women's Role in Buddhist Tibet." In *Studies in History of Buddhism,* edited by A. K. Narain, 155–66. Delhi: B. R. Publishing.

Mohapatra, Sagarika. 1981. "Introduction of Female Deities in Buddhist Pantheon." *Transactions of the International Conference of Orientalists in Japan* 26: 128.

Monier-Williams, Monier. 1899, 1976. *A Sanskrit-English Dictionary.* Oxford: Oxford University Press.

Mullin, Glen H. 1985. *Selected Works of the Dalai Lama II: The Tantric Yogas of Sister Niguma.* Ithaca, N.Y.: Snow Lion Publications.

Mumford, Stan Royal. 1989. *Himalayan Dialogue: Tibetan Lamas and Gurung Shamans in Nepal.* Madison: University of Wisconsin Press.

Nālandā Translation Committee. 1982. "The Life of Tilopa." *Chos byung bstan pa'i padma rgyas pa'i nyin byed*, vol. 2 of Collected Works of *Kun-mkhyen Padma-dkar-po*. Halifax, N.S.: Nālandā Translation Committee. 1997. Excerpt reprinted in *Religions of Tibet in Practice*, edited by Donald Lopez, 137–56. Princeton: Princeton University Press.

Nālandā Translation Committee. 1975–1998a. "Pacifying the Turmoil of the Mamos" by Karma Chagme. Halifax, N.S.: Nālandā Translation Committee.

Nālandā Translation Committee. 1975–1998b. "Ekajāṭī" by Chögyam Trungpa. Halifax, N.S.: Nālandā Translation Committee.

Namdak, Neldjorpa Tsultrim, tr. 1997. *Hagiographies de Nigouma et Soukhasiddhi*. Combaudet, France: Editions Yogi Ling.

Nebesky-Wojkowitz, René De. 1975. *Oracles and Demons of Tibet: The Cult and Iconography of the Tibetan Protective Deities*. Graz, Austria: Akademische Druck–u. Verlagsanstalt.

Neumaier-Dargyay, E. K. 1992. *The Sovereign All-Creating Mind—The Motherly Buddha: A Translation of the Kun byed rgyal po'i mdo*. Albany, N.Y.: State University of New York Press.

Norbu, Namkhai, and Kennard Lipman. 1987. *Primordial Experience: An Introduction to rDzog-Chen Meditation*. Boston: Shambhala Publications.

Norbu, Thinley. 1981, 1985. *Magic Dance: The Display of the Self-Nature of the Five Wisdom Dakinis*. New York: Jewel Publishing.

Nyoshul Khenpo. 1995. *Natural Great Perfection: Dzogchen Teachings and Vajra Songs*, translated by Lama Surya Das. Ithaca, N.Y.: Snow Lion Publications.

Obermiller, E., tr. 1964. *The Jewelry of Scripture, the History of Buddhism by Buston*. Reprint series 5. Tokyo: Suzuki Research Foundation.

O'Flaherty, Wendy Doniger. 1980, 1982. *Women, Androgynes, and Other Mythical Beasts*. Chicago: University of Chicago Press.

Ortner, Sherry B. 1974. "Is Female to Male as Nature Is to Culture?" In *Woman, Culture, and Society*, edited by Michelle Zimbaist Rosaldo and Louise Lamphere. Palo Alto: Stanford University Press.

———. 1983. "The Founding of the First Sherpa Nunnery, and the Problem of 'Women' as an Analytic Category." In *Feminist Re-Visions: What Has Been and What Might Be*, edited by Vivian Paraka and Louise A. Tilly, 98–135. Ann Arbor: University of Michigan Press.

———. 1989. *High Religion: A Cultural and Political History of Sherpa Buddhism*. Princeton: Princeton University Press.

———. 1996. *Making Gender: The Politics and Erotics of Culture*. Boston: Beacon Press.

Ortner, Sherry B., and Harriet Whitehead. 1981. *Sexual Meanings: The Cultural Construction of Gender and Sexuality*. Cambridge: Cambridge University Press.

Padmakara Translation Group, tr. 1994. *The Words of My Perfect Teacher: Patrul Rinpoche's Kunzang Lama'i Shalung.* San Francisco: HarperCollins.

———. 1999. *Lady of the Lotus-Born: The Life and Enlightenment of Yeshe Tsogyal, by Gyalwa Changchub and Namkhai Nyingpo.* Boston: Shambhala Publications.

Padoux, Andre. 1981. "A Survey of Tantric Hinduism for the Historian of Religions." *History of Religions* 22, 4: 345–60.

Palmo, Anila Rinchen. 1987. *Cutting Through Ego-Clinging.* (Montignac, France: Dzambala).

Paul, Diana. 1979. *Women in Buddhism.* Berkeley: Asian Humanities Press.

———. 1983. "Kuan-Yin: Saviour and Saviouress in Chinese Pure Land Buddhism." In *The Book of the Goddess,* edited by Carl Olson, 161–75. New York: Crossroad.

Pay, Phyllis. 1997. "Meeting Vajrayoginī." In *Being Bodies: Buddhist Women on the Paradox of Embodiment,* edited by Lenore Friedman and Susan Moon. Boston: Shambhala Publications.

Piburn, Sidney, ed. 1990. *The Dalai Lama: A Policy of Kindness.* Ithaca, N.Y.: Snow Lion Publications.

Pintchman, Tracy. 1994. *The Rise of the Goddess in the Hindu Tradition.* Albany: State University of New York Press.

Plaskow, Judith, and Carol Christ. 1989. *Weaving the Visions: New Patterns in Feminist Spirituality.* San Francisco: Harper and Row.

Poussin, Louis de la Vallée. 1922. "Tantrism (Buddhist)." In *Encyclopedia of Religion and Ethics,* edited by James Hastings, vol. 12, 193–97. New York: Scribner's.

———. 1971. *L'Abhidharmakośa de Vasubandhu, vols. 1–14.* Brussels: Institut Belge Des Hautes Études Chinoises; 1988. *Abhidharmakośabhāṣyam,* translated into English by Leo M. Pruden. Berkeley: Asian Humanities Press.

Prats, Ramon. 1978. "The Spiritual Lineage of the Dzogchen Tradition." In *Tibetan Studies Presented at the Seminar of Young Tibetologists, Zurich, June 26–July 1, 1977,* edited by Martin Brauen and Per Kvaerne, 199–208. Zurich: Völkerkündemuseum der Universität Zürich.

Purkiss, Diane. 1996. *The Witch in History: Early Modern and Twentieth-Century Representations.* London and New York: Routledge.

Rahula, Walpola. 1959. *What the Buddha Taught.* New York: Grove Press.

Ray, Reginald. 1980. "Accomplished Women in Tantric Buddhism of Medieval India and Tibet." In *Unspoken Worlds: Women's Religious Lives in Non-Western Cultures,* edited by Nancy Auer Falk and Rita M. Gross, 225–41. San Francisco: Harper and Row.

———. 1994. *Buddhist Saints in India.* Oxford: Oxford University Press.

Reis, Ria. 1983. "Reproduction or Retreat: The Position of Buddhist Women in

Ladakh." In *Recent Research on Ladakh: History, Culture, Sociology, Ecology,* edited by Detlef Kantowsky and Reinhard Sander. Munich: Weltforum Verlag.

Rhys Davids, Caroline A. F., tr. 1900, 1975. *A Buddhist Manual of Psychological Ethics: Dhammasangani.* London: Royal Asiatic Society.

Ricard, Matthieu, tr. 1994. *The Life of Shabkar: The Autobiography of a Tibetan Yogin.* Albany: State University of New York Press.

———. 1996. *Enlightened Journey: The Life and World of Khyentse Rinpoche, Spiritual Teacher from Tibet.* New York: Aperture Foundation.

Ricoeur, Paul. 1965, 1970. *Freud and Philosophy: An Essay in Interpretation,* translated by Denis Savage. New Haven: Yale University Press.

———. 1972. "The Symbol Gives Rise to Thought." In *Ways of Understanding Religion,* edited by Walter H. Capps. New York: Macmillan. Originally published as "The Symbol—Food for Thought." *Philosophy Today* 4 (1960): 196–207.

———. 1976. *Interpretation Theory: Discourse and the Surplus of Meaning.* Fort Worth: Texas Christian University Press.

———. 1978a. "Existence and Hermeneutics." In *The Philosophy of Paul Ricoeur: An Anthology of His Work,* edited by Charles E. Reagan and David Stewart. Boston: Beacon Press.

———. 1978b. "The Hermeneutics of Symbols and Philosophical Reflection." In *The Philosophy of Paul Ricoeur: An Anthology of His Work,* edited by Charles E. Reagan and David Stewart. Boston: Beacon Press.

———. 1981. "Hermeneutics and Critique of Ideology." In *Hermeneutics and the Human Sciences,* edited and translated by John B. Thompson, 63–100. Cambridge: Cambridge University Press.

Robinson, James B. 1979. *Buddha's Lions: The Lives of the Eighty-Four Siddhas.* Berkeley: Dharma Publishing.

Roerich, George N., tr. 1949. *The Blue Annals,* vols. 1 & 2. Delhi: Motilal Banarsidass.

Roy, Satindra Narayan. 1928. "The Witches of Orissa." *Journal of the Anthropological Society of Bombay* 14, 2: 185–200.

Ruegg, David Seyfort. 1989. "Allusiveness and Obliqueness in Buddhist Texts: Saṃdhā, Saṃdhi, Saṃdhyā and Abhisaṃdhi." In *Dialectes dans les litteratures indo-aryennes,* edited by C. Caillat, 295–328. Paris: College de France.

Ruether, Rosemary. 1983. *Sexism and God-Talk: Toward a Feminist Theology.* Boston: Beacon Press.

Samuel, Geoffrey. 1989. "The Body in Buddhist and Hindu Tantra: Some Notes." *Religion* 19: 197–210.

———. 1990. *Mind, Body and Culture: Anthropology and the Biological Interface.* Cambridge: Cambridge University Press.

———. 1993. *Civilized Shamans: Buddhism in Tibetan Societies.* Washington: Smithsonian Institution Press.

Saunders, E. Dale. 1962. "A Note on Shakti and Dhyānibuddha." *History of Religions* 1, 2: 300–06.

Schmidt, Erik Pema Kunsang, tr. 1993. *The Lotus-Born: The Life Story of Padmasambhava, by Yeshe Tsogyal.* Boston: Shambhala Publications.

———. 1994. *Advice from the Lotus-Born: A Collection of Padmasambhava's Advice to the Dakini Yeshe Tsogyal and Other Close Disciples.* Boudhnath: Rangjung Yeshe Publications.

———. 1996. *Tibetan-English Dictionary of Buddhist Teaching and Practice.* Computer disk format only. (Boudhnath: Rangjung Yeshe Translation and Publications.)

Schuster, Nancy. 1981. "Changing the Female Body: Wise Women and the Bodhisattva Career in Some Mahāratnakūtasūtras." *Journal of the International Association of Buddhist Studies* 4, 1: 24–69.

Schuster-Barnes, Nancy. 1987. "Buddhism." In *Women in World Religions,* edited by Arvind Sharma. Albany: State University of New York Press.

Shahidullah, M. 1928. *Les Chants Mystiques de Kāṇha et de Saraha.* Paris: Adrien-Maisonneuve.

Shaw, Miranda. 1994. *Passionate Enlightenment: Women in Tantric Buddhism.* Princeton: Princeton University Press.

Simmer-Brown, Judith. 1994. "An Interview with Miranda Shaw." *Shambhala Sun* (July), 67–69.

Singer, June. 1976, 1989. *Androgyny: The Opposites Within.* Boston: Sigo Press.

Sircar, D. C. 1973. *The Śaktā Pīṭhas.* 2nd ed. Delhi: Motilal Banarsidass.

Situpa, Khentin Tai. 1988. *Tilopa: Some Glimpses of His Life.* Eskdalemuir, Scotland: Dzalendara Publishing.

Skorupski, Tadeusz, ed. 1990. *Indo-Tibetan Studies: Papers in Honour and Appreciation of Professor David L. Snellgrove's Contributions to Indo-Tibetan Studies.* Tring, U.K.: Institute of Buddhist Studies.

Smith, Kendra. 1987. "Sex, Dependency, and Religion—Reflections from a Buddhist Perspective." In *Women in World's Religions, Past and Present,* edited by Ursula King, 219–31. New York: Paragon House.

Snellgrove, David, tr. 1954, 1964. "The Tantras." In *Buddhist Texts Through the Ages,* edited by Edward Conze. New York: Harper and Row.

———, tr. 1959, 1980. *The Hevajra Tantra: A Critical Study.* London: Oxford University Press.

———. 1957. *Buddhist Himālaya.* Oxford: Bruno Cassirer.

———. 1987. *Indo-Tibetan Buddhism: Indian Buddhists and Their Tibetan Successors.* Boulder: Shambhala Publications.

Snyder, Jeanette. 1979. "A Preliminary Study of the Lha Mo." *Asian Music* 10, 2: 23–62.

Sogyal Rinpoche. 1992. *The Tibetan Book of Living and Dying.* San Francisco: HarperCollins.

Sopa, Geshe. 1985. "The Subtle Body." In *The Wheel of Time: The Kālacakra in Context,* 139–58. Madison, Wisc.: Deer Park Books.

Sponberg, Alan. 1992. "Attitudes Toward Women and the Feminine in Early Buddhism." In *Buddhism, Sexuality, and Gender,* edited by José Cabezon, 3–36. Albany: State University of New York Press.

Spretnak, Charlene. 1982. "Feminist Politics and the Nature of Mind." In *The Politics of Women's Spirituality: Essays on the Rise of Spiritual Power with the Feminist Movement,* edited by Charlene Spretnak, 565–73. Garden City, N.Y.: Doubleday.

Stewart, Jampa Mackenzie. 1995. *The Life of Gampopa, The Incomparable Dharma Lord of Tibet.* Ithaca, N.Y.: Snow Lion Publications.

Stott, David. 1989. "Offering the Body: The Practice of gCod in Tibetan Buddhism." *Religion* 19: 221–26.

Strong, John S. 1977. "Gandhakuṭi: The Perfumed Chamber of the Buddha." *History of Religions* 16: 390–406.

Sutherland, Gail Hinich. 1991. *The Disguises of the Demon: The Development of the Yakṣa in Hinduism and Buddhism.* Albany: State University of New York Press.

Sutton, Florin Giripescu. 1991. *Existence and Enlightenment in the Laṅkāvatāra-sūtra: A Study in the Ontology and Epistemology of the Yogācāra School of Mahāyāna Buddhism.* Albany: State University of New York Press.

Suzuki, D. T. 1932, 1978. *The Laṅkāvatāra Sūtra.* London: Routledge and Kegan Paul.

Templeman, David. 1989. *Tāranātha's Life of Kṛṣṇācārya/Kāṇha.* Dharamsala: Library of Tibetan Works and Archives.

———. 1994. "Buddhist Tantric Song: Dohā, Vajragīti, and Caryā Songs." *Tantra and Popular Religion in Tibet,* edited by Geoffrey Samuel, Hamish Gregor, and Elisabeth Stutchbury. New Delhi: Aditya Prakashan.

Thanissaro Bhikkhu. 1993. *The Mind Like Fire Unbound: An Image of the Early Buddhist Discourses.* Barre, Mass.: Dhamma Dana Publications.

Thinley, Karma. 1980. *The History of the Sixteen Karmapas of Tibet.* Boulder: Shambhala Publications.

Thomas, Louis-Vincent. 1980. *Le Cadavre: De la biologie à l'anthropologie.* Brussels: Editions Complexe.

Thondup, Tulku. 1982. *The Dzog-chen Preliminary Practice of the Innermost Essence: The Long-chen Nying-thig Ngon-dro with Original Tibetan Root Text Composed by the Knowledge-Bearer Jig-me Ling-pa (1729–1798).* Dharamsala: Library of Tibetan Works and Archives.

———, tr. 1983, 1992. *The Queen of Great Bliss of Long-Chen Nying-Thig by Kun-Khyen Jigme Ling-pa.* Gangtok, Sikkim: Dodrup Chen Rinpoche.
———. 1986. *Hidden Teachings of Tibet: An Explanation of the Terma Tradition of the Nyingma School of Buddhism,* edited by Harold Talbott. London: Wisdom Publications.
———. 1995. *Enlightened Journey: Buddhist Practice as Daily Life.* Boston: Shambhala Publications.
———. 1996. *Masters of Meditation and Miracles.* Boston: Shambhala Publications.
Thrangu, Khenchen. 1978, 1990. *The Open Door to Emptiness.* Manila: Isarog Printing.
———. 1990. *The Uttaratantra: A Treatise on Buddha Nature.* Boulder: Namo Buddha Publications.
———. 1992, 1995. *The Spiritual Biography of Marpa the Translator.* Boulder: Namo Buddha Publications.
———. 1993. *The Spiritual Biographies of Tilopa and Gampopa.* Boulder: Namo Buddha Publications.
———. 1997. *Songs of Nāropa: Commentaries on Songs of Realization,* translated by Erik Pema Kunsang Schmidt. Hong Kong: Rangjung Yeshe Publications.
Thurman, Robert A. F. 1976. *The Holy Teaching of Vimalakīrti.* University Park: Pennsylvania State University Press.
———. 1986. "Female Deities." Ithaca, N.Y.: Snow Lion Audio Tapes.
Thurman, Robert A. F., and Marylin M. Rhie. 1991. *Wisdom and Compassion: The Sacred Art of Tibet.* New York: Harry N. Abrams.
Tobgyal, Orgyen. 1988. *The Life of Chokgyur Lingpa,* translated by Tulku Jigmey and Erik Pema Kunsang. 3rd ed. Kathmandu: Rangjung Yeshe Publications.
Trinh, Minh-ha. 1989. *Woman, Native, Other: Writing Postcoloniality and Feminism.* Bloomington and Indianapolis: Indiana University Press.
Trungpa, Chögyam. 1973a. *Born in Tibet.* Berkeley: Shambhala Publications.
———. 1973b. *Cutting Through Spiritual Materialism.* Berkeley: Shambhala Publications.
———. 1973c. "Femininity." *Woman: Maitreya IV.* Berkeley: Shambhala Publications.
———. 1975. *Visual Dharma: The Buddhist Art of Tibet.* Berkeley: Shambhala Publications.
———. 1976. *The Myth of Freedom and the Way of Meditation.* Berkeley: Shambhala Publications.
———. 1980. *The Rain of Wisdom: The Essence of the Ocean of True Meaning, The Vajra Songs of the Kagyü Gurus.* Boulder: Shambhala Publications.
———. 1982a. "Sacred Outlook: The Vajrayoginī Shrine and Practice." In *The Silk Route and the Diamond Path: Esoteric Buddhist Art on the Trade Routes of the*

Trans-Himalayan Region, edited by Deborah Klimburg-Salter. Los Angeles: UCLA Art Council Press.

———. 1982b. *The Life of Marpa the Translator,* by Tsang Nyon Heruka. Boulder: Shambhala Publications.

———. 1991a. *Crazy Wisdom.* Boston: Shambhala Publications.

———. 1991b. *Secret Beyond Thought: The Five Cakras and the Four Karmas.* Halifax, N.S.: Vajradhatu Publications.

———. 1991c. *The Heart of the Buddha.* Boston: Shambhala Publications.

———. 1994. *Illusion's Game: The Life and Teaching of Nāropa.* Boston: Shambhala Publications.

———. 1999. *Glimpses of Space: The Feminine Principle and EVAM.* Boston: Shambhala Publications.

Trungpa, Chögyam, and Herbert Guenther. 1975. *The Dawn of Tantra.* Berkeley: Shambhala Publications.

Tsomo, Karma Lekshe. 1982. "Vajrayoṣidbhageṣu Vijahāra: Historical Survey from the Beginnings to the Culmination of Tantric Buddhism." In *Indological and Buddhist Studies: Volume in Honour of Professor J. W. de Jong on his Sixtieth Birthday,* edited by L. A. Hercus et al., 595–616. Canberra: Faculty of Asian Studies.

———. 1987. *Sakyadhita: Daughters of the Buddha.* Ithaca, N.Y.: Snow Lion Publications.

Tsuda, Shinichi, tr. 1974. *The Samvarodaya-Tantra: Selected Chapters.* Tokyo: Hokuseido Press.

Tucci, Giuseppe, 1961, 1969. *The Theory and Practice of the Mandala.* New York: Samuel Weiser.

———. 1977. "On Swāt. The Dards and Connected Problems." In *East and West,* 27, 9–103.

Tulku, Chagdud, 1989. "Ḍākinī Wisdom." Taped from a seminar in Seattle, Washington, November 16, 1989. Distributed by Chagdud Gonpa Foundation.

Tulku, Tarthang. 1975. "The Life and Liberation of Padmasambhava." *Crystal Mirror* 4: 3–34.

———, tr. 1983. *Mother of Knowledge: The Enlightenment of Ye-shes mTshorgyal,* by Nam-mkha'i snying-po. Berkeley: Dharma Publishing.

Urgyen, Tulku. 1995. *Rainbow Painting: A Collection of Miscellaneous Aspects of Development and Completion,* translated by Erik Pema Kunsang. Boudhanath: Rangjung Yeshe Publications.

Van Herik, Judith, 1982. "Feminist Critique of Classical Psychoanalysis." In *Challenge of Psychology to Faith,* edited by David Tracy and Stephen Kepne. *Concilium Revue internationale de theologie* 156: (Edinburgh: T. and T. Clark), 83–86.

Van Lysebeth, André. 1988. *Tantra, le culte de la Féminité.* Paris: Flammarion.

Van Tuyl, C. 1979. "Mila-ras-pa and the gCod Ritual." *The Tibet Journal,* 4: 1.

Wayman, Alex. 1962. "Female Energy and Symbolism in the Buddhist Tantras." *History of Religions* 2, 1: 73–111.

———. 1973. *The Buddhist Tantras: Light on Indo-Tibetan Esoterism.* New York: Samuel Weiser.

———. 1977. *Yoga of the Guhyasamājatantra: The Arcane Lore of Forty Verses.* New York: Samuel Weiser.

Wehr, Demaris S. 1987. *Jung and Feminism: Liberating Archetypes.* Boston: Beacon Press.

White, Erin. 1995. "Religion and the Hermeneutics of Gender: An Examination of the Work of Paul Ricoeur." *Religion and Gender,* edited by Ursula King, 77–100. Oxford: Blackwell.

Wiethaus, Ulrike. 1991. "Sexuality, Gender and the Body in Late Medieval Spirituality: Cases from Germany and the Netherlands." *Journal of Feminist Studies in Religion* 7, 1 (Spring): 35–52.

Willemen, Ch. 1983. *The Chinese Hevajratantra: The Scriptural Text of the Ritual of the Great King of the Teaching, The Adamantine One with Great Compassion and Knowledge of the Void.* Orientalia Gandensia, vol. 8. Louvain, Belgium: Uitgeverij Peters.

Willis, Janice Dean. 1972. *The Diamond Light of the Eastern Dawn: A Collection of Tibetan Buddhist Meditations.* New York: Simon and Schuster.

———. 1985. "Nuns and Benefactresses: The Role of Women in the Development of Buddhism." In *Women, Religion and Social Change,* edited by Yvonne Yazbeck Haddad and Ellison Banks Findly, 59–85. Albany: State University of New York Press.

———. 1987a. "Ḍākinī: Some Comments on Its Nature and Meaning." In *Feminine Ground: Essays on Women and Tibet,* edited by Janice Willis, 57–75. Ithaca: Snow Lion Publications.

———. 1987b. "Tibetan Anīs: The Nun's Life in Tibet." In *Feminine Ground: Essays on Women and Tibet,* edited by Janice Willis, 96–117. Ithaca: Snow Lion Publications.

———. 1999. "Tibetan Buddhist Women Practitioners, Past and Present." In *Buddhist Women Across Cultures: Realizations,* edited by Karma Lekshe Tsomo, 145–58. Albany: State University of New York Press.

Willson, Martin. 1986. *In Praise of Tārā: Songs to the Saviouress.* London: Wisdom Publications.

Wilson, Liz. 1995. "Seeing Through the Gendered 'I': The Self-Scrutiny and Self-Disclosure of Nuns in Post-Aśokan Buddhist Hagiographic Literature." *Journal of Feminist Studies in Religion* 11, 1: 41–80.

———. 1996. *Charming Cadavers: Horrific Figurations of the Feminine in Indian Buddhist Hagiographic Literature.* Chicago: University of Chicago Press.

Woodroffe, Sir John. 1918, 1929. *Shakti and Shākta: Essays and Addresses on the Shākta Tantrashāstra.* Madras: Ganesh.

Wylie, Turrell. 1959. "A Standard System of Tibetan Transcription." *Harvard Journal of Asiatic Studies* 22: 261–67.

Young, Katherine K., and Arvind Sharma, eds. 1974. *Images of the Feminine—Mythic, Philosophic and Human—In the Buddhist, Hindu, and Islamic Traditions: A Bibliography of Women in India.* Chico, Calif.: New Horizons Press.

Young, Serinity. 1999. *Dreaming the Lotus: Buddhist Dream Narrative, Imagery, and Practice.* Boston: Wisdom Publications.

Zangpo, Ngawang, tr. 1997. *Enthronement: The Recognition of the Reincarnate Masters of Tibet and the Himalayas,* by Jamgön Kongtrül Lodrö Thaye. Ithaca, N.Y.: Snow Lion Publications.

TIBETAN TRANSLITERATIONS AND SANSKRIT EQUIVALENTS

This word list, alphabetized in the Roman alphabet according to Tibetan phonetic spelling, provides the Wylie system of transliteration of Tibetan words and their Sanskrit equivalents, where appropriately available. Although there is no commonly accepted system for phonetically rendered Tibetan words, the Nālandā Translation Committee, based in Halifax, Nova Scotia, has developed conventions for spelling that are used here. Sanskrit spellings follow commonly accepted scholarly norms.

PHONETIC	WYLIE TRANSLITERATION	SANSKRIT
bap tang	babs stang	
chag-gya chenpo	phyag rgya chen po	mahāmudrā
chag-gya druk	phyag rgya drug	ṣaṇ-mudrā
chag-gya	phyag rgya	mudrā
chag-lam	chags lam	
chagdral	chags 'bral	
changchup sem	byang chub sems	bodhicitta
che	mched	bhaginī
Chenresik	spyan ras gzigs	
chi	phyi	
Chö	gcod	
chöjung	chos 'byung	dharmodaya
chöku	chos sku	dharmakāya

PHONETIC	WYLIE TRANSLITERATION	SANSKRIT
Chöku Yum Chenmo	chos sku yum chen mo	
chökyong	chos skyong	dharmapāla
chöpa la shekpa	spyod pa la gshegs pa	
chogga	mchog dga'	paramānanda
Chomo Menmo	jo mo sman mo	
da	brda or brda'	
da-thim	brda thim or brda' thim	
Dagmema	bdag med ma	Nairātmyā
dakki jemo	dak ki rje mo	ḍākima
Dechok Yab-yum Kodok	bde mchog yab yum go zlog	
delok	'das log	
dewa chenpo	bde ba chen po	mahāsukha
dökham wangmo	'dod khams dbang mo	
Dö-pe Tenchö	'dod pa'i bstan bcos	
Dorje Naljorma	rdo rje rnal 'byor ma	Vajrayoginī
Dorje Phagmo	rdo rje phag mo	Vajravārāhī
dralhe gyalmo	dgra lha'i rgyal mo	
dren	'dren	
drip-pa	sgrib pa	āvaraṇa
Drölma Karmo	sgrol ma dkar mo	Śukla-tārā
drup-thap	sgrub thabs	sādhana
drup-thop	sgrub thob	siddha
druppa ka-gye	sgrub pa bka' brgyad	
dü	bdud	māra
dül	rdul	rakta
dütsi	bdud rtsi	amṛta
dütsi men-gyi phap	bdud rtsi men gyi phab	
Dzogchen	rdzogs chen	Mahāsāṃdhi
dzog-rim	rdzogs rim	sampannakrama
gadrel	dga' bral	vilakṣana
Gampopa	sgam po pa	
Garap Dorje	dga' rab rdo rje	Prahevajra
gawa	dga' ba	ānanda
geshe lharampa	dge bshes lha rams pa	
gomchen	sgom chen	
gongpe-ke	dgongs pa'i skad	sandhā-bhāṣā
Gyalkün Kyeyum	rgyal kun skyed yum	
gyalwa gonggyü	rgyal ba dgongs brgyud	
gyepa	rgyas pa	puṣṭika
gyü	rgyud	tantra
gyu-lü	sgyu lus	māya-deha
ja-lü	'ja' lus	
Jamgön Kongtrül	'jam mgon kong sprul	

PHONETIC	WYLIE TRANSLITERATION	SANSKRIT
jetsünma	rje btsun ma	
jik-tsok la tawa	'jig tshogs la lta ba	sat-kāya-dṛṣṭiḥ
jikten chötö	'jig rten mchod bstod	
jikten kyi chögye	'jig rten kyi chos brgyad	aṣṭau lokadharmāh
jikten kyi khandro	'jig rten kyi mkha' 'gro	loka-ḍākinī
jiltang	skyil stang	
kabap lungten	bka' babs lung bstan	
Kagyü	bka' brgyud	
kama (abb.)	ring brgyud bka' ma	
kangsak nyengyü	gang zag snyan brgyud	
karak	ska rags	mekhalā
Karmapa	ka rma pa	
kartap (abb.)	gar gyi stangs stabs	
kartap gu	gar stabs dgu	nava-rasa
kasung	bka' srung	
Khachö (abb.)	mkha' la spyod pa	Khecara
khachöma	mkha' spyod ma	khecarī, vyomacarī
Khakhyap Dorje	mkha' khyab rdo rje	
khandro dayik	mkha' 'gro brda yig	
khandro khalung	mkha' 'gro kha rlung	
khandro ling-gi nyül-le	mkha' 'gro gling gi nyul le	
Khandro Nyingthik	mkha' 'gro snying thig	
khandro shallang	mkha' 'gro'i zhal rlangs	
khandro te-gya	mkha' 'gro gtad rgya	
khandro trölung	mkha' 'gro drod rlung	
khandro-me nying-trak	mkha' 'gro ma'i snying khrag	
khandro-me sog-nying	mkha' 'gro ma'i srog snying	
khandroma	mkha' 'gro ma	ḍākinī
khekham su khyappar droma	mkha'i khams su khyab par 'gro ma	
khenpo	mkhan po	
Khenpo Jigme Phüntsok	mkhan po 'jigs med phun tshogs	
khorlo	'khor lo	cakra or cakrī
khu-wa	khu ba	śukra
Khyungpo Naljor	khyung po rnal 'byor	
Kö Karmo	gos dkar mo	
könchok sum	dkon mchog gsum	triratna
ku	sku	kāya
Künga Bumpa	kun dga' 'bum pa	
Künje Gyalpo	kun byed rgyal po	
Küntusangmo	kun tu bzang mo	Samantabhadrī
Küntusangpo	kun tu bzang po	Samantabhadra

PHONETIC	WYLIE TRANSLITERATION	SANSKRIT
kyangma	rkyang ma	lalanā
kyemen	skye dman	strī
kyerim (abb.)	bskyed pa'i rim pa	utpattikrama
kyil-khor	dkyil 'khor	maṇḍala
Lachi (abb.)	la phyi gnas yig	
lag-drup	lag gdub	haste rucaka
lam-yik	lam yig	
lana me-pe gyü	bla na med pa'i rgyud	anuttara-yoga
lang	glang	vṛṣa
langpo	glang po	hastinī
lekyi chag-gya	las kyi phyag rgya	karmamudrā
lekyi khandro	las kyi mkha' 'gro	karma-ḍākinī
Lekyi Wangmo	las kyi dbang mo	Karmeśvarī
lhak thong	lhag mthong	vipaśyana
lhasin degye	lha srin sde brgyad	
lhe ngagyal	lha'i nga rgyal	
lhen-chik kye pe yeshe	lhan cig skyes pa'i ye shes	sahajā-jñāna
lhen-chik kyepa gawa	lhan cig skyes pa'i dga' ba	sahajā-sukha
lhen-kye khandroma	lhan skyes mkha' 'gro ma	sahajā-ḍākinī
Lodrö Thaye	blo gros mtha' yas	
Longchen Rabjam	klong chen rab 'byams	
longku	klongs sku	sambhogakāya
lu	klu	nāga
lü-kyi-kyil	lus kyi dkyil	
lung	rlung	prāṇa
ma-gyü	ma rgyud	
Machik Lapdrön	ma gchig lab sgron	
mamo bötong	ma mo rbod gtong	
Marpa	mar pa	
menmo	sman mo	
mikpa	dmigs pa	
Mikyö Dorje	mi bskyod rdo rje	
mögü	mos gus	adhimukti
mönlam wangkur	smon lam dbang bskur	
möpa trag-ngak	dmod pa drag sngags	
nacha	rna cha	kuṇḍala
naljorma	rnal 'byor ma	yoginī
naljorpa	rnal 'byor pa	yogin
namkha	nam mkha'	ākaśa
namthar	rnam thar	
nang	nang	
Nāropa	na ro pa	Nāropa
neluk	gnas lugs	

PHONETIC	WYLIE TRANSLITERATION	SANSKRIT
ne-yik	gnas yig	
ngak	sngags	mantra
ngak sungma	sngags srung ma	
ngak-kye khandroma	sngags skyes mkha' 'gro ma	dhāraṇijā-ḍākinī
ngak-phang	ngag 'phang	
ngakpa	sngags pa	tāntrika, tāntrikā (fem.)
Ngawang Lhamo	ngag dbang lha mo	Vākīśvarī
ngedön	nges don	nītārtha
ngöndro	sngon 'gro	
ngotrö	ngo sprod	
nöjin	gnod sbyin	yakṣa
norbu	nor bu	kaṇṭhi
nyachi	nya phyis	
nyam-gur	nyams mgur	
nyen-gyü	snyan brgyud	karṇa-tantra
nyer-len zuk kyi pungpo	nyer len gzugs kyi phung po	
nyingje	snying rje	karuna
Nyingma	rnying ma	
nyönmong	nyon mongs	kleśa
nyong-dröl	myong grol	
nyug me sem	gnyug ma'i sems	
ösel	'od gsal	
ösel chenpo	'od gsal chen po	
Orgyen	o rgyen	Uḍḍiyāṇa
orgyen khandro ling	o rgyen mkha' 'gro gling	
padma	pad ma	padminī
Palden Lhamo	dpal ldan lha mo	Vetalī
pamo	dpa' mo	vīrinī
pardo	bar do	anantarabhava
Pardo Thödröl	bar do thos grol	
pawo	dpa' bo	vīra (or ḍāka)
Pema Kethang	pad ma bka' i thang	
Pema Lendreltsel	pad ma las 'brel rtsal	
Pema Ö	padma 'od	
Pemasel	pad ma gsal	
pharöltu chinpa	pha rol tu phyin pa	pāramitā
phünsum tsokpa nga	phun sum tshogs pa lnga	
Ralchigma	ral gcig ma	Ekajaṭī
rang-rik yeshe	rang rig ye shes	
Rangjung Dorje	rang byung rdo rje	
Ri-me	ris med	
ribong	ri bong	śaśa
ridak chen	ri dvags can	hastinī

PHONETIC	WYLIE TRANSLITERATION	SANSKRIT
ridakpo	ri dvags po	
rigdzin dayi gyü	rig 'dzin brda yi brgyud	
rimochen	ri mo can	citriṇī
rimpa	rim pa	
rinpoche	rin po che	maṇi
ro-chik	ro-gcig	ekarāsa
roma	ro ma	rasanā
Rumtek	rum bteg	
sabön	sa bon	bīja
sang	gsang	
Saraha	sa ra ha	Saraha
Sarma	gsar ma	
selnang	gsal snang	
sem-de	sems sde	
senmo	bsen mo	
sepa	sred pa	tṛṣṇā
shanak	zhva nag	vajra mukut
shasa khandro	sha za mkha' 'gro	
shedra	bshad grva	
Shelkar Dorje Tsomo	shel dkar rdo rje mtsho mo	
sherap kyi pharöltu chinpa	shes rab kyi pha rol tu phyin pa	prajñā-pāramitā
sherap	shes rab	prajñā
shi-ne	zhi-gnas	śamatha
shing-kye khandroma	zhing skyes mkha' 'gro ma	kṣetrajā-ḍākinī
zhing-kyong kyi khandroma	zhing skyong kyi mkha' 'gro ma	kṣetrapāla-ḍākinī
shiwa	zhi ba	śantika
shok-ser	shog ser	
sibur	bzi bur	
sinmo	srin mo	rākṣasī
sipa	srid pa	gatiḥ
sog-lung	srog rlung	
sog-nying	srog snying	
sok	srog	
ta-chok	rta mchog	aśva
tag-nang	dag snang	
tamla tak	dam la btags	
Tampa Sanggye	dam pa sangs rgyas	Bodhidharma
tamtsik	dam tshig	samaya
tangka	thang ka	
tashi tag-gye	bkra shis rtags brgyad	
tatang sum	lta stangs gsum	
tendel (abb.)	rten cing 'brel bar 'byung ba	pratītyasamutpāda
tenma chu-nyi	brtan ma bcu gnyis	

PHONETIC	WYLIE TRANSLITERATION	SANSKRIT
tepa	dad pa	śraddhā
terma (abb.)	nye brgyud gter ma	
tertön	gter ton	
thab-lam	thabs lam	upāya-mārga
thabla khepa	thabs la mkhas pa	upāya-kauśalya
thalwa	thal ba	bhasma
thap	thabs	upāya
thigle	thig le	bindu
thong-dröl	mthong grol	
Thöpa Bhadra	thod pa bha tra	
thorang	tho rangs	
Thötreng Tsal	thod phreng rtsal	
thrap	'khrab	
Tilopa	ti lo pa	Tilopa
togden	rtog ldan	
togme	rtog med	
tong-pa-nyi	stong pa nyid	śūnyatā
torma	gtor ma	bali
trak	khrag	rakta
trak-thung	khrag 'thung	heruka
trak-thung chenmo	khrag 'thung chen mo	
trakpo	drag po	abhicāraka
tramen	phra man	vetāla
trenrik detong chenpo	dran rig bde stong chen po	
triguk	gri gug	kartari
trin-le shi	'phrin las bzhi	catuḥ-karmā
Tröma Nagmo	khros ma nag mo	Kālikā or Khrodhakāli
trül-yik	'phrul yig	
tsa	rtsa	nāḍī
tsa-lung	rtsa rlung	prāṇa-nāḍī
tsa-we tungwa	rtsa ba'i ltung ba	mūlāpatti
tsasum	rtsa gsum	trimūla
tsawe lama	rtsa ba'i bla ma	mūla-guru
tse-sum	rtse gsum	khaṭvāṅga
tsok-khor (abb.)	tshogs kyi 'khor lo	gaṇacakra
tsöndrü	brtson 'grus	vīrya
tülku	sprul sku	nirmāṇakāya
tummo	gtum mo	caṇḍālī
tung-gye kyil	dung gye kyil	
tungchenma	dung can ma	sáṅkhinī
tungwa	ltung ba	
turtrö	dur khrod	śmaśāna
uma	dbu ma (or kun 'dar ma)	avadhūti

PHONETIC	WYLIE TRANSLITERATION	SANSKRIT
wang (abb.)	dbang skur	abhiṣeka
wang	dbang	vaśī-karaṇa
Wangchuk Dorje	dbang phyug rdo rje	
yab-yum	yab yum	yuga-naddha
Yangchenma	dbyangs can ma	Sarasvatī
yeshe	ye shes	jñāna
yeshe chölwa	ye shes 'chol ba	
yeshe khandro	ye shes mkha' 'gro	jñāna-ḍākinī
Yeshe Tsogyal	ye shes mtsho rgyal	Jñāna-sāgara
yidam (abb)	yid kyi dam tshig	iṣṭa-devatā
ying	dbyings	dhātu
yül	yul	pīṭha
yülchen nyershi	yul chen nyer bzhi	
Yum Chenmo	yum chen mo	

CREDITS

Excerpts from "Pacifying the Turmoil of the Mamos" by Karma Chagme and "Ekajaṭī" by Chögyam Trungpa were translated by and used with the permission of the Nālandā Translation Committee, copyright ©1975–1978 by the Nālandā Translation Committee, 1619 Edward Street, Halifax, N.S., Canada B3H 3H9.

Cakrasaṃvara drawing by Gega Lama, reproduced from Gega Lama, *Principles of Tibetan Art* (Schoten, Belgium: Kunchab Publications). With kind permission of the publisher.

Photograph of Ven. Khandro Rinpoche, 1993, by Diana Church, photographer, Halifax, Nova Scotia. With kind permissions of the lama and the photographer.

Two photographs of sculptures from the Great Stūpa of Dharmakāya at Rocky Mountain Shambhala Center, Red Feather Lakes, Colorado, photographed by Marvin Ross, Boulder, Colorado. Vajrayoginī was sculpted by Joshua Mulder. Sculptors of the retinue ḍākinī are Kunchok Lama and Joshua Mulder; Cakrasaṃvara and Vajrayoginī sculptors are Tsewang Dorje and Tsewang Dorje, with the assistance of Senge Lama, Sangye Wangdi, Kunchok Lama, and Joshua Mulder. With kind permission of the artists.

Vajrayoginī drawing, drawn by Glen Eddy, ornamented by Greg Smith. With kind permission of the artists.

Nine line drawings of ḍākinīs by Cynthia Moku: Yeshe Tsogyal, Machik Lapdrön, Samantabhadrī and Samantabhadra, Ekajāṭī, Niguma, Sukhasiddhi, Maṇḍāravā, Kurukullā, and Yum Chenmo. With kind permission of the artist.

Index